JUDAISM AND THE

BY THE SAME AUTHOR

Jewish Prayer

A Guide to Rosh Ha-Shanah

A Guide to Yom Kippur

Jewish Values

Studies in Talmudic Logic and Methodology

The Palm Tree of Deborah
(Translated from the Hebrew of Moses Cordovero, with Introduction and Notes)

Tract on Ecstasy
(Translated from the Hebrew of Dobh Baer of Lubavitch, with Introduction and Notes)

*Principles of the Jewish Faith:
An Analytical Study*

*Jewish Preaching
Homilies and Sermons*

The Talmudic Argument

Helping with Inquiries

God, Torah, Israel

Religion and the Individual

We have Reason to Believe
(Fifth revised edition)

*Their Heads in Heaven:
Unfamiliar Aspects of Hasidism*

Rabbinic Thought in the Talmud

JUDAISM AND THEOLOGY

Essays on the Jewish Religion

LOUIS JACOBS

VALLENTINE MITCHELL
LONDON • PORTLAND, OR

First published in 2005 in Great Britain by
VALLENTINE MITCHELL & CO. LTD
Suite 314, Premier House, 112–114 Station Road,
Edgware, Middlesex HA8 7BJ

www.vmbooks.com

and in the United States of America by
VALLENTINE MITCHELL
c/o ISBS,
920 NE 58th Avenue, Suite 300, Portland, OR 97213-3786 USA

Copyright collection © 2005 Vallentine Mitchell & Co. Ltd

British Library Cataloguing in Publication Data
have been applied for

Library of Congress Cataloging in Publication Data
have been applied for

ISBN 0 85303 563 6 (cloth)
0 85303 567 9 (paper)

All rights reserved. No part of this publication may be reproduced in any form or by any means, electronic, mechanical, photocopying, reading or otherwise, without the prior permission of Vallentine Mitchell & Co. Ltd.

Printed in Great Britain by
MPG Books Ltd, Bodmin, Cornwall

Contents

INTRODUCTION *vii*

1. The Jewish Approach to God — 1
2. The *Via Negativa* in Jewish Thought — 10
3. Jewish Cosmology — 22
4. The Problem of the *Akedah* in Jewish Thought — 39
5. Holy Places — 51
6. The Jewish Tradition — 66
7. The Body in Jewish Worship: Three Rituals Examined — 83
8. Attitudes Towards Christianity in the *Halakhah* — 102
9. Rabbi Ephraim Ha-Kohen and a Heretical Sermon — 117
10. Hasidism and the Dogma of the Decline of the Generations — 126
11. The Relevance and Irrelevance of Hasidism — 134
12. Praying for the Downfall of the Wicked — 144
13. Rabbi Aryeh Laib Heller's Theological Introduction to his *Shev Shematata* — 159
14. Rabbi Meir Simhah of Dvinsk — 196
15. Zionism after 100 Years — 209
16. Sanctity and Meaning of Human Life in Relation to the Present Situation of Violence — 218
17. Concept of Power in Jewish Tradition — 225
18. Contemporary Judaism — 238
19. Angels and Feminism — 251

Index — 255

For my granddaughter Paula
and her
husband David Ward

Introduction

All these essays (with the exception of the last) have been previously published. Diverse though they are, they have a common theme, that of Jewish theology and topics arising from this, especially of a comparative nature. The essays, having been published at various times, are bound to be somewhat different in emphasis and may even seem to contradict one another here and there. I have also treated these themes in my books on Jewish theology, so there is a degree of repetition. Nevertheless, I have thought fit to present them to the interested reader for discussion and perhaps as a stimulus.

Here is a short run-through of the essays.

Chapter 1 is a contribution I was invited to make to the journal *Twentieth Century*. The previous issue of this journal had been devoted to pornography. This had aroused the ire of some readers and, perhaps in repentance, the next issue bore the heading Where is God? This opened with a comical dialogue between Peter Cook and Dudley Moore, as the well-known characters Pete and Dud, in which the two discussed how to discover the truth of religion. This was followed by a number of writers from different traditions. I was invited to write on the Jewish attitude. In the circumstances I was obliged to be more subjective than objective in trying to describe *the* Jewish view.

Chapter 2 takes up the mystical approach to the divine as seen by two near contemporaries.

Chapter 3 is similarly comparative in nature, as is Chapter 4 on the Jewish response to Kierkegaard.

Chapter 5 deals with this universal question from the point of view found in Jewish sources.

Chapter 6 explores the Jewish point of view of the idea of tradition as developed by Wilfred Cantwell Smith.

Chapter 7 is also comparative, and appeared in a work devoted to the general question of the use of the body in worship.

Chapter 8 turns towards Christianity and Chapter 9 towards heretical sermonizing.

Chapters 10 and 11 consider theological aspects of Hasidism.

Chapter 12 examines what Jewish thinkers had to say on the legitimacy of praying to God to harm or destroy the wicked.

Chapter 13 deals with the comprehensive theological essay by Rabbi Aryeh Laib Heller, important and interesting in that Rabbi Heller was known chiefly as a distinguished Halakhist.

Chapter 14 discusses Rabbi Meir Simhah, another famed Halakhist who devoted part of his work to theological investigation.

From Chapter 15 onwards the turn is towards modern life and thought from a number of theological aspects. Chapter 15 concerns the 100th anniversary of the beginning of the Zionist movement.

Chapter 16 addresses the concept of sanctity as applied to human life, and Chapter 17 the concept of power in Jewish tradition. Chapter 18 was originally contributed to a work on the contemporary religious scene.

In Chapter 19 I consider the semi-amusing question of whether angels are male or female or both. This is a theological jaunt with which to finish the book and not to be treated too seriously.

The following notes the original home of each chapter.

Chapter 1: *Twentieth Century*, Vol. 174, No. 1027, Autumn 1965, pp. 7–10.

Chapter 2 (full title 'The *Via Negativa* in Jewish and Christian Thought: The Zohar and the *Cloud of Unknowing* Compared'): Annual Sachs Lecture, Essex University, Colchester, 1997.

Chapter 3: Carmen Blacker and Michael Lowe (eds), *Ancient Cosmologies*, George Allen and Unwin, 1975, pp. 66—86.

Chapter 4: Richard L. Perkins (ed.), *Kierkegaard's Fear and Trembling: Critical Appraisals*, University of Alabama Press, Tuscaloosa, 1981, pp. 1–9.

Chapter 5: *Conservative Judaism*, Vol. XXVII, No. 3, Spring 1984, pp. 4–16.

Chapter 6: Frank Whaling (ed.), *The World's Religious Traditions*, T. and T. Clark, Edinburgh, 1984.

Chapter 7: Sarah Coakley (ed.), *Religion and the Body*, Cambridge University Press, Cambridge, 1997.

Chapter 8: Zeev W. Falk (ed.) *Gevurath Haromah*, Jewish studies addressed at the eightieth birthday of Rabbi Moses Cyrus Weiler, Jerusalem, 1987, pp. xvii–xxxi.

Introduction

Chapter 9: Abraham Karp, Louis Jacobs and Chaim Zalman Dimitrovsky (eds), *Three Score Years and Ten: Essays in Honour of Rabbi Seymour G. Cohen*, Ktav, Hoboken, NJ, 1991, pp. 133–41.

Chapter 10: Ada Rapoport-Albert (ed.), *Hasidism Reappraised*, Littman Library of Jewish Civilization, London, 1996, pp. 208–13.

Chapter 11: Nathaniel Stampfer (ed.), *The Solomon Goldman Lecture*, Vol. 2, Chicago, IL, 1979, pp. 19–27.

Chapter 12: *Modern Judaism*, Vol. 2, Johns Hopkins University Press, Baltimore, MD, 1982, pp. 297–310.

Chapter 13: *Modern Judaism*, Vol. 1, Johns Hopkins University Press, Baltimore, MD, pp. 184–216.

Chapter 14: Memorial address for Rabbi Salzberger, London, 1978.

Chapter 15: *Proceedings of the Rabbinical Assembly of America*, New York, 1982, pp. 56–63.

Chapter 16: *Fifteen Years of Catholic–Jewish Dialogue*, Vatican, Rome, 1988, pp. 191–6.

Chapter 17: *Conservative Judaism*, Vol. XXXIII, No. 2, Winter 1980, pp. 16–28.

Chapter 18: Ian Harris, Stuart Mews, Paul Morris and John Shepherd (eds), *Contemporary Religion: A World Guide*, Longmans Group, Lancaster, 1997, pp. 31–8.

— 1 —

The Jewish Approach to God

A famous eighteenth-century Rabbi was the author of a slim volume on God which became a classic of Jewish devotional literature running into many editions. One of his colleagues on reading the book remarked: 'What an achievement to contain such a big God within the covers of such a little book!'

Anyone who writes on this theme must be painfully aware of the absurdity inherent in an attempt at describing the source of all being in a few thousand or even in many hundreds of thousands of words. Here it is certainly true that the more one knows the less one is able to speak. Moses, observed a Jewish teacher, is said to have been 'slow of speech' precisely for this reason. Wittgenstein's 'Whereof one cannot speak, thereof one must be silent' is surely correct. From one point of view all theology is indeed a futile enterprise.

On the other hand there must be some talk of Deity in any vital form of religion. Unless *something* can be uttered there can be no prayer and no worship. The way out of the dilemma, as seen by many notable Jewish thinkers, including the greatest Jew of the Middle Ages, Moses Maimonides (1135–1204), is to draw a distinction between God in His essence and God in manifestation. Of God as He is in Himself, as the Neo-Platonists say, nothing can be said. The nature of the Divine Being can only be known to Himself. But the religious life is not concerned with this at all but with God as He is revealed to mankind and with the relationship man can have with him. Judaism teaches that it is God's power which moves the stars. His voice is heard in the storm and tempest. The heavens declare His glory and the earth is filled with it. His is the force giving life to the beasts of the field, causing the rain to descend and the grass to grow. Moreover man can approach Him in personal relationship. The urge to worship in the human breast is seen as a reaching out for the Infinite which can alone fully satisfy it. God is described in the Bible as compassionate, just and merciful to imply that by pursuing justice and loving mercy man can become God-like, near to his creator.

In this way a good deal of Jewish teaching affirms both the nearness of God and His remoteness. God is very near – 'closer than breathing and nearer than hands and feet'– because all things owe their existence to Him and because man can walk in His ways, imitating Him in working righteousness. God is very near so that it is not unfitting to address Him as Father. And yet, Judaism teaches, God is remote. His true nature is utterly beyond man's comprehension. And one of the ways in which Judaism asserts this remoteness is in its uncompromising refusal to permit any plastic image of God. The Romans called the Jews 'atheists' because they worshipped an invisible God. The mental image, implied in various Biblical descriptions of God in human terms, is as far as Judaism is prepared to allow its adherents to go and even here, it urges, there must be a constant mental reservation that what is spoken of does not represent the reality. Pictorial representation is forbidden because its concrete form renders such qualification impossible. Idolatry is the worship of that which is finite, and hence not God, as if it were God.

For the same reason Judaism rejects utterly the claim that God ever took on human flesh. It treats the very suggestion as blasphemous. Theoretically such a stern and utter rejection of every form of imagery of the divine might have resulted in a coldly abstract faith, starkly unemotional and over-intellectualized, a philosophy rather than a religion. In practice the result has been otherwise, as Pascal saw when he contrasted the 'God of the philosophers' with the 'God of Abraham, Isaac and Jacob'. The God of the Hebrew Bible and of subsequent Judaism, of whom no image may be made, is the 'living God' obedience to whose will is man's greatest privilege and deepest joy.

The very emphasis in Judaism on the remoteness of God's essence has made for greater awareness of His manifestations in the concrete universe by which alone He can be apprehended. If God can only be known in the world He has brought into being then holiness is not to be thought of as something apart from the world. This is why there is no simple answer to the question whether Judaism is this- or other-worldly. It is both. To be sure it teaches that the death of the body is not the end of life and that man can enjoy God's goodness for ever. But it is in this life that man learns to grow in spirituality and he does so by engaging in worldly matters in a spirit of consecration. It is only when Jews have been influenced by Greek notions of a dichotomy between flesh and spirit that they are tempted to think of a God at war with His creation so that, somehow, losing the world becomes the inescapable price one has to pay for gaining one's soul. Celibacy, for instance, was hardly ever considered particularly virtuous in Judaism. The Jewish ideal is of the consecration of human life in obedience to the laws of justice and equity in family and social relationships. Marriage is a religious duty, the first command issued by God to man according to the Rabbis. Children are a blessing. Kierkegaard accused the Christians of his day of Judaizing when they celebrated their weddings with joy and Judaism looks upon this as a compliment. Extreme no doubt, but typical of a definite tendency in Judaism, is the saying of one of the teachers of the Talmud that on judgment day man will be obliged to give an account before the heavenly throne for every legitimate pleasure he denied himself.

On the psychological level man's rebellion against God is all too frequently due to the suggestion, fostered unfortunately by a good deal of religious teaching, that the very idea of God is anti-life. Religion is seen as being rather like the Victorian mother who says to the nanny: 'Go and see what the children are doing and tell them not to.' While not a few Jewish teachers have expressed themselves in ways which do little to remove the suspicion, the basic philosophy of Judaism that God is the Creator of the world who saw all that He had made and pronounced it good, acts as a brake on that religious outlook which would turn the world grey. The Rabbis were no world-haters or life-haters when they taught that it is the task of man to become a co-partner with God in building a just and righteous world. The old tale is told of a Rabbi who rebuked for being a deserter a miserly rich man he observed reciting Psalms with devotion. Why a deserter? he was asked. Because, he replied, the infantryman who goes over to the cavalry without his superior officer's permission is a shirker and by the same token the man blessed with worldly goods can best sing God's praises by doing something towards the alleviation of suffering.

Whatever he may think about some of the other ideas of the Bishop of Woolwich, the believing Jew can respond wholeheartedly to the chapter in *Honest to God* entitled: "Worldly Holiness", for this is pure Judaism. It is odd that the Bishop, in this chapter, seems to imply that this way of looking at religion is foreign to Judaism. In that little gem of Rabbinic wisdom and spirituality *Ethics of the Fathers*, a Rabbi is reported as saying that while one hour of spiritual bliss in the Hereafter is worth more than the whole of this life, yet one hour of good deeds in this life is better than the whole of the Hereafter. The Bishop also seems to be unaware that the saying of Jesus regarding the Sabbath being made for man, not man for the Sabbath, is sound Rabbinic teaching and is found as such in the Talmud.

The Jewish declaration of faith, known, after its opening Hebrew word, as the *Shema*, is the verse in Deuteronomy: 'Hear, O Israel! The Lord is our God, the Lord is One' (Deut. 6:4). The verse is recited twice daily by the devout Jew. It is mouthed by those around the deathbed of a Jew as he breathes his last. It is taught to Jewish infants as soon as they learn to speak. It is the great affirmation of ethical monotheism.

The Jewish doctrine of God as one meant, in the first instance, a total rejection of polytheism. The question much debated by Biblical scholars whether the doctrine erupted spontaneously, as it were, or evolved gradually from henotheism is beside the point for a theological appraisal. The facts are that, whatever its origin, the doctrine that there is only one God and that He loves righteousness and that He is on the side of the oppressed against the oppressors, eventually came like a breath of fresh air into the murky world of gods and goddesses fighting among themselves and greedy for man's propitiation. Baal, Marduk and the rest came to be called *elil-im*, a Hebrew word meaning 'non-entities'. For all the colossal temples erected to them and the elaborate worship offered they were mere figments of the human imagination. It took much insight to become aware of this and believing Jews see it all as part of God's self-revelation through their ancestors. A recent Israeli scholar has gone so far as to put forward the view that the complicated pagan mythologies were so foreign to the Biblical authors that they were ignorant of their nature, describing idolatry in terms of simple fetish worship. Certainly the Bible is silent on the myths of the gods and, although this may be purely fortuitous, there is no Hebrew word for goddess which has survived in the Bible. Even in speaking of God, the creation myth with which the Bible opens spends no time at all in describing what took place before creation but comes down immediately to earth: *'In the beginning God created the heaven and the earth. And the earth...'*

With the rise of dualistic theories about the universe, that there are two gods, one evil the other good, the 'One' of the *Shema* was made to yield the thought that God is Lord of all, that He creates darkness as well as light, that evil, too, is subordinate to Him and that those who fight it are doing His work. The problem of how the All-good can tolerate evil in his creation has always been a problem for Theism from, on the Jewish scene, the massive probings of the book of Job to the Rabbi who declared that it is beyond our power to explain the prosperity of the wicked and the suffering of the righteous. The standard theistic reply that a world in which evil was unknown could not serve, in Keats's words, as a vale of soul-making, that without a choice between good and evil there could be no meaning in the free choice of the good which makes man God-like, satisfies some minds but fails to satisfy others completely. Many Jews have preferred to walk by faith. What no representative Jewish thinker ever did was to fall back on theories suggesting that while God is a supreme Artist He is indifferent to the sufferings of His creatures. Judaism has always stood firmly on the belief in the goodness of God. Even when the figure of Satan came into Judaism, probably under the influence of Zoroastrianism, he was always seen as being completely subordinate to God. God is One and there is no power in heaven or earth beside Him. In the words of the great prophet of exile, almost certainly directed against early Persian dualism: 'I form light, and create darkness; I make peace, and create evil; I am the Lord, that doeth all these things' (Isaiah 45:7).

From the rejection of polytheism and dualism the deeper meaning of the *Shema* was developed to suggest far more than that God is one and not two or more. The Hebrew word for 'One' can also mean 'unique'. The idea, its roots in the Bible but stressed particularly under the influence of philosophical thinking in the Middle Ages, gradually came to the fore that God is 'wholly other', different entirely from anything in His creation. God came to be thought of as the source of goodness and of being in general but with His true nature altogether incomprehensible to man. A well-known Jewish hymn declares:

> *They told of Thee, but not as Thou must be,*
> *Since from Thy work they tried to body Thee.*

To countless visions did their pictures run,
Behold, through all the visions Thou art one.

Hence the distinction we have noted between God as He is in Himself and God in His manifestations. With highly questionable exegetical licence but with deep insight in this matter, the Jewish mystics interpret the verse: 'Lift up your eyes on high, and behold who hath created these' (Isaiah 40:26) to mean that behind the visible manifestations of His wisdom in the wonders of creation there is the hidden and unknown God. 'Who' (= God in His essence, of whom only the question: 'Who is He?' can be asked without an answer being forthcoming) has created 'these' (= the visible manifestations of His power and glory).

This is not to say that Judaism has never known inferior notions of Deity. There were not lacking, for instance, in the Middle Ages Jewish scholars who took the anthropomorphisms in Bible and Talmud quite literally, thinking of God as a being among others, elevated on a throne in heaven surrounded by the ministering angels. One of them even used the bizarre illustration of a wizard who can change himself into a hare, arguing that God can assume many guises, appearing, for example, to the Biblical heroes in the form of a man. These men dubbed thinkers like Maimonides heretics for daring to spiritualize the God concept. The significant thing for Judaism is, however, that it was men like Maimonides whose views won out, so much so that it can safely be said that no thinking Jew today would look upon the location of God 'up there' in outer space as anything but grotesque in the extreme and heretical to boot.

In the eighteenth century Baron von Holbach advanced as an argument for atheism the view that if God exists He would surely make His existence known to man in such a way as to preclude the possibility of doubt. It is interesting that a Jewish contemporary of Holbach, the founder of the Hasidic movement, also raised the question of the purpose of atheism. Why does God allow men to doubt His existence? His answer was that if God were immediately evident to all then faith in Him would be so powerful as effectively to preclude any endeavours on behalf of others. The psychological phenomenon of doubt is allowed to exist that a certain lack of faith might be brought into play where the needs of others are concerned. To have faith that God will provide for one's own needs is laudable. To have this kind of faith on behalf of others is no virtue at all. Unless this were so all charity, all kindliness and sympathy would lose their meaning.

This is no doubt a rather naïve way of expressing a great truth seen by Judaism. There is no Prometheus legend in Judaism. Far from being jealous of man's creativity, God endows man with the capacity for adapting the world to his needs. God gives man freedom of choice so that he can freely choose the good rather than have it given to him as a gift. It is man's glory that he can become God-like in making the good his own without any kind of divine coercion. It follows that there must be an ebb and flow in the life of faith, creative tensions stemming from the nearness of God at certain times and His remoteness at others. When God hides Himself, said a Hasidic master, it is to be compared to a father who plays hide and seek with his little child. The harder it is for the child to find his father the greater the joy when the discovery is made. 'Seek ye the Lord while He may be found, call ye upon Him while He is near' (Isaiah 55:6). The Rabbis conclude from this verse that there are times when God is especially near, especially to be found by those who seek Him. And they suggest that one of these times is the period of self-examination which traditionally ushers in the Jewish new year. On the wider level this means that Judaism has evolved a whole range of observances, such as the Sabbath and the dietary laws, which have as their avowed aim the discovery of God and His revelation in human lives. These observances are not flights of poetic ritual undertaken in isolation from the world. They have to do with eating and drinking and the world of men and women of flesh and blood. It is in normal human life in society that the hidden God becomes revealed.

The most misunderstood aspect of the Jewish God concept is the Jewish claim that God has chosen the Jews. The choice appears odd, as the old jingle has it, because of the incongruity of universal truth being the preserve of a tiny group.

The first thing to be noted is that the doctrine of the chosen people is not tribal. A choosing God is the exact opposite of a tribal god. The fortunes of a tribal god depend on those of his tribe. When the tribe is vanquished he is conquered with it. A choosing God can only make the choice because He is the God of all. It is not without significance that when reference is made in the Bible to the choice of Israel there is generally a reference to God's universal reign. 'Now then, if you will obey Me faithfully and keep My covenant, you shall be My treasured possession among all the peoples *for all the earth is Mine'* (Exodus 19:5).

The second aspect of this whole matter to be noted is implied in the above verse. God chooses Israel because Israel chooses God. The relationship is reciprocal. The whole idea, historically considered, arose out of the recognition by the seers and prophets of Israel that Israel was, at the time when the doctrine was first put forward, the only people which acknowledged the one God as Lord of the universe. They felt that God would remain unknown to mankind unless His truth was kept alive in Israel. Right from the beginning, therefore, particularism was itself a form of universalism. It cannot be denied, however, that there were times, especially when Jews suffered from discrimination and oppression, when the particularistic aspects were over-stressed. Some Jewish thinkers have spoken as if there were a qualitative difference between the souls of Jews and non-Jews. But a living faith is no simple uncomplicated matter not open to abuse. The fruitful idea of a group dedicated to God and His truth is in danger when interpreted in a narrow fashion. Yet it has produced creative tensions and in the best Jewish thinking the idea of Israel's dedication is for the sake of mankind.

In discussing the Jewish concept of God it must be noted, too, that Judaism has never had a central authority to regulate belief. Maimonides, it is true, did draw up thirteen articles of faith, five of them having to do specifically with the doctrine of God. Whatever authority they enjoy among Jews today is due to the emergence of a consensus of opinion over the centuries that these represent Jewish teaching. One of Maimonides's principles, for instance, is that of the incorporeality of God. For Maimonides any Jew who believes that God has image or form is a heretic. But other teachers did not share Maimonides's view. Now no Synod or Council was ever summoned (apart from other considerations this would have been physically impossible until modern times) representing the Jews of the world to determine whether Maimonides or his opponents were right and to define the true faith. Maimonides's view won out because it seemed right to the majority of Jews, more in accordance with the general tendency in Jewish thinking from the earliest times and through the centuries.

All this has made for a certain elasticity in Judaism in matters of dogma. When this becomes, as it sometimes does, an excuse for avoiding entirely theological considerations and a preoccupation with observances without reference to their spiritual meaning it is harmful to the religious life. But in itself the absence of hard, clearly defined statement of what a Jew must believe is no bad thing. For it has produced the realization that the divine cannot be contained in a formula, that behind the affirmation that there is a Supreme Being there lies a mystery too deep for man's comprehension. This in turn has produced among Jews what a modern Jewish theologian has called 'normal mysticism'. 'Normal mysticism' implies an attitude of reverence towards the sheer wonder of an existence permeated by the divine, an attitude capable of inspiring men towards the realisation of their spiritual natures without either removing them from the world of our daily concerns or allowing them to become lost in the obscurities of abstruse theological speculation.

This, then, is the Jewish concept of God. That there is a Supreme Being, All-good and All-powerful. That He is the ground of all there is and that the way to Him is by the pursuit of justice, mercy and holiness. That the people of Israel have their role to play in making these ideals common to mankind. The faith of Israel has been on earth a long time. It has won notable successes and has also suffered serious reversals. Jews believe that their faith is true and that one day it will win over the hearts and minds of all men. Jews believe that when that day comes, to use the language of tradition, the Kingdom of heaven, with us now even if we do not see it, will be firmly established upon earth.

— 2 —

The *Via Negativa* in Jewish Thought

Theologians, Jewish, Christian and Muslim, have grappled with the problem of how to speak of God. If a theist says too much about the nature of God he is guilty of trying to impose finite human limits on the Infinite. The theologian's greatest temptation is familiarity. In reaction to over-confident theological claims an anonymous writer composed the limerick:

> O God, forasmuch as without Thee
> We are not even able to doubt Thee,
> Lord, give us the grace
> To convince the whole race
> We know nothing whatever about Thee.

On the other hand, if too little is said about God there is the danger of belief shading off into atheism. Most theists, in the interest of a vital faith, have preferred the risk of saying too much rather than too little. But some theists, concerned with refining their religious notions, have preferred to adopt the *Via Negativa*,[1] a theology of negation which sometimes goes so far as to say that the only thing we can say about God is that we cannot say anything about God. The *Via Negativa*, generally preferred by the mystics of the three religions, was never seen by them as negative in the pejorative sense. The mystic's fascination with the Object of his contemplation derives in no small measure from the fact that It is so wonderful, so majestic, so utterly different from anything in heaven and earth, that it cannot be contained in human speech. The mystic bows before God in adoration not in spite of God's ineffability but because of it.

In this lecture I want to compare and contrast the *Via Negativa* as found in the Zohar, on the Jewish side, and in the work, by an unknown author, *The Cloud of Unknowing*,[2] on the Christian side. The Zohar first appeared at the end of the thirteenth century in Spain, *The Cloud of Unknowing* in the second half of the fourteenth century in England. The Zohar is written largely in an artificial Aramaic, *The Cloud of Unknowing* in Middle English. *The Cloud of Unknowing* is imbued with the spirit of Christian mysticism. The Zohar is the great work of Jewish mysticism, eventually becoming in some Jewish circles a sacred book of divine revelation next to the Bible and the Talmud. Yet, different though the two works are in aim, treatment, language, religious dogma and, to a lesser extent, in time, in both there is evident the crystallization, through their respective traditions, of Greek philosophy.

Long before the Zohar and *The Cloud of Unknowing*, Greek philosophy in its Arabic garb had led Jewish and Christian thinkers to a fresh interpretation of their religious traditions in the light of the new systematic modes of thought, the rise of Scholasticism in Christianity with its culmination in Aquinas and of mediaeval Aristotelianism in Judaism culminating in Maimonides. Side by side with these trends a strong degree of Neo-Platonic thought emerged. In both faiths, the question of anthropomorphism was widely discussed, of how human thought can legitimately be applied at all to God who, according to the philosophers, is indescribable in human language. In the *Via Positiva*, while God is infinitely greater than any weak attempt at human reasoning can reach, there is still sufficient correspondence between, say, God's goodness and human goodness that it is possible to apply positive attributes to Him. In the *Via Negativa* only negative attributes of God are legitimate. A description of what God is not can be attempted, never of what He is. (The actual Latin terms *Via Negativa* and *Via Positiva* are not of course found in Jewish sources but the phenomena the terms denote are certainly present and, occasionally, the Hebrew equivalents are found in connection with the divine attributes: *sholeli* and *hiyyuvi*.) Neo-Platonism is particularly emphatic that very little can be said of God as He is in Himself. For Plotinus[3] the 'One' is unknowable. If it is called 'Good' this is not to affirm any quality within itself. To affirm its existence means no more than that it does not fall within the realm of non-existents so that it is false even to say that the 'One' exists because it is beyond all essence and existence: 'Its definition, in fact, could only be "the indefinable"; what is not a thing is not some definite thing. We are in agony for a true expression; we are talking of the untenable; we name, only to indicate for our own use as best we may. And this name, The One, contains really no more than the negation of plurality ... If we are led to think positively of The One, name and thing, there would be more truth in silence; the designation, a mere aid to inquiry, was never intended for more than a preliminary affirmation of absolute simplicity to be followed by the rejection of even that statement: it was the best that offered, but remains inadequate to express the nature indicated. For this is a principle not to be conveyed by any sound; it cannot be known on any hearing, but, if at all, by vision, and to hope in that vision to see a form is to fail even of that.'

It is generally accepted that the *Via Negativa* as found in pseudo-Dionysius, a teacher whose influence on *The Cloud of Unknowing* is evident throughout, owes much to the doctrines taught by the heathen Neo-Platonist Proclus[4] who was lecturing in Athens in the year 430. This author, too, prefers to use the non-personal term 'It' when speaking of the Godhead. Pseudo-Dionysius became familiar to Western Christians through a Latin translation made by an Irish scholar in the ninth century, and to the Greek Church even earlier, in the seventh century. Following Proclus, St Denis, as he is called by the author of *The Cloud of Unknowing*, writes:

> Now concerning this hidden Super-Essential Godhead we must not dare, as I have said, to speak, or even to form any conception Thereof, except those things which are divinely revealed to us from the Holy Scriptures. For as It hath lovingly taught us in the Scriptures concerning Itself, the understanding and contemplation of Its actual nature is not accessible to any being; for such knowledge is super-essentially exalted above them all. And many of the Sacred Writers thou wilt find who have declared that It is not only invisible and incomprehensible, but also unsearchable and past finding out since there is no trace of any that have penetrated the hidden depths of Its infinitude. Not that the Good is wholly incommunicable to anything, nay, rather, while dwelling alone by Itself, and having there firmly Its super-essential Ray, It lovingly reveals Itself by illuminations corresponding to each separate creature's powers, and thus draws upwards holy minds into such contemplation, participation and resemblance of Itself as they can attain – even them that holily and duly strive thereafter and do not seek with impotent presumption the Mystery beyond that heavenly revelation which is so granted as to fit their powers, nor yet through their lower propensity slip down the steep descent, but with unwavering constancy press onwards towards the ray that casts its light upon them and through the love responsive to these gracious illuminations, speed their temperate and holy flight on the wings of a godly reverence.[5]

The author of *The Cloud of Unknowing* states (chapter 70) that Dionysius's work clearly endorses all that he has said in his treatise, that 'the most godlike knowledge of God is that which is known by unknowing'... All rational beings, he says (chapter 4), possess two faculties, the power of knowing and the power of loving but God cannot be known by knowing but by love. It is by an act of the naked loving will that the contemplative can penetrate the 'cloud of unknowing'. But this very ability to love and know Him would not be possible without His prior love for us. We are able to approach Him by His grace or free gift. In contemplation all remembrance, even of the holiest things, is a hindrance rather than a help (chapter 9). The author advises the contemplative (chapter 3): 'When you begin, you will find only darkness, and as it were a cloud of unknowing. You don't know what this means except that in your will you feel a steadfast intention reaching out towards God. Do what you will, this darkness and this cloud remain between you and God, and stop you both from seeing him in the clear light of rational understanding, and from experiencing his loving awareness in your affection. Reconcile yourself to wait in the darkness as long as is necessary, but still go on longing after him whom you love. For if you are to feel him or to see him in this life, it must always be in this cloud, in this darkness. And if you will work hard at what I tell you, I believe that through God's mercy you will achieve this very thing.' According to this Christian mystic, the love of which he speaks is only possible through the love of Jesus (chapter 4). If the contemplative asks 'how am I to think of God himself, and what is he?', the author replies (chapter 6) that all he can say is: 'I do not know!' 'For with this question you have brought me into the same darkness, the same cloud of unknowing, where I want you to be.' God may well be loved, but not thought. By love he can be caught and held, but by thinking never.

The author of *The Cloud of Unknowing* (chapter 7) continues that when the mystic's thought asks him what he is seeking he should reply that it is God he wants. If his thought then asks him: 'What is this God?', he should answer that it is the God who made him and redeemed him who, through his grace, called him to his love. 'So when you feel by the grace of God that he is calling you to this work, and you intend to respond, lift your heart to God with humble love. And really mean God himself who created you, and bought you, and graciously called you to this state of life. And think no other thought of him. It all depends on your desire. A naked intention directed to God, and himself alone, is wholly sufficient.' In this contemplation the mystic should not even think of God's kindness or worth (chapter 5): 'For though it is good to think about the kindness of God, and to love him and praise him for it, it is better to think about him as he is, and to love and praise him for himself.'

To turn now to the Zohar, it has first to be appreciated that this work is based entirely on the system known as the Kabbalah, which arose in the Provence in the twelfth century, from whence it spread to Spain. It is better to speak of the Zoharic corpus since, in addition to the Zohar proper (it is the verdict of modern scholarship that this was composed by Moses de Leon), there are additions such as the Tikkuney Zohar and the Rayya Mehemna by later authors.[6]

The mediaeval Jewish thinkers, before the Kabbalistic system was fully developed, argued that reason must be brought into play in order to refine the idea of God. In a memorable passage in his 'Duties of the Heart', Bahya Ibn Pakudah (eleventh century) quotes[7] with approval the saying of a 'philosopher' that the only men who serve the 'Cause of causes' are the prophet by virtue of his nature and the philosopher by virtue of his reason. The prophet knows God intuitively, the philosopher knows what God is because his reasoning about God has freed him from cruder conceptions. All other men, Bahya observes, in their worship of God, are not really worshipping God but something other than he, a mere figment of the imagination. The reasoning process to which Bahya alludes consists in negating from God all human and finite limitations. If we wish to determine the nature of a thing, says Bahy,[8] we must ask two questions – if it is and *what* it is. But of God one can only ask if he is. Once having established that God is we cannot go on to ask *what* he is for his true nature is utterly beyond all human comprehension. In that case what are we to make of the description of God's attributes found in Scripture and used in the liturgy? Bahya claims that the three main attributes are to be understood in a negative not a positive sense. These three attributes of God, his existence, his unity and his eternity, even when expressed in positive terms, as they are in Scripture, are negative attributes. Thus to say that God exists means that he is not nonexistent; to say that he is one is to say that there is no multiplicity or plurality in him; to say that he is eternal is to say that he is not temporal or transient. Inscrutable though God's nature is, this we

The Via Negativa in Jewish Thought

do know, that there is a God, that there is no plurality in him and that he is not involved in the temporal process. As for the other attributes, such as God's goodness and wisdom, these can be expressed in positive form because they deal, unlike the first three, with God's acts not his essence. These have a psychological value in that they afford human beings a vocabulary of worship. If no attributes at all were to be allowed, man would have no means of communicating with his Creator.

Maimonides (1135–1204) takes up the question of negative attributes, developing the doctrine at length in his 'Guide for the Perplexed'.[9] For Maimonides, to ascribe to God positive attributes is a form of polytheism because it suggests that other beings, namely, his attributes, are co-existent with him for all eternity. According to Maimonides, even to say that God is One is not to say anything significant about his true nature but only to negate all plurality from his being. Even to say that God exists is simply to say that his non-existence is impossible. Like Bahya, Maimonides does allow positive attributes to be used if these refer to God's acts but attributes referring to God's nature are only permissible in their negative form. Furthermore, the attributes referring to God's acts imply only the acts themselves not the emotions responsible for them. Thus the Biblical references to God's mercy do not imply that God is influenced by feelings of mercy but 'that acts similar to those which a father performs for his son, out of pity, mercy and real affection, emanate from God solely to the benefit of his pious men, and are by no means the result of any impression or change'.

The Kabbalists were evidently influenced by the philosophical negation of attributes and yet, at the same time, sensed that, if God is to be worshipped in mystical prayer and contemplation, God talk and God thought are required. For the Kabbalists, Neo-Platonic negation (though the Kabbalists never actually refer to Neo-Platonic thinkers) and traditional Jewish positive statements about God are combined in a very unconventional way. The Kabbalists draw a distinction between God as he is in himself and God in manifestation, between *deus absconditus* and *deus revelatus*. God as he is in himself is called *En Sof,* 'That which is limitless'.[10] By a process of emanation ten powers or potencies emerge from *En Sof*. These are the Ten Sefirot. These ten represent God's wisdom and emotions is the creative processes. There is much debate among the Kabbalists as to whether the Sefirot are themselves part of the Godhead or are the instruments of *En Sof* but, in the Zohar, the Sefirot are separate from *En Sof* and yet infused by It.[11] The Kabbalists go beyond the philosophers with regard to *En Sof*, from which even negative attributes are negated. One cannot speak or even think of *En So*, not even, strictly speaking, to call It *En Sof*, according to the eighteenth-century Talmudist and Kabbalist, Elijah Gaon of Vilna. But in speaking and thinking of the Sefirot even positive attributes are allowed. The Kabbalists are always on guard against dualism, that there are two Gods, the *En Sof* and the world of the Sefirot or ten Gods distributed among the Sefirot. The Kabbalists employ various metaphors such as that of colourless water poured into bottles of different hues which assumes for the time the colour of the vessels into which it is poured.[12]

In the doctrine of *En Sof* the *Via Negativa* receives the most radical expression in Jewish mystical thought. The Kabbalist Azriel of Gerona (1160–1238) remarks: 'Know that *En Sof* cannot be thought of, much less spoken about, even though there is a hint of in all things, for there is nothing apart from*It*. Consequently, *It* can be contained neither by letter nor writing nor any thing.'[13] Another Kabbalist, contemporaneous with the Zohar, writes: 'Know that the *En Sof* we have mentioned is hinted at neither in the Pentateuch nor the Prophets nor the Hagiographa nor in the Rabbinic literature but the masters of worship [the Kabbalists] received a faint hint of *It.*'[14]

The Zohar, obedient to the Kabbalistic conception of the incomprehensibility of *En Sof*, rarely refers to this aspect of Deity and on the rare occasions when it does it is only to stress the utter failure of thought to penetrate the great Mystery. Even of the higher stages of God in manifestation, that is to say, of the stages represented by God's will, his wisdom and understanding, the Zohar prefers to speak in negative terms. God's will, represented by the Sefirah *Keter* ('Crown') is called *Ayin*, 'Nothing'. So elevated is *Keter*, the link between *En Sof* and the other Sefirot, beyond all human thought, that it can only be represented by complete negation. *Keter* is not even the will to create but the emergence of a will to will *En Sof* to create, that is, to cause the other Sefirot to be emanated from it. From *Keter* there is the further emanation of *Hokhmah* ('Wisdom'). This is the will to create. At this stage all the details of the whole process of emanation of the Sefirot exist in potentia but are not realized in the divine thought until the emergence of *Binah* ('Understanding'). The Zohar states that of *Binah* one can ask what it is but no answer can be forthcoming.[15]

Scholem[16] calls this the apotheosis of the Jewish penchant for answering a question with a question. Of *Hokhmah* one cannot even ask the question.

Reference should be made in this connection to the Zoharic understanding[17] of the first verse in Genesis, usually translated as: 'In the beginning God created the heavens and the earth'. The Hebrew word for 'in the beginning' is *bereshit* which can be rendered 'with the beginning', representing *Hokhmah*, the first impulse in the Godhead to create, that is, to cause to be emanated... 'God created' in the verse is, in the Hebrew, 'created God', *bara elohim*, *elohim* standing for *Binah*. Thus the verse is rendered: By means of *reshit* (=*Hokhmah*) he (the unknown, the *En Sof*) created *elohim* (=*Binah*) i.e. the God of religion, God in manifestation, comes into being, so to speak, through the process of emanation from *Hokhmah*. This is the *Via Negativa* with a vengeance. *Keter*, as the link between *En Sof* and the other Sefirot, is not mentioned here at all since it is so far above all human thought. In the scheme in which colours are allotted to the Sefirot,[18] *Keter* has the colour of impenetrable blackness and darkness, the 'dazzling darkness' of which *The Cloud of Unknowing* speaks. Similarly, when describing the beginning of the process, the Zohar uses the imagery of a darkness beyond darkness emerging to produce colours:

> In the beginning, when the will of the King began to take effect, he engraved signs into the divine aura. A dark flame sprang forth from the innermost recess of the mystery of the Infinite, *En Sof*, like a fog which forms out of the formless, enclosed in the ring of this aura, neither white nor black, neither red nor green, and of no colour whatever. But when the flame began to assume size and extension it produced radiant colours. For in the innermost centre of the flame a well sprang forth from which flames poured upon everything below, hidden in the mysterious secrets of *En Sof*. The well broke through, and yet did not entirely break through, the ethereal aura which surrounds it. It was entirely unrecognisable until under the impact of its break-through a hidden supernal point shone forth. Beyond this point nothing may be known or understood, and therefore it is called *Reshit*, that is 'Beginning', the first word of creation.[19]

Thus the Zohar, like the author of *The Cloud of Unknowing*, knows of the 'cloud' which knowledge cannot penetrate, the difference appearing to be that, in the Zoharic scheme, *Keter* and a fortiori *En Sof* cannot really be spoken of at all. The 'cloud' is not a barrier to be penetrated by means of love but is the ultimate aspect of God to which no direct access at all is allowed. To be sure, the Zohar also knows of mystical contemplation in love[20] but this is contemplation of the Sefirot. Through contemplation of the Sefirotic process the soul of the mystic is engaged in love with the Sefirot and through these his soul is attached to *En Sof.* Whereas for the author of *The Cloud of Unknowing* it is the naked will to love God, in which all thought about the Godhead is abandoned, that is the task of the mystic, for the Zohar, while thought on *En Sof* is utterly impossible, contemplation of the Sefirot is the means of becoming attached to God. In *The Cloud of Unknowing* the mind has to be emptied of all thought about God's mercies and goodness to be concentrated on God alone, for the Zohar there is to be a filling of the mind of thoughts about the Sefirotic processes through which alone the mystic becomes attached to God.

The author of *The Cloud of Unknowing* also wrote a brief commentary to the Prayer of St Denis[21] in which his basic ideas on contemplation are contained. It might be helpful to compare this with the similar Prayer of Elijah in the Tikkuney Ha-Zohar.[22] The Prayer of St Denis reads in modern English:

> You are wisdom, uncreated and eternal, the supreme First Cause, above all being, sovereign Godhead, sovereign goodness, watching unseen the God-inspired wisdom of Christian people
> Raise us, we pray, that we may totally respond to the supreme, unknown, ultimate and splendid height of your words, mysterious and inspired.
> There all God's secret matters lie covered and hidden under darkness both profound and brilliant, silent and wise.
> You make what is ultimate and beyond brightness secretly to shine in all that is most dark.
> In Your way, ever unseen and intangible, You fill to the full with most beautiful splendour those souls who close their eyes that they may see.
> And I, please, with love that goes beyond mind to all that is beyond mind, seek to gain such for myself through this prayer

The opening of the Zoharic passage reads:

> Elijah began by saying: Lord of the universe! You are One but are not numbered. You are higher than the highest. You are the mystery above all mysteries. No thought can grasp You at all. It is You who produced the Ten Perfections which we call the Ten Sefirot. With them You guide the secret worlds which have not been revealed and the worlds which have been revealed, and in them You conceal Yourself from human beings. But it is You who binds them together and unites them. Since

You are in them, whoever separates any one of these ten from the others it is as if he had made a division in You.

Further on in Elijah's Prayer it is said:

> Lord of the universe! You are the Cause of causes, the Ground of grounds, who waters the tree [of the Sefirot] by means of a spring and that spring is as the soul to the body by which the body survives. Of You there is no likeness or image of anything within or without.
>
> No one can know anything about You. Apart from You none is unique and there is no unity apart from You in the upper and lower worlds. You are known as Lord of all there is. Among all the Sefirot each has a special name by which the angels are called. But you have no special name for You fill all names and You are the perfection of them all and when You remove Yourself from them all names remain as body without soul.

The correspondences as well as the differences between these two approaches of the *Via Negativa* are clear. In both, God, as He is in himself, is beyond human wisdom. In both, he is the sovereign Godhead. But in the Prayer of St Denis he 'watches unseen the God-inspired wisdom of Christian people' i.e. he is concealed in that God-inspired wisdom, whereas in the Zoharic passage, the *En Sof is* concealed in the Sefirot. For the author of *The Cloud of Unknowing* the contemplation to be engaged in is the negation of all thoughts, even holy thoughts regarding the goodness of God and his mercies, so as to allow the naked intent to love God to be receptive to God himself. In the Zoharic scheme, contemplation involves profound reflection on the Sefirot, that is, precisely on the goodness of God as revealed in the Sefirot. Since the Sefirot are the 'garments' of *En Sof*, it is through them, and through them alone, that thought can approach the great Unknown. It can perhaps be put in this way: in the Zoharic scheme the *Via Negativa* utilizes the *Via Positiva* whereas in *The Cloud of Unknowing* the *Via Negativa* involves a repudiation, during contemplation, of the *Via Positiva*.

It is interesting to find that, centuries after the Zohar, Hasidic contemplation, while still utilizing the *Via Positiva* of reflection on the Sefirot, still ultimately negates this, too, in order for the soul to reach out to *En Sof*. The mind does dwell on the Sefirotic realm and the four worlds of Emanation, Creation, Formation and Action but only in a casual way and the whole scheme is interiorized, that is to say, the interest is far less in what goes on in the higher worlds but rather in the way the counterparts of the Sefirot in the human psyche find expression therein, with the ultimate aim of losing the self in *En Sofas* revealed in the Sefirah of Wisdom. In a well-known Hasidic text the technique of mystical prayer is described as follows:

> When he prays a man should put all his strength into the utterances and so he should proceed from letter to letter until he has forgotten his corporeal nature. He should reflect on the idea that the letters become combined and joined one to the other and this is great delight. For if in the material world unification is attended by delight how much more so in the spiritual realms! This is the stage of the World of Formation. Afterwards he should reach the stage of having the letters in his thoughts alone so that he no longer hears that which he speaks. At this stage he actually enters the World of Formation. Afterwards he should reach the quality of Nothingness at which all his physical powers are annihilated. This is the stage of the World of Emanation, the quality of Wisdom.[23]

It is fascinating to trace the evolution of Jewish mystical thought from the Zohar through to Hasidism but this would take us beyond the aim of this lecture ...

It is perhaps fitting for the great exponent of the Zoharic doctrine, Moses Cordovero (1522–70), to have the last word. Cordovero advises the contemplative to follow the 'living creatures', seen in Ezekiel's vision of the Chariot, to allow his mind to run 'to and fro': 'And the living creatures ran and returned as the appearance of a flash of lightning' (Ezekiel 1:14). Cordovero writes:

> When your intellect conceives of God do not allow yourself to imagine that there is really a God as depicted by you. For if you do this you will have, God forfend, a finite and corporeal conception. Instead your mind should dwell only on the affirmation of God's existence and then recoil. To do more than this is to allow the imagination to reflect on God as he is in himself and such reflection is bound to result in imaginative limitation and corporeality. Put reins, therefore, on your intellect and do not allow it too great a freedom, but assert God's existence and deny your intellect the possibility of comprehending him. The mind should run to and fro–running to affirm God's existence and recoiling from any limitations produced by the imagination, since man's imagination pursues his intellect.[24]

A statement to which, one can imagine, the author of *The Cloud of Unknowing* would give his assent.

The Via Negativa in Jewish Thought

NOTES

1. This lecture is partly based on my Alan Bronfman Lecture, delivered in Montreal, entitled 'The *Via-Negativa* in Jewish Religious Thought', Judaica Press, New York, n.d. On the *Via Negativa* in general see the article by Veselin Kesich 'Via Negativa' in *The Encyclopedia of Religion*, ed. Mircea Eliade, New York, 1987, vol. 15, pp. 252–4 with a full bibliography. For Jewish views see also: Daniel C. Matt: *'Ayin:* The Concept of Nothingness in Jewish Mysticism' in: *The Problem of Pure Consciousness: Mysticism and Philosophy*, ed. K. C. Forman, Oxford University Press, New York and Oxford, 1990, pp. 121–59.
2. I am indebted, in my account of *The Cloud of Unknowing* to the edition of Clifton Wolters and Wolters's Introductions and notes: *The Cloud of Unknowing* and Other Works. Translated into Modem English with an Introduction by Clifton Wolters, Penguin Books, 1978.
3. See Plotinus: *The Enneads*, translated by Stephen MacKenna, 2nd edition, revised by B.S. Page, Faber and Faber, London, 1956 p. xxiv, *Enneads*, v, 5.6, p. 408.
4. See B. R. Dodds: *Proclus - The Elements of Theology*, Oxford, The Clarendon Press, 1933, p. 195, in which Dodds refers to the influence of Proclus on Dionysius, and Appendix 1: 'The Unknown God in Neoplatonism', pp. 3 10–313.
5. Quoted in the section on Dionysius the Areopagite in A.C.Bouquet: *Sacred* Books of the World, Cassell, London, 1963, Part 111, 7 (iv), pp.218-220. *Cf* Dean Inge: *Mysticism in Religion*, London, 1969, pp. 164–166, that the author of *The Cloud of Unknowing* was also influenced by Richard of St victor, Augustine and probably Bonaventura and Inge's comparison with the views of Eckhart. Eckhart was, in fact, a contemporary of the Zohar.
6. The two essential accounts of the authorship and doctrine of the Zohar are: Gershom G. Scholem: *MaJor Trends in Jewish Mysticism*, Thames and Hudson, London, 1955, pp. 156–243; Isaiah Tishby: *The Wisdom of the Zohar*, translated from the Hebrew by David Goldstein, The Littmann Library of Jewish Civilization, Oxford University Press,1989.
7. Shaar Ha-Yihud, chapter 2.
8. *Shaar Ha-Yihud*, chapters 4 and 10.
9. Guide Part I, chapters 5 1–60.
10. On the doctrine of *En Sof* see the section on *'En Sof* and the World of Emanation' in Tishby, *op. cit.*, pp.229–269.
11. See the section on the 5eflrot in Tishby, *op. cit.*, pp.269–370.
12. *Cf* the discussion in Tishby *op. cit.*, pp.232–235.
13. *Perush Eser Sefirot* in Meir Jbn Gabbai's *Derekh Emunah*, Berlin, 1850, pp.2a–4a.
14. Maarekhet Ha-Elohut, Mantua, 1558, chapter 8, beg., quoted by Scholem op. cit., p.353 note 8.
15. Zohar I, ib.
16. Scholem *op.cit.*, p.220.
17. Zohar I, 3b.
18. On the Sefirot and colours see my Friends of Dr. Williams's Library Trust Lecture, 'Symbols for the divine in the Kabbalab', London, 1984.
19. Zohar I, 15a in the translation of Scholem, *op. cit.*, pp.218-219
20. See Tishby *op.cit.*, p.232. *Cf* Elijah de Vidas on 'love' in his *Reshit Hokhmah*, ed. Jerusalem, 1980, *Shaar Ha-A havah*, chapter 4:18, pp.417-421, quoting, among other passages, Zohar II, 198b on 'the desire of the heart in love' through which the very self is surrendered.
21. In Wolters ed. *op. cit.*, p206 in modem English; the author's translation is, of course, into Middle English.
22. Tikkuney Ha-Zohar, 5econd introduction. I have translated this passage with explanatory notes in my: *Jewish Ethics, Philosophy and Mysticism*, Behrman House, New York, 1969, pp. 115–120.
23. *Keter Shem Toy*, ed. Jerusalem, 1968, pp.48 a-b. *Cf.* the chapters on contemplative prayer in Hasidism in my: *Hasidic Prayer*, The Littman Library of Jewish Civilization, London Washington, 1993, pp.70–92.
24. *Elimah*, Lemberg, 1881, 1, 10, p.4b. *Cf* Cordovero's remarks *(Tomer Devorah*, chapter 5; in my translation: *The Palm Tree of Deborah*, Vallentine Mitchell, London, 1960, pp.99—100) that when carrying out the religious duty of burying the dead the mystic should have in mind that the counterpart in the Sefirotic Realm is the 'burial' i.e. the loss of separate life of the Sefirot in *En Sof.*

— 3 —

Jewish Cosmology*

A study of the Jewish sources demonstrates that the Jews did not develop in any period of their history a special cosmology of their own. They adopted or accepted the cosmologies of the various civilizations in which they lived, but utilized these for the religious purposes with which they were primarily concerned. Judging by the classical Jewish writings, Jewish preoccupation was with the God of cosmos not with the cosmos itself. There was, to be sure, a profound interest in natural phenomena but chiefly as pointers to God who initiated them and whose glory was revealed through them.

> Lift up your eyes on high,
> And see: who hath created these?
> He that bringeth out their host by number,
> He calleth them all by name;
> By the greatness of His might, and
>   for that He is strong in power,
> Not one faileth   Isa. 40:26)

> The heavens declare the glory of God,
> And the firmament showeth forth His handiwork
>   (Ps. 19:2)

The vivid description of the universe and its creatures in Psalm 104 begins with:

> O Lord my God, Thou art very great;
> Thou art clothed with glory and majesty

It is preferable, therefore, to speak not so much of Jewish cosmology as of cosmologies that have been entertained by Jews. For

---

* A brief explanation of some of the technical expressions used in this chapter will be found on pp. 37–8.

Jewish Cosmology

Figure 1
Heaven, the earth and the abysses
(Source: W. F. Warren, *The Earliest Cosmologies* (New York, 1909))

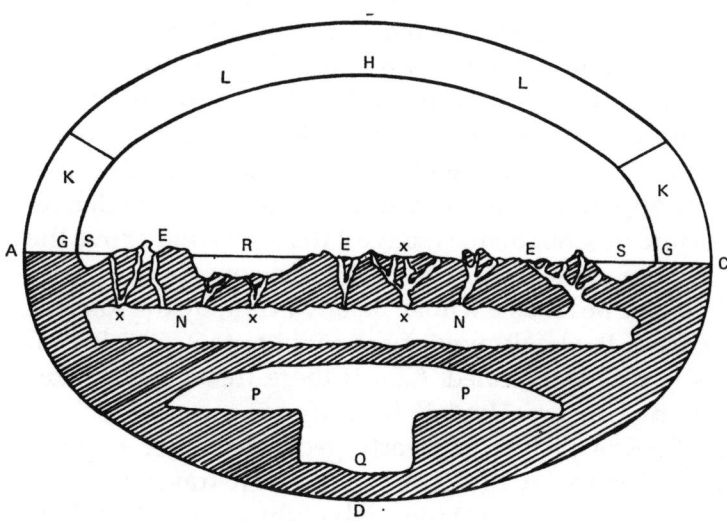

Explanatory Key:
ABC = the upper heaven; ADC = the curve of the abyss; AEC = the plane of the earth and seas; SRS = various parts of the sea; EEE = various parts of the earth; GHG = the profile of the firmament or lower heaven; KK = the storehouses of the winds; LL = the storehouses of the upper waters, of snow, and of hail; M = the space occupied by the air, within which the clouds move; NN = the waters of the great abyss; xxx = the fountains of the great abyss; PP = Sheol or limbo; Q = the lower part of the same, the inferno properly so called.

these it is necessary to examine the picture of the world as portrayed in the Bible and the Rabbinic literature, in mediaeval Jewish philosophy and the *Kabbalah*, with a glance at later Jewish thought. The consideration of mediaeval notions in a series of chapters concerning ancient cosmologies is, I think, justified when we observe that many of these notions are themselves ancient. Even when they are stressed particularly by the mediaeval thinkers, they go back in the main to the period with which this series is concerned.

Although the Biblical writings extend over a period of several hundred years, the cosmological picture in these writings is remarkably uniform. One can, without distortion, refer, therefore, to the 'Biblical' view and quote in its support passages from the different books of the Bible. A moot point first to be noted is whether the Biblical record knows of the concept of a cosmos. T. H. Gaster[1] suggests that to the ancient Hebrews 'the world was not an organic unity but a collection of disparate phenomena individually controlled and collectively disposed at the will and pleasure of their common Creator'. There is, in fact, no word in the Bible for 'universe' or 'cosmos'. The word *olam*, later (in the Rabbinic literature, for instance) meaning 'world' or 'universe', means, in the Bible, 'eternity', with the possible exception of the use of this word in the late book of Ecclesiastes (3:11). However, the use of 'very good' at the end of the creation narrative in Genesis (1:31), as opposed to the simple 'good' in which the details of the creation are described, does suggest that, over and above the excellence of each particular, the writers had a concept of the excellence of the cosmic order as a whole.[2] In any event, by the Rabbinic period (i.e. from the beginning of the civil era to *c.* 500) the idea of a cosmos is well established. God is there frequently spoken of as 'King of the Universe' (*melekh ha-olam*).

The Biblical picture is clearly geocentric. The earth has the shape of a flat disc[3] so that if one were able to travel far enough one would eventually arrive at the 'ends of the earth' (Deut. 13:8; 28:64; Isa. 5:26; Ps. 135:7). This term can simply refer to far-distant places, but its use is evidence of the cosmological picture. The 'corners' or 'wings' (*kanefot*) of the earth (Isa. 11:12; Ezek. 7:2; Job 37:3) may be a synonym for the 'ends of the earth'. If, on the other hand, the earth is not conceived of as a disc but as a square strip, the 'corners' may be understood literally. It is also possible that the term *kanefot* refers to the four directions, north, south, east and west. The earth rests on pillars (Job 9:6). Stretched above the earth is the sky, 'heaven' (*shamayim*) or 'firmament' (*rakia*), a solid substance[4] (Gen. I:6–8) resting on pillars (Job 26:1 1).[5] Just as the earth has an 'end' so does the sky (Deut. 4:32). The sun, moon and stars are positioned in, or just beneath,[6] the firmament (Gen. I:14–17) and they move across it (Ps. 19:1–7). Beneath the earth is *Sheol*[7] the abode of the dead (Num. 16:28–34; I Sam. 28:13–15; Isa. 14:9–11; Eccles. 9:10). There are waters above the firmament (Gen. 1:6–7) as well as beneath it. Some of the waters beneath the firmament were gathered together at the beginning of creation to form the seas (Gen. 1:9–10) but, in addition, these waters flow beneath the earth (Exod. 20:4; Deut. 4:18; Ps. 24:2) where they are connected to the waters of *Tehom*, the great deep (Gen. 1:2). Fountains, wells and springs flow from these waters beneath the earth. The Deluge was caused by a tremendous outpouring of the fountains of *Tehom* as well as by the opening of the windows of heaven (Gen. 7:11). Rain is pro-

Figure 2
Biblical conception of the world
(Source: N. M. Sarna, *Understanding Genesis* (New York, 1966))

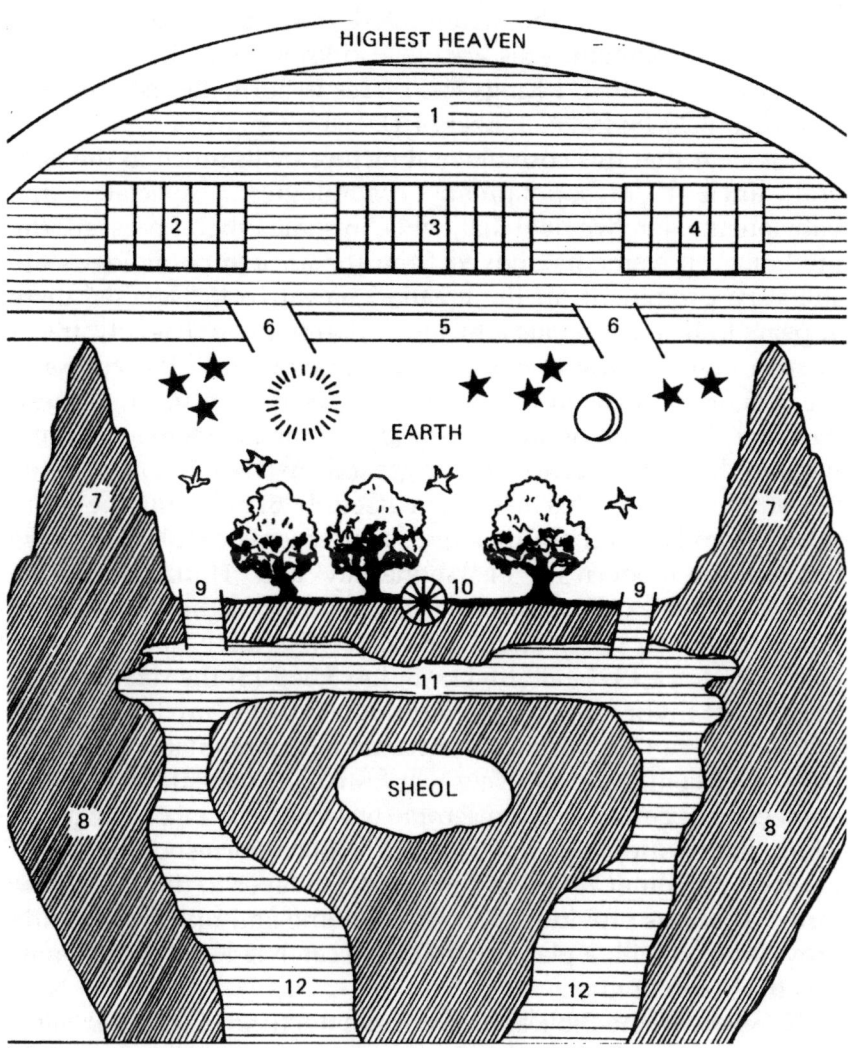

Biblical conception of the world: 1. waters above the firmament; 2. storehouses of snows; 3. storehouses for hail; 4. chambers of winds; 5. firmament; 6. sluice; 7. pillars of the sky; 8. pillars of the earth; 9. fountain of the deep; 10. navel of the earth; 11. waters under the earth; 12. rivers of the nether world.

duced by the clouds (Gen. 9:11–17; Job 26:8; Eccles. 11:3). The water in the clouds comes from the waters above the firmament so that when the heaven is 'shut up' there is no rain (Deut. 11:17) while when the 'good treasure' of heaven is opened the rain falls in abundance (Deut. 28:12).

While the word 'heaven' (*shamayim*) is used of the firmament or sky, it is also used of the area located above the waters that are above the firmament. This area is also known as 'the heaven of heavens' (Deut. 10:4; I Kings 8:27). This is normally the abode of God (Exod. 20:19; Isa. 66:I; Ezek. 1:1).

It is clear that this cosmological picture owes much to the general ancient Mesopotamian cosmologies, especially the Babylonian. Here we note that, while in some Biblical passages the mythological elements derived from the ancient cosmologies are still very prominent, in the creation narrative in Genesis[8] there appears to be a conscious effort to suppress them. Possibly, traces of such mythological themes as the battle between the gods and the dragon of chaos in the deep are present even in the Genesis narrative in the use of the word *Tehom* (= the Babylonian *Tiamat**) without the definite article for the great deep (Gen. 1:12) and in the use of the plural 'Let us make man' (Gen. 1:26) reflecting the counsel of the gods. But these are largely matters of vocabulary or usage only (cf. the modern use of 'Wednesday' and 'Thursday' for the days of the week). The narrative as a whole breathes the spirit of monotheism. In other Biblical passages (Isa. 27:1 30:7; 5 1:9–10; Hab. 3:8; Ps. 74:13–14; 89:10–11; 93; Job 3:8; 9:13) the references to the ancient myths are far more pronounced. The 'myth and ritual' school has even purported to detect an annual re-enactment of the primordial conflict on the New Year festival in ancient Israel.[9] It has also been suggested that the Temple was constructed on the parallel of the world, e.g. the Holy of Holies corresponds to the heavens, the outer house to the earth, the laver to the sea and so forth.[10] God has provided man with a home and man in gratitude provides God with a place in which He can reside and which mirrors the home of man.

Nowhere in the Biblical record is the doctrine of *creatio ex nihilo* clearly mentioned. Although the root *bara*, 'to create', is used only of God's activity, never of man's, it does not in itself imply *creatio ex nihilo*; indeed, the root meaning seems to be that of 'cutting out' i.e. of an existing material. As Abraham Ibn Ezra (1089–1164)[11] pointed out in the Middle Ages, the root *bara* is used in the Genesis narrative not alone for the original creation (Gen. 1:1) but also for the later creation of the sea-monsters (Gen. 1:21) and of man (Gen. 1:27). The earliest reference in Jewish literature to *creatio ex nihilo* is in the second book of Maccabees (late second to early first century BC; see 7:28). In the Wisdom of Solomon (first century BC to first century AD), on the other hand, creation is out of 'formless matter' (11:17).

On the whole the cosmological picture as it appears in the vast Rabbinic literature is not very different from the Biblical picture. The world of nature was thoroughly familiar to the Rabbis and they introduced special benedictions to be recited when a man observes its marvels. There are benedictions on observing the sea, mountains, comets, thunder and lightning, strange creatures and trees in bloom.[12] But side by side with this there is a strong attempt to discourage speculation on cosmic origins and on those cosmic matters that are beyond human experience, in all probability because of the heretical, especially dualistic, views, which could follow from these.[13] Ben Sira (early second century BC) is quoted in the Talmud[14] for his, according to the Rabbis, sound advice: 'Do not pry into things too hard for you or examine what is beyond your reach. Meditate on the commandments you have been given; what the Lord keeps secret is no concern of yours.[15] (Eccles. 3:21–22). Thus the *Mishnah*[16] states: 'Whosoever reflects on four things, it were better for him if he had not come into the world – what is above; what is beneath; what is before; and what is after.' In the comment of the Jerusalem Talmud to this passage in the *Mishnah* it is said that the *Mishnah* follows the opinion of Rabbi Akiba (c. 50–150 BC) but that according to Rabbi Ishmael (early second century AD) it is permitted to 'expound the work of creation'. In any event there are to be found in the Rabbinic literature discussions on the manner of God's creation and the nature not alone of the terrestrial but also of the celestial realms.

The School of Shammai (first century AD) held that heaven was created first and the earth afterwards. The School of Hillel (first century AD) held that the earth was created first and afterwards the heavens. But the Sages held that heaven and earth were created simultaneously.[17] We are told[18] that a philosopher said to Rabban Gamaliel (first century AD): 'Your God is a great craftsman, but He found good materials to help Him in the work of creation, namely, *Tohu* and *Bohu*, darkness, wind, water and the deep', to which Rabban Gamaliel retorts that these, too, were created by God and he quotes scriptural verses in support. This is the Rabbinic equivalent of the discussion concerning *creatio ex nihilo*. As late as the third century, however, the Palestinian teacher Rabbi

Johanan could say that God took two coils, one of fire and the other of snow, wove them into each other and created the world.[19] According to one Rabbinic theory all things were created simultaneously on the first day of creation but made their appearance at different stages in the other six days, just as figs are gathered simultaneously in one basket but each selected in its time.[20] The opinion that the primordial light was a garment with which God wrapped Himself before creation[21] is probably a reference to a theory of emanation which became especially prominent in the *Kabbalah*.[22] The idea is found that God created several worlds and destroyed them before creating this one.[23] God is, as it were, proud of the world He has created. He declares that His creation is 'very good' (Gen. 1:31). If the Creator praises His wonderful works who would dare to criticize them?[24] There was a belief in Rabbinic times that originally the sun and the moon were the same size but that because the moon protested that 'two kings cannot wear the same crown' God told her to make herself smaller.[25]

The fondness of the Rabbis for descriptions of the immense size of the universe has undoubtedly an apologetic motivation. The aim is either to praise God or to defend Israel's worth in creation. It is, in fact, difficult to know how far these statements were intended to be taken literally. For instance, a sage declares, in opposition to his colleagues, who say that the world rests on twelve or on seven pillars, that the earth rests on one pillar and its name is 'Righteous', for it is said: 'But *Righteous* is the foundation of the world' (Prov. 10:25).[26]

Similarly, a heavenly voice is made to taunt Nebuchadnezzar when he said: 'I will ascend above the heights of the clouds; I will be like the Most High' (Isa. 14:14). The heavenly voice replies: 'Man has only seventy years in which to live.' But the distance from the earth to the firmament is a journey of five hundred years, and the thickness of the firmament is a journey of five hundred years, and likewise the distance between one firmament and the other. Above them (the seven firmaments) are the holy living creatures:

> the feet of the holy living creatures are equal to all of them together; the ankles of the living creatures are equal to all of them together, the legs of the living creatures are equal to all of them; the knees of the living creatures are equal to all of them; the thighs of the living creatures are equal to all of them; the bodies of the living creatures are equal to all of them; the necks of the living creatures are equal to all of them; the heads of the living creatures are equal to all of them; the horns of the

living creatures are equal to all of them. Above them is the throne of glory: the feet of the throne of glory are equal to all of them; the throne of glory is equal to all of them. The King, the Living and Eternal God, High and Exalted, dwelleth among them. Yet thou didst say: 'I will ascend above the heights of the clouds, I will be like the Most High'![27]

(Ezek. 1:5)

Again, when Israel is apprehensive that God has forgotten her, He replies (significantly in terms taken from the Roman army):

My daughter, twelve constellations have I created in the firmament, and for each constellation I have created thirty hosts, and for each host I have created thirty legions, and for each legion I have created thirty cohorts, and for each cohort I have created thirty maniples, and for each maniple I have created thirty camps, and to each camp I have attached three hundred and sixty-five thousands of myriads of stars, corresponding to the days of the solar year, and all of them I have created only for thy sake, and thou sayest, Thou hast forgotten me and forsaken me![28]

As for the time the universe will endure, Rabbi Kattina (third century AD) said that the world will endure for six thousand years and it will be desolate for a thousand, but Abaye (early fourth century) said that it will be desolate for two thousand years.[29]

The Rabbis believed in the possibility of miracles happening, seeing in miracles not a suspension of natural or universal law (of which there was no such conception in their thinking) but, as they put it, a 'change in the order of creation'. They believed that miracles did not only occur in the past but occur also in their own day, although there are differences of opinion whether it was praiseworthy or otherwise for a miracle to be performed on behalf of a contemporary. Revealing in this connection is the bizarre anecdote about a man whose wife died, leaving him with a babe for whom he was unable to afford a nurse. A miracle was performed for him and his breasts became as a woman's that he might suckle his child. One of the Rabbis said: 'How great this man must have been that such a miracle was performed for him!' But another Rabbi said: 'On the contrary! How unworthy this man must have been that the order of creation was changed on his behalf!'[30]

In a well-known Rabbinic passage it is said that ten things were created on the eve of the first sabbath of creation in the twilight, among them: the mouth of the earth (Num. 16:32); the mouth of the well (Num. 21:16); the mouth of the ass (Num. 22:28); the rainbow, the manna, and the rod (Exod. 4:17).[31] Similarly, it is said that

Figure 3
Maimonides' cosmology

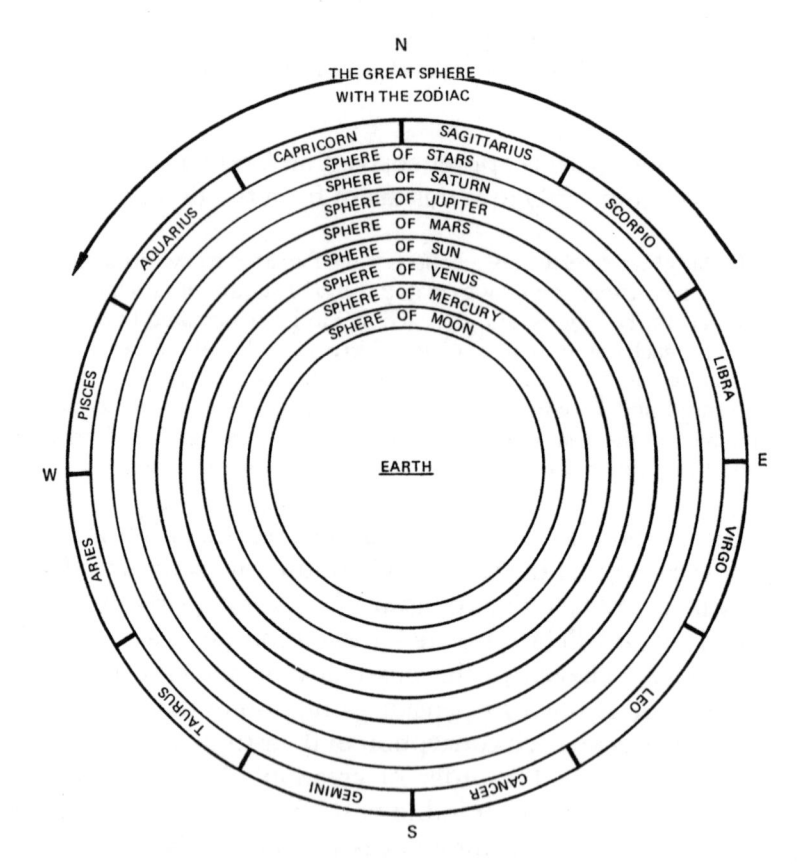

when God created the sea He imposed a condition on it that it be divided before Israel, as He did with the fire that it should not harm the three young men, with the lions that they should not harm Daniel, and with the fish that it should vomit out Jonah.[32] With the exception of the remark about 'universal law', which, as we have noted, is anachronistic when applied to the thought of the Rabbis, Zangwill's[33] explanation comes close to the meaning of these passages: 'The Fathers of the *Mishnah*, who taught that Balaam's ass was created on the eve of the Sabbath, in the twilight, were not fantastic fools, but subtle philosophers, discovering the reign of universal law through the exceptions, the miracles that had to be created specially and were still a part of the order of the world, bound to appear in due time much as apparently erratic comets are'

It is extraordinary how the ancient creation myths reappear in the Rabbinic, especially the Midrashic, literature. Thus, while it is stated that the Leviathan was created on the fifth day, together with the other fishes,[34] the fins of the Leviathan are said to radiate such brilliant light as to obscure the light of the sun.[35] The Leviathan is said to be the plaything of God.[36] There are references to a male and female Leviathan, God slaying the female.[37] But, interestingly enough, the conflict with the Leviathan is projected into the future. At the end of days the angels will engage the Leviathan in combat without success and eventually it will be slain by Behemot, and its flesh will be fed to the righteous.[38] The mythological *motif* is similarly pronounced in the legends which tell of the rebellion of the Prince of the Sea at the time of creation.[39] The astonishing feature in all this is that the mythological passages are late, dating from the Amoraic period (third century onwards) not from the earlier Tannaitic period. It would seem that the Mesopotamian creation myths lived on among the people and were at first refused any recognition by the official Rabbinic teachers.[40] Mythological *motif* of very ancient vintage similarly re-emerge in the Kabbalistic literature from the thirteenth century.

Mediaeval Jewish cosmology, generally speaking, is the standard Greek cosmology in its Arabic garb. The central problem for the Jewish thinkers in this area was the doctrine of *creatio ex nihilo*. All the Jewish thinkers reject the Aristotelian view that matter is eternal but while Maimonides (1134–1205) and the majority of these thinkers have an unqualified belief in *creatio ex nihilo*, considering this to be a cornerstone of the Jewish faith, Gersonides (1288–1344) adopts the Platonic view of a formless matter, existing from all eternity, upon which God imposed form.[41]

Maimonides devotes the opening sections of his great Code to a description of the universe in his conviction that man's contemplation of the vastness and the marvels of God's creation would evoke his sense of awe and lead eventually to the love and fear of God.[42] For Maimonides[43] there are three types of being in the universe: (1) beings having both form and matter but who suffer decay, such as humans, animals, plants and minerals; (2) beings having form and matter but which do not suffer decay, such as the spheres and the heavenly bodies attached to them; (3) beings that are non-corporeal, having only pure form, such as the angels. There are in all nine spheres. The nearest of these is the sphere to which the moon is attached. In ascending order there are then the spheres of Mercury, Venus, the Sun, Mars, Jupiter and Saturn. Above these is the eighth sphere to which all the other stars are attached and above all these is the great ninth sphere which revolves each day from east to west and through its revolutions the other spheres revolve. The spheres are translucent so that when seen from the earth all the stars appear to be attached to a single sphere. But each of the eight lower spheres is subdivided into many other spheres 'like the layers of an onion' (the comparison is made by Maimonides), some of these revolving from east to west, others from west to east. The spheres are both colourless and weightless. The blue appearance of the sky is an optical illusion.[44] The ninth sphere is divided into twelve sections each named after the planet situated beneath it. These are the twelve signs of the Zodiac.[45] Some of the stars seen in the sky are smaller in size than the earth, some of them larger. The earth is forty times larger than the moon but the sun is 170 times larger than the earth. The smallest of the stars is Mercury and none of the stars is larger than the sun.[46] The stars and spheres are intelligent beings who offer praises to their Creator.[47] All sublunar beings are composed of the four elements, fire, air, water and earth.[48] Maimonides concludes:[49] 'When man reflects on these topics and comes to recognise all creatures, from the angels and the spheres to human beings like himself and when he observes the wisdom of the Holy One, blessed be He, as manifested in all things and in all creatures, his love for God grows, his soul thirsts and his flesh longs to love God, blessed be He. Such a man is filled with awe and dread at the thought of his own lowliness, poverty and insignificance when compared with one of the great and holy bodies to say nothing of one of the pure, disembodied spirits, so that he becomes aware of himself as a vessel full of shame and confusion, empty and lacking.'

Although the mediaeval Jewish thinkers believed in miracles there is a marked tendency to interpret these as uncommon but natural phenomena. For Gersonides, for example, the regularity of nature is itself the most powerful evidence of God's work. Miracles only occur when there is a special and pressing need to demonstrate God's power. All miracles are the result of the Active Intellect, the mediator between the higher Intelligences, which move the heavenly spheres, and the human intellect. The Active Intellect only operates, therefore, in the sublunar world. Furthermore, miracles are only a temporary, never a permanent, interruption of the natural order, which latter is guaranteed by the orderly movements of the heavenly bodies not subject to the influence of the Active Intellect. It follows that no miracle can ever occur in the realm of the spheres and hence the Biblical passages which seem to say that the sun stopped for Joshua and the shadow moved back for Hezekiah have to be understood otherwise than appears on the surface.[50]

The idea, which goes back to the Greeks, of a close correspondence between man, the microcosm, and the universe, the macrocosm, was utilized by some of the mediaeval Jewish thinkers but was virtually ignored by others.[51]

In the *Kabbalah* the theory of emanation is the central feature. *Creatio ex nihilo* means, for the *Kabbalah*, the emergence of 'somethingness' out of God's *Nothingness*. Remarkably reminiscent of Far Eastern cosmogonic theories, is the Zoharic comparison of the way in which the *Sefirot*, the creative powers or potencies in the Godhead, emerge from *Ein Sof*, the Limitless, the unknown and unknowable Ground of Being, to the silkworm which spins its cocoon out of itself.[52] In Hasidic thought, strongly influenced by the *Kabbalah*, the simile is changed to that of the snail 'whose garment is from itself' and applied to the world which is God's garment.[53] In some versions of Hasidism this results in a completely acosmic view. From God's point of view, as it were, there is no cosmos at all. The cosmos only enjoys existence from the point of view of God's creatures.[54]

The main concern of the *Kabbalah* is, in any event, not with the physical universe but with the 'upper worlds'. Thus the Rabbinic saying regarding God creating worlds and destroying them is referred, in the Lurianic *Kabbalah*, to the creative processes in the Godhead in which the 'vessels' of the *Sefirot* were at first shattered because they were too weak to contain the splendour of the light of the limitless (*Ein Sof*). In fact, for the *Kabbalah*, the details of the cosmic order as perceived by man are no more than a pale reflection in the physical world of the spiritual entities and their various combinations on high.[55]

The ancient theory of cosmic cycles (*Shemmitot*) won much support in the early *Kabbalah* but was eventually repudiated. The theory, as it appears in the *Kabbalah*, runs that there are time cycles each lasting six thousand years followed by a thousand-year sabbath. There are seven of these cycles in all culminating in the great Jubilee after 49,000 years have passed. In one version the whole process begins afresh after the Jubilee. Again in some versions the daring view was put forward that each cycle has its own *Torah*. Thus we are now living in the cycle governed by the *Sefirah* 'Judgment' and the *Torah* we have is one that is adjusted to such a situation. Therefore our *Torah* contains negative as well as positive precepts. But in the cycle of 'Lovingkindness' a different *Torah* prevails containing only positive precepts. It was this idea, in flat contradiction to the dogma of the immutability of the *Torah*, that caused the later Kabbalists to reject the whole doctrine.[56] But the doctrine was resurrected by more recent post-Darwinian thinkers in a somewhat forlorn attempt at coping with the problems raised for believers by the evolutionary theories and the new picture of the great age of the earth.[57]

Modern Jewish thinkers, with few exceptions, adopt the view that the nature of the physical universe is to be investigated by the methods of science and that it is not a matter of religious faith; so that for these thinkers there is no Jewish cosmology any more than there is a Jewish mathematics. Even a completely traditionalist thinker like Rabbi A. I. Kook accepts, for example, the theory of evolution in his contention that the creation narrative in Genesis belongs to the 'secrets of the *Torah*' and hence must not be taken literally. With a strong resemblance to the views of Teilhard de Chardin, Kook believes that an evolutionary theory is in the fullest accord with the basic optimism of the *Kabbalah* of which he was an adherent.[58]

The new picture of the universe revealed by modern science has produced hardly any new theological speculations among Jews but some little consideration has been given to the problems raised by space travel and the possibility that there are intelligent and moral beings on planets other than earth. In the encyclopedia of human knowledge compiled by Rabbi Phineas Elijah Hurwitz of Vilna (d. 1821), entitled *Sefer Ha-Berit*,[59] there is speculation on this theme as early as the beginning of the nineteenth century. Hurwitz[60] believes, on the basis of Isa. 45:18, that there are creatures on planets other than earth. He refers to the Talmudic passage[61] in which, according to one opinion, *Meroz* (Judges 5:23) is a star and yet, says Hurwitz, *Meroz* is cursed for not coming to the help of the Israelites, which indicates that it is inhabited. Hurwitz goes on to admit that the creatures on other planets may have intelligence but refuses to believe that they are endowed with freewill, for this, he argues, is only possible for creatures with a human constitution.

More recently Rabbi Gunther Plaut[62] asks: 'Will the possibility that there are intelligent creatures on other planets impose any strain on our religious beliefs?' He replies: 'The modern Jew will answer this question with a firm "No". An earlier generation, rooted in beliefs in an earth-centered universe, might have had some theological difficulties, but we have them no longer. That God should, in His vast creation, have caused only one earth and one manlike genus to evolve, is in fact harder to believe than that His creative power expressed itself in other unfathomable ways. This does not in any way diminish our relationship to Him or His to ours. Just as a father may love many children with equal love, so surely may our Father on high spread His pinions over the vastness of creation.'[63] A more detailed and acute examination of the problem is that given by Rabbi Norman Lamm under the title: 'The Religious Implications of Extraterrestrial Life'.[64] Among other matters, Lamm discusses whether Judaism holds the doctrine of man's cosmic significance to be a cardinal principle of the Jewish faith.

To sum up, the Jews never invented a cosmology of their own. Still less has there been any official Jewish cosmology dictated by Jewish orthodox belief. But certain cosmological themes, deriving from Babylonian, Greek or Arabic sources, have been stressed or rejected according to the doctrinal bent of individual Jewish thinkers in the various periods of their history.

NOTES

1. 'Cosmogony' in *International Dictionary of the Bible*, Vol. I, 702–9.
2. See U. Cassuto, *From Adam to Noah*, trans. I. Abrahams, Jer. (1961), 59.
3. This is possibly the meaning of the *hug* ('circle') of the earth in Isa. 40:22. Kimhi and many moderns, however, understand the *hug* of the earth to be the vault of the sky. But it is worth noting that in Job 22:14 there is a reference to the *hug* of heaven, which would suggest that the verse in Isaiah refers to the earth.
4. In Exod. 39:3 the root *raka* is used for beating gold into thin plates. When the 'heaven' fails to produce rain it is described as being like iron (Lev. 26:19). No significance is to be attached to the dual form *shamayim* (as in *yadayim*, 'hands', *raglayim*, 'feet') since this word, like the word for 'water', *mayim*, is really a plural and not a true dual form. The correct translation is 'heavens' but *shamayim* is used in our verse as a synonym for *rakia* which is the singular form. Cf. Gesenius, *Grammar*, 88:1.
5. The earth, too, rests on pillars, Job 9:6. Presumably these pillars were at either end of the sky and earth. In the diagram in *Interpreter's Bible*, op. cit., 703 (also reproduced in Nahum M. Sama's *Understanding Genesis*, McGraw-Hill, New York, 1966, 5), the pillars of earth and heaven are depicted as two huge masses reaching to and supporting the sky at either end with the earth crossing them in the middle, but I have been unable to discover the evidence to warrant this.
6. The expression used is 'God *set* (or *put*) them' (*va-yitten*) in the 'firmament' (Gen. 1:17). See S. R. Driver, *The Book of Genesis* (London, 1926), 9–11.

7. In the diagram referred to, the 'waters beneath the earth' are depicted as dividing the earth and *Sheol, Sheol* being beneath these waters. But from Num. 16:28–34 it appears that Sheol is immediately beneath the earth's surface with nothing else in between.
8. There are two different creation narratives. The first (Gen. 1:1–2:4a) is ascribed by the critics to 'P' (sixth century BC), the second (Gen. 2: 4b–25) to 'J' (tenth century BC).
9. The 'myth and ritual' school was inaugurated by S. Mowinckel's *Psalmenstudien*. Cf. Snaith's *The Jewish New Year Festival* (1947), and the bibliography in O. Eissfeldt, *The Old Testament: An Introduction*, trans. Peter A. Ackroyd (Oxford, 1966), 110, note 29.
10. See R. Patai, *Man and Temple* (London, 1967). The belief that Palestine is at the exact centre of the earth is probably referred to in the 'navel' of the earth (*tabbur ha-aretz*) in Ezek. 38:12. (But in Judges 9:37, where the same term is used, the reference is simply to the centre of that district.) Cf. the Rabbinic legend that when David began to dig for the site of the Temple the waters of *Tehom* welled up and threatened to engulf the earth (Makkot 11a).
11. *Commentary* to Gen. 1:1.
12. See *Mishnah Berakhot*, Ch. 9, and the Babylonian Talmud on this.
13. See the remarkable illustration in the Jerusalem Talmud (*Hagigah* 1:2) of the king whose palace was erected over the sewers. The honour of the king demands that no one is allowed to inquire as to what was there before the palace had been erected. Cf. H. Albeck's *Commentary to the Mishnah*, Jer.-Tel-Aviv (1964), *Moed*, Supplementary Note to *Hagigah* 2:1, 5:10–11.
14. Babylonian Talmud, *Hagigah* 13a. Cf Genesis Rabbah 8:2, Theodor-Albeck (ed.), 58 and Theodor's note 1.
15. New English Bible Version.
16. *Hagigah* 2:1. The terms *le-fanim* and le-ahor used in this passage of the Mishnah can either mean (as appears from the Babylonian Talmud and is generally assumed) 'before' and 'after' in time or they can mean 'before' and 'after' in space, i.e. what is beyond the confines of the earth. Cf. *Genesis Rabbah* 1:10.
17. Babylonian Talmud, *Hagigah* 12a.
18. *Genesis Rabbah* 1:9.
19. *Genesis Rabbah* 10:3.
20. *Genesis Rabbah* 12:4.
21. *Genesis Rabbah* 3:4.
22. See A. Altmann, *Studies in Religious Philosophy and Mysticism* (London, 1969), 128–39.
23. *Genesis Rabbah* 9:2.
24. *Genesis Rabbah* 12:1.
25. Babylonian Talmud, *Hullin* 60b.
26. Babylonian Talmud, *Hagigah* 12b.
27. Babylonian Talmud, *Hagigah* I3a. The number seven is the general Semitic sacred number. While this passage is not necessarily the earliest reference to the 'seven heavens' in the Rabbinic literature (for further references see Ginzberg, *Legends of the Jews*, Philadelphia, 1942, Vol. V, pp. 10–11, note 22), the concept appears only from the third century. This lengthy note of Ginzberg should be consulted on the whole question as well as his notes 20 and 21 on p. 19. In note 20 Ginzberg remarks that the use of the apparent plural form for *shamayim* (see note 4 above) led to the conception that the idea of several heavens is already met with in the Bible.
28. Babylonian Talmud, *Berakhot* 32b.
29. Babylonian Talmud, *Rosh ha-Shanah* 31a; *Sanhedrin* 97a.
30. Babylonian Talmud, *Shabbat* 13b.
31. *Avot* 5:6. The other four are: the Shamir-worm, used by Solomon miraculously to cut the stones for the Temple; the letters of the Two Tablets of Stone on which the Decalogue was engraved; the engraving tool for these; and the Two Tablets themselves.
32. Genesis *Rabbah* 5:6.
33. Zangwill's comment is quoted by J. M. Hertz, *Commentary to the Daily Prayer Book* (London, 1947), 687f.
34. Babylonian Talmud, *Baba Batra* 74b.
35. *Pesikta de Rab Kahana*, Buber (ed.), p. 188a.
36. Babylonian Talmud, *Avodah Zarah* 3b; *Baba Batra* 74b.
37. Babylonian Talmud, *Baba Batra* 74b.

Jewish Cosmology 37

38. *Pesikta de Rab Kahana*, Buber (ed.) p. 188 a–b.
39. Babylonian Talmud, *Baba Batra* 74b. On the whole question of these ancient myths in the Rabbinic literature see the lengthy note by Ginzberg, *Legends of the Jews* (Philadelphia, 1942), Vol. V, note 127, pp. 43–6.
40. On this see E. Urbach, *Hazal*, Jer. (1969), pp. 169f.
41. See Saadia, *Emunot Ve-Deot*, 1:1–15; Maimonides, *Guide for the Perplexed*, II, 13–25; Albo, *Ikkarim*, I, 23; Gersonides, *Milhamot*, VI.
42. *Yesodei Ha–Torah* 2:2.
43. *Yesodei Ha–Torah* 2:3.
44. *Yesodei Ha–Torah* 3:1–3.
45. *Yesodei Ha–Torah* 3:6.
46. *Yesodei Ha–Torah* 3:8.
47. *Yesodei Ha–Torah* 3:9.
48. *Yesodei Ha–Torah* 3:10–11 .
49. *Yesodei Ha–Torah* 4:12.
50. See Gersonides *Commentary* to Joshua 10:12.
51. See I. Broydé in *Jewish Encyclopedia*, Vol. VIII, 544–5.
52. Zohar I, 15a.
53. Jacob Joseph of Pulnoye, *Toledot* (ed. Warsaw, 1881), 39a; *Keter Shem Tov* (ed. Jer., 1968), 12a. The actual wording about the snail is found in *Genesis Rabbah* 21:5 but in an entirely different context.
54. This view is especially pronounced in the Habad school of Hasidism and more particularly in the writings of R. Aaron Hurwitz of Starosselje, see my study of R. Aaron's thought, *Seeker of Unity* (London, 1966).
55. See G. Scholem, *Major Trends in Jewish Mysticism*, 3rd ed. (London, 1955), 205–86.
56. An excellent account of the doctrine of cosmic cycles in the Kabbalah is I. Weinstock's *Studies in Jewish Philosophy and Mysticism* (Heb.) (Jer., 1969) 151–241.
57. See Weinstock, op. cit., 230—41.
58. See Kook's *Orot Ha–Kodesh* (Jer., 1938), Part IV, 19–22.
59. 2nd ed. (Warsaw, 1881).
60. Part I, *Maamar* 3, Chs 2–4, 30-2.
61. Babylonian Talmud, *Moed Katan* 16a.
62. *Judaism and the Scientific Spirit* (New York, 1962), 36–9.
63. In a note (p. 79) Plaut observes: 'There is some reason to believe that even the Jewish ancients were already hinting at a wider view. Judaism knows various expressions for God. It calls Him "King of the World" and also, "King of All Worlds". A *Midrash* states that before our earthly creation God created and destroyed many worlds (Gen. R. 3:7).' But, of course, the ancients had no notion of 'worlds' inhabited by non-human, intelligent beings (other than angels), and the reference in the *Midrash* is to God creating and destroying many worlds before the creation of this one.
64. In Tradition, Vol. 7, No. 4–Vol. 8, No. 1, Winter 1965–Spring 1966, 5–56.

EXPLANATION OF TECHNICAL TERMS

1. AMORAIM. Amoraic; see TALMUD.
2. LURIANIC KABBALAH. The mystical doctrine evolved by the great Jewish mystical teacher and poet Isaac Luria (1534–72), associated especially with the Galilean town of Safed, where Luria settled not long before his death.
3. MIDRASH. Interpretation of Scripture. The term is also used for the considerable non-legal part of the anonymous Rabbinic literature. Some of this is dated to the Tannaitic (Mishnaic) period, but most of it is later, some as late as the twelfth and thirteenth centuries. The Midrashic literature contains a widely ranging assortment of Rabbinic teachings, many of which do not strictly fall under the heading of exegesis.
4. MIDRASH RABBAH ('Great Midrash'). A collection of *Midrashim* on the Pentateuch and the Five Scrolls (Ruth, Lamentations, Esther, Ecclesiastes and the Song of Songs). In fact these are quite separate compilations produced at widely differing dates. Although based on the Biblical books, they mostly consist of homilies, legends and edifying religious teachings.
5. MISHNAH ('teaching'). A codification of mainly legal teachings of the early Rabbis

(Tannaim). In its present form the Mishnah is generally assumed to be the work of the Patriarch Rabbi Judah (end of the second century AD), but it contains a good deal of much earlier material and some slightly later authorities are mentioned in it. For a translation, see H. Danby, *The Mishnah* (Oxford 1933).
6. PESIKTA DE RAB KAHANA. A collection of midrashic homilies for certain special sabbaths and the festivals, named after the teacher who is mentioned at the beginning of the work. It is probably seventh-century, but contains much early material.
7. TALMUD ('teaching'). Compendium of the teachings of the later Rabbis (Amoraim), presented in the form of a running commentary on the Mishnah. There are two Talmuds, the Babylonian and the Palestinian (or Jerusalem) Talmud, which are quite distinct although they contain much material in common. The Palestinian Talmud was compiled in the Rabbinic schools of Palestine in the later fourth century; the Babylonian Talmud (often referred to simply as 'The Talmud', in consequence of the wider currency it has enjoyed), was compiled in the Babylonian schools in the late fifth century, but was somewhat edited and added to in the following century.
8. TANNAIM. Tannaitic; see MISHNAH.
9. TORAH. The Pentateuch or 'Five Books of Moses'. Sometimes applied to Scripture as a whole, to the Biblical law, or to religious teaching in general.
10. ZOHAR, THE ('The Book of Splendour'). The classic text of the mediaeval Jewish mysticism (Kabbalah). The principal part of the Zohar, written in a peculiar form of Aramaic, sets out the mystical doctrine under the guise of discussions on parts of the Bible by Rabbi Simeon bar Yohai and other second-century Palestinian Rabbis. In fact it was composed in Spain towards the end of the thirteenth century by Moses de Leon.
11. *Translations of Rabbinic texts*:
    The Mishnah, tr. H. Danby (Oxford, 1933).
    The (Babylonian) Talmud (London [Soncino] 1935–52).
    Midrash Rabba (London [Soncino], 1939).
    The Zohar (London [Soncino], 1934).
    Jerusalem Talmud, French tr. by M. Schwab (Paris, 1932–33).

— 4 —

The Problem of the *Akedah* in Jewish Thought

The narrative in the twenty-second chapter of the book of Genesis, in which Abraham is instructed by God to offer up his son Isaac as a burnt offering, is known in the Jewish tradition as the *Akedah*,[1] 'the binding' (of Isaac on the altar). The *Akedah* features prominently in the Jewish liturgy. It is, for instance, the Pentateuchal reading in the synagogue on the second day of the New Year festival, and it is recited daily by some pietists. It became the prototype for Jewish martyrdom. And it has exercised a powerful fascination over the minds of Jewish biblical exegetes and Jewish thinkers generally throughout the ages, each of whom has tried to bring his own understanding to the narrative.

This essay is concerned with Jewish attitudes towards the most difficult problem connected with the *Akedah*: How could God have ordered a man to murder his son? The problem is aggravated by the fact that in no fewer than sixteen other passages in the Bible (Leviticus 18:21; 20:1–8; Deuteronomy 12:31;18:10; 2 Kings 13:27; 16:3; 17:17, 31; 21:6; 23:10; Jeremiah 7:31; 19:5; Ezekiel 20:31; Micah 6:7; 2 Chronicles 28:3; 33:6) child sacrifice is condemned as an abomination before God. Arising out of the initial problem are the further questions regarding Abraham's intention to carry out the terrible deed. How could Abraham have been so sure that God had, indeed, commanded him to kill his innocent child? Even if he was convinced that God had so commanded him, was it his duty to obey? Is obedience to God's will so supreme an obligation that it can override man's moral sense, demanding of him that he commit a criminal act of the very worst kind for the greater glory of God? Can or should one worship a being who wishes to be served by an act of murder? Moreover, the very God who demanded the sacrifice of Isaac had himself performed the miracle of giving Isaac to Abraham and Sarah when they were of advanced age and had promised Abraham that, through Isaac, Sarah would be a mother of nations (Genesis 17:15–19; 18:10–15; and 21:1–12).

Three different attitudes to the problem have been adopted by Jewish thinkers. The first stresses the story's 'happy ending'. Abraham is, in fact, eventually commanded not to slay his son. The whole episode was only a 'test', a divine vindication of Abraham's absolute trust in God. There was never any divine intention for Abraham to kill Isaac. God, being God, could never so deny his own nature as to wish a man to commit a murder in obedience to him. The second attitude stresses, on the contrary, the original command. This view, very close to Kierkegaard's attitude, can imagine God commanding Abraham to slay his son. True the order is revoked at the last moment but the point has been made, none the less, that, in Kierkegaard's terminology, there can be, so far as 'the knight of faith' is concerned, a 'teleological suspension of the ethical'. As 'ethical man' as well as 'knight of faith', Abraham goes in 'fear and trembling' but the ultimate for him is not the ethical norm but his individual relationship to his God. A third attitude seeks to dwell on both aspects of the narrative. On this view, it is impossible that God could ever, in reality, be false to his own nature and command a murder, and yet if he could, then Abraham would indeed be obliged to cross the fearful abyss. These three attitudes, it must be said, are rarely given sharply defined expression in the Jewish sources. They tend to shade off into one another, and among some of the Jewish thinkers, all three are combined without any awareness that a contradiction is involved. It is thus far more a matter of where the emphasis is placed than one of precise categorization.

The first attitude seems to have been the earliest among the Jewish thinkers. It is not without significance that the *Akedah* hardly appears at all as a distinct theme in the early rabbinic literature. The only reference to it before the third century is in the Mishnah (Taanit 2:4). Here there is a vivid description of the procedure adopted on a public fast-day when the rains had failed to come. The people congregated, we are told, in the town square where they were led in prayer by a venerable man free of sin and experienced in offering supplication to his maker. One of the prayers he was to offer is given as: 'May He who answered our father Abraham on Mount Moriah answer you and hearken to the voice of your crying this day.' But this is said to be only one of the special 'May He who answered ...' prayers. Others recited on that day contained references to other biblical characters, such as Joshua and Jonah, whose prayers in a time of crisis and danger were answered. Abraham's crisis, it is implied, was basically no different from that of the other heroes. When God answered Abraham's prayer it was to spare Isaac. Implied, too, is the idea that God's 'answer', his true will, was revealed not in the original command but in the second command for Abraham to stay his hand and save Isaac. In a later talmudic passage (Taanit 4a) it is stated explicitly that God never intended Abraham to kill his son any more than God wishes Baal worshippers to carry out human sacrifices. In a comment to Jeremiah's fierce castigation of the people for burning their sons in fire as burnt offerings for Baal 'which I commanded not, nor spoke it, neither came it into My mind' (Jeremiah 19:5), this passage elaborates: '"which I commanded not" refers to the sacrifice of the son of Mesha, the king of Moab (2 Kings 3:27); "nor spoke it" refers to the daughter of Jephtah (Judges 11:31); "neither came it into My mind" refers to the sacrifice of Isaac, son of Abraham'. Similarly, a rabbinic midrash (Genesis Rabbah 56:8) describes Abraham, after the angel had told him in the name of God to spare Isaac, puzzled by the contradictory statements: 'Recently Thou didst tell me (Genesis 21:12): "In Isaac shall seed be called to thee," and later Thou didst say (Genesis 22:5): "Take now thy son." And now Thou tellest me to stay my hand!' God is made to reply in the words of Psalm 79 verse 35: 'My covenant will I not profane, nor alter that which is gone out of My lips.' 'When I told thee: "Take thy son," I was not altering that which went out from My lips [i.e., the promise that Abraham would have descendants through Isaac]. I did not tell thee: "Slay him" but bring him up [i.e., take him to the mountain and make him ready to be sacrificed]. Thou didst bring him up. Now take him down again.'

In addition to this idea emerging from specific comments to the *Akedah*, it seems to be implied in the typical rabbinic view that God himself keeps his laws. In the Jerusalem Talmud (*Rosh Ha-Shanah* 1:3), for example, the Greek maxim is quoted that the law is not written for the king (i.e., the law is for the king's subjects whereas the king himself is beyond the law). God, it is said, is not like a human king who decrees laws for others but need not keep them himself. God orders man to rise in respect before the aged and God did this himself, as it were, out of respect for Abraham.

All this lends powerful support to an anti-Kierkegaardian understanding of the *Akedah*. Drawing on passages such as those we have quoted it is easy (far too easy, as we shall see) to generalize and to argue that there is no room in Judaism for a doctrine that accepts any teleological suspension of the ethical.

This is, in fact, the attitude adopted by the late Milton Steinberg in an essay entitled: 'Kierkegaard and Judaism'.[2] In a lethal attack on the Danish thinker's interpretation of the *Akedah*, Steinberg roundly declares that there is nothing in Judaism to correspond to Kierkegaard's teleological suspension of the ethical and continues:

> From the Jewish viewpoint – and this is one of its highest dignities – the ethical is never suspended, not under any circumstances and not for anyone, not even for God. *Especially not for God* [italics Steinberg's]. Are not supreme Reality and supreme Goodness one and co-essential to the Divine nature? If so, every act wherein the Good is put aside is more than a breach of His will; it is in effect a denial of His existence. Wherein the rabbis define sin as constituting not merely rebellion but atheism as well.
>
> What Kierkegaard asserts to be the glory of God is Jewishly regarded as unmitigated sacrilege. Which indeed is the true point of the *Akedah*, missed so perversely by Kierkegaard. While it was a merit in Abraham to be willing to sacrifice his only son to his God, it was God's nature and merit that He would not accept an immoral tribute. And it was His purpose, among other things, to establish that truth.[3]

The opposite view, the 'pro-Kierkegaardian' interpretation of the *Akedah*, is, however, also found in Jewish thought, and certainly not as infrequently as Steinberg implies. Philo (*De Abrahamo*, 177–99) replies to hostile critics of Abraham who point out that many others in the history of mankind have offered themselves and their children for a cause in which they believed. Among examples these critics cite are the barbarians whose Moloch worship was explicitly forbidden by Moses, and Indian women who gladly practise suttee. Philo retorts that Abraham's sacrifice was unique in that he was not governed by motives of custom, honour, or fear but solely by the love of God. It is, then, for Philo a token of Abraham's great love that he was ready to suspend the ethical norm; his love for God overriding all else.

The Talmud (*Sanhedrin* 89b), in a legal context, asks why Isaac (who, in one tradition, was not a docile infant but a mature man) allowed himself to be led to the slaughter. True Abraham was a prophet but is even a prophet to be heeded when he orders another in the name of God to commit an illegal act, in this instance, what amounts to suicide? The reply given is that, indeed, an established prophet can be relied upon, not to cancel any of God's laws entirely but to demand, in God's name, a temporary suspension of them. The commentators[4] rightly remark that no question is even raised about Abraham's readiness to kill his son since the prophet himself is obviously obliged to heed God's command even if it involves an illegal act. In the 'Remembrance' prayer, dating, according to the majority of historians, from the third century and still recited in synagogues on the New Year festival, there occurs the phrase: 'Remember, unto us, O Lord our God, the covenant and the loving kindness and the oath which Thou swore unto Abraham our father on Mount Moriah: and consider the binding with which Abraham our father bound his son Isaac on the altar, how he suppressed his compassion in order to perform Thy will with a perfect heart. So may Thy compassion overbear Thine anger against us; in Thy great goodness, may Thy wrath turn aside from Thy people, Thy city and Thine inheritance.'

Indeed, there was current in the Middle Ages a curious legend that Abraham actually killed Isaac at the command of God and that later Isaac was resurrected from the dead, the call of the angel to Abraham, commanding him to stay his hand, coming too late. The mediaeval Spanish commentator, Abraham Ibn Ezra (to Genesis 22:19) quotes this opinion (which, he says, seeks to explain why there is no reference in the narrative to Isaac returning home with his father) but rejects it as completely contrary to the biblical text. Yet in a splendid monograph Shalom Spiegel[5] has demonstrated how widespread such views were in the Middle Ages, possibly, Spiegel suggests, in order to deny that Isaac's sacrifice was in any way less than that of Jesus; or as a reflection of actual conditions when the real martyrdom of Jewish communities demanded a more tragic model than that of a mere intended sacrifice. It was not unknown for parents to kill their children and then themselves when threatened by the Crusaders.[6]

It is highly improbable that Kierkegaard knew of it, but the Talmud (*Sanhedrin* 89b), in the passage following the legal one we have quoted, has a Midrashic exposition of the drama of the *Akedah* in which there is expressed all the 'fear and trembling' of which Kierkegaard speaks, as Abraham, both 'ethical man' and 'knight of faith', is torn in his anguish. The passage deserves to be quoted in full:

'And it came to pass after these words that God did tempt Abraham' (Genesis 22:1). What is the meaning of *after*? Rabbi Johanan said in the name of Rabbi Jose ben Zimra: *After* the words of Satan. It is written: 'And the child grew up and was weaned: and Abraham made a great feast the same day that Isaac was weaned' (Genesis 21:8). Satan said to the Holy One, blessed be He: 'Sovereign of the Universe! Thou didst give a son to this old man at the age of a hundred, yet of all the banquet he prepared he did not sacrifice to Thee a single turtle-dove or pigeon!" God replied: 'Did he not do all this in honour of his son! Yet were I to tell him to sacrifice that son to Me he would do so at once.' ... On the way (as Abraham was leading Isaac to be sacrificed) Satan confronted him and said to him: *'If we assay to commune with thee, wilt thou be grieved?... Behold, thou hast instructed many, and thou hast strengthened the weak hands. Thy words have upholden him that was falling, and thou hast strengthened the feeble knees. But now it is come upon thee, and thou faintest"* (Job 4:2–5) (i.e., Abraham is being asked to commit a wrong against which his whole teaching has hitherto been directed7). Abraham replied: *"I will walk in my integrity'* (Psalm 26:2). Satan said to him: *'Should not thy fear be thy confidence?'* (Job 4:6). He replied: *'Remember, I pray thee, whoever perished being innocent?"* (Job 4:6). Seeing that Abraham would not listen to him, Satan said to him: *'Now a thing was secretly brought to me'* (Job 4:12). I have heard from behind the Veil *'the lamb, for a burnt offering'* (Genesis 22:7) 'but not Isaac for a burnt offering.' Abraham replied: 'It is the punishment of a liar that he is not believed even when he tells the truth.' In the parallel passage in the Midrash (Genesis Rabbah 56:4) Satan says to Abraham: 'Tomorrow He will condemn thee as a murderer'[8] but Abraham replies: 'Nevertheless!'

The analysis of the *Akedah* given by Moses Maimonides (1135–1204),[9] the greatest of the mediaeval Jewish thinkers, similarly comes very close to the Kierkegaardian understanding. Maimonides observes that the *Akedah* teaches two fundamental ideas (neither of these, it should be noted, has anything to do with the 'happy ending' of the narrative). The first of these is that man, out of the love and fear of God, is obliged to go even to the limits to which Abraham was prepared to go. According to Maimonides' reading of the *Akedah*, the 'test' was not in order to provide God with information about Abraham's steadfastness that God did not possess, but rather it was to provide a 'test case' of the limits to which a man can and should go in his love for God. Maimonides stresses not alone the natural love that Abraham had for the child of his extreme old age but the fact that in this child was centred all Abraham's hope of establishing a religious community to carry on his teachings. Maimonides adds: 'Know that this notion is corroborated and explained in the *Torah*, in which it is mentioned that the final end of the whole of the Torah, including its commandments, prohibitions, promises and narratives, is one thing only–namely, fear of Him, may He be exalted. This is referred to in its dictum: *If thou wilt take care to observe all the words of this Law that are written in this book, that thou mayest fear this glorious and awful Name, and so on* (Deuteronomy 28:58).'

The second idea contained in the *Akedah*, according to Maimonides, is that the prophets consider as true what comes to them from God in a prophetic revelation. If the prophetic vision ever allows the prophet to remain in some doubt, Abraham would not have hastened to commit an act so repugnant to nature. The man, Abraham, who taught that God does reveal himself to man, was the most suitable instrument for conveying the further truth that there is complete conviction in the mind of the prophet that he is really the recipient of a divine communication so that he is ready to act on it no matter how severe the moral as well as physical demands it makes on him. Maimonides' statement, that the final end of the whole Torah (as he says, including its commandments, which means, the ethical as well as the purely religious commandments) is one thing only, the fear of God, is as close to the idea of, at least, a possibility that the ethical can be suspended for this particular telos as makes no difference. The thirteenth-century exegete Bahya Ibn Asher[10] develops the same line as Maimonides, that the *Akedah* teaches the great love of Abraham and adds that the reason that Abraham took only two lads with him (and ordered even these to remain at the foot of the mountain) was because Abraham knew that if others were present they would, in their horror of the deed he intended to perform, seek to prevent him from carrying it out.[11]

The renowned contemporary Orthodox teacher Professor J. B. Soloveitchick is the most determined exponent of a Kierkegaardian interpretation of the *Akedah*. In a famous essay, entitled 'Ish Ha-Halakhah' ('The Man of Halakah'),[12] Soloveitchick observes that the midrash (to which reference has previously been made) in which Abraham's dialogue with Satan conveys all the anguish and uncertainty of the man of faith, is much closer to Kierkegaard than any idea of religion as offering 'peace of mind'. The ultimate aim of 'the man of Halakah', the man who follows the *Halakah*, the legal side of Judaism, is to obey God's revealed will which transcends man's merely rational aspirations for the good life. The psalmist who speaks of the Lord as his shepherd who leads him beside the still waters (Psalm 23), affirms this only as the ultimate aim of the religious life. He does not mean to imply, according to Soloveitchick, that the religious way itself has anything to do with 'still waters'. On the contrary, as Kierkegaard affirms, the deeper aspects of religious faith are only to be found in the man tormented by the demands God seems to be making both on his intelligence and his conscience. Soloveitchick only refers to Kierkegaard's interpretation in connection with Abraham's anguish and doubt, not with regard to the teleological suspension of the ethical, but J. B. Agus[13] may be right in reading Soloveitchick's essay as a statement that the full Kierkegaardian view is compatible with Judaism.

Although some Jewish thinkers have stressed the 'happy ending' as the chief point of the *Akedah* narrative and others have stressed the original command to sacrifice as the chief point of the story, a compromise position in which both aspects are avowed is not as contradictory as might appear at first glance. It can be argued that, after all, the story does consist of these two parts, the original command and the 'happy ending'; that this is the only occasion on which God is said to have commanded a man to commit murder as a test of obedience; that, on the other hand, to read the story simply as a homily on the sacredness of human life tends to reduce it to banality; and, at the same time, to overlook the finale is to ignore an element that the narrator never intended should be overlooked. For this reason some modern thinkers, especially, have tried to preserve both insights as essential parts of the *Akedah*.

W. Gunther Plaut,[14] in an essay entitled 'Notes on the Akedah', implying, perhaps, an avoidance of too tidy a schematic presentation of the complicated narrative, states the problem but offers more than one solution. Plaut first quotes Franz Rosenzweig's understanding[15] of the whole idea of God tempting man. God must, at times, conceal his true purpose. He must mislead man (as he misled Abraham into thinking that he was the kind of God who demanded that a murder be committed for his glorification) because if everything were clear men would become automatons. In Rosenzweig's words, 'the most unfree, the timid and the fearful would be the most pious. But evidently God wants only the free to be His: He must make it difficult, yea, impossible, to understand His actions, so as to give man the opportunity to believe, that is, to ground his faith in trust and freedom.' Plaut continues: 'What kind of God is He? How can the compassionate God of the Bible be presented as asking the sacrifice of a child?' Plaut replies by referring to two different solutions that have been offered. The first is that the test came out of a time when human sacrifice was still an acceptable possibility; in terms of its own age, therefore, it was merely the extreme test and, after all, God did not exact the final price. The real test of faith and obedience consists in being ready to do the totally unexpected, the impossible, for the sake of God. Another solution is that God never intended the sacrifice to be made. According to this way of reading the narrative, concludes Plaut, Abraham's test both succeeded and failed. It succeeded in that it proved Abraham to be a man of faith and obedience. And it failed in that Abraham's understanding of God's nature remained deficient. This latter observation does not seem to tally, however, with the narrative. It is nowhere suggested that Abraham failed in any way in his test, as Plaut would have it. Even if the *Akedah* be interpreted as a lesson on the sacredness of human life and the true nature of God it is nowhere implied that Abraham was mistaken in his understanding of the demand made on him.

The religious thinker and educationist Ernst Simon,[16] in a discussion of how the *Akedah* narrative should be taught in religion classes, refers to the two different interpretations of the *Akedah* in the Jewish tradition. He calls them the 'rationalist' and the 'existentialist' and believes that between these two extremes some intermediate possibilities exist, 'not necessarily of a compromising nature, but authentic in themselves'. Simon refers to Kierkegaard's analysis in his *Fear and Trembling* and remarks that though Kierkegaard was not aware of the Jewish traditions his attitude towards Abraham as the 'knight of faith' is, in some ways, kindred to them.

Simon formulates the basic problem of the *Akedah* as: 'How could Abraham believe that God asked from him the sacrifice of his son? Is that a moral demand? And if not, how can it be a religious one?' The 'rationalist' view is that God never intended the sacrifice to be made. This line of interpretation can be followed all the way to Maimonides' view[17] that God does not really want even animal sacrifices and that these are commanded only as a concession to the psychology of the ancient Israelites who, under the influence of their milieu, could not conceive of divine worship without sacrificial offerings. The 'existentialist' school of thought, on the other hand, sees man's highest perfection in the absolute submission of his will to God's command, even when this seems most absurd. 'According to this view', writes Simon, 'the real victim was not the innocent Isaac, but the knowing Abraham who brought a sacrifice of his intellect and his will, of his emotions and even of his morals, that is, of his whole human personality, *ad maiorem gloriam Dei*'.[18]

Yet Simon believes that it is possible to read the narrative in a way in which both extremes are avoided but in which justice is done to the insights provided by both. The command to sacrifice can be read as a warning against too facile an identification of religion with naturalistic ethics. Ultimately, it is in the command of God that ethical conduct is grounded. The 'happy ending', on the other hand, precludes any religious approach that encourages ideas repugnant to our moral feelings. An anti-ethical religion such as that described in Gustave Flaubert's historical novel *Salammbô*, about Moloch worship in Semitic Carthage, is a real possibility. Thus the *Akedah* teaches that Judaism is neither a secular system of morals nor a blind devotion to a supernatural power. Furthermore, the *Akedah* is the great exception, not the rule. The rule in Judaism is that religious and moral commands are very close to each other.

To sum up, there is more than one Jewish interpretation of the *Akedah*. In this and similar matters of biblical interpretation there is no such thing as an 'official' Jewish viewpoint and it is extremely doubtful whether the whole concept of 'normative Judaism' is more than a myth. Both Steinberg and Soloveitchick are, therefore, correct in claiming that their understanding of the *Akedah* is authentically Jewish. They are both wrong in appearing to claim that theirs is the only possible authentically Jewish interpretation. It is not as if there is any question of the Jew ever being obliged to emulate Abraham's example. Judaism supplies a categorical answer to the question whether a murder is ever permitted when it is believed that God has so commanded and the answer in all the Jewish sources is in the negative. The command to Abraham was, on any showing, a once-and-for-all matter, never to be repeated and not carried out in practice even in the instance of Abraham himself. Yet this does not allow a Jewish thinker to dimiss the Kierkegaardian 'midrash' as utter nonsense. There is point in the reminder, and sufficient support from the classical Jewish writings, that a true religious outlook demands of 'ethical man' that he acquire a vertical direction to his life and that when the brave 'knight of faith, goes out to do battle he does not tilt at windmills.

The Problem of the Akedah in Jewish Thought

NOTES

1. Louis Jacobs 'Akedah' in *Encyclopedia Judaica*, Vol. 2 (1972), pp. 480–4.
2. In his *Anatomy of Faith* (New York: Harcourt, Brace, 1960), pp. 130–52.
3. Ibid., p. 147.
4. See the discussion in Reuben Margaliout's commentary to tractate Sanhedrin, entitled *Margaliyot Ha-Yam* (Jerusalem: Mosad Harav Kook, 1958), Part II, No. 10, p. 128.
5. Shalom Spiegel, *The Last Trial* (New York: Schocken, 1969).
6. Relevant to this question is a Responsum of Rabbi Meir ben Baruch of Rothenburg (d. 1293). Here (*Teshuvot Pesakim U-Minhagim*, ed. I. Z. Kahana [Jerusalem: Mosad Harav Kook, 1957–62], Part II, No. 59, p. 54) Meir discusses a case arising out of certain tragic events that occurred in the city of Koblenz, where on 2 April 1265 a man killed his wife and four children in order to save them from torture and forcible conversion; he had intended also to kill himself, but the Gentiles prevented him from doing so. Asked whether the unfortunate man must do penance for the murder of his family, Meir replies that he is quite sure that it is permitted – indeed, obligatory – to commit suicide in order to avoid apostasy, but that he is not at all sure that it is permitted to murder others for the sake of the 'sanctification of God's name'. Nevertheless, Meir concludes that this, too, must be permitted, since we know that many of the saints killed themselves and their families when threatened with forcible conversion. He concludes that the man must not be allowed to undergo any penance, for if he did penance it would imply that the saints of old were wrong.
7. This does seem to be the meaning of the quotation by Satan from Job, see Reuben Margaliout, op. cit., No. 17, p. 129, and the sermon by Hayyim Jeremiah Plensberg (nineteenth century) in his *Divrey Yirmiyahu*, S. P. Garber, Part I, Viona, n.d., to the *Akedah* narrative, pp. 157–60.
8. Cf. the comment of the Hasidic master Rabbi Mordechai Joseph Leiner of Izbica (d. 1854) in his *Mey Ha-Shiloah*, Vol. II, ed. M. J. Leiner (New York: Sentry Press, 1973), p. 12, that the command to Abraham was conveyed in an ambiguous manner and that Abraham had doubts as to whether it was really a divine command, since it involved the prohibited act of murder. Abraham emerged victorious from the test because he refused to allow his love for Isaac to persuade him that God could not really have commanded him to commit murder. This author quotes the Zohar (I, 120a) to the effect that Abraham saw his vision of this command 'as in a glass darkly'.
9. *The Guide for the Perplexed*, III, 24, Vol. I, trans. S. Pines (Chicago: University of Chicago Press, 1963), pp. 500–2.
10. Bahya Ibn Asher, *Commentary to the Pentateuch*, Vol. I, ed. C. B. Chavel (Jerusalem: Mosad Harav Kook, 1966), pp. 192–4.
11. Plensberg, op. cit., states that, on the face of it, the *Adekah* is extremely strange. The command to commit a murder seems 'a very ugly thing' for God to do and appears to involve, in fact, a profanation of God's name. But Abraham had hitherto only known the love of God. In order to become the perfect man of faith he had to learn to obey God and fear him even when commanded to do something that made it extremely hard to believe in God's goodness.
12. J. B. Soloveitchick, 'Ish Ha-Halakhah', *Talpiot* 2 (1944): 651–735.
13. J. B. Agus, *Signposts in Modern Judaism* (New York: Bloch, 1954), pp. 37–8.
14. W. Gunther Plaut, 'Notes on the Akedah', *Central Conference of American Rabbis Journal* 17 (January 1969): 45–7.
15. Franz Rosenzwieg, *Star of Redemption*, second edn (1930), trans. William W. Hallo (London: Routledge and Kegan Paul, 1971), Part III, Introduction, pp. 265–7.
16. Ernst Simon, 'Torat Hayyim', *Conservative Judaism* 12 (Spring 1958): 16–19.
17. *Guide for the Perplexed*, III, 32.
18. Cf. Jiri Langer, *Nine Gates*, trans. Stephen Jolly (London: James Clarke, 1961), p. 156. Under the heading And now something for Kierkegaard, Langer gives this interpretation of the *Akedah*, which he attributes to the eighteenth-century Hasidic master Rabbi Shmelke of Nikolsburg:

> The significance of Abraham's testing lies not in the fact that his obedience to the Lord's command made him prepared to offer up his only son for love of God, but in

the way he behaved when God ordered him to set his son free and let him live. In other words, its significance lies in the fact that God declined the offering the moment after He had demanded it. If Abraham had rejoiced because the life of his beloved son was saved, or if he had grieved because he had not been allowed to show his love for God by actually carrying out his sacrifice – in either of these cases he would have failed the test. But Abraham rejoiced – as can be seen from a careful reading of the Scriptures – that, in carrying out God's new command, to spare his son, he was allowed to bring to God a still greater sacrifice than the actual offering up of Isaac would have been. In being prepared to offer his son to God, he showed that for him the command to sacrifice was something even higher than his love for his child. But when God gave His second command, Abraham gave up the performance of this sacrifice, in other words, he sacrificed even that sacrifice which had previously become so dear to him, for this was the only way he could show his infinite love to the Creator. He rejoiced in the new sacrifice whose significance lay essentially in the fact that he had renounced the offering up of his son. This is the climax of his testing.

— 5 —

Holy Places

Every religion has its holy places; monotheistic faiths are no exception. The concept of a holy place does, however, present difficulties peculiar to monotheism. When earth is seen as inhabited by a multiplicity of gods, it seems natural to assume that each of these has his own particular abode, the plot where he actually resides, zealously maintaining his right of possession. Like a king in his palace, the god in his temple awaits the homage of his subjects, exercising control of his realm, which may be far-flung but is limited by the area over which it extends. All-powerful though he may be in his own domain, the god's existence is at peril if he ventures forth into a province governed by other deities as passionately concerned as he is in maintaining their territorial rights. For monotheism, on the other hand, it is hard to understand how the God whose glory fills the earth can be said to reside in one place rather than another. Why is the building in which He is worshipped more His 'house' than any other spot on earth? And what meaning can be given to the idea that there are degrees of sanctity in which one place is more holy than another? Does this mean that there is a greater degree of in-dwelling in the holier place, and if it does how can it be said that God is located more definitely in one place, less in another?

Here an attempt is made to analyse the problem, relying chiefly on the classical Jewish sources. The task is rendered difficult by the absence of anything like a systematic treatment of the topic. What exist are voluminous rules and regulations regarding the practical consequences which result from the sanctity of certain places; casual theological deliberations on the significance of the idea that God dwells in those places; observations on the psychological effects of man's confrontation with the numinous (a term, needless to say, not found in ancient Jewish writings); and mystical speculations on the spiritual realm invading the secular. Any attempt at systemization, therefore, is to try to impose on the sources a neat order they do not possess. Complex material, large enough to contain contradictions, cannot be delivered in a neat package.[1]

TWO APPROACHES

There are basically two different ways within monotheism of understanding the concept of a holy place. The first is to see the divine as somehow actually located in a quasi-physical manner in the sacred spot or, better, as especially manifested there. The second way is to see the holy place as hallowed by experience and association. On this view there is numinous power in the holy place, not due to any special in-dwelling of the divine but to the evocation of intense religious emotion due to the fact that it is believed to have been the scene of divine revelation or of sustained and fervent worship. It is history that hallows the shrine. We can refer to these two ways of looking at the matter as the objective and the subjective.

One gains the impression that the majority of sophisticated theists today favour the subjective interpretation and there would seem to be several reasons for their preference. First, this way of looking at it does appear to be less crude than the perception of God coming down to earth rather like a traveller from outer space taking care to land his capsule is a hospitable clearing. (The illustration is not inappropriate in view of the bizarre notion that the origin of sacred places is actually to be found in the landings of extraterrestrials on earth in the infancy of the human race.) Second, in a generation that has gone overboard on psychology it appears to be more cogent if the truth and value of religion are expressed in terms of their influence on human emotions and conduct. We tend to prefer religious existentialism to attempts at discovering or locating a divine essence. Third, comparative religious studies have made us aware, to an unprecedented extent, of the rival claims that this or that spot is sacred. Instead of engaging in an argument, which leads nowhere, as to where God is really to be found, we prefer to stand on the surer ground of where humans have found Him – at Bethlehem and in a church by Christians; at Mecca and in a mosque by Muslims; in Jerusalem and in a synagogue by Jews. Fourth, we fear that the objective understanding is a hangover from primitive animism, an attitude unbecoming to man who, as the current jargon has it, has now come of age.

Can we nevertheless put in a word for the objective interpretation? The charge of crudity can be met once it is appreciated that in any event there is the problem for the theist, as the later Kabbalists were fond of pointing out, of how there can be a world at all, of how the universe, time-bound and space-bound, can have emerged from the Infinite, beyond space and time. The Kabbalists postulate a withdrawal of the Infinite (the *Ein Sof*) 'from Itself into Itself' to leave room for the emergence of the finite universe in the 'empty space' it has voluntarily vacated.[2] Whether or not this Kabbalistic idea has significance – and the Kabbalists themselves can hardly avoid spatial images in their very formulation – the problem has still to be faced for all theists, the problem of how God can be everywhere without the universe ceasing to be anywhere or, conversely, if the universe is everywhere, how can God be anywhere? We are bound to conclude that statements such as 'God is everywhere' are themselves spatial and can be no more than metaphors. In a well-known Talmudic homily,[3] God's residence in the world is compared to the soul's residence in the body. 'In' is the operative word here. The soul is 'in' the body in the sense that its separate identity is determined in this material world by the particular body it inhabits, but it is not to be found beneath the skin of that particular body. And our various religious traditions have affirmed that it will survive the death of the body.

Once it is accepted, as theists do, that it is not meaningless to speak of God in the world, once it is accepted that God is present in space and time, although He is beyond space and time; once, in other words, the mystery of God being both transcendent and immanent is referred to as God being in the world, there is no sound reason for denying that His Presence may be located in one spot on earth to a greater degree than in other places.

As far as the other arguments against the objective interpretation are concerned, if we take these too far it is not the location of God in a particular spot that is challenged but the whole theistic position. It is no doubt correct that we generally tend nowadays to see religion in terms of its effect on our personal lives, and that we have a great awareness of religious pluralism. But unless we are prepared to surrender all the truth content of our beliefs, we cannot really opt for religious relativism. Even if we prefer to look for the values inherent in the idea of holy places, as we do when we consider religion as a whole, and even if we are fully conscious of the rival claims of the theist religions, and even if we accept that religious ideas did not drop down ready made from Heaven but had their origin early in the human race and have gone through a process of development and refinement; all this tells us nothing about the truth of the statement that God resides in a particular place or places. There is, of course, no method of investigating the truth of such a claim. If it is held, it is held on faith, but that is true of much else in a theistic philosophy of existence.

FROM THE SOURCES

Let us now examine some typical passages from the sources of Judaism in which our problem is considered. albeit, as we have noted, in a non-systematic way. There are many references in the Bible to sacred spots, the most famous being Mount Moriah, the place of the binding of Isaac (Genesis 22:14), which later tradition identified with the Temple site in Jerusalem; Beth-El where Jacob dreamed of the ladder linking heaven and earth (Genesis 28:10–22); the burning bush when Moses was instructed to remove his shoes because the ground on which he stood was holy ground (Exodus 3:1–5); and Mount Sinai when the Lord descended upon it in fire (Exodus 19:1–25). Interestingly enough, however, Sinai was only held to be sacred at the time of the theophany. In subsequent Jewish tradition Sinai possesses no sanctity whatsoever, probably because, as the Rabbis say[4] and it was believed, the command for the people to keep away from the mount was rescinded once the Decalogue had been given. The Promised Land is the Holy Land (Leviticus 18:24–30; 30:22–24; Zechariah 2:16) and the Temple Mount the most sacred portion of the land (Psalms 15:1; 24:3). The Levitical laws applied especially to the Sanctuary (Leviticus 12:4; Numbers 5:1-4; 19:1–22). Only the High Priest on the Day of Atonement was allowed to enter the Holy of Holies (Leviticus 16:1–34). Anyone who entered the Sanctuary in a state of unfitness committed a grave offence (Leviticus 21:21–23). To this day there is a notice at the entrance to the Temple Mount warning pious Jews to proceed no further. The reasoning behind this is that the area has retained its sanctuary, even though the Temple has long been destroyed, and that all Jews are held to be in a state of ritual contamination, having come into contact with the dead while the ashes of the red heifer (Numbers 19: 1–22) are no longer available for the purification rites.[5]

The Mishnah, compiled around the year 200 CE but containing much earlier material, gives a list of ten places with an ascending degree of sanctity (*Kelim* 1:6–9). Thus the Land of Israel is holier than any other land. The walled cities in the Land of Israel are still more holy in that lepers must be sent forth from their midst. Within the walls of Jerusalem is still more holy. Only therein may the meat of those sacrifices possessing a lower degree of sanctity be eaten. The Temple Mount is still more holy, for no man or woman who has a flux, no menstruant, and no woman after childbirth may enter therein. The Rampart is still more holy, for no Gentile may enter therein and none that has contracted contamination from a corpse. The Court of the Women is still more holy, for none that has immersed himself that day may enter therein. Israelites may not enter therein except when bringing their sacrifices. The Court of the Israelites is still more holy, for none whose atonement is incomplete may enter therein. The Court of the Priests is still more holy, for Israelites may not enter therein except when bringing their sacrifices. The area between the Porch and the Altar is still more holy, for no priest who has a blemish or whose hair is unloosed may enter therein. The Sanctuary is still more holy, for no priest may enter therein without first washing his hands and feet. The Holy of Holies is still more holy, for none may enter there at all save the High Priest on the Day of Atonement at the time of the service. The Mishnah states,[6] incidentally, that when the walls of the Holy of Holies had to be repaired, the workmen were lowered down from the roof in enclosed cages so that their eyes would not feast on other parts of the sacred section.

All this would certainly seem to support the objective interpretation, that the divine actually resides in the sacred place.[7] Yet any attempt at really confining God to a particular spot on earth is repudiated in Solomon's prayer when he dedicated the Temple: 'But will God in very truth dwell on the earth? Behold, heaven and the heaven of heavens cannot contain Thee, how much less this house that I have built' (I Kings 8:27). And the great, unknown prophet of the return from exile declares: 'Thus saith the Lord: The heaven is My throne and the earth My footstool. Where is the house that you may build unto Me? Where is the place that may be

My resting place? For all these things has My hand made, and so all these things came to be, says the Lord. But on this man will I look, even on him that is poor and of a contrite spirit, and trembles at My word' (Isaiah 66:1–3).

Even when it is implied that God does actually reside in His house there is recoil from any suggestion that the place is God's permanent home. He is always there and yet not there.. Modern Biblical scholarship[8] has noted that the word *mishkan*, the word used for the Tabernacle in the wilderness, suggests a temporal not a permanent building. (The same root is found in the Rabbinic term for for the Divine Presence, *Shekhinah*.) God 'tabernacles' in the midst of the people like one who pitches his tent in a place only to move on later. As Cassuto observes,[9] the Ugaritic texts show that the god was conceived of as actually living in the Temple. There he was provided with his needs by his worshippers: his furniture was a throne on which he sat, a table at which he took his meals, a bed on which he slept, a chest of drawers for his clothes and the candelabrum to illumine his darkness. The Biblical account of the building of the Tabernacle appears to be derived from this, while avoiding the grosser anthropomorphism – the bed and the chest of drawers. There was, however, an ark, representing the throne, a candelabrum and a table. But the bread on the table was eaten by the priests; the candelabrum became, at least in the later tradition, the symbol of the spiritual light which proceeds from the Sanctuary (the candelabrum was outside the Holy of Holies where all was dark); and the ark was the container of the tablets of stone upon which the divine law was written.

With regard to the lesser sanctity of the synagogue, the emphasis does seem to be on the subjective interpretation. The place is sacred because worship takes place there. Worship does not take place there because it is sacred. Although Ezekiel's 'minor sanctuary' (Ezekiel 11:16) is applied to the synagogue[10] and although, the synagogue is occasionally called 'the house of God',[11] the sanctity of the synagogue is derived from the prayers and the readings of the Torah which take place there. Zeitlin[12] has advanced the ingenious theory, unsupported, alas, by any evidence and therefore pure guesswork, that the *bet knesset* was originally not a place of worship at all but the local town hall where the town notables discussed public affairs, the proceedings of which were opened by prayer, thus eventually converting the place of assembly into a synagogue. Very revealing in this connection is the Rabbinic ruling[13] that the house of study – *ha-midrash* – has a higher degree of sanctity than the synagogue since the study of the Torah occupies a higher rung on the ladder of Jewish piety than prayer. Jewish law has it that the sanctity of the synagogue is conditional on its use so that when it is no longer in use it may be sold to be used even for secular purposes.[14] It is true that the Jewish mystics did tend to see the synagogue as holy in the objective sense,[15] but they, too, accepted the provisions of Jewish law with its clear implication that the sanctity of the synagogue derives from association. A latter-day Rabbinic authority[16] goes so far as to argue that, strictly speaking, it is permitted to smoke in a synagogue but that this should not be done since Christians do not smoke in church and Jews must not give the impression of having less respect for their house of worship than Christians have for theirs.

MEDIAEVAL PHILOSOPHERS

The mediaeval philosophers were concerned with our problem. In his great Code of Jewish law,[17] Maimonides, after stating the laws governing the trespass offering, the sacrifice brought by one who had inadvertently made use of some object belonging to the Temple, by sitting on a Temple stone, for example, writes: 'It is fitting that man reflect on the laws of the holy Torah, knowing to the best of his ability, their full meaning. When he comes across a matter for which he can find neither reason nor cause, let him not proceed to go up to the Lord [i.e. to question its truth] lest He punish him, and let not his thoughts on that subject be like his thoughts on secular matters. Come and see how strict the Torah is with regard to trespass. Now if mere wood and stones, dust and ashes, become holy by virtue of their having the name of the Lord of the universe called upon them, merely by word of mouth, so that whoever treats them in secular fashion commits a trespass and requires atonement even if he does it inadvertently, how much more so with regard to the precepts ordained by the Holy One, blessed be He, that man should not reject them because he knows not the reason for them.' The wood and stones of the Temple possess no inherent sanctity. They are sacred because the name of God has been called upon them, i.e. they have been dedicated verbally by human beings. They are, therefore, associated with the divine and in this respect are like the divine commandments.

In his *Guide for the Perplexed*[18] Maimonides is more explicit. Here he observes that the Holy of Holies is at the west end of the Temple and the Rabbis say[19] that the *Shekhinah* is in the west. Maimonides refuses to give all this a spatial interpretation. The site of the Temple, he says, is the place on which Abraham bound his son Isaac. Abraham taught us that we should face west, the direction of the Holy of Holies, when we pray as a protest against the sun-worshippers who bow to the rising sun in the east. The ancient pagan idolaters, when they built their temples, placed therein the images of their gods. The Torah, consequently, commanded that the ark, containing the two tablets of stone, should be placed in the holiest part of the Sanctuary, since the Decalogue, recorded on the tablets, begins with the first two commandments: 'I am the Lord thy God' and Thou shalt have no other gods'. Elsewhere in the *Guide*[20] Maimonides writes that the whole command to build a Temple and offer sacrifices was to wean the people away from idolatry. It was a concession to human frailty, as if to say, since you believe that God can only be worshipped in a special place, so be it, but have that place under the control of the law and so learn the truth that there is only One God and He alone is to be worshipped. 'Through this divine ruse it came about that the meaning of idolatry was effaced and that the grandest and true foundation of our belief – namely, the existence and oneness of the deity – was firmly established, while, at the same time, the souls had no feelings of repugnance and were not repelled because of the abolition of modes of worship to which they were accustomed and than which no other mode of worship was known at that time.' There could hardly be a more explicit statement that the sanctity of the holiest of all places derived not from the divine residence there but solely because of the divine command, a command, moreover, issued as a 'ruse' for the purpose of encouraging sound and true ideas and banishing the unreal and the false.

The historical aspect is stressed by Maimonides when he writes:[21] 'There is a tradition accepted by all that the place where David and Solomon built the altar on the threshing floor of Arauna is the very place where Abraham built the altar on which he bound Isaac, and it is the place where Noah built his altar when he emerged from the ark. It is the altar upon which Cain and Abel offered their sacrifices and on it Adam offered a sacrifice as soon as he had been created and it was from (the dust of) that very place that he was created. The Sages say:[22] "Adam was created from the place of his atonement". 'It is not surprising, therefore, that Maimonides, when discussing the obligation to be in dread of the Sanctuary, can write[23]: 'It is a positive commandment to to be in fear of the Sanctuary, as it is said: "And venerate My Sanctuary" [Leviticus 19:30]. But it is not of the Sanctuary that you must be in fear, but of the One who commanded that you must be in fear of it.' This is, in fact, a Talmudic saying[24] but it is no accident that Maimonides refers to it here in order to avoid any impression that the Sanctuary is itself an object of worship or an end in itself.

For all that, Maimonides does not reject the possibility that God may have created a special light which becomes manifest in certain places and on certain occasions. Discussing[25] the verse: 'And the glory of the Lord filled the Sanctuary' (Exodus 10:34) he first observes that 'filling' refers to the evidence for God's perfection as apprehended in the Sanctuary. But he goes on to write: 'Every mention of filling that you will find referring to God is used in this sense, and not in the sense of there being a body filling a place. However, if you wish to consider that *the glory of the Lord* is the created light that is designated as *glory* in every passage and that *filled the Tabernacle*, there is no harm in it.' Elsewhere Maimonides states[26] less ambiguously that there really is a created light that God causes to descend in a particular place in order to confer honour upon it in a miraculous way and this is the glory that descended on Mount Sinai and which filled the Tabernacle.

This latter idea of the created light or glory which fills the Sanctuary is a kind of compromise between the objective and subjective interpretations, according to which there is an objective reality in certain holy places but that reality is not God's essence but a miraculous light that becomes manifest at times. This idea is found in Saadiah Gaon (882–942) who writes:[27] 'Apropos of *place*, I say that it is inconceivable for several reasons that the Creator should have need for occupying any place whatsoever. First of all, He is Himself the Creator of all space. Also He originally existed alone, when there was no such thing as place. It is unthinkable, therefore, that as a result of His act of creation He should have been transported into space. Furthermore, space is only required by a material object which occupies the place of the object that it meets and comes in contact with, so that each one of the two contiguous objects form the place of the other. This is, however, out of the question as far as the Creator is concerned. As for the assertion of the prophets that God dwells in heaven, that was merely a way of indicating God's greatness and His elevation, since heaven is for us the highest thing we know of. This is borne out by such explanations offered by Scripture as: "For God is in heaven, and thou upon the earth" [Ecclesiastes 5:1] as well as: "Behold, heaven and the heaven of heavens cannot contain Thee" [I Kings 8:27]. The same applies to statements that God dwells in the Temple, such as: "And I will dwell among the children of Israel" [Exodus 29:15], and " the Lord dwelleth in Zion" [Joel; 4:21]. The purpose of all this was to confer honour upon the place and upon the people in question. Besides that, it is to be remembered that God had also revealed in that place His specially created light, of which we have made mention previously, that was called *shekhinah* and *glory*.'

The fifteenth century Spanish philosopher and Biblical exegete, Isaac Arama, has a lengthy excursus on our theme in his *Akedat Yitzhak*.[28] Arama follows Maimonides[29] in his understanding of the command to build a Sanctuary. What can be the meaning, asks Arama, of this strange command, as if God is like a human king who requires to be housed in special apartments when he visits his subjects? 'Heaven forfend that God should occupy a place in the Temple or in any other place famed for His Presence [*shekhinatol*] since one who occupies a place is limited by the confines of that place and His blessed name and splendour is totally beyond this.' Arama's understanding of the matter is that the philosophers, in their eagerness to reject all anthropomorphism, go to the opposite extreme, to deny God's Providence. It is in reaction to such an attitude that God is said metaphorically to dwell in the Sanctuary. The Rabbis, too, speak of God as *Ha-Makom*, 'the Place', because He is the place of the world and the world is not His place.[30] This, too, must be metaphor. God behaves like a healer who sometimes avails himself of medicines the value of which the patient does not understand. God was prepared, as it were, to take the risk that the people would really believe that He is confined in holy places. He was prepared to do this in order to make them aware that His Providence extends over them. God, in fact, for the purpose of training His people, made seem possible to them that which in reality was quite impossible. Thus, when Scripture says: 'And Moses was not able to enter into the tent of meeting, because the cloud abode therein, and the glory of the Lord filled the house of the Lord' (Exodus 10:35), the reference is to a kind of illusion wrought by God for its psychological advantages. 'He allowed Israel to believe three things that are really impossible for the One who is beyond all these. When He said: "And Moses was not able to enter into the tent of meeting", He surrendered the idea that anthropomorphism must be rejected, as if something tangible were really there. When He said: "because the cloud abode therein", He allowed them to believe that He moves from one place to another. And when He said: "and the glory of the Lord filled the house of the Lord", He allowed them to believe that He occupied space.'

A somewhat different way of looking at the matter is developed in the mystical tradition. The sixteenth-century preacher and mystic of Safed, Moses Alsheikh, for instance, describes[31] this tradition as postulating that the Temple on earth is a counterpart to the Temple on high: it is the channel through which the divine grace flows from on high to the whole world. Commenting on the verse commanding the making of the Sanctuary so that God will dwell among the people (Exodus 25:8), Alsheikh remarks: 'The ears tingle when they hear this strange thing, for how can the light of His Shekhinah have dwelt in this earth in a Temple built by human hands? But the reply is that there is the gate of Heaven, the place where the supernal grace flows downwards to illumine the earth and the inhabitants thereof. From the time the world was created the Shekhinah has dwelt in that spot. The reason is that it corresponds to the Temple on high. Consequently, there is nothing strange in God dwelling in the Sanctuary on earth, for there is His residence on high as if He dwells in both worlds at the same time.'

As we have seen, there are to be found in the Jewish tradition varying degrees of sanctity. At one extreme is the Temple, where the Biblical seems to imply an actual in-dwelling of the divine. At the other extreme is the synagogue, the sanctity of which depends on those who worship there. Somewhere in the middle is the Holy Land. Nowhere in the Middle Ages is the high sanctity of the Land of Israel so warmly affirmed than in the *Kuzari* and the religious poetry of Judah Halevi (d. 1141). Halevi was obviously bothered by the problem of particularism, both in connection with the choice of the people of Israel and the special distinction of the Land of Israel. The book *Kuzari*[32] consists of an imaginary dialogue between the King of Khazars and a Jewish sage. The King cannot understand why God should have singled out a special people. The sage manages to convince him that such a choice makes sense but then the King, while admitting this, cannot see why one land should be holier than any other. The sage replies that just as vines, for example, require good and proper cultivation, so, too, the Holy Land promotes holiness, but it requires cultivation by the Chosen People, this cultivation consisting of the observance of specific obligations on that land by that people. All the prophets, he observes, either prophesied there or prophesied concerning that land. The sanctity of the Holy Land is, then, for Halevi a spiritual endowment by virtue of which greater holiness, even to the extent of prophecy, can be realized if the divine Torah is obeyed. It is this spiritual influence that 'dwells' in the land.

Nahmanides (1194–1270)[33] has a different approach, seeing the sanctity of the Land of Israel in that all other lands are governed each by its own Prince, its guardian angel, whereas the Holy Land is under the direct control and providence of God Himself. That is why Scripture warns the children of Israel so sternly against immoralities; if they will be guilty of these the land will spew them out as it spewed out the Canaanites. The specially holy place, under God's special providence, cannot tolerate its pollution by these offences.[34]

It is clear that there is considerable tension in the sources between the objective and subjective understanding of the phenomenon and there are recognitions that while a more objective understanding might be more appropriate for a place of higher sanctity it is less appropriate for one of a lesser degree of sanctity. But even so far as the synagogue is concerned, the lowest in the degrees of sanctity, the interpretation is not entirely unknown that something is really there in an objective sense. We have argued that the objective interpretation cannot be ruled out *a priori*. Nor can a religion like Judaism, with its strong emphasis on the material as the vehicle for the spiritual and on the physical world as the arena for the struggle against evil and the pursuit of the good, necessarily reject the objective understanding as too materialistic, literally too earth-bound. For it is on earth that humans meet their God in this life.

Yet, granted that there are no cogent reasons for rejecting the objective interpretation, the question still remains, how can we know whether or not holiness or the divine influence dwells in a particular place? The traditional answer, so far as Judaism is concerned, is that we know it through revelation; it has been told to us by God in the Torah. That is how Maimonides, Halevi, Arama and the others quoted 'knew' it. The modernist Jew, however, has learned to see the Torah more in terms of a divine–human encounter than as a direct communication by God to passive recipients. The Torah, for him, has a human element though it is still God's Torah. The sources, including the Biblical sources, in which it is implied that the divine glory actually resides in the holy places, are themselves seen by the modernist as profound *human* reflection on events. Historically speaking, these sources themselves are subjective and do not convey anything like a divine guarantee that this or that place is sacred. It seems right for the modernist to have an open mind on the question of whether or not a presence is 'really' there in the sacred spot while treating that place as sacred, none the less, because, as a historical reality, that place has been associated with the most sacred religious experiences of his tradition. I cannot see that there is much practical difference between the objective and subjective view except that the latter might encourage a more tolerant and respectful attitude towards the holy places of theistic religions other than one's own. To say this is far from adopting a relativistic position. The adherents of all the monotheistic faiths continue to have their own holy places of supreme importance to them. There is no need for triumphalism, not, at least, in the pre-Messianic age. What happens in the Messianic age is another matter. Of that age it is said in the Jewish tradition: 'Even them will I bring to My holy mountain, and make them joyful in My house of prayer. Their burnt offerings and their sacrifices shall be acceptable upon My altar: for My house shall be called a house of prayer for all peoples' (Isaiah 56:7).

NOTES

1. For Jewish sources on the significance of holy places see *Encyclopedia Talmudit*, S. J. Zevin (Jerusalem 1947–); for the Land of Israel, vol. 2, pp. 199–235, for the synagogue,, vol.3, pp. 190–205, for the Temple, vol. 3, pp. 224–41; S. A. Adler: *Aspaklaria*, vol.3 (Jerusalem, 1978) for the Land of Israel, pp. 170–90, for the synagogue, pp. 358–363, for the Temple, pp. 354–82; M. Guttman, *Mafteah Ha-Talmud* (Breslau, 1924), vol. 3, 'The Land of Israel in Midrash and Talmud' [Hebrew];. On the general question see Hastings, *Encyclopedia of Religion and Ethics*, vol. 10 (Edinburgh, 1918 'Places (Sacred)', pp. 50–2; *The Encyclopedia of Religion*, ed. Mircia Eliade, New York, 1987, s.v. 'Hierophany', vol. 6, pp. 313–17. The famous work on the 'numinous' is: *The Idea of the Holy* by Rudolf Otto, trans. J. W. Harvey, London, 1957.
2. On the Kabbalistic doctrine see G. Scholem: *Major Trends in Jewish Mysticism* (London 1957), pp. 246–86; I. Tishby: *Torat ha-Ra ve-ha-kelipah be-torato shel ha-ari*, Jerusalem, 1968. Interestingly enough for the purpose of our discussion, the term *tzuntzum* in the Lurianic Kabbalah, to denote God's withdrawal in order to bring the universe into being, is derived from the use of this term in the Midrash to denote God's concentration (the term has the associated meaning of withdrawal from one place and concentration into another) in the Sanctuary. See Midrash Exodus Rabbah 34:1: 'When God said to Moses: "Make a tabernacle for Me", Moses exclaimed in amazement: "The glory

of the Holy One, blessed be He, fills heaven and earth and yet He commands me to make a tabernacle." God said: "Not as you think do I think; twenty boards on the north, twenty on the south and eight in the west; moreover, I will descend and even confine [*metzamtzem*] my Shekhinah within one square cubit'" .Cf. *Pesikta de-Rav Kahana*, ed. Buber, p. 2b, English translation by William G. Braude and Israel J. Kapstein (London, 1975, p. 8) : 'Rabbi Joshua of Siknin said in the name of Rabbi Levi: With what is the Tent of Meeting to be compared? With a cave situated on the edge of the sea. When the sea rises and floods it, the cave, of course, is filled by the sea, yet the sea is not diminished. Likewise, the Tent of Meeting was filled with the Splendour of the Presence'. Immediately before this there occurs the passage: 'A heathen put the following question to Rabban Gamaliel: Why did the Holy One, blessed be He, reveal Himself in a thorn bush? Rabban Gamaliel replied: Had He revealed Himself in a carob tree or high in a fig tree, what would you have said? As it is, you see that no place on earth is devoid of His Presence.' Cf. the comment on this Midrash of R. Moshe Teitelbaum in *Yismah Moshe* (Jerusalem ed. 1976, *Noah*, p. 29a). 'The divine power was in the bush because it is everywhere. What was revealed to Moses was the power and vitality already there.' This comment is reminiscent of Elizabeth Barrett Browning:

> *Earth's crammed with heaven,*
> *And every common bush afire with God,*
> *But only he who sees, takes off his shoes.*

3. *Berakhot* 10a.
4. See *Betzah* 5b.
5. The Talmud (*Shavuot* 16a) discusses whether the sanctity still remains after the destruction of the Temple. Maimonides (*Yad, Bet Ha-Behirah* 6:15–16) rules that it does, whereas the *Rabad* holds that it does not. According to the latter, the Talmudic discussion concerns only the Land but all agree that the Temple site is only sacred when the Temple stood. Maimon ides, on the contrary, holds that the sanctity of the Temple site depends on the presence there of the Shekhinah and this has never departed.
6. *Middot* 4:5; *Pesahim* 26a.
7. Cf. the Rabbinic comment (Exodus Rabbah 33:3) to the verse.'Open to me, my sister, my spouse' (Song of Songs 5:2): 'Until when shall I walk about homeless? Therefore, make Me a Sanctuary, so that I shall not be obliged to walk in the streets.'
8. See Frank M. Gross Jr: 'The Priestly Tabernacle' in: *Old Testament Issues*, ed. Samuel Sandmell, London, 1969, pp. 39–67
9. U. Cassuto: *A Commentary on the Book of Exodus*, translated Israel Abrahams, Jerusalem, 1967, pp. 319–24. Cf. the statement of the fifteenth century statesman and Biblical exegete, Don Isaac Abravanel in his Commentary to Exodus (trans. in Nehama Leibowitz: *Studies in Shemot, Exodus*, Part 2, Jerusalem, 1978,p. 472): 'The divine intention behind the construction of the Tabernacle was to combat the idea that God had forsaken the earth, and that His throne was in the heaven, remote from humankind. To disabuse the Israelites of this erroneous belief, He commanded them to make a Tabernacle, as if to imply that He dwelt in their midst, that they should believe that God lived in their midst and His Providence was always with them. This is the meaning of: "and I shall dwell amidst the children of Israel' ... who dwells with them in their defilement". It is all a parable and allegory representing the immanence of His Presence and Providence. This, indeed, was the implication of of the statement in Isaiah [66:1]: "The heaven is my throne and the earth My footstool, where is the house that you may build for Me, where is the place of My rest? – I do not need the Tabernacle for My dwelling place for "all these things has My hand made" [ibid. 2], but I commanded these to be made in order to implant My providence in their midst. And this is what is stated [at the end of the verse] "but to this man will I look, even to him that is pure and of a contrite spirit and he who trembles at My word."'
10. *Megillah* 29a.
11. *Shabbat* 10a. Cf. Bahya Ibn Asher, *Kad Ha-Kemah*, ed. Chavel, Jerusalem, 1970, s.v. *bet ha-Kenesset*, pp. 87–91, who, p. 88, refers to the synagogue as 'the house of God' and compares (p.88) the synagogue to the Temple, yet states that the reason why prayers are especially acceptable in the synagogue is because public prayer is more acceptable and makes no suggestion that it is because of the special sanctity of the place.
12. Solomon Zeitlin: 'The Origin of the Synagogue' in his: *Studies in the Early History of*

Judaism, vol. 1,, New York, 1973, pp. 1–8.
13. *Megillah* 26b–27a.
14. *Megillah* 26a–b.
15. See e.g. Elijah de Vidas: *Reshit Hokhmah, Shaar Ha-Yirah*, chapter 15: 'Now although the whole earth is filled with His glory yet because of His love for us He concentrates His Shekhinah among us as He used to do between the staves of the ark and the place of the Holy of Holies in the Temple. Of the Tent of Meeting we also find that once it had been finished Scripture says: "And Moses was not able to enter into the tent of meeting because the cloud abode therein, and the glory of the Lord filled the tabernacle" [Exodus 40:35]. Similarly, of the Temple, when Solomon brought the ark into the Holy of Holies, Scripture says: "The priests could not stand to minister by reason of the cloud, for the glory of the Lord filled the house of the Lord" [I Kings 8:11]. The synagogue, too, is filled with the light of the glory of the Lord, Even though we see nothing of it, it is essential that we believe this with perfect faith.'
16. David Hoffman: *Melammed le-hoil* (New York, 1954), *Orah Hayyim*. No. 11.
17. *Yad, Meilah* 8:8.
18. *Guide* III, 45.
19. *Bava Batra* 25a cites this as one of the reasons given for the rule in the Mishnah (*Bava Batra* 2:9) that a tannery must not be set up to the west of the town. Cf. Maimonides' comment to this Mishnah and the remarks (*Bava Batra*) of Menahem Meiri of Perpignan (1249–131 6) on the statement that the Shekhinah is in the west. 'This is a hint to keep away from sun-worship ... not, Heaven forfend, to limit Him to space'; as well as the note to this Mishnah by Israel Lipshitz Tiferet Yisrael, *Nezikin*, p. 59 in the standard large edition.
20. *Guide* II, 32, trans. S. Pines: *The Guide for the Perplexed* (Chicago University Press, 1974) pp. 526–7.
21. *Yad, Bet Ha-Behirah* 2:2.
22. JT, *Nazir* 7:2 (56b).
23. *Yad, Bet Ha-Behirah* 7:1.
24. *Yevamot* 6b. Cf. the remarkable observation by the nineteenth- century Hasidic master, Jacob of lzbica (*Bet Yaakov*, Lublin, 1905, vol. 2, p. 256) on the second commandment. The 'graven image' in the heavens above refers to the Sabbath and on the earth beneath refers to the Temple. The Sabbath and the Temple are the instruments for approaching God but only God Himself is an object of worship. It is possible to make an idol of the holy place!
25. *Guide* I, 19.
26. *Guide* I, 64.
27. *Emunot ve-Deot* II, 11, trans. *The Book of Beliefs and Opinions* by Samuel Rosenblatt, Yale University Press, 1955, pp. 124–5.
28. *Akedat Yitzhak*, ed. H. J. Pollack, Vienna, 1847.
29. *Akedat Yitzhak, terumah, Shaar* 48, ed. Pollack, vol. 2, pp. 135b–140b. Cf. Arama's comment on Jacob's dream, Genesis, *Shaar* 25, ed. Pollack, vol. 1, pp. 187b–8a.
30. See Mishnah *Berakhot* 5:1; *Taanit* 3:8; *Avot* 3:3; *Shabbat* 12b. The explanation:'He is the place of the world but the world is not His place' is given in Genesis Rabbah 68:9. C f. A. Marmorstein: *The Old Rabbinic Doctrine of God* (New York, 1968) pp. 92–3.
31. *Torat Moshe* (Warsaw, 1979), Exodus, pp. 87a–89b. On this idea see Responsa *Hatam Sofer, Yoreh Deah*, No. 234, especially the quotation from the *Hesed le Avraham* by Abraham Azulai.
32. *Kuzari*, Part II, 9–24, ed. Kaufman (Tel-Aviv, 1972), pp. 52–64.
33. Commentary to the Torah to Leviticus 18:25 (ed. Chavel, Jerusalem, 1960, pp. 109–112).
34. Reference should also be made here to the Talmudic accounts of Rabbis who kissed the earth and stones of the Land of Israel when visiting there for the first time, see *Ketubot* 112a.

— 6 —

The Jewish Tradition

An inquiry into the relationship between faith and tradition in Judaism must begin with the linguistic problem. The classical sources – the Bible and the Talmudic literature – know neither the Greek-inspired term 'Judaism' nor the term 'religion'. Zangwill put it neatly when he said: the Rabbis were the most religious of men but they had no word for religion. As for 'tradition', while this is roughly equivalent to *masorah* and *kabbalah*, words which are found in the sources, the modern connotation of the word is quite different. In contemporary language a religious tradition generally refers to the practices, forms and rituals of a religious community as the creation of that community in the past. When the community appeals to its tradition the appeal is to the past as a guide for the future. But *masorah* and *kabbalah* refer, respectively, to the handing over and the acceptance of a body of truth independent of the transmission. It is the truth that is said to be binding; those who handed it down and those who received it, to hand it down in turn, are merely the instruments for the conveyance of that truth. Take, for instance, the Biblical appeals to consider the past such as:

> Remember the days of old, consider the years of many generations, ask thy father and he will tell thee, thy elders and they will declare it. (Deuteronomy 32:7)

The father who tells the tale of God's mighty acts in history and the elders who declare these are to be heeded, it is implied, not because there is any virtue in listening to them *per se* but because they are the links in the chain reaching back to the original events. They are reliable witnesses, faithful transmitters and no more than that. Or take the opening section of 'Ethics of the Fathers' (another modern name, for what, in the original, is simply *Avot*, 'Fathers', meaning the teachings of the fathers of the community, the sages). This tractate, *Avot*, records the particular sayings or maxims of the Jewish sages down to the end of the second century and as such constitutes a chain of tradition. But it is noteworthy that the opening passage reads:

> Moses received [*kibbel*] a Torah at Sinai and he handed it down [*mesarah*] to Joshua and Joshua to the Elders and the Elders to the Prophets. And the Prophets handed it down to the Men of the Great Assembly.

The picture is of a body of truth handed down intact from generation to generation, though each generation added something of its own in elaboration of the truth. It is beside the point that, from the historical point of view, the notion of a static truth, uninfluenced by external conditions and communicated in such a neat order, is untenable. The fact remains that this is how tradition is thought of in the sources.

The word for 'faith' – *emunah* – never means, in the early sources, 'belief *that...*' but always 'belief *in...*'. Naturally, belief in God implies that God exists. Theoretical atheism was, in any event, virtually unknown in Biblical and Rabbinic times. But the explicit meaning of *emunah* is trust in God, confidence in His power to help, acknowledgement of His concern with justice and righteousness. Anselm's famous ontological argument begins with the 'fool' of Psalm 14 who 'hath said there is no God', which Anselm understands as a denial of God's existence. The whole tenor of the Psalm, however, shows that this cannot be correct. The Psalmist continues:

> They are corrupt, they have done abominable works, there is none that doeth good. The Lord looked down from heaven upon the children of men, to see if there were any that did understand, and seek God.

The *naval* of the Psalm is, in reality, not 'foolish' but ethically insensitive. His obtuseness is moral not intellectual. Of the people at the crossing of the Sea it is said (Exodus 14:31):

> And Israel saw that great work which the Lord did upon the Egyptians; and the people feared the Lord, and believed in the Lord and in Moses His servant.

The people believed in the Lord in the same way in which they believed in Moses. They had not previously doubted whether

Moses existed. It was their faith and trust in him that had wavered. Now that they had been delivered they saw that God was reliable and Moses His true servant. We need only quote one Rabbinic passage among many to make the point so far as the Talmudic literature is concerned: 'Rabbi Eliezer the Great said: "Whoever has bread in his basket and yet says: 'What shall I eat tomorrow' is of those of little faith"', *ketaney emunah*.[1]

Apart from the linguistic difficulties, any attempt to treat systematically a question of this nature from the Jewish sources is to impose upon these sources a meaning they simply do not possess. It is in the nature of neither Biblical nor Rabbinic texts to explore this, or, for that matter, any other idea in a systematic way. The very idea of an 'idea' is foreign to Biblical and Rabbinic modes of thought. These, in the words of Isaac Heinemann and Max Kadushin, are 'organic'.[2] They grow out of the experiences of prophets, sages and teachers and are rather like popular proverbs in which one response is required in one situation, a different response in another. 'Too many cooks spoil the broth'. 'Many hands make light work'. Both are true, depending on the circumstances. This means, in effect, that, until the Middle Ages, when the Jewish thinkers were influenced by Greek philosophy in its Arabic garb, there was no such thing as Jewish theology. The conclusion to be drawn, however, is not, as Moses Mendelssohn would seem to have had it in the eighteenth century, that Judaism has no dogmas. It must have beliefs for it to have an identity. But it is a valid contention that beliefs of the 'belief that...' variety are never too closely defined and that their acceptance (or rejection) is less cognitive than moral and religious, less due to thought processes than to personal choice, less the result of reflection than of response, less because they have been worked out in reason than because they 'ring a bell'.

To be sure the great mediaeval thinkers were systematic in their approach. But since they accepted the Bible and the Talmudic literature as sacred and binding, they were reduced to the attempt, one that could hardly succeed, of incorporating into their system material that, by its nature, defies systematization. The price they paid was to be meta-historical, not to say, unhistorical. They saw no incongruity in reading Greek ideas into the ancient texts, as when Maimonides finds his golden mean in Rabbinic teachings[3] and when he identifies,[4] to the scandal of the traditionalists, the Rabbinic 'Work of Creation' and 'Work of the Chariot' (in the context mystical speculations and reflections on God bringing the world into being and God's providence as seen in Ezekiel's vision of the Chariot) with, respectively, Aristotelian physics and metaphysics.

An instructive illustration of the varying attitudes is provided by the treatment of what amounts to the basic Jewish dogma, the revelation of the Torah. The Mishnah[5] lists among those who have no share in the World to Come one who declares (*ha-omer*, not 'one who does not believe *that*', a form impossible for the Rabbis, as noted above): 'There is no Torah from Heaven'. This statement is elaborated on in an early source mentioned in the Talmud:[6] '*Because he hath despised the word of the Lord* (Numbers 15:31) – this refers to one who declares that the whole of the Torah is from Heaven, with the exception of a single verse which (he maintains) was not said by the Holy One, blessed be He, but by Moses of his own accord, the verse: *Because he hath despised the word of the Lord* still applies to him. And even if he declares that the whole of the Torah is from Heaven, with the exception of a single inference, a single argument from the minor to the major, or a single derivation by means of similar expression (*gezerah shavah*), the verse: *Because he hath despised the word of the Lord* still applies to him.'

The statement about the argument from the minor to the major has puzzled the commentators since it is everywhere acknowledged that this hermeneutical principle is based solely on human reasoning and may be rejected, as happens frequently in the Talmud, by those who advance counter-arguments for its refutation. But anyone familiar with the nature of Talmudic literature will appreciate that what we have here is Rabbinic hyperbole; as if to say, the Torah is a revelation from God and there must be no compromise with this doctrine, not even with the process of inference from the Torah by human reasoning since this is how God wishes His Torah to be interpreted. The one who declares that Moses made up any part of the Torah despises *the word of the Lord*, i.e. he denigrates God's word by declaring it to be the mere human word of Moses. It is the divine character of the Torah that the Rabbis are eager to affirm, that, as it would be expressed today, Judaism is a revealed religion. The Rabbis were certainly not concerned with the question of the Mosaic authorship of the Pentateuch. That was no problem in their day. Even the heretics believed that Moses wrote the Pentateuch, only they declared that some of it was not given by God at all but was made up by Moses out of his own head.

Another passage in the Talmud[7] of similar import tells of the wicked king Manasseh who 'sat and expounded false homilies' (*haggadot shel dofi*). Manasseh said: Had Moses nothing better to do than to record *And Timna was concubine to Eliphaz* (Genesis 16:12)? Krochmal[8] and other modern students of the Talmudic literature have taught us to see that when the Rabbis put words into the mouths of the Biblical characters, especially when, as here, the vocabulary is that of Rabbinic institutions ('sat and expounded false homilies'), they were, in effect, addressing themselves to the faults and offences, as they saw them, of their own times. In all probability there were sceptics in Rabbinic times who refused to believe that God was responsible for every single verse in the Torah, even for verses which seemed quite pointless or which imparted information no one wished to have. There is nothing here at all like a precise theological statement about the content of the divine revelation. It is rather a homiletical device for the purpose of strengthening belief in the sanctity of the whole of the Torah, a free response on the part of the Rabbis to the challenges of their day. The Rabbis are here sermonizing. They are not doing theology.

Maimonides, on the other hand, in obedience to his theological stance in which precision is all and totally clear definition an imperative (perhaps in response to and influenced by Islamic claims for the Koran and undoubtedly as part of his dogmatic system-building), states the Rabbinic view[9] (which, for him, is now *the* Jewish view) as: 'The eighth principle of the Jewish faith is that the Torah has been revealed from Heaven. This implies our belief that the whole of the Torah found in our hands this day is the very Torah that was handed down to Moses and it is all divine in origin. By this I mean that the whole of the Torah came to him from before God in a manner metaphorically called "speaking"; but the real nature of that communication is not known to anyone apart from Moses (peace to him!) to whom it came. Moses was like a scribe writing from dictation the whole of it, its chronicles, its narratives and its precepts. It is in this sense that he is termed *mehokek* ("copyist"). And there is no difference between verses like: *And the sons of Ham were Cush and Mizraim, Phut and Canaan* (Genesis 9:6), or *And his wife's name was Mehetabel, daughter of Matred* (Genesis 36:39), or *And Timna was concubine* (Genesis 36:12), and verses like *I am the Lord thy God* (Exodus 20:2) and *Hear, O Israel* (Deuteronomy 6:4). They are all equally of divine origin and all belong to the law of

God, perfect, pure, holy and true. In the opinion of the Rabbis, Manasseh was the greatest of all infidels because he thought that in the Torah there is a kernel and a husk, and that these histories and anecdotes have no value and emanate from Moses.' What had previously been exhortation and preachment, directed, in all probability, against some Jewish sceptics in a particular period, now becomes a 'principle of the faith' (the very notion is not found in any of the earlier sources), a dogma eternally binding upon Jews. Under the great weight of Maimonides' authority, this statement was, indeed, accepted by the majority of Jews until the rise of modern historical investigation into the sources of Judaism and of Biblical Criticism. It is still the Orthodox position in Jewry, although, even in the middle ages, thinkers like Abraham Ibn Ezra were prepared to admit to a number of post-Mosaic additions to the Pentateuch, evidently understanding the above-mentioned Rabbinic passages as leaving scope for mild literary criticism of the Pentateuch, provided no actual laws of the Torah were affected.

A few years ago a Swiss scholar, I. S. Lange, published from manuscript a series of Commentaries to the Pentateuch[10] by Judah the Saint of Regensburg (twelfth–thirteenth centuries), a recognized authority for all Orthodox Jews. The book was declared to be heretical on the grounds that it maintains there are (a very few) post-Mosaic additions to the Pentateuch. Attempts were made to suppress the book, one of the rare instances in modern times of Jewish censorship of books alleged to contain heresy. The renowned, contemporary Halakhist, Rabbi Moses Feinstein,[11] fiercely objected that the work could not possibly have been written by the Saint of Regensburg and he refers to both the Talmudic statements and those of Maimonides, whereas it would appear that some of the mediaeval scholars, even if they were 'saints', did not understand the doctrine of 'Torah from Heaven' as precluding entirely every suggestion that this or that Pentateuchal verse may have been added after Moses.

Biblical Criticism and historical investigation in general have presented a mighty challenge to the whole doctrine of 'Torah from Heaven'. If the Documentary Hypothesis is correct and the sources J, E, D and P were put together by a Redactor or a series of Redactors; if many of the textual variants found in the Septuagint and other ancient versions may be a record of a better preserved text; if the Rabbinic teachings and expositions are not seen as having dropped from Heaven directly but as having had a history and best understood in terms of responses to the particular needs of their time; if all this appears convincing, what is to become of the dogma that the whole of the Torah in its present textual form and with all the explications of it in the 'Oral Torah' was delivered by God to Moses? Some Jews in the last century and more in this have been unable to reconcile the new learning with the older tradition, going so far as surrender completely the idea of Judaism as a revealed religion. But, in varying degrees, many other Jews have remained believers in 'Torah from Heaven' by reinterpreting the doctrine in the light of the new knowledge, which, after all, on the believer's own premiss, is also part of God's truth, as is all truth. If I may repeat something I wrote in this connection, it is still possible to believe in 'Torah from Heaven' but it all depends on what one means by 'Torah', by 'Heaven' and, more especially, by 'from'. From one point of view the divide among Jews on this matter is between Orthodoxy on the one hand and Reform and Conservative Judaism on the other. Yet, in reality, the divide is more accurately between the fundamentalist and liberal-critical approach. Orthodoxy itself has sometimes been understood by its adherents more as Orthopraxy, a religious position which does not necessarily mean: 'Believe what you like provided you keep the *mitzvot* (precepts)' but can mean that God intended the emphasis to be on the practical. From these considerations the question we are examining is, in the language used by Jews, that of the relationship between the Torah and the *mitzvot* and the personal convictions of the individual, faithful and loyal Jew. Put in this way there can only be one answer, the relationship is complicated, with considerable tensions between the two. This is obviously true for the 'liberal' Jew, less so for the traditionalist or fundamentalist. Yet even the Jew who believes that the whole of the Torah is God-given in a direct sense, including the verse *And Timna was concubine,* believes it, presumably, because that is his own personal conviction. Moreover, whatever his actual affirmation, he does see more significance in some verses of the Torah than in some others because his history and traditions have made some verses more significant than others. Throughout the ages devout Jews have been ready to sacrifice life itself for the idea expressed in: *Hear, O Israel* and *I am the Lord thy God.* We have yet to hear of a Jew suffering martyrdom for *And Timna was concubine to Eliphaz.* The principle of selectivity has been at work in the history of Judaism.

Keeping in mind the non-systematic nature of the classical

Jewish sources and without expecting to find there too much consistency, we are still able to note how the tension between the Torah and personal faith has been expressed by looking at a number of passages in these and in later sources.

As early as the Song of Moses, God is described as both 'my' God and as God of the fathers (Exodus 15:2):

> He is my God, and I will glorify Him;
> my father's God and I will exalt Him.

The famous French commentator, Rashi (whose commentary is printed in practically every edition of the Pentateuch), no doubt relying on earlier teaching, remarks in exposition of the verse: 'The sanctity did not begin with me but has been established for me by my ancestors.' In other words, the individual is sustained in his belief by the fact that he did not invent it but has received it by tradition. It is noteworthy that Rashi, writing in eleventh century France, speaks of the sanctity (*kedushah*) not the belief. It is the experience of God rather than the mere belief in His existence that is fortified. It is as if Rashi is saying, what I imagine to be an encounter with the holiness of God might have been construed as an illusion were it not that my ancestors have handed down the record of their experiences, encouraging me to regard mine as authentic. Here the tradition fortifies personal faith.

The further idea that the tradition itself becomes significant by the personal choice in which it is appropriated seems to be implied in the Talmudic account[13] of the debate on whether a teacher of the Torah can renounce the honour due to him. The fourth-century Babylonian teacher, R. Joseph, argued that he is permitted to renounce his honour, quoting in support the verse: *And the Lord went before them by day* (Exodus 13:21) i.e. God, the Teacher of Israel, renounced His honour to act as their guide. Just as the divine Teacher renounced the honour due to him so, too, an earthly teacher of the Torah may renounce the honour due to him, if he so wishes. To this, R. Joseph's colleague, Rava, objected that with regard to God the whole world is His and the Torah is His and so He can renounce the honour due to Him. It does not follow that a human teacher of the Torah may renounce the honour due to him because of the Torah. Is, then, asks Rava, the Torah his own possession that he may renounce the honour due to him because he is skilled in learning and teaching the Torah? But, the passage continues, eventually Rava came to agree with R. Joseph. Yes, indeed, declared Rava, the Torah is his, the scholar's, quoting in support the verse: *and in his Torah doth he meditate day and night* (Psalm 1:2). That is to say, Rava interprets homiletically the personal pronoun in the verse as referring not to God, as in the plain meaning ('His Torah'), but to the student of the Torah mentioned in the first clause: *But his delight is in the Torah of the Lord.* The student of the Torah makes the Torah his own by his diligent studies. It is no longer something external to him to which he owes allegience. It has become his own; intimate and personal.

The personal aspect of faith finds its expression in the Rabbinic concept of *lishmah* ('literally "for her sake" i.e. for the sake of the Torah'). The motives of the student of the Torah and of the Jew who observes its laws should ideally be purely for the sake of God. The religious act should not be carried out with ulterior motives but solely because it is God's will. Before the performance of a *mitzvah* a benediction is to be recited: 'Blessed art Thou, O Lord our God, King of the universe, who has sanctified us with His commandments and has commanded us to …', thereby demonstrating the devotional character of the act. It is one performed in obedience to God's will not as a mere mechanical following of the tradition and not in order to acquire a reputation for piety. Faith is expected to infuse constant life into the observances. For all that, there is a realistic appraisal of human nature, an appreciation by the Rabbis that it is demanding too much that the motive for observance must be pure at all times. The early-third-century teacher Rav is quoted[14] as saying: 'Let a man engage in the Torah and carry out the *mitzvot* even if it is not *lishmah*. For out of engagement that is lacking in *lishmah* he will eventually attain to observance *lishmah*.'

That the motive be pure is, none the less, always the ideal. The impure motive is only tolerated because it will eventually lead to observance with pure motive. The oft-quoted and frequently misinterpreted passage in the Midrash[15] notwithstanding, the Rabbis perceived no value in mechanical observance in itself. A secular Judaism, in which the observances are carried out as picturesque folkways, would have been quite repellent to the Rabbis if they had been able to conceive of such a thing. The Midrash in question reads: 'R. Huna and R. Jeremiah said in the name of R. Hiyya bar Abba: It is written: *They have forsaken Me and have not kept My Torah* (Jeremiah 16:11). This means that God says: Would that they had forsaken Me if only they had kept My Torah.' It is preposterous to understand the Midrash as advocating a God-less Judaism. A Judaism without God but with observance of the Torah would have been totally incomprehensible to the Rabbis of the Midrash or to any other representative Jewish teacher in the pre-modern era. Nor is the paraphrase of M. Friedländer, in his popular handbook of the Jewish faith,[16] anywhere near the mark. Friedländer renders the meaning of the Midrash as: 'theologians would do better if they were less eager to investigate into the essence of God and His attributes and were more anxious to study and to do God's commandments'. There were, in fact, no theologians in Rabbinic times who were eager to investigate into the essence of God and His attributes. That exercise did not emerge in Judaism until the Middle Ages. What the Midrash means is that even if the people kept the Torah without having their thoughts on God the power and healing force of the Torah would bring them back to Him. It is astonishing how many have quoted the Midrash without noting its conclusion: 'since by occupying themselves with the Torah the light contained therein would have led them back to the good way'. And this conclusion is immediately followed by the statement that the Torah should be studied and the *mitzvot* observed even if it is not *lishmah* because it will eventually lead to *lishmah*.

In Hasidism, the vibrant, mystical movement which arose in the eighteenth century in Eastern Europe, the concept of *lishmah* was deepened. The Hasidic ideal was for the worshipper to have God constantly in mind. This ideal of *devekut* ('attachment'), of a being-with-God in the mind at all times, was held by the Mitnaggedim, the traditionalists who opposed the new movement, to be undesirable. Awareness of God, the Mitnaggedim argued, was an essential preliminary before the Torah is studied and the *mitzvot* carried out but was a hindrance if engaged in during study or observance. Study in particular is impossible unless the mind is directed not to God but is concentrated on the subject studied. How can the student master, say, a difficult passage in the Talmud if his mind is not on its intricacies but on God? To attempt to study the Torah *lishmah* in the Hasidic sense of *devekut* is not to study at all. The would-be worshipper will be left with the *lishmah* without the Torah, or so the Mitnaggedim argued. In Hasidism, too, there are tensions in the matter of *lishmah* and *devekut*. To be with God in the mind at all times is far more difficult than it sounds. Among the later Hasidim the Mitnaggedic critique was partially accepted. Moreover, the Hasidic doctrine of the Zaddik, the Guru-like saint and master, developed in such a way that, it was generally maintained, he alone was fully capable of *devekut*; his followers could only approximate to the ideal by becoming attached to him and through him to God. Yet Hasidic criticism of a blind, mechanical observance continued to be voiced. An early Hasidic text, frequently quoted, shocked the Mitnaggedim. This text remarks that a man should not be over-scrupulous in his observances since this leads to morbidity, obsession and anxiety, all in opposition to Hasidic stress on serving God with joy. A similar Hasidic saying has it that the difference between the Hasidim and the Mitnaggedim is that the former fear God whereas the latter fear the standard Code of Jewish observances, the Shulhan Arukh. Again, there is the Hasidic tale of the man who repeatedly had a dream in which he saw God. The man took himself off to a professional interpreter of dreams who observed that the interpretation was all too easy. 'You think of God all the time and so, naturally, you see Him in your dreams.' That cannot be the explanation, the man retorted. My whole day is taken up with prayer and worship and study of the Torah. When have I the time to think of God!

On this question of personal faith and the Torah it must be noted that, for the Rabbis, the Torah is never an object of worship. The sixteenth-century Italian author, Joshua Boaz, quotes an earlier authority who forbids bowing to the Torah or to the Ark containing the Scrolls of the Torah.[17] It is the custom in many places to bow when the Scrolls are taken in procession around the synagogue but this is understood not as an act of worship but simply a mark of respect as would be paid, for example, to a man of high rank. The Talmud[18] refers to sages who would interpret every single word of the Torah, even the word *et*, which is no more than the sign of the accusative. In their exposition this little word was made to include, in the verses in which it occurs, something not stated explicitly in the verse. But what were these sages to make, in that case, of *thou shalt fear the Lord thy God* (Deuteronomy 6:13), a verse containing the word *et*? What could have been included in a command to fear, that is, to worship, since only God is to be worshipped? Rabbi Akiba is said to have interpreted the *et* to include students of the Torah. They have to be 'feared', that is, treated with respect, just as God is 'feared'. It is interesting to find students of the Torah included but not the Torah itself. Evidently, 'fear' of scholars would not be misunderstood whereas to use such a term of the Torah might give rise to the idea that the Torah is a legitimate object of worship. In fact, to my knowledge, with only one exception, the term 'fear of the Torah' (unlike 'love of the Torah' which is found frequently in the literature) is never found in the whole of the Talmudic literature. The exception is in the Palestinian Talmud[19] where the word *et* in the above-mentioned verse is said to include both the Torah and its students. But obviously this only means that for the Palestinian Talmud the term 'fear' can be used of the Torah but only in the sense in which it is used of scholars. There is a prayer in the Zohar,[20] still recited in many synagogues when the Torah Scroll is brought out of the Ark on the Sabbath, which contains the clause: 'I am the servant of the Holy One, blessed be He, before whom I bow and before the glory of His Torah at all times'. In the Kabbalistic thought represented in the Zohar, the Torah is, in a sense, a kind of divine incarnation, at least of one of the *Sefirot*, the powers of potencies in the Godhead. Yet even in this prayer the worshipper who bows to the Torah first declares himself to be a servant of God alone.

It is also at times implied that the sacred institutions of Judaism can act as barriers to faith if they are treated not as means but as ends, though only very rarely do we find this expressed so starkly as in the comment of the unconventional, nineteenth-century Hasidic master, R. Jacob of Izbica.[21] The comment is on the second commandment which forbids the making of an image of that which is in the heavens above and the earth beneath (Exodus 20:4). This author first observes that the more highly regarded and spiritually valuable a thing is the greater is the danger of it becoming an object of worship, an idol. That which is in the heavens above refers to the Sabbath, commanded from the beginning of creation and the most sacred institution in time. That which is in the earth beneath is the Temple, the most sacred institution in space. The second commandment, in this interpretation, is an injunction not to make an idol of the institutions of the Jewish tradition. These are instruments to be used for the purpose of coming nearer to God. They are never to be treated as objects of worship and to do so is to be guilty of idolatry. The author finds this thought in the Talmudic saying:[21] 'One does not stand in fear of the Sabbath but of Him who ordered its observance and one does not stand in fear of the Temple but of Him who gave the command concerning the Temple'. Once again, in the Babylonian Talmud, the term fear (*yirah*), denoting worship, is used of God alone.

That priority must be given to faith over the tradition, that it is the former which breathes life into the latter, is implied in the statement in the Mishnah[23] regarding the order of the sections recited in Israel's declaration of faith, the Shema. The first section (Deuteronomy 6:4–9) deals with God's unity. The second section (Deuteronomy 11:13–21) deals with the performance of the *mitzvot*. Thus the Mishnah records R. Joshua b. Korhah saying, the reason the first section precedes the other is because one is first obliged to take upon oneself 'the yoke of the Kingdom of Heaven' and afterwards 'the yoke of the *mitzvot*'. Faith without its translation into action is meaningless, so it is implied, but practice not infused with faith has similarly little value. There are two 'yokes', that of the Kingdom of Heaven and that of the *mitzvot*, both of which have to be accepted but the first of these has priority in the scale of values.

None of the traditional thinkers ever thought for one moment that it is possible to have Judaism without observance of the Torah. But by the same token they all held mere observance of the law insufficient. Nowhere is this given more powerful expression than in a comment, which became very influential in Jewish religion and ethics, by the great Spanish Talmudist and mystic, Nahmanides (1195–1270). The comment[24] is on the Biblical injunction to be holy (Leviticus 19:2). Nahmanides seeks to analyse the holiness concept. Holiness cannot mean an avoidance of the illicit since that is taken care of by the laws of the Torah, each sinful act being explicitly forbidden. Holiness means, according to Nahmanides, self-denial over and above the demands of the law. It is perfectly possible, he remarks, for a man to be thoroughly disreputable and profligate without actually infringing any law of the Torah. Unless he is a Nazirite he can drink as much wine as he pleases; he can have many wives with whom he can indulge his sexual appetites to excess; he can avoid eating forbidden food but still make a pig of himself when eating kosher food. Such a man, in Nahmanides' pungent formulation, is 'a scoundrel with the full permission of the Torah'. This is why man is commanded to be holy. He is called upon not only to obey the actual dictates of the law but must deny himself even legitimate pleasures where these tend to corrupt his character. There could hardly be a more cogent statement of the idea that the Torah in itself is not sufficient or, better, that the demand of holiness over and above the actual laws of the Torah is itself a demand of the Torah.

A striking passage in the Talmud[25] is indicative of the tension between faith and tradition among the Rabbis. The passage begins with the remark by the third-century Palestinian, Rabbi Simlai, that there are 613 precepts of the Torah given to Moses. The later prophets, the passage continues, gave shorter principles for the leading of the good life. (This is without doubt the meaning of *heemidan,* literally, 'they made them stand' i.e. they based all the precepts on certain brief but embracing rules.) After describing these 'reductions' of the prophets, the passage concludes: 'Habakkuk based them on one single statement: *But the righteous shall live by his faith* (Habakkuk 2:4).' Trust in God is thus the basic principle in Judaism from which all else follows. There is also a recognition that not all men have the same capacity for faith and that apprehension of the divine is arrived at in many different ways. This idea is found in a Midrash[25] on revelation. Psalm 24 verse four is translated as: *The voice of the Lord is with power*, taking 'power' as referring not to God but to the power of the individual to hear God's voice. The voice of God, says the Midrash, was heard by the men according to their capacity, by the women according to theirs. Young men heard it differently from old men. Each individual heard it according to his own capacity. Human nature and individual temperament have a role to play if God's voice is to be heard.

For many of the mediaeval thinkers the way to faith, though supported by the tradition, was to reason for it by the philosophical proofs, particularly the cosmological. The famous moralist and philosopher Bahya Ibn Pakudah, influenced in his work by Sufi ideas, goes so far as to see the tradition itself demanding the attainment of faith through reason.[26] Bahya neatly quotes in his support (though the Biblical knowledge of God is not cognitive, as Bahya would have it, and his rendering of the verse, consequently, is anachronistic): *And thou, Solomon my son, know thou the God of thy father and serve him with a perfect heart* (II Chronicles 28:9). But Judah ha-Levi (d. 1141) in his *Kuzari* bases faith entirely on tradition. In reality, as ha-Levi sees it, the appeal to tradition is an appeal to the reasonableness of the tradition. He argues (and in his day, when both Christianity and Islam accepted the truth of the Scriptural narratives, the argument was convincing) that the events at Sinai are attested to by the evidence of two million people, as are the events of the Exodus. The book *Kuzari* is in the form of a dialogue between a Jewish sage and the King of the Khazara. The King, troubled by the question of which religion is the true one, invites first a Christian and a Muslim to convince him. They begin their discourse with the creation of the world. But when the Jewish sage is invited to defend his faith he begins not with creation but with the Exodus. The only sure way to faith is by an appeal to history which is why, the sage observes,[28] the Decalogue begins with: 'I am the Lord thy God who brought thee out of the land of Egypt', not with: 'I am the Creator of the world and your Creator.' 'And so did I reply to thee, O King of the Khazara, when thou didst ask me to substantiate the truth of my faith and I informed thee of that which obligates me and which obligates all the people of Israel, that which, in the first instance, the children of Israel became convinced of because they saw it with their own eyes and was then handed down by tradition, the equivalent of seeing with the eyes, from man to man.'

Judaism knows, too, of the mystic's way to faith, that of direct experience. But while the theosophical system known as the Kabbalah is based on mystical speculation and meditation, the mystics were extremely reticent in recording their personal mystical testimonies. Only around thirty of these are extant. The word Kabbalah itself means 'tradition' because the mystics believed that the Kabbalistic gnosis was handed down in a tradition reaching back to Moses or even to Adam. Yet the Kabbalists were fully aware of their originality, stating frequently that the mysteries revealed to them had never before been revealed to man. The link between the traditional gnosis and the new, the device used to bring the personal insights into the Kabbalah, was the figure of the prophet Elijah, who, in Jewish legend, returns to earth from time to time to impart teachings to the saints. For the mystics 'the appearance of Elijah' is a mystical state but since Elijah is a disciple of Moses that which he imparts is both new and at the same time part of the Torah of Moses. In this way personal, mystical experience became part of the tradition.

It was not only the mystics who acknowledged the idea of a developing tradition in which not everything is given and then simply handed down from generation to generation. An oft-quoted Talmudic tale[29] speaks of Moses transported across time to the school of Rabbi Akiba where Moses is unable to understand anything of Akiba's teachings. But when a student asks Akiba how he knows the law he is expounding, Akiba replies: 'I have it by a tradition from Moses at Sinai' and Moses' mind is set at rest. The new Torah taught by Akiba was really new and yet, because implicit in the Torah given to Moses, it is the same Torah. How far this dynamic view of the Torah was preserved in subsequent Jewish thought is a moot point but the idea is present in this and in other Talmudic and post-Talmudic sources.[30]

What of conflicts between the demands of the tradition and personal choice in faith? There are references to the sin for the sake of God (*averah lishmah*), the Biblical prototype being the sinful act of Jael (Judges chapters four and five) who allowed herself to be seduced by Sisera in order to save her people.[31] In circumstances where an individual believes that an act must be carried out for the greater glory of God that act overides the demands of the law. But it must be appreciated that this whole idea occupies a very peripheral place in traditional Jewish thought. It was developed in a radical way by the followers of Shabbatai Zevi, the seventeenth century false Messiah, but that was due to Shabbatai's conversion to Islam which required, for those who still believed in him, theological justification on the lines of the sin for the sake of God. The prevailing attitude was expressed by Hayyim of Volozhyn, the chief disciple of the eighteenth-century Gaon of Vilna and leading traditionalist Rabbi, who maintained[32] that once the Torah has been given the doctrine can no longer operate. If it could, he continues, what is the point of the Torah and its laws since the sole guide will be the individual conscience. Where this demands that a certain act be carried out or not carried out, it would depend not on what the Torah says but on whether the motive is pure and for God. The antinomianism implicit in the doctrine of *averah lishmah* is rejected in the name of the Torah.

This has been an attempt at surveying Jewish attitudes to faith in relation to tradition. Since Judaism is not monolithic but consists of the response of a variety of Jewish communities and their teachers even on the idea of revelation, consistency is not to be expected. What we do have is tension between faith and tradition, a tension never completely resolved but which, Jews would hold, has generally been creative. This essay might fittingly conclude with a comment of the Midrash[33] which, perhaps, comes closest to the thinking of Wilfred Cantwell Smith on faith and tradition: 'And ye are My witnesses, saith the Lord, and I am God (Isaiah 43:12). When you are My witnesses I am God. But when you are not My witnesses I am not God, as it were. Similarly: *Unto Thee I lift up mine eyes, O Thou that art enthroned in the heavens* (Psalm 123:1). If not for me, Thou, as it were, would not be enthroned in the heavens.'

NOTES

1. Sotah 48b.
2. Max Kadushin: The Rabbinic Mind, sec. ed., New York, 1965; Isaac Heinemann: *Darkhey ha-Aggadah*, Jerusalem, 1974.
3. *Yad*, Deot 1:2–7.
4. *Yad, Yesodey ha-Torah* 4:10.
5. *Sanhedrin* 10:1.
6. *Sanhedrin* 99a.
7. *Sanhedrin* 99b.
8. N. Krochmal: *Moreh* Nevukhey ha-Zeman, ed. S. Rawidowicz, London, 1961, Ch. 14, pp. *238–56*.
9. *Commentary to the Mishnah* to Sanhedrin 10:1.
10. Jerusalem, 1975.
11. *Iggerot Moshe*, VI, Bene Berak, 1981, Nos. 114 and 115.
12. *Students, Scholars and Saints,* New York, 1958, p. 206.
13. *Kiddushin* 32a–b.
14. *Pesahim* 50b.
15. *Lamentations Rabbah*, Proem 2.
16. The Jewish Religion, sec. ed., London, 1900, page 3, note 1.
17. Shiltey ha-Gibborim to Alfasi, Kiddushin 14b.
18. *Pesahim* 22b.
19. *Berakhot* 9:5, 14b.
20. II, 206a.
21. *Bet Yaakov,* Lublin 1906, II, p. 256.
22. *Yevamot* 6b.
23. *Berakhot* 2:2.
24. Commentary of Ramban, ed. B. Chavel, Jerusalem, 1960, pp. 115–17.
25. Makkot 23b–24a.
26. *Exodus Rabbah* 5:9 .
27. *Hovot ha-Levavot*, ed. P. J. Liebermann, Jerusalem, 1968, *Shaar ha-Yihud*, Ch. 3, p. 97.
28. *Kuzari* ed. Y. Even Shmuel, Tel-Aviv, 1972, I, 25, p. 12.
29. *Menahot* 29b.
30. Some of these are given in Louis Jacobs: *We Have Reason to Believe,* third ed., London, 1965, pp. 70–81.
31. *Nazir* 23b.
32. *Keter Rosh* in the Prayer Book of the Vilna Gaon, *Ishey Yisrael*, Tel-Aviv, 1968, p. 539.
33. *Sifre,* ed. L. Finkelstein, New York, 1969, par. 346, pp. 403–4.

— 7 —

The Body in Jewish Worship: Three Rituals Examined

In this chapter the relationship is examined between body and soul as expressed in three Jewish rituals – the sabbath rituals, the death and burial rites, and the priestly blessing – with a view to uncovering some of the nuances of this relationship in Judaism in general. It is hoped that in the process the lie will be given to the caricature of Judaism as a religion with its stress above all on the physical body in its relationship to the divine. Any neat distinction, say, between Christianity, supposedly concerned primarily with the soul, and Judaism, supposedly concerned primarily with the body, must be rejected if only because of the complexity of the issue. There is no single, official view in Judaism (and, I imagine, the same is true of Christianity) on this and on similar extremely involved topics. Modern scholarly investigation has succeeded in demonstrating that religions have a history in which ideas, forms, and rituals have developed in response to changing social, economic, political, and even climatic conditions, and that the particular temperament of religious teachers has also had its effect. These facts go a long way to explaining why no article on the body is found in the standard Jewish encyclopedias; nor has any monograph been published on Jewish attitudes to the body. The task of the historian of Jewish ideas and rituals is to try to collate stray references in diverse sources, produced over lengthy periods of time, so as to produce some kind of systematic picture, being fully aware that in the very process he is imposing categories not really present in the sources.

Here is not the place for anything like a history of Jewish thought on the body through the various stages of Jewish civilization; but a brief, preliminary and tentative overview cannot be dispensed with altogether if the rituals we are examining are accurately to be understood.

The minds of Old Testament scholars have been much exercised in discovering whether the biblical authors ever entertain the notion of body and soul as two distinct entities that have become conjoined, or whether, for these authors, there is only a single entity, what we (but not the biblical authors themselves) call the human being or human person. In the second creation narrative (Genesis 2:7) the formation of Adam is described as: 'And the Lord God formed man of the dust of the ground, and breathed into his nostrils the breath of life; and man became a living soul.' But the original Hebrew, *nefesh hayyah*, translated as 'living soul', certainly has no reference to the soul as a separate entity – this is ruled out, in any event, by the context. The nearest in our language to what is implied is rather 'a living person'. Similarly, in the parallel to Genesis it is said of the death of the body: 'Then shall the dust return to the earth as it was; and the spirit shall return unto God who gave it' (Ecclesiastes 12:7). It is true that the later Jewish tradition reads into this latter verse the idea that at the death of the body the soul leaves to return to God, residing with Him for ever, but it is a moot point whether the author of Ecclesiastes himself was thinking of an immortal soul which leaves its temporal abode, the body, when the latter dies. It has often been noted that, while it would be too much to say that the Old Testament knows nothing at all of an immortal soul, belief in the Hereafter generally is only faintly implied; possibly because, in the early biblical period, at least, the other world was the domain of the gods against the worship of whom the biblical authors so strongly protest.

Under the influence of Greek thought, ideas such as the complete distinctiveness of body and soul and conflict between the two did emerge in Judaism, especially in the Greek-speaking community of Alexandria, the foremost representative of which is Philo, whose eschatology is confined to the immortality of the soul and who knows nothing of the later Rabbinic doctrine of bodily resurrection at the end of time. The most pronounced element, however, in subsequent Jewish thought is that of the Talmudic rabbis (Philo is not mentioned at all in the traditional Jewish sources until as late as the sixteenth century). The Rabbinic views, much closer to religious poetry than to precise, theological statement, are found in the Mishnah (edited around the year CE 200); the Jerusalem Talmud (edited around CE 400); and the Babylonian Talmud (edited around CE 500). In the Talmudic/Rabbinic literature the dichotomy between body and soul is everywhere present but

The Body in Jewish Worship: Three Rituals Examined   85

the holistic implications of many of the earlier, biblical passages are also, though somewhat paradoxically, acknowledged, as the following typical passages demonstrate:

1. Rabbi Eleazar son of Rabbi Zadok said: 'To what are the righteous compared in this world? To a tree standing wholly in a place of purity, but its bough overhangs to a place of impurity; when the bough is lopped off, it stands entirely in a place of purity. Thus the Holy One, blessed be He, brings suffering upon the righteous in this world, in order that they may inherit the World to Come... And to what are the wicked compared in this world? To a tree standing wholly in a place of impurity, but its bough overhangs a place of purity; when the bough is lopped off, it stands entirely in a place of impurity. Thus the Holy one, blessed be He, provides them with goodness in this world, in order to destroy them, consigning them to the nethermost rung.' (*Kiddushin* 40b)

2. Antoninus said to Rabbi Judah the Prince: 'The body and soul can both free themselves from judgment. The body can plead: It is the soul that has sinned since the moment it left me. I am like a dumb stone in the grave. And the soul can say: It is the body that has sinned since from the day I departed from it I fly in the air like a bird.' He replied: 'Let me tell you a parable. A human king had a beautiful orchard containing splendid figs. He appointed two watchmen over the orchard, one lame, the other blind. The lame man said to the blind man: "I see splendid figs in the orchard. Take me up on your shoulders and we can get them to eat." The lame man bestrode the blind and they got hold of the figs and ate them. When the owner of the orchard asked them what had happened to the figs, the lame man protested: "Have I feet with which to walk?" and the blind man protested: "Have I eyes with which to see?" What did the owner do? He placed the lame man on the shoulders of the blind man and judged them together. So will the Holy One, blessed be He, bring the soul, place it in the body, and judge them together.' (*Sanhedrin* 91a–b)

The mediaeval Jewish thinkers, influenced by Greek thought in its Arabic garb, went far beyond the idea of the lameness of the soul and the blindness of the body to stress the struggle, rather than the co-operation between the two, with the corollary that a strong dose of denial of bodily pleasures is essential to the religious life. The greatest of the mediaeval thinkers, Maimonides (1135–1206), writes that the destruction of the soul is in direct proportion to the building up of the body (*Commentary to the Mishnah*, Kapah, 22). Bahya Ibn Pakudah (twelfth century), while advocating for his contemporaries a balanced attitude towards asceticism, can still admire the world-losers, the hermits and ascetics (*Duties*, IX, ed. Hyamson 1962, 288–337). In the Talmud a great variety of views is found on the question of asceticism. In the very same Talmudic passage (*Taanit* 11a) two conflicting opinions are recorded. According to one rabbi, the Nazirite is a holy man because he denies himself wine and the man who fasts, denying himself all food and drink, is an even holier man. According to the other rabbi, the Nazirite is a sinner because he denied himself God's gift of wine, and the man who fasts, denying himself all food and drink, is an even greater sinner. In the Jerusalem Talmud (*Kiddushin* 66d) there occurs the astonishing anti-ascetic saying that a man will be obliged to give an account before God for every legitimate pleasure he denied himself. Even the ascetically inclined among the Jewish pietists, and they were many, followed the Rabbinic injunction to offer thanks to God in the form of a benediction for every bodily pleasure they enjoy (Singer 1962, 385–90). The popular seventeenth-century book, *Meah Berakhot* ('One Hundred Blessings'), as its name implies, is a list of such blessings to be recited daily.

In both the Rabbinic and the philosophical traditions the many *mitzvot* ('precepts') of the Torah to be carried out by bodily activity are binding upon Jews. The Talmudic homily (*Makkot* 22b) that there are 248 positive precepts, corresponding to the 248 parts of the human body, and 365 negative precepts, corresponding to the days of the solar year, became a powerful slogan for Jewish piety; the Jew who kept the 613 precepts was held to be sanctifying his body and his years. For the rabbis of the Talmud, observance of the *mitzvot* is not a means to an end but the end itself – obedience to the will of God. The philosophers, on the other hand, tended to see the *mitzvot* as the means to what, for the philosophers, is the true aim of religion, contemplation on the divine truths. The rabbis, too, demand proper concentration (*kavvanah*) when carrying out the *mitzvot* and they condemn mere mechanical observance, but the *kavvanah* demanded is simply: 'I do this for the sake of God who has commanded it.' The rabbis were not primarily interested in why God commanded this or that. It was sufficient that He had so commanded. Not so the philosophers who were mightily concerned with 'the reasons for the *mitzvot*', arguing that to carry out certain acts merely because God had so commanded, without asking why, would result in less than enthusiastic observance; would constitute a poor defence of Judaism as a rational faith; and would tend to treat God as a tyrant who issues arbitrary dictates (Heinemann 1949, 10–11). Yet, for all their attempts at explanation, the philosophers had to admit that many of the details of the *mitzvot* remained opaque. As Maimonides (*Guide*, III, 26) puts it:

> Know that wisdom rendered it necessary that there should be particulars for which no cause can be found; it was, as it were, impossible in regard to the law that there could be nothing of this class in it. In such a case the impossibility is due to the circumstances that when you ask why a lamb should be prescribed instead of a ram, the same question would have to be asked if a ram had been prescribed instead of a *lamb*. But one particular species had to be chosen. The same holds for you asking why *seven lambs* and not *eight* have been prescribed. For a similar question would have been put if *eight* or *ten* or *twenty* had been prescribed. (trans. Pines 1914, 509)

For Maimonides, then, the ordered rules and regulations of the sacrificial system – and the same would hold good for all the other *mitzvot* – are the necessary means to the general aim of intellectual and moral perfection. But, once rules have become necessary, it is futile to ask why these details in particular since one cannot have rules without them being detailed and such details are, indeed, quite arbitrary. It was left to the Kabbalists to develop a system in which every detail of the *mitzvot* is highly significant because it represents one or other of the divine processes on high.

The Kabbalah is the theosophical system which arose in Provence in the twelfth century to reach its culmination in Spain in the book Zohar, which first saw the light at the end of the thirteenth century. A more elaborate version of the Kabbalah was produced in Safed by Isaac Luria (1534–1572), known as the *Ari* ('The Lion'). In both the Zoharic and the Lurianic systems, bodily acts of worship have a highly charged mythological significance in that the human body is a pale reflection of the divine corpus. Long before the rise of the Kabbalah, the work *Shiur Komah* ('The Measurements of God's Stature') sought to describe the mystical dimensions of God's 'body' (Scholem 1974, 16–18). *Tikkuney ha-Zohar*, the work that supplements the Zohar proper, states that each 'limb' of the king is a *mitzvah*, i.e., the *mitzvot* represent the divine corpus (No. 30, ed. Margaliot, 1978, 74a).

Basic to the Kabbalah is the idea that there are two aspects of the Deity–God as He is in Himself and God in manifestation. The former is known as *En Sof* ('The Limitless') and is the impersonal Ground of Being, known only to Itself and utterly beyond all human comprehension. The latter is the revelation of *En Sof* through the *Sefirot*, the powers or potencies in the Godhead, of which there are ten. These, in descending order, are: (1) *Keter* ('Crown'), the divine will; (2) *Hokhmah* ('Wisdom'); (3) *Binah* ('Understanding'); (4) *Hesed* ('Love'); (5) *Gevurah* ('Power'); (6) *Tiferet* ('Beauty'); (7) *Netzah* ('Victory'); (8) *Hod* ('Splendour'); (9) *Yesod* ('Foundation'); (10) *Malkhut* ('Sovereignty'). The *Sefirot* proceed from *En Sof* by a process of emanation and are, in a favourite Kabbalistic simile, like bottles of various colours into which transparent water is poured, the water taking on the colour of the bottle into which it is poured. The *Sefi rot* represent the body of God, that is, they are the cosmic forces that are thecounterparts on high of the human body on earth. *Hesed*, for example, is God's right arm which assumes in this world a human right arm and which is the ultimate source of all human love.

Here lies the significance of the body and bodily actions according to the Kabbalah. The 'image of God' in which man is created (Genesis 1:26–27) means for the Kabbalists that the human body mirrors forth the Godhead. The idea of the image of God referring to the actual physical body of man is not unknown in earlier sources. The Midrash (Leviticus Rabbah 34:3), for example, tells of the sage, Hillel, who, on his way to the bath house, said to his disciples that he was going to carry out a *mitzvah*. 'Is it a religious obligation to bathe?' they asked. 'Yes,' replied Hillel, 'if the statues of kings erected in theatres and circuses are regularly scoured and washed by the person appointed to look after them, how much more, I, who has been created in God's image and likeness.' But this whole idea comes to mean for the Kabbalists that the human body mirrors forth the *Sefirot* and can influence them by the actions it performs. When human beings, at the end of a great chain of being reaching back to the *Sefirot*, perform acts of virtue, they send beneficent impulses on high to promote harmony among the *Sefirot* and then the divine grace can flow unimpeded through all creation. Conversely, when humans are vicious they send baneful impulses on high to disturb the harmony of the *Sefirot* and arrest the flow of the divine grace.

It follows that every detailed act in the performance of the *mitzvot* has its correspondence in the Sefirotic realm and each detail contributes to the formidable task of literally holding up the heavens. The body is significant precisely because it alone can provide the cosmic energy required if the divine purpose in creation is to be realized. Unlike the rationalists, the Kabbalists do see in every detail of the *mitzvot* a way of influencing the upper worlds. Some of the hymns composed by the Kabbalists to invoke the *Sefirot* 'read like the hymns of a mystery religion' (Scholem 1967, 143).

A further refinement is found in the Lurianic Kabbalah, where the doctrine runs that at one stage in the emanation process, as the infinite light of *En Sof* poured into the vessels of the *Sefirot*, the vessels, too weak to sustain the overpowering light, were shattered under the impact, with the result that, even after their reconstitution, there were 'holy sparks' imprisoned among the demonic forces, the *kelippot* ('shells'). Every virtuous act helps towards the rescue of the 'holy sparks' from their imprisonment by the dark powers.

In the Hasidic movement, which arose in the eighteenth century, the doctrine of the 'holy sparks' receives further elaboration. It is not only through the performance of the *mitzvot* that the 'holy sparks' are rescued. Every bodily act performed in the spirit of holiness – eating, drinking, sex, even smoking a pipe – has the effect of releasing the 'holy sparks' from their prison. In Hasidism 'serving the Creator with the body' means not alone that the body be engaged in the performance of the *mitzvot*, but that ordinary physical acts, neutral in themselves, become vehicles for the sacred if carried out for the glory of God.

Before turning to the three rituals, it has to be added that these and all other Jewish rituals became codified. The major Codes are: *Mishneh Torah* of Maimonides; *Tur* of Jacob ben Asher (d. 1340); and *Shulkan Arukh* of Joseph Karo (1488–1575), the last, once it had received the glosses of Moses Isserles of Cracow (d. 1572), becoming the standard Code for observant Jews. Karo and Isserles introduced here and there rituals of Kabbalistic origin, and so did their commentators, especially Abraham Gombiner (d. 1683) in his *Magen Avraham*. There is, in addition, a special Code devoted entirely to the Kabbalistic meaning of the rituals – *Shulhan Arukh ha-Ari*. Local custom also has a voice in these matters, for example, in the different forms adopted by the Sephardim – Jews hailing from Spanish countries – and Ashkenazim – German and French Jews. We can now look at the rituals and observe how the above actually operates.

THE SABBATH

The body is engaged positively in a large number of sabbath rituals, but the very institution of the Sabbath, with its requirement that there be total cessation of all creative manual labour on the day, constitutes in itself worship with the body, albeit by negation. In the Rabbinic tradition, the biblical injunctions to refrain from 'work' on the Sabbath (Exodus 20:8–11; 35:2–3; Deuteronomy 5:12–15) are understood as referring not to all physical actions, but only to those which involve creative manipulation of the material world. The Mishnah (*Shabbat* 7:2) spells it out:

> The main classes of work are forty save one; sowing, ploughing, reaping, binding sheaves, threshing, winnowing, cleansing crops, grinding, sifting, kneading, baking, shearing wool, washing or beating or dyeing it, spinning, weaving, making two loops, weaving two threads, separating two threads, tying a knot, loosening a knot, sewing two stitches, tearing in order to sew two stitches, hunting a gazelle, slaughtering or flaying or salting it or curing its skin, scraping it or cutting it up, writing two letters, erasing in order to write two letters, building, pulling down, putting out a fire, lighting a fire, striking with a hammer and taking out something from one domain to another.

Thus what are forbidden are evidently acts involved in the preparation of food, clothing, and housing. Naturally these are types of creative labour that were the norm in second-century Palestine when the Mishnah was compiled. The idea behind it all seems to be that God is acknowledged as the Creator by refraining on this day from that which is, on the other days of the week, a divine gift to man, his creative talent (see Genesis 2:1–3 and Exodus 20:11).

While the body is to be restrained from working on the Sabbath, the satisfaction of bodily needs and appetites on the day is enjoined as a religious duty. The prophetic injunction (Isaiah 58:13) to 'call the Sabbath a delight' forms the basis of the Rabbinic idea of *oneg shabbat* ('Sabbath delight'), defined by Maimonides in his Mishneh Torah (1983, *Shabbat* 30:7–8) on the basis of Talmudic statement, as the enjoyment on the Sabbath of special juicy dishes and good wine. The Talmud (*Berakhot* 31b) states that while it is forbidden to fast on the Sabbath, yet if a man has had a bad dream which disturbs him he is allowed to fast on the sacred day in order to counteract its baneful effects. Nevertheless, he must undertake another fast as a penance for having offended against the principle of Sabbath delight. The Talmud (*Shabbat* 1 18a) also states that, unlike on weekdays when it is normal to partake of only two meals each day, on the Sabbath one should partake of three meals, one on Friday night (when the Sabbath begins), one at lunchtime and one on Sabbath afternoon.

Sabbath delight thus involves a degree of indulgence of the body. Rashi (1040–1105), the famous French commentator, understands the Talmudic notion (*Betzsah* 16a) of the 'additional soul' with which a man is said to be endowed on the Sabbath as: 'A heart with an extended capacity for tranquillity and joy, open to enlargement, so that he is able to eat and drink without feeling ill.' This attitude has been captured exquisitely in Heine's pen portrait of the poor packman Moses Lump who works hard during the day to earn his meagre living:

> But when on Friday evening he comes home, he finds the candlestick with seven candles lighted, and the table covered with a fair white cloth, and he puts away his pack and his cares, and he sits down to table with his squinting wife and yet more squinting daughter, and eats fish with them, fish which has been dressed in beautiful white garlic sauce, sings therewith the grandest psalms of David, rejoices with his whole heart over the deliverance of the children of Israel out of Egypt, rejoices, too, that all the wicked ones who have done the children of Israel hurt, have ended by taking themselves off, that King Pharaoh, Nebuchadnezzar, Haman, Antiochus, Titus, and all such people, are well dead, while he, Moses Lump, is yet alive, and eating fish with his wife and daughter; and I can tell, Doctor, the fish is delicious and the man happy. (Roth 1960, 26)

For the Kabbalists, such an approach, admirable enough for ordinary folk, is far too pedestrian. The Zohar (II, 88b) understands the 'additional soul' in its literal sense; on the Sabbath the *Shekhinah* (in the Zohar this represents the personification of the female principle in the Godhead, the *Sefirah* called *Malkhut*) is present at the table. Based on this passage, the Lurianic Kabbalists see one of the *Sefirot* being especially present at the first meal, another at the second, and another at the third. In Hasidism the three sacred meals are partaken of in the presence of the Zaddik, the spiritual leader and saint, who tastes a little of each dish, the remainder being distributed to his followers so that some of his close attachment to God might be carried over to them through the food he has tasted and blessed. The third meal has special numinous qualities because at this meal the Zaddik delivers his homilies, his Torah; it being believed by the Hasidim that at this awesome moment the *Shekhinah* speaks through the throat of the Zaddik (Wertheim 1960, 151–3; 167–9).

The Talmud (*Bava Kama* 32b) speaks of welcoming the Sabbath as Israel's bride; but for the Kabbalists the Sabbath represents the *Shekhinah*, the *Sefirah Malkhut*, while Israel is the *Sefirah Tjferet*, the male principle in the Godhead. The Safed mystics used to dress in white on the eve of the Sabbath and go out to welcome the Sabbath/*Shekhinah*. The poem composed for the purpose by Solomon Alkabetz (d. 1576) is now recited on Friday night in synagogues all over the world, when, during the evening prayers, the whole congregation turns towards the door to welcome the Sabbath with the words of the poem, 'Come my friend, to meet the bride: let us welcome the presence of the Sabbath', sung in a melody of hope and yearning (Singer 1962, 146–7).

The Friday-night meal at the beginning of the Sabbath is a family occasion. The table is covered with a white cloth on which are set two candles, two whole loaves of bread, corresponding to the double portion of manna on the Sabbath (Exodus 16:5), and a goblet of wine over which the *kiddush* ('sanctification') is recited in which God is praised as Creator and for giving the Sabbath to Israel. Since the kindling of fire cannot be done on the Sabbath itself the candles are lit just before Sabbath begins by the mistress of the house who covers her eyes with her hands while she prays for her family. The Midrash (Genesis Rabbah 8:8) sees the duty of kindling the Sabbath lights as devolving particularly on women, because when Eve was responsible for Adam's sin she extinguished 'the light of the world'. The husband recites the verses in Proverbs (31:10–31) in praise of the 'woman of worth', referring to his wife, although in the Kabbalah these verses were introduced in praise of the *Shekhinah*, the female principle, united with Her Spouse, *Tiferet*, the male principle in the Godhead. From this union souls are born.

This is why Friday night is the special time for marital relations. The Talmud (*Ketubot* 62b) quotes the third-century Babylonian teacher, Samuel, as saying that scholars are obliged to make love to their wives on Friday night; in context, this is because they are often away from home studying during the rest of the week. But

Figure 1
Illustration in a seventeenth-century Jewish devotional work (the *Meak Berakhot*) showing the use of the five senses in worship.

in another Talmudic passage (*Bava Kama* 82a) it is implied that this duty is not confined to scholars, presumably because other people, too, can be preoccupied during weekdays. Here it is said that Ezra introduced the practice of eating garlic, presumed to be an aphrodisiac, on the eve of the Sabbath. The Kabbalists built on this to construct the Friday-night union into a sacred ritual, mirroring forth the 'Sacred Marriage' on high, a ritual to be carried out, so far as possible, as a mystical rite to be engaged in without pleasure or passion (Vital 1890, 10). It is difficult to know how far the Kabbalists were able to succeed in banishing pleasure and passion from the act. Karo, in his *Shulhan Arukh*, section *Orak Hayyim* (280:1) follows earlier authorities in extending the concept of Sabbath *delight* so as to include the marital act. Jacob Emden (1697–1776), in his extraordinarily detailed guide to marital relations on the Sabbath, writes that, while a man should not speak lewdly to his wife, he should speak loving words to her to make her happy and responsive to his caresses (Emden 1904, 159).

The *havdalah* ('division') ceremony takes place when the Sabbath ends on Saturday night (Singer 1962, 292–4). Over a cup of wine the benediction is recited in which God is praised for making a distinction between holy and profane, between light and darkness, between Israel and other nations, between the Sabbath and the six working days. Sweet spices are smelled in order to restore the soul saddened by the departure of the 'additional soul' of the Sabbath. Since fire cannot be kindled on the Sabbath but is now permitted, a taper is lit over which God is praised for giving man the precious gift of fire and light. The order of the *havdalah* rituals is first the wine, representing the sense of taste; then the spices, representing the sense of smell; then the light, the sense of sight; and, finally, the mind is brought into play in reflection on the meaning of the rite as a whole. Thus, at the beginning of the new week, the Jew resolves to elevate his bodily senses from taste to smell to sight, each more refined and more subtle than the other, and to have them controlled by his intellect (Gaguine 1955, 470).

The curious custom is still followed of looking at the fingernails by the light of the *havdalah* taper. Karo (298:3) simply states that it is the custom to gaze at the palms and the fingernails, but Isserles adds: 'One should gaze at the nails of the right hand while holding the cup of wine in the left hand and one should bend the fingers towards the palm so that one looks at the palm and the nails at the same time and sees the inside of the fingers.' Some see in all this an echo of ancient forms of divination (see Finesinger 1937–38). The Kabbalists see it as part of the distinction between the upper world, represented by the flesh of the palm, and the demonic powers, represented by the nails (Ginsburg 1989, 271–2). There is a further custom of extending afterwards the hands towards the light, said to denote that the hands, held back from work during the Sabbath, can now freely be employed.

DEATH AND BURIAL RITES

Attitudes towards a dead body differ widely in the history of Judaism. In the Bible a corpse is a severe source of ritual contamination. Anyone who has been in contact with a corpse must undergo the rite of sprinkling with the ashes of the red heifer before being allowed to enter the sacred camp (see Numbers 19). The priests were forbidden to come into contact with a corpse other than that of a near relative (Leviticus 21:1–4). This latter is still the rule for observant Jews. A *kohen*, a descendant of the ancient priests (hence the name Cohen), does not enter a house in which there is a corpse and does not walk near the graves in the cemetery. There was a view, however, in the Middle Ages, that the bodies of the saints do not contaminate. The French scholars known as the Tosafists, authors of glosses to the Talmud, quote (*Ketubot* 103b) a Rabbi Hayyim Kohen who said that if he had been present at the funeral of the great teacher, Rabbenu Tam (d. 1171), he would have participated in the burial since the body of a saint does not contaminate. While this view still prevails in some circles, the weight of opinion is against it (see Langauer 1977). Legends are told of Jewish saints whose corpses suffered no decomposition and emitted a sweet fragrance, the reward of their holy life while in the body.

The Mishnah (*Yadaim* 5:6) records a debate between the Sadducees and the Pharisees on the strange Pharisaic law that a scroll of the Torah renders the hands unclean, i.e., the hands have to be ritually washed before handling sacred food. Why, asked the Sadducees, should sacred scripture contaminate and yet the works of Homer do not contaminate? The Pharisees reply that scripture is treated as a taboo for the same reason that a corpse is a source of contamination, not because it is abhorrent, but, on the contrary, to prevent it being treated in an overfamiliar way. The comparison with scripture is also found in the Talmudic statement (*Moed Katan* 25a) that those present at the death must rend their garments as if they had witnessed the burning of a Scroll of the Torah.

In any event, the corpse has to be treated with respect, though the author of a popular compendium on the laws of death and burial (Tykocinski 1960, 64–74) goes too far in suggesting that because of the comparison with the scroll of the Torah a corpse possesses a degree of sanctity. In most Jewish communities the preparations of the corpse for burial are carried out by the members of a special society known as the *hevra kaddisha* ('Holy Brotherhood') to which only the most learned and most pious members of the community are allowed to belong. On the basis of the Talmudic rule (*Hullin* 11b) that it is forbidden to mutilate a corpse, Orthodox law frowns on autopsies and the dissection of corpses, though in some circumstances, where lives can be saved as result, for instance, for organ transplants are permitted.

Many of the practices in connection with death and burial are due to Kabbalistic influences and, naturally in these matters, superstitions have crept in, for instance, that the water in the vicinity of a death must be poured out. This practice is not found in Jewish sources earlier than the thirteenth century, but it has been noted that the practice was followed by Christians in France and Germany at a still earlier date so that borrowing seems plausible. A Jewish interpretation given to the practice is that the Angel of Death may have let fall into the water a drop from the poison on the sword with which he slays (Trachtenberg 1970, 176). The practice of watching over a corpse is mentioned in the Talmud (*Berakhot* 18a), but there the reason is in order to keep the rats away. Later on the reason given was to frighten off the demons who are attracted to a dead body (Trachtenberg 1970, 175). The Kabbalistic treatise, *Maavar Yabok* ('Ford of Yabok') by Aaron Berachiah of Modena was first published in Mantua in 1623, but the rites and ceremonies of death and burial mentioned in the book are still largely followed in the more traditional Jewish communities. The book contains a vivid eschatological scheme according to which the soul has three parts: *nefesh*, the lowest, *ruah*, the next highest, and *neshamah*, highest of the three. The *nefesh* remains in the body and suffers with the body in the grave. The *ruah* is punished for its sins, but twelve months after its departure from the body it is allowed to enter the 'Lower Garden of Eden'. The *neshamah* departs at once for the 'Higher Garden of Eden'. These complex relationships between the three parts of the soul and between them and the body are variously interpreted by the Kabbalists (Scholem 1974, 333–6).

The Mishnah (*Shabbat* 23:5) refers to the practice of washing the corpse before burial, but eventually there developed an elaborate rite of purification known as the *tohorah*, 'purification' (Rabbinowicz 1967, 39; Levine 1985, 300–12). The procedure followed is to place the corpse on its back on a flat board. It is then held upright while approximately four and a half gallons of water are poured over it. The hair is washed and combed and the nails trimmed. The mediaeval German work, *Sefer Hasidim* ('Book of the Pious') bases the *tohorah* on the verse in Ecclesiastes (5:15): 'as he came so shall he go', understanding it to mean, as he was bathed when he came into the world so is he to be bathed when he departs from the world (par. 560, ed. Margaliot 1973, 370). The corpse is then dressed in shrouds made of linen or cotton. These are usually a cap, a shirt, breeches, a neckcloth, a surplice, and a girdle. It can be seen that the shrouds resemble the garments worn by the priests in the Temple (Exodus 28:40–3). At the burial, as the coffin is lowered into the grave, all present declare: 'May he/she come into his/her place in peace.' For a female all these rites are carried out by women members of the *hevra kaddisha*.

The nearest relatives of the deceased (father, mother, brother, sister, son, daughter, husband, wife) rend their garments before the funeral. This is known as the *keriah* ('rending') and is referred to in the Bible (for example, in Genesis 37:34). The *keriah* is performed with the mourners standing upright, symbolic of their faith in God which allows them to face grief without becoming prey to despair. Nowadays, except for the very pious, the *keriah* is done on a token item of clothing such as a necktie or cardigan (Klein 1979, 279).

THE PRIESTLY BLESSING

The biblical source for the priestly blessing is the book of Numbers (6:23–7): 'And the Lord spake unto Moses saying, Speak unto Aaron and his sons, saying, Thus ye shall bless the children of Israel, saying unto them, The Lord bless thee, and keep thee; The Lord make His face shine upon thee, and be gracious unto thee; The Lord lift up His countenance upon thee, and give thee peace. And they shall put my name upon the children of Israel and I will bless them.' In Temple times the priests blessed the people daily as part of the Temple service. After the destruction of the Temple, the priestly blessing is recited in the synagogue at the section in the liturgy containing references to worship in the Temple but, in many communities, only on the festivals. In Temple times the priests recited the blessing from a special platform, the *dukhan*; hence the popular Yiddish expression for the rite, *duchaning*, 'platforming'. The full rite is given in the standard prayer books (Singer 1962, 324–5).

At the suitable place in the liturgy, the cantor recites: 'Our God and God of our fathers, bless us with the threefold blessing of the Law written by the hand of Moses thy servant, which was spoken by Aaron and his sons, THE PRIESTS', reciting the last two words in a loud voice in order to invite the priests to proceed to bless. As above, the *kohanim* ('priests') are men who claim descent by family tradition from the ancient priesthood. Before they ascend to take their place for the blessing in front of the holy Ark, the priests remove their shoes (see Gold 1981; Sperling n.d., 54–6). The hands of the priests are washed by the Levites in the congregation (men believed to be descended from the ancient Levites, people called Levy or Levine, for example). The Zohar (III, 146b) observes that the priest requires further sanctity to his own to be added before he can become worthy to recite the blessing, hence the washing of his hands by the Levites. If no Levite is present, the hands of the priests are washed by a first-born, who also possesses a special degree of sanctity (Gombiner, 128,7). The priests then station themselves in front of the Ark to await the cantor's invitation, at which they turn their faces to the congregation, raise their hands, and recite the blessing. Before reciting the blessing the priests say: 'Blessed art thou, O Lord our God, King of the universe, who hast sanctified us with the sanctity of Aaron and hast commanded us to bless thy people Israel in love.'

A good deal is made of the positioning of the hands of the priests. The custom as stated in the *Tur* (128) is for the ten fingers of the priest to be positioned in such a way that five apertures are formed. This is based on a Midrashic comment on the verse: 'gazing through the lattices' (Song of Songs 2:9), God sending His blessing, as it were, through the openings between the fingers of the priests. Gombiner (128,9) records a custom (this not usually followed) of the priests, before reciting the blessing, drawing in the air with their fingers the four Hebrew letters of the Tetragrammaton. The Kabbalist, Shabbetai Sheftel Horowitz (d. 1619) in his *Shefa Tal* (6) notes that there are fifteen Hebrew words in the priestly blessing. There are 14 joints of the hand – 3 on each of the 4 fingers and 2 on the thumb – representing 14 of the words, while the final word *shalom-*, 'peace', is represented by the palm of the hand. In the Zohar (III, 146b) the ten fingers of the priest represent the ten *Sefirot*, the right hand being raised a little above the left so that love should prevail over the 'left side' of rigorous judgment (Zohar, III, 145a). A further symbolic interpretation in the Zohar (III, 145b) is that the priest represents *Hesed* and the blessing itself the *Shekhinah, Malkhut*, the priest bringing down the divine grace from one to the other so that it might flow through all creation.

The Talmud (*Hagigah* isa) states that the eyes of the man which gaze on the hands of the priests while they are reciting the blessing will become dim, which Rashi (*Megillah* 24b) says is because the *Shekhinah* rests on their hands. The Tosafists to the passage say that this only applied in Temple times, when a special divine name, kept secret by the priests, was used for the blessing. Nevertheless, even nowadays, it is discouraged to gaze at the hands of the priests. The idea that the *Shekhinah* rests on the hands of the priests is stated in the Zohar (III, 147a), where it is said that although no man can actually behold the *Shekhinah* while he is still in the body, yet one should still refrain from gazing at the hands of the priests in reverence for the *Shekhinah*.

The Talmud (*Berakhot* 32b) quotes the verse: 'And when ye spread forth your hands, I will hide mine eyes from you ... your hands are full of blood' (Isaiah 1:15), to yield the thought that if a priest had been guilty of homicide, according to some, even of manslaughter, he must never again raise his hands to recite the priestly blessing.

CONCLUSIONS

Although the Sabbath rituals, the death and burial rites and the priestly blessing have no direct connection with one another – it would not have been too difficult to choose other examples for our purpose – yet these three in particular are all good examples of how Jewish religious practices give expression to the inevitable tensions that exist between the striving for spirituality and the need to keep religion earthbound in some measure by means of physical activity. In these practices performed by the body or on behalf of the body the spiritual side is never overlooked. Earth is rarely seen, except by the Jewish mystics, as crammed with heaven, but neither is the heavenly dimension ignored. There is much truth in Max Kadushin's description of Rabbinic Judaism as 'normal mysticism' (Gillman 1990, 122).

Sabbath delight involves eating and drinking and other forms of physical pleasure, but it is all in the spirit of sanctity and spiritual awareness through the symbols of light and fragrance and the love of God. The Talmud (*Berakhot* 57b) can state without irony that the Sabbath is a foretaste (the Talmud actually says a sixtieth) of the World to Come, which itself is referred to in the tradition as the 'Sabbath'. Nothing can be more earthbound than a dead body, yet, in the burial rites, it is treated with reverence and prepared (at least according to the conventional view) for its eventual resurrection, even though a thinker like Nahmanides thinks of the resurrected body as so refined that it has become itself a kind of soul, and even though Maimonides holds that the resurrection will be only temporary, the soul alone enjoying eternal bliss (Jacobs 1973, 3 12–15). In the priestly blessing it is material well-being that is promised and bodily movements attend the blessing, yet behind the whole notion of blessing lies the mystery of divine providence with God as the lover who gazes at his beloved through the lattices.

Naturally, since Judaism is not monolithic, there are various shades of emphasis. The Sabbath delight of a Moses Lump is quite different from what the Kabbalists understand by the concept. And it would be pointless to deny that on the popular level the burial rites imply that somehow the body is still alive, and that many believe the *Shekhinah* to be present in a quasi-physical sense when the priests recite their blessing, so that to look at them is to go blind. How could it be otherwise in view of the many forms of Jewish religious expression?

It should be added that this chapter describes rituals practised by Orthodox Jews, some of which, like the priestly blessing, have been abandoned by Reform Jews. Nor is this an essay in comparative religion, though many a parallel can easily be found in the practices of other religions. The priestly blessing, to give only the most obvious illustration, has been taken over by the Christian Church; the Christian priest becoming the 'kohen' of the 'New Israel'.

The blend of the physical and the spiritual in these rituals can be found often in Judaism. Is Judaism 'religious materialism', as it has been called, or is it a religion of pure spirituality; does Judaism place the emphasis on the body or on the soul; is the Jewish religion this-worldly or other-worldly? The only possible answer, from the historical point of view, is that both ways of looking at it are true. There is no avoiding the paradox expressed so cogently in the section of the Mishnah (*Avot* 4:17) known as 'Ethics of the Fathers': 'One hour of repentance and good deeds in this world is better than all the life of the World to Come and yet one hour of spiritual bliss in the World to Come is better than all the life of this world.' Eternity finds its expression in time and time is an expression of eternity.

BIBLIOGRAPHY

Aaron Berachiah of Modena (1896), *Maavar Yabok*, Vilna.
Bahya Ibn Pakudah (1962), *Hovot ha-Levavot* ('*Duties* of the Heart'), ed. and trans. by M. Hyamson, Jerusalem, New York.
Emden, J. (1904), *Siddur Bet Yaakov*, Lemberg.
Finesinger, S. (1937–38), 'The Custom of Looking at the Fingernails at the Outgoing of the Sabbath', in *Hebrew Union College Annual*, 12–13, 347–65.
Gaguine, S. (1955), *Keter Skein Tov*, London.
Giliman, N. (1990), *Sacred Fragments; Recovering Theology for the Modern Jew*, New York.
Ginsburg, E. K. (1989), *The Sabbath in the Classical Kabbalah*, Albany.
Gold, A. (1981), *The Priestly Blessing*, Brooklyn.
Gombiner, A. *Magen Avraham*, in *Shulkan Arukh*, var. eds.
Heinemann, I. (1949), *Taamey ha-Mitzvot*, Jerusalem.
Horowitz, S. S. (1712), *Shefa Tal*, Hanover.
Jacobs, L. (1973), *A Jewish Theology*, London.
    (1992), *Religion and the Individual: A Jewish Perspective*, Cambridge.
Kadushin, M. (1952), *The Rabbinic Mind*, New York.
Klein, I. (1979), *A Guide to Jewish Religious Practice*, New York.
Langauer, E. (1977), 'Contamination of Priests at the Graves of the Saints' (Heb.) in *Noam* 21, 184–232.
Levine, A. (1985), *Zikhron Meir*, Toronto.
Maimonides, M. (1883), *Mishneh Torah*, Warsaw.
    (1963), *Commentary to the Mishnak* (Heb.) ed. J. Kapah, Jerusalem.
    (1914), *Morek Nevuk/tim*, trans. S. Pines, Vilna.
    (1974), *Guide for the Perplexed*, Chicago University Press.
Meah Berakhot ('One Hundred Benedictions') (1687), Amsterdam.
Midrash Rabbah, ed. Vilna, 1911; English trans. H. Freedman and M. Simon, Soncino, London, 1977.
Mishnah, ed. H. Albeck, Tel-Aviv (1959); English trans. H. Danby, Oxford University Press.
Rabbinowicz, H. (1967), *A Guide to Life: Jewish Laws and Customs of Mourning*, New York.
Rashi: Standard Commentary to Talmud by Rabbi Shlomo Yitzhaki, in all editions of the Babylonian Talmud.
Roth, L. (1960), *Judaism, A Portrait*, London.
Scholem, G. (1967), *On the Kabbalah and Its Symbolism*, London.
    (1974), *Kabbalah*, Jerusalem.
Sefer Hasidim (1973), ed. R. Margaliot, Jerusalem.
Shulhan Arukh, Joseph Karo and Moses Isserles, var. eds.
Shulhan Arukh ha-Ari, Isaac Luria, Munkacs, n.d.
Singer, S. (1962), *Authorised Daily Prayer Book*, London.
Sperling, A. I., *Taamey ha-Minhagim*, Jerusalem, n.d.
Talmud, Babylonian, Vilna, 1936; English trans. I. Epstein, I. Soncino, London, 1948.
Talmud, Jerusalem, Krotoschin, 1866.
Tikkuney ha-Zohar, ed. R. Margaliot, Jerusalem, 1978.
Tosafists, mediaeval glosses to the Talmud, in most eds.
Trachtenberg, J. (1970), *Jewish Magic and Superstition*, New York.
Tur, Jacob ben Asher, var. eds.
Tykocinski, Y. M. (1960), *Gesher ha-Hayyim*, Jerusalem.
Vital, H. (1890), *Etz Hayyim*, ed. Warsaw.
Wertheim, A. (1960), *Halakhot ve-Halikhot ba-Hasidut*, Jerusalem.
Zohar, ed. R. Margaliot, Jerusalem, 1964; English trans. H. Sperling and M. Simon, Soncino, London, 1949.

— 8 —

Attitudes Towards Christianity in the *Halakhah*

An attempt is made in this essay to analyse Halakhic attitudes towards Christianity, an aspect of the relationship between the two religions that has not received much detailed treatment.[1]

In Talmudic times the question regarding the status of a Jew converted to a religion other than Judaism could not have arisen. The Jew who worshipped the pagan gods did not become 'converted' to paganism, abandoning his faith for another. He was treated, to be sure, very severely in Talmudic law as a *meshummad* to idolatry and, according to some opinions, he was given the status of a non-Jew for certain purposes. For instance, any act of *shehitah* carried out by him was invalid, even if performed in the correct manner, as if it had been carried out by a non-Jew.[2] But, even according to this opinion, he remained a Jew for other purposes of the law. If he contracted a marriage with a Jewish woman the marriage was valid,[3] the woman requiring a *get* from him to release her to marry someone else. The Jew who worshipped idols was still a Jew, though a very sinful one. He had not gone over to another religion, impossible in Talmudic times. In the Tannaitic period, when the status of the Jewish Christians was first discussed, these Jews were seen as Jewish heretics – *minim* – and, as for the Gentile Christians, later the vast majority, these were not treated as non-Jews because of their Christian beliefs but simply because they were non-Jews i.e. they had not been converted to Judaism.[4] The whole problem of Halakhic attitudes towards other religions could have no meaning until the emergence of the 'daughter' religions, Christianity and Islam. That is why all the Halakhic discussions on the question date from the Middle Ages.

The basic problem in the middle ages was whether the Talmudic rules about *avodah zarah* ('strange worship', idolatry) applied to the new religions. For a Gentile to worship idols was for him to offend against one of the seven Noahide laws.[5] It has not been sufficiently appreciated that all the Talmudic discussions about the seven laws of the sons of Noah were purely theoretical. It is unlikely in the extreme that the Talmud Rabbis were ever consulted by Gentiles who, while not wishing to convert to Judaism, were eager to keep the 'Torah' for them. In the post-Talmudic period as well there are no records, so far as I am aware, of, say, a Muslim or a Christian approaching a Rabbi to ask him where his 'salvation' was assured as one of the righteous of the nations of the world even though he did not convert to Judaism but remained in his own faith, keeping the seven Noahide laws.

It was far different with regard to the practical implications of the question whether Islam and Christianity were idolatrous faiths. If they were, then all the rigorous laws in tractate *Avodah Zarah* against fraternization with pagan idolaters were still in force. If they were not held to be idolatrous faiths then some of the ancient rules could be relaxed. On the other hand, it could be argued that while a Jew who worships idols is still held to be a Jew in some respects, it was theologically intolerable that a Jew who actually takes the step of embracing another religion should still remain a Jew. In other words, whatever the Talmudic Halakhah might say, the theological problem demanded an approach to the Halakhah that would allow it to be interpreted so as not to give the authority of the law to what was clearly an act of apostasy. The fact that a new theological dimension had to be given to the Halakhah accounts for the ambiguities in the whole post-Talmudic discussions. There was a new situation unenvisaged by the Talmud and yet the Talmud was the final court of appeal in matters of Halakhah.

It was Islam that was first considered by the Halakhists, that is, by the Geonim, who lived in an Islamic environment. Some of the Talmudic regulations forbidding Gentile wine were relaxed in the Geonic period on the grounds that Muslims were not idolaters, the original prohibition having stemmed from the fear that the pagans may have used the wine for idolatrous purposes, though later Rabbinic prohibition was based on the need to prevent social intercourse, possibly leading to intermarriage, and this would apply even to Gentiles who were not idolaters. The general tendency in the Geonic period was to forbid the actual drinking of Muslim wine but to permit its sale and the enjoyment of other benefits. In the Talmudic period it was not only forbidden to drink pagan wine but also to enjoy any benefit from it. The Geonic distinction was thus a compromise, a kind of reluctant recognition that the situation had changed together with a need to preserve the *status quo*. The Geonim[6] also debated whether a Jew converted to Islam was still a Jew for the purposes of the law. Some of the Geonim argued that a conversion to Islam severed all the apostate's connections with Judaism so that if a man had died without issue and had a brother who was a convert to Islam, the widow could remarry without having to undergo the *halitzah* ceremony, it being considered as if there were no surviving brother so that levirate marriage or its alternative, *halitzah,* did not apply (Deuteronomy 25:5–10). Other Geonim refused to treat the apostate differently from the Talmudic *meshummad* who, as above, did not lose his Jewish status and whose wife required a *get* to release her from him before she could marry another. Those Geonim who do not require *halitzah* have, in fact, introduced a theological *motif* into the Halakhah, according to which the death of the levir mentioned in the Torah as severing the levirate bond is not only physical death, as was hithero thought, but death to the faith, a concept unknown and which could not have been known in the Talmudic Halakhah.

A much more serious problem was whether a Jew must be prepared to lay down his life rather than embrace Islam; the Talmudic law requiring a Jew to suffer martyrdom rather than worship idols. Maimonides[7] rules that Islam is not an idolatrous faith, the Muslims being pure monotheists. He carries this to the extent of ruling that if a Jew is threatened with death if he refuses to adopt Islam no martyrdom is required and he may embrace Islam without guilt.[8] Later authorities, while agreeing with Maimonides that Islam is not an idolatrous faith, take issue with him on the question of martyrdom since a conversion to Islam involves, inevitably, a rejection and denial of the Torah of Moses.[9] According to these authorities, a Muslim commits no offence against the Noahide laws since the faith is not idolatrous but for a Jew to become converted to Islam is to commit an act of apostasy worse than idolatry and rather than be guilty of such an act of disloyalty to his own religion the Jew must give up his life. Here again the theological *motif* has been introduced into the Halakhah. To the authorities who do demand martyrdom in this instance it must have seemed intolerable that a Jew could forsake his faith with the blessing, so to speak, of the Halakhah, of which there was no technical infringement. The Halakhah had to be developed so that there would be an infringement.

The question of attitudes towards Christianity in the Halakhah was complicated by questions that could not be asked of Islam. Was Christianity considered Halakhically to be idolatrous because of the doctrines of the Trinity and the Incarnation? Did bowing to the cross or to icons constitute an idolatrous act? All the early Halakhists living in Christian lands held Christianity to be a form of idolatry. On the grounds of expediency, however, some of the more burdensome Talmudic rules governing relations between Jews and Gentiles were relaxed; the change in law then being defended casuistically in such a manner as to suggest that no actual abolition of the Talmudic regulations was being proposed, only that the older rules no longer applied in the new situation.[10] It was not until the thirteenth century that R. Menahem Meiri of Perpignan argued, and he was the first Halakhist of note to do so, that Christians were not to be treated as idolaters, that many of the Talmudic rules could not, in justice, be referred to those whom Meiri calls 'nations governed by religion'.[11] To all intents and purposes Meiri has created a third category, unknown in the earlier sources, between Jews and pagans. For Meiri, Christians were certainly not Jews but they were not pagans either. They did not have the Jewish religion but they did have a religion which made strong ethical demands on them in the same way as Judaism does for its adherents. Meiri, embarrassed by the Talmudic ruling[12] that it is forbidden to have any business dealings with Gentiles on the first day of the week because of the *Notzerim*, feels obliged to make the very fanciful suggestion that the term does not denote Christians (the Nazarines, of Nazareth) but the Babylonians (the successors of Nebuchadnezzer) and that 'the first day' is not because of the Christian Sunday but because sun-worship is alleged to have taken place on the first day of each new week.[13] Yet, even for Meiri, there was no total abolition of the older rules. With regard to the wine of Christians, the Geonic principle, in connection with the wine of Muslims, was adopted by the later Halakhists. The wine of Christians could be bought and sold but it was forbidden to drink this wine.[14] It is well-known that the great Rashi owned vineyards and employed Christian workers. No Halakhist ever thought of applying Maimonides' ruling in connection with Islam to Christianity and, of course, Jews throughout the ages were prepared to suffer martyrdom rather than embrace Christianity.

With regard to the status of a Jew converted to Christianity a new development took place, as Katz[15] has shown, in which a purely Aggadic statement was laid under tribute to provide what amounted to a new Halakhah. The Talmudic statement:[16] 'Though he sinned, he remains an Israelite' is Aggadic and means no more than that even when a Jew commits a serious sin he does not thereby forfeit the high rank of 'Israelite'. The context, makes it clear that the reference is not to an individual Jew at all but to the people and the text should really be translated as: 'The verse calls the people *Israel* even when the people has sinned.' Moreover, the passage does not speak at all of the sin of apostasy or idolatry. Rashi and his school, however, use the saying (in this they were followed by the later Halakhists) to deny that a Jew can ever be converted to another faith. He then remains a Jew even after his 'sin', now understood as his conversion, and is obliged to keep all the precepts as before.[17] As Katz remarks: 'The emphasis on an apostate remaining a Jew constituted a weapon employed by the Jewish community to counter Christian propaganda which intimated that the Jew achieves, through Baptism, a superior religious status, releasing him from any obligation to the law.' It is also highly likely that Rashi's school adopted the attitude it did in order to avoid any Halakhic recognition of Christianity. If the Halakhah had been allowed to acknowledge that the convert to Christianity had changed his legal status this would have had the effect of admitting the act of baptism into the Halakhah itself, hardly a desirable aim in an age when Judaism was on the defensive against Christian attack.

A similar misunderstanding was responsible for the idea, among the later Halakhists, that while Christianity was idolatry so far as Jews were concerned it was not idolatry for Gentiles. It was this misunderstanding of a passage in the Tosafists that was responsible for the oft-quoted and very influential statement that a Christian does not offend against the Noahide laws; he is not an idolater since *shittuf* ('association') is not forbidden to a Noahide.[18] The Talmud[19] rules that it is forbidden for a Jew to have a business partnership with a Gentile because, when a dispute arises, an oath may be required and the Gentile will take the oath by his gods, something it is forbidden for a Jew to bring about indirectly. The Tosafists defend the practice of their day in which this Talmudic rule was ignored, many Jews having business partnerships with Christians. The defence consists of the acknowledgement that when Christians take the oath they do so in God's name. Even though, continue the Tosafists, they associate God's name with that of Jesus, Gentiles (i.e. Noahides) are not forbidden *shittuf*. The meaning here is that a Noahide is not forbidden *shittuf when taking an oath* i.e. there is no prohibition for a Noahide, when he takes an oath, to associate the name of God with another. Hence a Jew may go into business partnership with a Christian and the Talmudic reason for forbidding Jewish–Gentile partnerships no longer applies. Even if it will lead to the Christian taking an oath, the Christian does no wrong, for which the Jew is indirectly responsible (unlike in the case of the pagan idolater who takes the oath solely in the name of his gods and makes no reference to God at all). This is, in fact, an illustration of the phenomenon, noted earlier, of the Halakhists finding accomodation with Christians even though, for them, Christianity is idolatry. The Tosafists never intended to imply that Christianity is not idolatry for Noahides. But subsequent commentators, instead of understanding the term *shittuf* correctly in its formal, legal sense (i.e. associating God's name with another *when taking an oath*) take the term to mean what it means in the very different discipline of mediaeval philosophy, namely, as denoting the *belief* that God has an associate or associates. They misunderstood the Tosafists as saying that a belief, by a Noahide, in the Trinity or the Incarnation is not idolatry, resulting in the new Halakhah that while Christianity is idolatry for Jews it is not idolatry for Christians. This cannot possibly have been the attitude of the Tosafists since the members of the French school never invoke the philosophical principle of *shittuf* and only allow accommodation *vis-à-vis* Christians on casuistic grounds having to do with expediency and necessity.[20] Isserles,[21] in the sixteenth century, states: 'Some authorities are lenient in the matter of a Jew becoming a business partner with a Gentile, nowadays, for their intention (when they take an oath) is to the Creator of heaven and earth.' According to the famous eighteenth-century authority, R. Ezekiel Landau of Prague,[22] Isserles had the true understanding of the Tosafists and only refers to the taking of an oath but this cannot be correct since elsewhere[23] Isserles himself applies the *shittuf* idea to laws other than those concerning the taking of an oath and clearly understands *shittuf* in its theological sense.[24] In any event, Isserles is frequently quoted by later Halakhists as ruling that a Noahide is permitted *shittuf* in the theological understanding of the term with the consequence that a Christian commits no offence against the Noahide laws by believing in the Trinity and in the Incarnation. This is as far as the Halakhists are prepared to go. None of the Halakhists are prepared to go further to affirm that Christianity does not even involve *shittuf* but is pure monotheism, a belief in a triune God. At the most, the Halakhists is prepared to acknow-ledge Christianity as a non-idolatrous faith for Gentiles because of the *shittuf* idea. Indeed, some later authorities, while understanding Isserles' reference to *shittuf* in its theological sense, yet hold that Christians are idolaters since, for these Halakhists, the *shittuf* principle can only be applied where there is belief in One Supreme Being (together with lesser deities) not to the Trinitarian doctrine of three equal Persons in the Godhead.[25]

Thus, among many of the Halakhists, a compromise position was adopted. In the Talmudic sources the distinction between a faithful Jew and an idolater is categorical. A Gentile who worshipped idols offended against the Noahide laws and a Jew who did so offended against the laws of the Torah. No distinction whatsoever was made between idolatry for 'them' and idolatry for 'us'. Whatever constituted idolatry (on this there are discussions) was considered to be idolatry for both 'us' and 'them'. Now, for the first time in the history of the Halakhah, a religion came to be recognized, by many of the Halakhists, as constituting an idolatrous faith so far as 'we' are concerned but a non-idolatrous faith so far as 'they' are concerned. In practice the distinction was hard to maintain since many of the regulations governing Jewish–Gentile relations have to do with 'our' relation to 'them'. This explains the lack of clarity in the whole discussion among the later Halakhists, of which some instances will now be noted.

Is it permitted, for example, for a Jew to enter a church? On the one hand, Christianity is not idolatry for 'them' and so the church is not a place of idolatrous worship it is forbidden for a Jew even to enter. But, on the other hand, it is 'we' who are entering the church and for 'us' Christianity is idolatry. Such a situation could not have arisen in the Talmudic period. A 'house of idols' was such both for Jew and Gentile. R. Zevi Hirsch Shapira[26] decides that it is forbidden for a Jew to enter a church but records it in a somewhat less than categorical manner. May a synagogue be sold to Christians for use as a church? Here the grounds for permissiveness are stronger. If it be granted that Christianity is not idolatry for 'them'[27] the sale in no way assists idolatrous worship. May a building that has been used as a church be used as a synagogue? Here the practice is to permit it but then, in any event, there is no clear ruling that a place in which idols have been worshipped may not be used as a synagogue. The proviso is naturally made that the building must contain no crosses.[28] May a Jew deal in selling crosses to Christians? Here the problem is complicated. If it is held that Christianity is not idolatry so far as Christians are concerned it ought to be permitted, on the face of it, since the Jew does no wrong by helping Christians to observe their own religion. But it is forbidden for a Jew to obtain any benefit from idolatrous objects and for 'us' Christianity is idolatry. Isserles[29] does permit the sale of crosses that are for purely decorative purposes (i.e. to be worn as ornaments not as objects to be worshipped) but not even for these purposes if the crosses have actually been worshipped. This is an interesting point. There is no intrinsic Halakhic objection to a Jew having in his home a work of art, for example, depicting Christian (or, for that matter, idolatrous) scenes (though, of course, there is the question of good taste and self-respect). The Halakhah knows nothing of any objection to a Jew enjoying some benefit of pleasure from the symbols of another faith *per se*. From the Halakhic point of view the sole criterion in all such cases is whether the object has been worshipped. On the basis of this principle, the nineteenth-century Halakhist, R. Joseph Saul Nathanson of Lemberg,[30] permits the wearing by a Jew of a medal in the form of a cross. Is it permitted for a Jew to give a donation towards the funds of a church since Christianity is not idolatry so far as Gentiles are concerned and there should be no objection on the grounds that it is encouraging idolatrous worship by Noahides? Rabbi Markus Horowitz of Frankfurt (1844–1910) not only permits it but considers donations by Jews towards the building of a church meritorious. It is, he argues, a sanctification of the divine name by demonstrating that Judaism is tolerant and, at the same time, calling attention to the differences between Judaism and Christianity, from which it emerges that Judaism is the purer faith.[31] Not all recent Halakhists come anywhere near to accepting Horowitz's tolerant attitude. R. David Hoffman (1843–1921), Rector of the Orthodox Rabbinical Seminary in Berlin, takes strong issue with Horowitz's view.[32] All the authorities agree, he argues, that Christianity is idolatry for the Jew. How, then, can a Jew be in any way responsible for what to him is idolatrous worship? If the Jew finds it hard and tactless to fail to contribute to the building of the church, he should simply give his donation without it being specified that it is for the building or repair of a church.

Many of the Halakhic questions in the context of Christianity have to do with the status of a convert to that faith. We have seen how the school of Rashi refuses to treat the apostate as if his connections with Judaism had been totally severed when he became converted. His wife requires a *get* and his sister-in-law *halitzah*. The view put forward by some of the Geonim, that the convert to another faith loses his Jewish status entirely, was rejected. Thus the *Shulhan 'Arukh*[33] does refer to this view but rejects it, ruling that the sister-in-law does require *halitzah*. Isserles quotes in this connection the ruling that when a man betrothes a woman and he has a brother who has been converted to Christianity, he may make the marriage conditional on his survival i.e. so that if he dies without issue and his widow becomes bound to the apostate for *halitzah* (the apostate naturally refusing to participate in a rite contrary to his new faith) the marriage is rendered null and void retrospectively.

The status of a *kohen* who has been converted to Christianity and had then returned to the Jewish fold was first discussed by Rabbenu Gershom of Mainz in the eleventh century.[34] The topic reoccurs in subsequent Responsa.[35] Gershom discusses whether the *kohen*, after his return to Judaism, may recite the priestly blessing in the synagogue. Gershom cites the Mishnaic ruling[36] that priests who had once worshipped idols may never again serve in the Temple, from which he concludes that it is only from participation in the Temple service that they are disbarred. The *kohen* who has now returned to the fold may again enjoy the other priestly privileges. He may be called up first to the reading of the Torah and he may recite the priestly blessing. After quoting Biblical and Rabbinic teachings on the power of repentence to wipe out all sin, Gershom is emphatic that it is wrong to brand the *kohen* publicly as a former apostate, which would be the effect of a ban on his carrying out the priestly blessing. We must provide apostates with every encouragement to revert to the fold instead of making their return an exposure to public ostracism. Gershon, in all this, has not the slightest doubt that Christianity is idolatry but he clinches his argument by referring to the Talmudic passage[37] which states that even when a brother has sunk so low as to sell himself to idols as their priest no stones must be cast at him and he must be redeemed from his captivity.

It is interesting to note how this same question of the *kohen* who had been converted to Christianity and has now returned surfaces centuries later in the Responsa of a Sephardi Rabbi,

Joseph Rahamim Franco (1838–1901) of Jerusalem; towards the end of his life, Chief Rabbi of Hebron.[38] Franco, living in Palestine, then under Turkish rule, is very circumspect when dealing with Islam (the quotes in this Responsum referring to Mohammed and Islam are omitted from the published version, evidently out of fear of the censor) but, by the same token, is completely unreserved when dealing with Christianity. The particular question discussed by Franco is that of a *kohen* who had been converted to Christianity by Protestant missionaries and who has now returned to Judaism. Franco, at pains to permit the *kohen* to recite the priestly blessing, introduces the novel idea that technically it is not, Halakhically speaking, the belief in Jesus that constitutes idolatry but the act of bowing to the cross. This constitutes the offence of bowing to an idol, though, strictly speaking, says Franco, the cross is a mere symbol and is not in itself an idol. Since among protestants there are no icons or crosses in their place of worship, the *kohen* has not been guilty technically of worshipping idols. He has, indeed, been guilty of entertaining false beliefs but, without any act of worship, he is not an idolater and may recite the priestly blessing and enjoy the other privileges of a *kohen* on his return to Judaism.

There are references in early Halakhic works to the son of Rabbennu Gershom of Mainz allegedly being converted to Christianity. Gershom is said to have mourned for his son for fourteen days, instead of the usual seven; one set of seven days because the son had been lost to his earthly father, the other because he had been lost to his Father in Heaven.[39] According to this report there is to be mourning even when an apostate dies but this is qualified in the note appended in the sources which implies that it is only if the apostate had been murdered by Gentiles, his unnatural death being an atonement for his sin. On the basis of this, Isserles[40] rules that there is to be no mourning for an apostate but that 'some say' he is to be mourned if he was murdered by Gentiles. It is clear from the context that the report is of Gershom mourning for his son when the son died. But the whole passage was later incorrectly understood to mean that Gershom mourned fourteen days when his son, who was still alive, became converted to Christianity, as if the son had died. Arising out of this misunderstanding was the popular opinion, frequently acted upon, that the near relatives of an apostate must mourn for him as if he had died even though he was still alive, his very conversion to Christianity being considered death. Generally speaking, however, the Halakhists reject the bizarre idea of mourning for a living person as if he were dead and they stress that to do so, in the case of a convert to Christianity, is to despair of his eventual return to the fold.[41]

In some respects a Jewish convert to Christianity is rejected by the Halakhists to a greater extent than born Christians. Isserles[42] rules that if Christians who are Gentiles give donations to a synagogue it is permitted to accept these for synagogue use but it is forbidden to accept donations from a Jewish convert to Christianity. It appears that in Hungary in the nineteenth- century it was far from unusual for Jews to solicit donations for the synagogue from their Christian neighbours. Rabbi Yekuthiel Judah Teitelbaum (1808–83) of Sighet seeks to defend the practice.[43] His questioner had raised the objection, among others, that to accept donations from Christians for synagogal use amounts to a profanation of the divine name. Teitelbaum defends the practice on the grounds that it is only done in an emergency; for example, when a new synagogue has to built or where the old synagogue requires extensive repairs.

Finally, we may note, at a period much later than that of the *Shulhan 'Arukh*,[44] a semi-Halakhic status was given to the folk-custom of refraining from certain activities on Christmas eve. Christmas is called *Nittel* (Latin, *Natale Dominus;* French 'Noël') in the late sources and in Yiddish parlance.[45] It was the custom to refrain from studying the Torah on this night and, in some places, to play cards instead. The prohibition of studying the Torah is very curious in view of the high value of Torah study in the Jewish tradition. In all probability its origin is to be found in the folk desire to treat the night as profane by avoiding sacred activities such as Torah study. But various other theories have been advanced to account for the custom. R. Moses Sofer[46] observes that in practice one only refrains from Torah study until midnight and so suggests that the custom was adopted in conscious reaction to the Christian practice of rising at midnight on Christmas eve in order to offer their prayers. To demonstrate that Jews are as least as assiduous as their Christian neighbours in the performances their religion, the custom developed of forbidding Torah study until midnight. This would serve to make sure that Jews would go early to bed and thus be encouraged to rise at midnight to make up their daily quota of learning. R. Moses Sofer cannot agree that the reason is because it is a night of mourning, a mourner being forbidden to study Torah, the Jew's most joyous activity, since, if that were the reason, why are there no other signs of mourning and why only until midnight? He adds that if the reason were because it is a night of mourning he could have understood the further custom of refraining from marital relations on this night. But he considers this latter custom to be ridiculous and demands that it should be stopped. On the other hand, it is reported, in a reliable source,[47] that the Munkacher Rebbe upheld the custom and, of course, that of refraining from Torah study until midnight.

If the above analysis of an important area of the Halakhah is correct, it throws light on the Halakhic process in general as one not uninfluenced by external conditions and by other values than that of Halakhah itself. About this there has been much discussion.

NOTES

1. S. Federbusch: 'The Attitude of Judaism to Christianity' (Heb.) in his *Hikrey Yahadut*, Jer., 1965, Pp. 217–36; Meir Lerner: *Hadar ha-Karmel*, Vol. 2, London, 1975, Nos. 44 and 45, pp. 33f.; H. B. Halevi: *'Aseh Lekha Rav*, Vol. 1, Tel-Aviv, 1975, pp. 178–181; Vol. 2, Tel-Aviv, 1978, pp. 158 f.; Vol. 3, Tel Aviv, 1979, pp. 19–22. On the whole subject see also my *Theology in the Responsa*, London, 1975, Index: 'Christianity' and 'church'; R. Margaliot: *Margalit ha-Yam* to Sanhedrin 63b, Vol. 2, Jer., 1958, No. 8, p. 22a; Lampronti's *Pahad Yitzhak*, ed. Mekor, Jer., 1970, s.v. 'avodah zarah; Jacob Schachter: *Sefer Mishley*, Jer., 1963, p. 231; Israel Abrahams: *Jewish Life in the Middle Ages*, Philadelphia, 1911, chapters xxiii and xxiv, pp. 399ff. On page 399 Abrahams makes the pertinent remarks: 'If the legal status of the Jews were our sole criterion, the picture of their relations with medieval Christians would seem to be painted in very sombre hues. Laws, however, were made to be broken, and the actual relations between Jews and Christians were for long periods far different to those which the Church Councils and, to a lesser degree, the Jewish ritual codes tended to produce. Jews and Christians often defied the laws which sought to keep them asunder.'
2. *Hullin* 4b–5a. The term *meshummad* is the original term, not the term *mumar* as in current editions of the Talmud. It was because the term *meshummad* came to be used for the convert to Christianity that the Talmudic texts were altered to read *mumar*, see Saul Lieberman's note in the Harry Wolfson Jubilee Volume, Jer., 1965, English Section, Vol. 2, pp. 531–2. The term *meshummad* occurs in *Tosefta*, Sanhedrin 13:5 and in *Rosh ha-Shanah* 17a (in uncensored versions see *Dikdukey Soferim* p. 32 note 50). Lieberman notes that the term *mumar* in *every* Talmudic text is a post-Talmudic substitution for *meshummad*. For instance in this passage, *Hullin* 4b (where the term occurs nineteen times in a single page) the Munich Codex has *meshummad* (erroneously quoted in *Dikdukey Soferim* as *mumar*). The Geonim were puzzled as to the meaning of the term *meshummad*, see *Arukh* s.v. *shemad*. Saul Lieberman (*Tosefta Kifshuto*, Vol. 2, New York, 1968, p. 402 note 45) connects it with *shemad*, 'destruction', as in the expression *dor hahemad* i.e. the generation in which Jews were compelled to worship idols and were hence 'destroyed'. This original meaning was later extended to wilful 'destruction' by the intentional sinner. Cf. *Iggerot Soferim*, ed. S. Sofer, Tel-Aviv, 1970, Letters of the *Hatam Sofer*, No. 10, pp. 10–11.
3. *Yevamot* 47b.
4. See the excellent treatment of Lawrence H. Schiffman: *Who Was a Jew? Rabbinic and Halakhic Perspectives on the Jewish Christian Schism*, New Jersey, 1985, especially chapter 7, pp. 75–6. Schiffman, p. 53, writes: 'By the time the Temple was destroyed, the Jewish Christians were a minority among the total number of Christians, and it was becoming clear that the future of the new religion would be dominated by Gentile Christians. Nevertheless, the tannaim came into contact primarily with Jewish Christians and so

continued to regard the Christians as Jews who had gone astray by following the teachings of Jesus.' The same, one might add, applies in the Amoraic period.
5. *Sanhedrin* 56b and see *Encyclopedia Talmudit*, Vol. 3 s.v. *ben noah*.
6. See the statement of Maimonides, *Yad, Maakhalot Asurot* 11:7, on Gentile wine and, on whether a Jew converted to Islam was still a Jew for his sister-in-law to require *halitzah*, see B. M. Lewin: *Otzar Ha-Geonim*, Vol. 7, *Yevamot*, Jer., 1936, pp. 36–7.
7. *Teshuvot ha-Rambam*, ed. J. Blau, Jer., 1960, No. 448, Vol. 2, pp. 725–8; *Yad, Maakhalot Asurot* 11:7.
8. *Iggeret ha-Shemad*, Rambam le-Am, Vol. 20, pp. 29–86. Cf. *Yad, Melakhim* 11:4, in the uncensored editions; Judah Halevi: *Kuzari* IV, 24 and Nahmanides' Sermon: 'The Law of the Lord is Perfect' in *Kitvey ha-Ramban*, ed. B. Chavel, Jer., 1963, Vol. 1, pp. 343–4.
9. See Responsa *Radbaz* (David Ibn Abi Zimra) No. 1163 (92) who quotes *Ritba* as having the same opinion.
10. See Tosafists to *Avodah Zarah* 2a, s.v. *asur* and *Shulhan Arukh, Yoreh De'ah* 148:12 and Isserles *ad loc*. Cf. Tosafists to *Berakhot* 57b s.v. *ha-roeh*.
11. See e.g. *Bet ha-Behirah* to *Bava Kama* 37b (ed. K. Schlesinger, Jer., 1973) p. 122 and to 113b p. 530. See J. Katz: *Exclusiveness and Tolerance: Jewish-Gentile Relations in Medieval and Modern Times*, Oxford, 1961, chapter 5, pp. 114–28 and the further passage from Meiri quoted there. The seventeenth-century Lithuanian scholar, Moses Rivkes, arrived at a similar position independently of Meiri. Rivkes' work *Beer ha-Golah* indicates the sources of the *Shulhan 'Arukh*. He remarks that the use of such terms as 'idolater' in the *Shulhan 'Arukh* do not refer to Christians who belong in the ranks of the righteous of the nations of the world and have a share in the World to Come, see *Beer ha-Golah* to *Hoshen Mishpat* 425:5 and Katz op. cit., pp. 164–6 (the reference is given incorrectly in Katz as 525:5).
12. In uncensored editions *'Avodah Zarah* 7b. Cf. *Ta'anit* 27b and Meiri *Bet ha-B ehirah ad loc*.
13. Meiri to *'Avodah zarah* beg. Cf. Katz's further essay: 'Religious Tolerance in the Religious System of Rabbi Menahem Meiri – A Reply' (Heb.) in *Zion*, XLVI, No. 3, 1981, pp. 243–244, where Katz defends his views on Meiri against the critics who argue that Meiri is not original in his stance.
14. See Isserles to *Yoreh De'ah* 123:1. Although there is some doubt as to whether it is permitted for a Jew to drink beer in the home of a Christian (see *'Avodah Zarah* 1b and Tosafists s.v. *ve-tarveihu*) it was the practice of Jews in pre-Expulsion England to do so (see the *'Etz Ijayyim* of R. Jacob of London, ed. I. Brodie, Jer., 1962, Vol. 2, p. 65).
15. 'Though He Sinned, He Remains an Israelite' (Heb.) in *Tarbitz*, XXVIII, Nos. 2–3, Jer., 1958, pp. 203–17.
16. *Sanhedrin* 44a.
17. For Rashi's view see *Teshuvot Rashi*, ed. I. Elfenbein, New York, 1942, Nos. 171, 173 and 175. Saadiah Gaon, though not in an Halakhic context, declares Christianity to be a form of idolatry, *Emunot ve-De'ot*, II, 5.
18. See *Encyclopedia Talmudit*, Vol. 3, s.v. *ben noah*, p. 350 note 72. On this see Katz: *Exclusiveness and Tolerance*, p. 163.
19. *Sanhedrin* 63b; *Bekhorot* 2b and Tosafists to these passages.
20. The first to note this was R. Nissim of Gerona (d c. 1375), the *Ran* (to Alfasi end of first chapter of *'Avodah Zarah*). *Ran* points out that the Tosafists, remark about *shitt uf* only refers to the case of a Gentile taking an oath. He is forbidden by the Noahide laws to be a Christian but there is no special prohibition, over and above this, to him taking a Christian oath. The Jew is not responsible for him being a Christian and there is no harm in the Jew being indirectly responsible for him taking a Christian oath. Maimonides (*Yad, 'Akum* 9:5) states that Christians (correct reading *Edomim* not *Kena'anim* as in the censored editions) are idolators; cf. his Commentary to the Mishnah, *'Avodah Zarah* 1:3 (in uncensored editions). On the other hand, Maimonides holds that while it is permitted to teach the Torah to Christians it is forbidden to teach the Torah to Muslims because the latter accuse the Jews of having falsified the Torah (see *Teshuvot ha-Rambarn*, ed. A. Freiman, Jer., 1937, No. 364). On the question of teaching the Torah to Christians see J. J. Weinberg: *Seriday Esh*, Vol. 2, Jer., 1977, *Yoreh De'ah*, Nos 90 and 92, that the prohibition only applies, in any event, if the teaching is done as a religious act, not to teaching at a University where it is purely academic activity.
21. *Orah Hayvfim* 156; cf. Isserles to *Yoreh De'ah* 147:3. See Isserles to *Orah Hayyim* 215:2 that it is permitted to answer 'Amen' to the benediction of a Christian and see Gumbiner:

Magen Avraham ad loc. who refers to Isserles *Orah Hayyim* 156.
22. Responsa *Noda' Biyhudah*, Second Series, *Yoreh De'ah*, No. 148 end.
23. *Darkhey Moshe* to *Tur*, *Yoreh De'ah* 151.
24. See *Pithey Tesuvah* to *Yoreh De'ah* 147 note 2.
25. See Zevi Hirsch Shapira: *Darkhey Teshuvah* to *Yoreh De'ah* 147, note 12 and *Encyclopedia Talmudit*, loc. cit., where this opinion is quoted in the name of R. Jacob Emden. The closest we get to a defence of Christianity by an Halakhist that is pure monotheism and a rejection of the view that the doctrine of the Incarnation compromises this, is in the recently published Responsum by the sixteenth-century Italian Rabbi Solomon Modena but this Responsum was written, in fact, as an apologia with an eye on the Church. For this Responsum see David B. Ruderman: 'A Jewish Apologetic Treatise from Sixteenth Century Bologna' in *HUCA*, Vol. L (1979), pp. 253–276.
26. *Darkhey Teshuvah* 150 note 2. Cf. the extreme view of the contemporary Halakhist. Rabbi E. Waldenberg of Jerusalem *(Tzitz Eli'ezer*, Vol. 14, Jer., 1981, No. 91) that it is forbidden to enter a church or a mosque even for the purpose of studying the architecture. In mediaeval England the view was put forward that it might be considered meritorious to use a church as a short cut on the grounds that since it is disrespectful to use a synagogue for this purpose it should follow that it is advisable to use a church for the purpose, see *Perushey Rabbenu Eliyahu mi-London*, ed. E. J. L. Zachs, Jer., 1956, p. 131. Cf. H. D. Halevi: *'Aseh Lekha Rav*, Vol. 1, pp. 178–81, who forbids a Jew to enter a church even for the purpose of studying the architecture. The source for the general prohibition of entering a house in which idols are worshipped is *Tosefta 'Avodah Zarah*, ed. Zuckermandel, 17b, top, and *Shulhan 'Arukh Yoreh de'ah* 150:1; *cf Sefer Hasidim*. ed. R. Margaliot, No. 1157.
27. See the discussion in S. Braun: *She'arim ha-Metzuyanim ba-Halakhah*, New York, 1949, Vol. 4, pp. 159–60.
28. See R. Joseph Saul Nathanson: *Shoel u-Meshiv*, Vol. 1, Part 3, Nos. 72 and 73 that in the case of a Protestant church building, containing no icons or crosses, it is not only permitted but meritorious to convert the building into a synagogue. The nineteenth- century Galician authority, R. Shalom Mordecai Schwadron (Responsa *Maharsham*, Vol. 4, No. 46) permits the melting down of the remains of tallow candles that have been used in a church to make new candles of them for Jewish use. R. Simhah Bunem Sofer (1842–1906) in his Responsa collection *Shevet Sefer, Orah Hayyim*, No. 12, discusses whether church pews may be used in a synagogue. R. Hayyim Eleazar Shapira (1872–1937) in his *Minhat Ele'azar* (Vol. 2, No. 73) and Rabbi J. J. Weiss (b. 1902) in his *Minhat Yitzhak* (Vol. 4, No. 87) both permit the telling of the time by a clock on a church tower. The clock is not an object of worship but has been placed on a high spot for the convenience of the townsfolk.
29. Isserles to *Yoreh De'ah*, 141:1 (in name of the *Mordekhai* but not found in current editions of this work) but only if they are purely for decorative purposes not those which have already been worshipped, see *Darkhey Teshuvah* 141 note 2.
30. *Shoel u-Meshiv*, Vol. 1, Part 3, No. 171; cf. *Jewish Encyclopedia*, Vol. IV, s.v. 'Cross', pp. 368–69 and Halevi: *'Aseh Lekha Rav*, Vol. 2, No. 46, pp. 168—169; Aaron Walkin: *Zekan Aharon*, Vol. 2, New York, 1976, No. 52, on tea and table cloths embroidered with a Maltese cross.
31. Responsa *Matteh Levi*, Part 2, Frankfurt, 1932, *Yoreh De'ah*, No. 28, see my *Theology in the Responsa*, p. 281.
32. *Melammed le-Ho'il*, Frankfurt, 1926–32, Part 2, No. 148, see *Theology in the Responsa*, pp. 299–300. The Gaon of Vilna, it might be noted, considers Christianity to be an idolatrous faith. Thus, on the basis of *Sanhedrin* 63b, the *Shulban 'Arukh (Yoreh De'ah* 147:1) rules that it is forbidden even to mention an idol by name, upon which the Gaon *(Biur ha-Gra* note 3) comments that while a Jew must not utter the name Christ he may speak of Jesus, which, as a proper name, is mentioned in the Talmud. On the subject of referring to Jesus, Mary etc. see the interesting Responsum of Yair Hayyim Bacharach: *Havot Yair*, No. 1, *Hasagot* 11/12.
33. *Een ha-'Ezer* 157:4 and Isserles gloss.
34. *Responsa of Rabbenu Gershom*, ed. S. Eidelberg, New York, 1955, No. 4, pp. 57–60.
35. See e.g. Rabbi Ezekiel Landau: *Noda' Biyhudah*, Second Series, *Orah Hayyim*, No. 10, the case of a *kohen* who had married a woman in a Hindu ceremony, and see *Theology in the*

Responsa, Index s.v. 'priestly blessing'. R. Hayyim Hezekiah Medini (1832–1904) in his *Sedey Hemed (Kelalim, mem,* 156, ed. Friedmann, New York, 1962, Vol. 4, pp. 267–8) seeks to prove from the sources that an apostate cannot help to make up the quorum for prayer, the *minyan,* and that his donation to a synagogue must not be accepted. Cf. Isserles to *Orah Hayyim* 154:11.
36. *Menahot* 13:10.
37. *'Arakhin* 30b.
38. *Sha'arey Rahamim,* Jer., 1881. *Orah Hayyim,* No. 5. Israel Abrahams tells of his visit to Franco in Hebron in: *The Book of Delight and Other Papers,* Philadelphia, 1905, pp. 82–3.
39. Notes to *Asheri, Mo'ed Katan,* chapter 3, No. 59.
40. *Yoreh De'ah* 340:5. Cf. *Yoreh De'ah* 345:5 that normally there is no mourning for an apostate when he dies.
41. On this subject see *Turey Zahav* to *Yoreh De'ah* 340 note 3; R. Simhah Bunem Sofer: *Shevet Sofer, Yoreh De'ah,* No. 108; Y. J. Greenwald: *Kol Bo CAlAvelut* New York, 1956, p. 317 and notes; Y.M. Tykochinsky: *Gesher ha-Hayyim,* Jer., 1960, Vol. 1, pp. 274/275; *Sefer Hasidim,* ed. R. Margaliot, Jer., 1973, No. 100 and the editor's notes, pp. 187–8.
42. *Yoreh De'ah* 254:2; cf. *Orah Hayyim* 154:11.
43. Responsa *Avney Tzedek,* Lemberg, 1885, *Orah Hayyim,* No. 14.
44. Isserles to *Yoreh De'ah* 148:12 refers to it only in a very indirect way.
45. On this see *Jewish Encyclopedia,* Vol. 9, p. 318 and J. Eisenstein: *Otzar Dinim u-Minhagim,* pp. 267—268, both articles very fragmentary with no attempt to date the emergence of the custom. Cf. J. D. Singer: *Ziv ha-Minhagim,* Jer., 1971, p. 265, who comments on the custom of fasting on the ninth day of the month of Tevet *(Shulhan 'Arukh, Orah Hayyim* 580:2) that he had seen somewhere in a book that this fast has its origin in the fact that Jesus was born on this day. Cf. A. S. Sperling: *Ta'amey ha-Minhagim,* ed. Jer., n.d. p. 500.
46. *Iggerot Soferim,* ed. S. Sofer, Tel-Aviv, 1970, Letter 2 of the *Hatam Sofer,* pp. 2–3.
47. Y. N. Gold: *Darkhey Hayyim vye-Shalom,* Jer., 1974, No. 825, p. 308. Cf. *No'am,* Vol. 20, Jer., 1978, pp. 325-7 on the customs of the Lubavitcher Rebbe. The Rebbe upholds the custom of refraining from studying the Torah on this night but observes that this is novel *(hiddush gadol).* Various Christian denominations observe Christmas at diverse times but the date observed by the majority of Christians in any particular place is the one on which the custom is to be observed. The Rebbe is less certain about forbidding marital relations on this night but remarks that perhaps it is better to abstain so as to prevent thoughts of Christianity, albeit negative ones, from entering the mind during what ought to be a sacred act.

— 9 —

Rabbi Ephraim Ha-Kohen and a Heretical Sermon

In the Responsa collection *Sha'ar Efrayim* by Rabbi Ephraim b. Jacob ha-Kohen (1616–78) of Vilna[1] there are two interesting Responsa concerning a Rabbi who had been accused of preaching a heretical sermon. This article seeks to uncover the issues beneath the surface in the dispute.

In the first Responsum we are told neither the identity of the Rabbi guilty of the alleged offence nor of the Rabbi who was moved to place the offender under the ban. As we shall see, however, the name of the alleged culprit is stated in the second Responsum. It appears from the first Responsum that the offending Rabbi was in the habit of allowing himself considerable homiletical licence, claiming that there was no need for a preacher to limit himself to the plain meaning of his Scriptural text. This attitude, so it was claimed, had led him seriously to distort the verse in which God said to Moses, 'When you have freed the people from Egypt, you shall worship *ha-elohim* at this mountain' (Exodus 3:12). The preacher interpreted the word *ha-elohim* in the verse to mean not God but 'a god', the meaning of the verse being, God warned Moses beforehand that the people would worship the Golden Calf. The Rabbi who turned to Ephraim for advice argued that the preacher deserved to be placed under the ban on three counts. First, according to his sermon, God had foretold that Israel would worship the Golden Calf, thereby implying that God compels man to sin. Secondly, he converted the word *elohim* from a sacred into a profane name. Thirdly, the preacher's stance has encouraged the ignorant to imagine that they, too, can exercise complete freedom in interpreting Scripture. For all these offences the preacher deserves to be excommunicated.

In his reply, Ephraim first discusses at length the sources in the Talmud and the Codes on the question of placing a scholar under the ban, coming to the conclusion that this should only be done if the scholar had been guilty of a very serious offence. It is praiseworthy to find extenuating circumstances for a scholar so as not to place him under the ban, and this Ephraim proceeds to do. To be sure, Ephraim remarks, the preacher erred grievously. Nevertheless, we are bound to find some excuse for him if we can, since he is a scholar. Did not R. Pappa say that when he had to find an excuse for a scholar, he refused to lay his head on his pillow until he had done so?[2]

Proceeding to his defence, Ephraim says it is possible that the preacher followed the example of Nahum of Gimzo, who expounded every *et* (the sign of the accusative) in the Torah as indicating something not stated explicitly in the text.[3] Our verse does not simply say *ha-elohim* but *et ha-elohim*, and the preacher, consequently, may have concluded that God had informed Moses that the people would worship God and the Golden Calf – the former from the word *ha-elohim*, the latter from the word *et*. The Talmud,[4] in fact, states that when the people worshipped the Golden Calf they had God in mind as well. Moreover, the Midrash[5] states that God had foretold to Moses that the people will worship the Golden Calf but with God in mind as well. This implies that their sin, grievous though it undoubtedly was, will not result in their utter destruction, since, God said to Moses, when they will worship the Golden Calf they will have Me in mind as well. Even if this is what the preacher intended, he certainly erred in preaching such a thing in public. But he does not deserve to be placed under the ban for this error, since even according to his erroneous interpretation the word *elohim* in the verse refers to God and thus retains its sanctity.

As for the objection that, according to the sermon, God compels man to sin when He foretells that the sin will be perpetrated, what of the verse (Deuteronomy 31:16) in which God tells Moses that after Moses' death the people will go awhoring after strange gods and what of the above-mentioned Rabbinic comment according to which God does tell Moses that the people will worship the Golden Calf? The truth is that all this is the old theological problem of how God's foreknowledge can be reconciled with human free will, and is really irrelevant to our question.[6] And, in fact, both Maimonides[7] and R. Abraham Ibn David have explained the Deuteronomic verse and other similar verses in such a way that they are not in conflict with the doctrine that the human will is free. The same kind of interpretation can be given here so that the preacher cannot be faulted on these grounds.

If, however, Ephraim continues, the preacher, Heaven forfend, did interpret the word *elohim* itself as referring to the Golden Calf, he should be rebuked for his error; yet, even if that is so, he does not deserve to be placed under the ban. The prosecuting Rabbi had argued that the preacher should be placed under the ban on the basis of a statement by R. Joseph Karo in the *Shulhan 'Arukh*.[8] Here Karo writes concerning a reader of the Torah in the synagogue who insisted on reading the *Ketiv* (the way in which certain words are written in the scroll) instead of the *Keri* (the traditional way of reading these words).[9] The great scholars present there at the time warned him sternly to desist and when he refused to listen to them, they placed him under the ban. *A fortiori*, then, should our preacher suffer the ban. Not so, retorts Ephraim. There the man had been warned not to continue and yet he persisted in following his own illegal practice, whereas our preacher, mistaken though he had been, was never warned that what he was doing is wrong.

The prosecuting Rabbi had quoted Maimonides,[10] who lists twenty-four offences for which the ban is imposed, among them offences of which our preacher had been guilty, such as one who brings others to a profanation of the divine name and one who causes the spiritually blind to stumble, both of which applied when the heretical sermon was delivered. Again Ephraim maintains that the case of the preacher is different in that he had never been warned to desist. R. Solomon Ibn Adret of Barcelona (1235–1310), the *Rashba*, engaged in a correspondence with the scholars of Provence on the question of the study of philosophy.[11] Jedaiah Bedersi (d. 1340) here defends his countrymen of Provence, pointing out that the whole controversy erupted when a Provençal scholar stated in a sermon that the Talmudic tale of R. Bana'ah[12] (who saw the patriarch Abraham reclining in the arms of his wife, Sarah) cannot possibly be taken literally. Although the views of this preacher were rejected, he was not placed under the ban. Another case of a heretical sermon is mentioned by R. Joseph Trani of Constantinople (1568–1639), the *Maharit*.[13] A preacher taught in his sermon that no charges of dishonest dealings can be brought against a scholar, implying that scholars are above the law. The *Maharit* vehemently objects to such an outrageous opinion and declares that the preacher must be silenced, but there is no record that according to the *Maharit* the preacher must be placed under the ban. All this is because no ban may be imposed without prior warning. And even though the prosecuting Rabbi had stated that a rebuke had been administered to our preacher, it all depends on how this was done. Furthermore, the warning to be given before the ban can be imposed must be delivered by a competent Court, not by an individual scholar. Ephraim concludes: 'All this I have brought up in my net in accordance with the inferior grasp of my mind. And may the Lord our God deliver me from error and bring about peace in the midst of the community of Israel and send us the Redeemer.'

From Ephraim's second Responsum we learn the identity of the preacher, who, evidently without consulting the Rabbi who had rebuked him, had sent his own inquiry to Ephraim, asking whether he had acted correctly and requesting Ephraim to support him in his dispute with his accusers. The preacher was none other than Joseph Almosnino (1642–89) of Belgrade,[14] a Rabbi and Kabbalist who had been won over eventually to Shabbateanism.

Ephraim, in his reply, addresses Almosnino in the most complimentary terms, referring to him as a great Talmudic scholar. He acknowledges the receipt of Almosnino's letter containing his complaint, from which we can glean further details of the whole episode. Almosnino's sermon began, in the typical manner of preachers of his time, with a difficulty in the verse in Exodus. Since it was God who was addressing Moses, the verse should not have said 'You will serve *ha-elohim*' but 'You will serve Me'. It was in order to meet this difficulty that Almosnino had suggested that the second *elohim* in the verse refers to the Golden Calf. It is obvious that the word *elohim* can mean, as is evident from other passages in the Torah, either 'God' or 'the gods'. As for the words "at this mountain' (they did not worship the Golden Calf at Sinai), the meaning is that despite the Torah, given at Sinai, prohibiting idolatry, they will still worship the Golden Calf (taking *'al* not as 'at' but as 'in spite of' – 'in spite of this mountain, upon which the Torah will be given, they will still worship the gods'). Almosnino complains that a 'fool' (i.e., the dissenting Rabbi who had turned to Ephraim) had called him an unbeliever who denies the living God, whereupon the members of the congregation insulted him as if he really were a foe of Judaism.

Ephraim first informs Almosnino that he had been approached by the prosecuting Rabbi, who only consulted him on whether such an offence is deserving of the ban. Ephraim had hitherto no knowledge of the Rabbi and it never entered his head that Almosnino was the Rabbi alleged to have committed the offence. He has learned this for the first time from Almosnino's own letter. Ephraim declares that his sole aim is to promote peace, and he provides Almosnino with the gist of his first Responsum.

There now follows an extremely involved discussion on the laws governing the injunction to rebuke sinners; a discussion interesting in itself but one not germane to this study. Ephraim agrees that the Rabbi should have spoken privately to Almosnino. He behaved badly when he reviled him in public. Yet Ephraim cannot help stating quite categorically that he does not accept Almosnino's defence. He proceeds to examine Almosnino's arguments in order to demolish them point by point.

Almosnino, in defence of his position, had quoted a passage from the Zohar.[15] In this passage the Zohar makes a distinction between the Tetragrammaton, used in Scripture only for the God of Israel, and other divine names, such as *elohim*, which refer to God in a more general way, i.e., not specifically to God as the God of Israel. The name *elohim* can even refer, on occasion, to the gods. The Zohar quotes in support the verse: '*Elohim* rules over the nations' (Psalm 47:9), *elohim* embracing the mystery of darkness from which realm Esau obtains his nourishment. After protesting his ignorance of the Kabbalistic mysteries, Ephraim none the less says that he cannot accept Almosnino's understanding of the Zoharic passage. The Zohar does not take the verse to mean that the gods rule over the nations (which would enable Almosnino to argue that if this *elohim* can mean the gods why not the *elohim* in the sermon). The Zohar says nothing of the sort. What the Zohar is saying is that *elohim* in the verse from Psalms is a divine name, but one denoting God's sternness and judgments (*Gevurah*) and it is from this holy name that the demonic forces, symbolized by Esau, derive their nourishment; unlike the Tetragrammaton, 'the glory (*Tiferet*) of Israel', which name denotes only compassion. If, on the other hand, Almosnino simply wants to point out that the name *elohim* sometimes has a 'profane' connotation, for this there was no need for him to quote the Zohar. Every schoolboy knows that the term is used occasionally in Scripture to denote 'judges' or even 'the gods'. What we must never do is interpret verses in which *elohim* refers to God as referring to the gods. Apart from the obvious objection, it will cause people to think that the name can be erased since it is not divine, and it is strictly forbidden to erase a divine name.[16]

In his further support, Almosnino had quoted the work *Ahavat 'Olam*,[17] in which there is an interpretation of a verse containing the word *elohim*. This is the verse:

> Wherefore should the nations say:
> 'Where is their God.'
> But our God (*elohenu*) is in the Heavens.
> Whatever pleaseth Him He does. (Psalm 115:2–3)

The author of *Ahavat 'Olam* renders this as

> and our god is in the Heavens,
> Whatever pleaseth him he does

i.e., this is the continuation of the declaration made by the nations, thus turning a divine name into a profane one. Ephraim states that he is unable to check the reference since the work in question is not in his possession, but if Almosnino has quoted the work correctly then he, Ephraim, must decline to treat the work with everlasting love *(ahavat 'olam)* and this author, too, requires to be pardoned for the offence of which he has been guilty.

Almosnino also quotes the famous sixteenth-century mystic of Safed, Isaac Luria, the *Ari*, who is supposed to have commented on the verse: 'Whoever sacrifices to *elohim* shall be proscribed' (Exodus 22:19). This is usually understood to mean: 'Whoever sacrifices to the gods', as the verse concludes: 'except to the Lord (the Tetragrammaton) alone'. But the *Ari* is said to have understood the verse to mean that it is sinful to dedicate a sacrifice to God by the name *elohim* (i.e., by declaring: 'this is a sacrifice to *elohim*') since this name, unlike the Tetragrammaton, is used occasionally for other gods. Thus the *Ari* understands a 'profane' *elohim* as a sacred one and by the same token we are entitled to do the opposite, as did Almosnino in his sermon.

To this Ephraim replies that here again he is unable to check the source but he is confident that if the *Ari* really made this comment, he only intended it as an interpretation of the second part of the verse. That is to say, the verse means: Whoever sacrifices to the gods will be proscribed, and even when a sacrifice is dedicated to God it should only be done with the use of the Tetragrammaton, not by *elohim*, since this term is used also for the gods. The *Ari* cannot possibly have intended to suggest that the word *elohim* in the verse refers to God.

Ephraim concludes by begging Almosnino to confess to his fault publicly in the synagogue where he had delivered his sermon: 'Through this we shall have the merit of seeing the pleasantness of the face of the Lord our God to serve Him with all our heart and all our soul and we shall have the merit of redemption by our Messiah, speedily in our days.'

We are in the dark about several details of the whole of this controversy. Who was the Rabbi who protested at Almosnino's sermon? Did the episode take place in Almosnino's own community or was he a visiting preacher in another community? Why did both Rabbis turn to Ephraim in particular? Where was Ephraim serving as Rabbi at the time? Since we know that Almosnino had Shabbatean leanings, were these already evident when he delivered his sermon and, if they were, was Ephraim conscious of them when he wrote his Responsa? If they had been and Ephraim was aware of them, it is unlikely in the extreme that he would have been so fulsome in his praise of Almosnino and so anxious to promote peace.

Although, so far as I am aware, none of the historians of the Shabbatean movement refers to these two Responsa of Ephraim, little imagination is required to detect Shabbatean overtones in the whole affair, even though the full details remain obscure. Almosnino, as has been noted, was eventually won over to Shabbateanism. The author of *Ahavat 'Olam*, Algazi, whom Almosnino quotes, was a determined opponent of Shabbateanism, as were Ephraim's grandson, the Hakham Zevi, and the latter's son, Jacob Emden. Moreover, a central theme in Shabbatean theology is the distinction between The Holy Ancient One and The God of Israel,[18] and in our debate references are made to the heresy involved in confusing *elohim* with other gods, and there are explicit references to The God of Israel (*Tifenet Yisnael*). It is also perhaps relevant that Shabbetai Zevi was wont to pronounce the Tetragrammaton.[19]

Another sermon delivered by Almosnino is referred to in Ephraim's Responsa. Almosnino had here interpreted the verse: 'He shall lay his hand upon the head of the burnt-offering' (Leviticus 1:4) as referring to Amalek. Ephraim, in his letter to Almosnino, remarks that he fails to grasp what possible meaning this can have. Is it just possible that there is a veiled hint to Shabbetai Zevi? On all these matters much further research is required. What does seem to emerge from the affair is that at a time when the Jewish world was about to be disrupted by the new Shabbatean heresy, the struggle had already begun and the attempt at enlisting support from established Rabbinic authority had been undertaken by both sides – unless it is all coincidence pure and simple, something hard to believe.

NOTES

1. For R. Ephraim ha-Kohen, see the article in *Encyclopedia Judaica*, Vol. 6, cols. 812–13. He was the maternal grandfather of Zevi Ashkenazi, the Hakham Zevi (1660–1718). In the introduction to the *Sha'ar Efrayim*, the author's son states that his mother, Ephraim's wife, Rachel, died in the year 1685 and that she was a daughter of Rabbi Elijah, grandson of R. Elijah Baal Shem of Chelm. To the latter is attributed in legend the creation of a Golem. See Responsa *Hakham Tzevi*, Amsterdam, 1712, No. 93, where the author, Zevi Ashkenazi, refers to this and speaks of Elijah of Chelm as his 'grandfather' meaning, of course, his ancestor. The first edition of the *Sha'ar Efrayim* was published by the author's son, Aryeh Laib, in Sulzbach in 1698. The edition used for this article is that of Lemberg, 1886, the second edition of the work. Cf. on Ephraim *Entziklopedia le-Toledot Hakhmey Yisrael*, ed. M. Margaliot, Jer., 1946, pp. 222–3. Although Ephraim served as Rabbi in a number of important communities after serving as a member of the Rabbinical Court in his native town of Vilna, he signs his Responsa 'Ephraim of the House of Aaron of Vilna'. Ephraim's Rabbinic positions were in the towns of Velke Mezerici in Moravia, Prague, Vienna, and Ofen (Buda). Zevi Ashkenazi studied with his uncle, Ephraim's son, see the son's introduction, beginning. R. Jacob Emden, Zevi Ashkenazi's son, fiery opponent of Shabbateanism, refers in his Siddur (*Bet Yaakov*, Lemberg, 1904, *shavuot*, p. 306) to his ancestor, R. Ephraim, with whose views on a liturgical question he takes strong issue but refers to as 'my great-grandfather the Gaon, the Hasid, author of *Sha'ar Efrayim*." The two Responsa studied in this article are Nos 64 and 65.
2. *Shabbat* 1 19a, in our texts Rava not R. Pappa, which, no doubt, is a printer's error.
3. *Hagigah* 12a; Ephraim also quotes *Pesahim* 22b.
4. *Sanhedrin* 63a.
5. Exodus Rabbah 3:2.
6. Ephraim refers to the discussion of the problem of divine foreknowledge versus human free will by Maimonides (*Yad, Teshuvah* 5:5) and by other mediaeval thinkers like Abraham Ibn David, see my article 'Divine Foreknowledge and Human Free Will' in *Conservative Judaism*, Vol. XXXIV, No. 1 (September/October, 1980) pp. 4–16.
7. *Yad Teshuvah* 5:5 and R. Abraham Ibn David's stricture *ad loc*.
8. *Orah Hayyim* 141:8.
9. On this subject see Robert Gordis: *The Biblical Text in the Making: A Study of the Kethib-Qere*, New York, 1971.
10. *Yad,Talmud Torah* 6:4 and *Tur, Yoreh De'ah* 334.
11. Responsa *Rashba*, Lemberg, 1811, No. 418 (p. 45b) and the collection of letters by Abba Mari Astruc: *Minhat Kenaot*, ed. Mordecai Laib of Brody, Pressburg, 1838. On the controversy see Joseph Saracheck: *Faith and Reason*, New York, 1935, and D. J. Silver: *Maimonidean Criticism and the Maimonidean Controversy*, Leiden, 1965.
12. *Bava Batra* 58a. *Bava Metzia* in *Minhat Kenaot*, p. 69, is a printer's error.
13. Responsa *Maharit*, Part I, No. 110, Lemberg, 1861. See my *Theology in the Responsa*, London, 1973, pp. 148–50.
14. On Joseph Almosnino, see *Encyclopedia Judaica*, Vol. 2, col. 669. During Almosnino's Rabbinate in Belgrade the community sent a delegation to Shabbetai Zevi, see G. Scholem, *Shabbetai Tzevi*, Tel-Aviv, 1957, Vol. 2, p. 535. Cf. the English translation and enlarged version of Scholem's work: *Sabbatai Sevi* by R. J. Z. Werblowsky, London, 1973, index, *s.v.* 'Almosnino, R. Joseph'.
15. Zohar II, 96a (the page given in the Lemberg edition of the *Sha'ar Efrayim* is 173 and is either a printer's error or refers to a different edition of the Zohar).
16. *Shevuot* 35a–b.
17. By the anti-Shabbatean R. Solomon Algazi (d. *c*. 1683). Almosnino only refers to the work; he does not mention the author by name.

18. See Scholem, op. cit., and Werblowsky, op. cit. On the proliferation of Shabbatean preachers and their extremely unconventional manipulation of Biblical texts in favour of their theology, see H. A. Sosland: *A Guide for Preachers: The OR HA-DARSHANIM of Jacob Zahalon, A Seventeenth-Century Preacher's Manual*, New York, 1987, pp. 39–49.
19. See Scholem's article 'Shabbetai Zevi' in *Encyclopedia Judaica*, Vol. 14, cols. 1219–54. See col. 1235 for Shabbetai signing some of his letters 'I am the Lord your God Shabbetai Zevi.' Cf. col. 1239, that, after Shabbetai's apostasy, his followers searched for and re-interpreted strange *aggadot* in order to discover the apostasy foretold there. The term used is *aggadot shel dofi*. The term used for Almosnino's sermon by his opponent is *derashot shel dofi*. Furthermore, the idea in the sermon that God had foretold that Israel would worship the Golden Calf fits neatly into the Shabbatean theme of the two deities; see Scholem, col. 1240, that for Shabbetai Zevi the first cause is distinct from the God of Israel and compare this with Almosnino's understanding of the *Ari* that the sacrifice must be dedicated to 'the God of Israel'.

—10—

Hasidism and the Dogma of the Decline of the Generations

From the very beginnings of hasidism enormous claims were made by the hasidim on behalf of the great masters, the zaddikim, who were seen as spiritual supermen endowed with the holy spirit, possessing a degree of sanctity unparalleled in many an age and with the power to work extraordinary miracles. The Baal Shem Tov came to be seen as a unique personality who came into the world to teach a new 'way' that amounted to a new revelation of God's truth. (Whether this 'way' is really original is beside the point since the hasidim themselves certainly saw it as such.) Even the *torot* of the later zaddikim were seen as fresh revelations hitherto undisclosed. These claims, as opponents of the movement were not slow to point out, were in flat contradiction to what had become virtually a dogma long before the rise of hasidism: that each successive generation after the revelation at Sinai exhibits further decline. This idea, implied in a number of rabbinic texts, was known to the hasidim, as it was to most learned Jews, but the problem became especially acute once the talmudic rabbis came to be viewed as infallible teachers who constituted the final court of appeal for all matters concerning the Jewish religion.

One of the rabbinic texts (Ber. 20a) refers specifically to miracle-working:

> R. Papa asked Abbaye: 'Why is it that miracles were performed for those of former generations but no miracles are performed for us? It cannot be because they were superior in their studies since in the days of R. Judah all their efforts were concentrated on *Nezikin*, whereas we study all the six orders . . . And yet when R. Judah drew off a single shoe the rains would come whereas we torment ourselves and cry out loudly and not the slightest notice is taken of us.' Abbaye replied: 'The former generations were ready to sacrifice themselves for the sanctification of the

divine name whereas we are not ready to sacrifice ourselves for the sanctification of the divine name.'

The passage concludes with a story illustrating the readiness for self-sacrifice on the part of a saint belonging to an earlier generation.

In this passage the power to work miracles through prayer is made to depend on readiness to sacrifice oneself for the sake of God, it being implied that the talmudic giants, Abbaye and R. Papa, were incapable of this degree of selflessness and hence miracles could not be performed for them. Since Abbaye and R. Papa said this about themselves and their contemporaries, it would seem to follow that it applied *a fortiori* to post-talmudic teachers, and yet the hasidim repeatedly made the claim that the zaddikim could work miracles by the power of their prayers.

Interestingly enough, the decline in the generations is not applied to learning. It is acknowledged that Abbaye and R. Papa are superior in learning to R. Judah. But that is because R. Judah was an *amora*. In another passage (Er. 53a) the learning of the *amora' im* is compared adversely to that of the *tanna 'im*:

> R. Johanan said: 'The heart of the earlier ones was open like the entrance to the Outer Hall of the Temple while the heart of the later ones was open only like the entrance to the Inner hall (which was smaller). But as for us the opening is no bigger than the eye of a fine needle' ... Abayye said: 'We are like a peg in a wall with regard to *gemara'*. Rava said: 'We are like a finger in wax with regard to *sevara'*. R. Ashi said: 'We are like a finger in a pit with regard to forgetfulness'.

However, the passage usually quoted for the doctrine of the progressive decline of the generations is one in which the doctrine is presented in the starkest terms (Shab. 112b): 'R. Zera said that Rava bar Zamina said: "If the early ones were like angels then we are like human beings, but if the early ones were like human beings then we are like donkeys; not like the donkey of R. Hanina b. Dosa or the donkey of R. Pinhas b. Yair but like ordinary donkeys."'[1]

The mediaeval Jewish teachers, refusing to allow themselves to become completely stultified by the dogma of inferiority *vis-à-vis* the talmudic sages, adopted various ploys in defence of their capacity for original thought. The best known of these is to use the famous illustration, going back to John of Salisbury, of the pygmy standing on the shoulders of a giant. Later teachers are, indeed, mere spiritual pygmies in relation to the giants of the past, especially to the talmudic rabbis, but they have the shoulders of the ancients upon which to stand and can therefore possess vistas quite impossible for them had they stood only on their own two feet. Now that they do have the shoulders of the ancients upon which to stand they can, on occasion, see further than the ancients themselves.[2]

For Maimonides the ancient teachers of the Talmud could possess less knowledge of such matters as astronomy than the Gentile scholars of his day possessed.[3] For the Geonim, the talmudic rabbis only had the medical knowledge of their day, so that cures found in the Talmud should not be relied on unless contemporary doctors concur.[4] For all that, very few Jews in the early eighteenth century were prepared to compromise in any way on the view that the talmudic rabbis were infallible in all matters. This was the problem hasidism had to face. Repeatedly one finds in the mitnaggedic polemics the taunt that the hasidim make claims for their zaddikim quite impossible for those in 'our orphaned generations'.[5]

Moreover, the pygmy on the shoulders of the giant idea could not be used as a defence by the hasidim since that would imply something far less than complete originality on the part of the Baal Shem Tov and his 'way',[6] and, in any event, such an idea could not apply to the alleged power to work miracles. The *torot* of the zaddikim could also not be defended in this way since, it was believed, these were in the nature of fresh divine communications, 'the Shekhinah speaking out of the throat of the zaddik'.[7]

In a sense, the kabbalists had to face the same problem. But the Zohar was believed to be the work of R. Simeon b. Yohai, himself a *tanna* and hence one of the ancients. The problem did, however, arise for the post-zoharic kabbalists, that is, those who lived after the Zohar had been 'revealed'. The usual device adopted by the kabbalists was to claim that the mysteries were revealed by Elijah, the link with Moses,[8] so that the 'new' teachings were really the old ones 'received' anew, as the name 'kabbalah' implies. For all that, some kabbalists did admit the possibility of entirely new revelations in spite of the doctrine of spiritual decline. Thus in the work *Berit menuhah*, attributed to Abraham of Granada,[9] it is suggested that the doctrine of spiritual decline does not apply to the very latest mystics. This is because there are cycles in mystical power, just as there are cycles in nature. Just as in the revolution of the great sphere the planets eventually come round full circle, so it is with regard to mystical illumination. Only those mystics who came in between the ancients and contemporaries are inferior because in their day the cycle was in mid-course. 'Nowadays' the cycle has begun again so that it is even possible for a contemporary to have greater illuminations than those teachers who lived in an earlier period but after the cycle had begun.

An early hasidic reply is to be found in the letter by Eleazar, son of R. Elimelekh of Lyzhansk.[10] Eleazar published his father's work *No'am Elimelekh* a year after his father's death. Eleazar's letter in defence of the zaddikim is appended to the work. Eleazar remarks that even the opponents of hasidism admit that the saints of old were gifted with the holy spirit and were able to perform miracles but they argue that such things are impossible for those who live in later generations. This, says Eleazar, is because saints are rarely acknowledged as such by their contemporaries. Even so elevated a holy man as the Ari was the object of criticism in his day, whereas now all acknowledge his great sanctity. This is the meaning of the saying, 'the righteous are greater when dead than in their lifetime' (Hul. 7b). Evidently, a man can only be acknowledged as a saint when he has died. The accolade is only awarded posthumously, the 'canonization' process, so to speak, can only be initiated after the candidate's death. (Needless to say, Eleazar would not have used such an illustration, though the comparison with the procedures of the Catholic Church is not without its own interest.)

In the name of R. Elimelekh it is even said that 'nowadays' it is far easier to attain to the holy spirit than in former times. This is because the Shekhinah, now in exile, is very near. R. Elimelekh quotes the parable given by the Maggid of Rovno (i.e., the Maggid of Mezhirech, residing at that time in Rovno).[11] When the king is in his palace he will only leave it to stay for a time in a splendid mansion where full regal honours can be paid to him. But when the king is on a journey he is prepared to enter the most humble of dwellings provided it is clean and he is offered hospitality.

R. Phinehas of Korets appears to be grappling with our problem. R. Phinehas is reported to have said that Abraham Ibn Ezra is not to be blamed for his rationalism in daring to criticize such ancient teachers as Kalir, held to be a *tanna*.[12] The *tanna'im*, who lived soon after the destruction of the Temple, were still able to avail themselves of the tremendous illuminations that proceeded from the holy place, even though these illuminations had begun to wane in their day. The mediaeval teachers like Ibn Ezra could not avail themselves of the Temple illuminations because in their day these had waned completely. But contemporary zaddikim, though even more distant from the Temple period, are very close to the dawning light of the Messianic Age. Distant in time and hence 'late' in relation to the illuminations of the past, they are very near and hence 'early' to the even greater illuminations of the future. One would have to be blind, remarks R. Phinehas, not to see now the dawning light of the messiah.

These ideas became current in hasidic circles. The reputed teachings of the hasidic master Uri of Strelisk (d. 1826) were published under the title of *Imrei kodesh*.[13] Here the editor's introduction deals with our problem. We are not supplied with the editor's name but, since he remarks that it is over 130 years since Uri died, it is obvious that he is writing around 1956. It is, consequently, a little dubious to use what he says for our purpose. Yet it is not irrelevant for the consideration of how our problem is treated in the hasidic tradition. After referring to the talmudic passages about the decline of the generations, this author quotes the passage from the *Berit menuhah* (he italicizes the words 'the later sages *are greater than the earlier ones*') and the passage from Phinehas of Korets. He concludes:

> Since this is so it is no cause for surprise that we see, after the darkness which prevailed in the middle ages, when the light was concealed and every vision blocked, all generations become progressively weaker, that the Lord should have illumined our way, that a star should have arisen in Jacob whose light has extended over all the earth, namely, Israel's illumination and holy one, the Baal Shem Tov, may his merits shield us. He is the man, the great lion of the supernal forest. He ascended the heights to become the disciple of Ahijah the Shilonite who had heard the Torah from Moses our teacher himself, on whom be peace. After all these generations the wheel has come full circle so that they are able to draw down the holy spirit from the Source and the word of the Lord has been spread abroad.[14]

Similarly relying on hasidic traditions are the remarks of Israel Berger in the introduction of his *Eser orot*, a collection of tales of the zaddikim including many miracle tales.[15] Fully aware of opposition even on the part of faithful Jews to the cult of the zaddik, Berger feels obliged to deal with four objections to the institutions: (*a*) Where do we find in the classical sources of Judaism that the saints can change the laws of nature in such radical ways as the zaddikim are said to be able to do? (*b*) Even if such things were possible for the ancients, how can they be possible nowadays, in view of the talmudic statements about the decline of the generations? (*c*) What basis is there for the strange methods of biblical exegesis employed by the zaddikim? (*d*) How can the zaddikim enjoy supernatural powers since some of them are unlearned in the Talmud and the Codes?

Berger's replies to questions (*c*) and (*d*), interesting in themselves, are not strictly relevant to our inquiry. In reply to the first objection, Berger has no difficulty in adducing a list of miracle tales in the Talmud and other sources where the laws of nature are set at naught by the powers of the saint. In reply to the second question, that is, to our problem, Berger advances the following arguments, obviously relying on what his predecessors have said.

First, he argues, the *amora'im* who spoke of the decline of the generations were not making any kind of categorical statement but were only thinking, in their humility, of themselves. All they were saying was that they themselves were inferior to the ancients, not that there is a dogma that all generations are necessarily inferior to early ones. Second, even if their statements applied to their whole generation, there could still be exceptions. Third, Berger quotes Abraham of Granada. Once the wheel has come full circle there is a fresh outburst of spiritual power. Fourth, in an age of spiritual darkness God sends down to earth a lofty soul that has previously been on earth in the time of the ancients. Thus the souls of the zaddikim do not belong to the generations in decline but to the generations in which they lived in their previous incarnation.

In every reformist or revisionist movement there is bound to be tension between the need for continuity and the need for originality, between the claims of the past and those of the present and future, between what the founding fathers said when they were alive and what it is imagined they would say were they to come back to earth to face the new situation. For hasidism the tensions were aggravated by the doctrine of the decline of the generations. In their attempted solutions they, too, tried to have their cake and eat it. All the attempted solutions are really an attempt to abolish the time sequence altogether. But then, on the hasidic view, the zaddikim can reach the world that is beyond time. In such a world it is not impossible to have one's cake and eat it.

NOTES

1. For the donkey of R. Phinehas see Hul. 7*a*–*b*; for the donkey of R. Hanina b. Dosa see *Avot deRabbi Natan*, ed. S. Schechter [1887] (New York, 1967), ch. 8, 38. Both R. Phinehas and R. Hanina are renowned in the rabbinic literature as saints and are often used as rabbinic models for the hasidic zaddik. In the Hul. narrative R. Phinehas (who is

described in the narrative as a 'zaddik') has the miraculous power to cause a river to part and his efforts are compared to those of Moses at the Sea of Reeds: The Zoharic statement (Zohar 3:2a) on the difference with regard to mystical knowledge between the earlier and later generations is obviously an amplification of the talmudic statement.
2. For the literature on the pygmy and the giant motif in Jewish thought see Jacob Haberman, *Maimonides and Aquinas* (New York 1979), 203–5.
3. *Guide*, iii. 14–end.
4. See the Geonic comments on Git. 68 f. quoted in B. M. Lewin, *Otsar hage'onim* (13 vols.; Haifa–Jerusalem, 1928–62), vol. on *Gittin* (1941), 152 f.
5. See Mordecai Wilensky, *Hasidim umitnaggedim* (2 vols; Jerusalem, 1970), index, s.v. *mofetim*, and esp. the polemics of Israel Loebel, *Sefer vikuah* [Warsaw, 1798], repr. in Wilensky, *Hasidim umitnaggedim*, ii. 320–2. Even if it be admitted, says this author, that the hasidic zaddikim do perform miracles they do so by means of the black art (*kishuf*) as did (in veiled reference) Jesus, Muhammad, and Shabbetai Zevi!
6. In every version of hasidism, the Baal Shem Tov's complete originality is stressed. See e.g. the well-known observation of the Baal Shem Tov's grandson Moses Hayyim Ephraim of Sudylkow in his *Degel mahaneh Efrayim* [1808] (Jerusalem, 1963), on Exod. 14: 8, 100–1. The *Targum* renders *beyad ramah* as *beresh gelei*. The children of Israel 'go out' of the Exile through the revelation of the Zohar–*beresh* stands for R. Shimon ben Yohai, *gelei* stands for the new 'revelation'. The word *beresh* also stands for R. Israel Baal Shem. The maskilim poured scorn on the hasidic glorification of the Baal Shem Tov; see e.g. Joseph Perl, *Megaleh temirin* (Vienna, 1819), 1, who quotes in this connection the famous saying: 'The word of the Lord was with the Baal Shem and whatsoever he decreed came to pass. He was unique. Of the earlier ones none arose like unto him and after him who can arise upon earth.' Perl quotes this derogatorily as the introduction to the Kopys ed. of *Shivhei haBesht* but the source is, in fact, *Peri ha'arets* of R. Menahem Mendel of Vitebsk [Kopys, 1814] (Jerusalem, 1965), 60, and the startling saying should be seen in context. A follower had asked R. Menahem Mendel to pray for him that he should be blessed with a child. In his humility, Menahem Mendel observes that he cannot compare in any way with the Baal Shem Tov and *in this* the Baal Shem Tov was unique. However, it is not only Perl who takes the saying out of context but all the subsequent hasidic hagiographers who quote the saying.
7. See Rivka Schatz-Uffenheimer, *Hahasidut kemistikah* (Jerusalem, 1968), 108, 118–19.
8. See Gershom G. Scholem, *On the Kabbalah and its Symbolism* (London, 1965), 19–21, on *gilui Ehyahu* as a device used by the mystics to justify their originality while preserving their links with the Jewish tradition.
9. Abraham of Granada, *Berit menuhah* [Amsterdam, 1648] (Warsaw, 1864), 24a. Cf. Zohar I: 118a 'The Holy One, blessed be He, does not desire that so much be revealed to the world, but when the days of the Messiah are near at hand, even children will discover the secrets of wisdom.'
10. *No'am Elimelekh* [Lemberg, 1788], ed. G. Nigal (2 vols; Jerusalem, 1978), ii. 593–602.
11. Ibid. i. 109–10, on Gen. 37:1. As Nigal notes, the parable is found in the writings of the Maggid, *Maggid devanav leYa'akov* [Korets, 1784], ed. Rivka Schatz-Uffenheimer (Jerusalem, 1976), no. 49, p. 70.
12. *Midrash Pinhas*, [Warsaw, 1876]. Repr. in *Sefarim kedoshim migedolei talmidei Ba'al Shem Tov* (35 + 3 vols; Brooklyn, NY, 1981–86), i, no. 7, p. 82.
13. *Or olam: Sefen imrei kodesh hashalem* (Jerusalem, 1961), ch. 1 (no pagination, but at beginning of the work).
14. The reference to Ahijah as the mystical mentor of the Baal Shem Tov occurs in the first hasidic work to be printed, Jacob Joseph of Polonnoye, *Toledot Ya'akov Yosef* Korets, 1780] (Jerusalem, 1966). The *Toledot* (on 'Balak', 156a) observes: 'Ahijah received (*kibel*) from Moses our Teacher and he was one of those who came out of Egypt and afterwards from the Court of David and he was the mentor of Elijah and of my master.' This is obviously based on the chain of tradition as portrayed in the introd. to M. Maimonides, *Mishneh torah*, but Maimonides only uses the term *kibel* when speaking of Ahijah receiving from David. In relation to Ahijah and Moses he uses the term *shama*, 'he heard it'. Possibly, R. Jacob Joseph was quoting from memory. In any event the purpose is clear. The Baal Shem Tov's teacher Ahijah is the link, skipping the generations of the usual chain of tradition, with Moses. Louis Ginzberg's suggestion (*Jewish Encyclopedia*, 12 vols,

Hasidism and the Dogma of the Decline of the Generations 133

New York, 1901–06, ii. 383–6, s.v. 'Ba'al Shem Tov, Israel B. Eliezer') that Ahijah features as the mentor of the Baal Shem Tov because the prophet, at the bidding of God, brought about the breach between the Davidic line and Jeroboam, as the Baal Shem Tov broke with the rabbinic tradition, is extremely unlikely. The hasidim would never have implied that the Baal Shem Tov can be compared to Jeroboam.

15. I. Berger, *Eser onot* [Piotrkow, 1907] (Warsaw, 1913), 4–15. Berger's remarks are quoted verbatim in Zevi Moskovitch, *Ma'aseh Nehemiah* (Jerusalem, 1956), 5. 13, 27–31. Cf. the opening passage in R. Shneur Zalman of Lyady, *Likutei amosim: Tanya* [Slavuta, 1796; Vilna, 1900], bilingual ed. trans. N. Mindel, N. Mangel, Z. Posner, and J. I. Schochet (London, 1973), 5a–b on the statement by Rabbah in the Talmud (Ber. 61b) that he was only an average man (*beinoni*), not even a zaddik. The *Tanya* solves the problem by elevating the *beinoni* to an extraordinary stage of spiritual attainment.

—11—

The Relevance and Irrelevance of Hasidism

The Hasidic movement has now been on the Jewish scene for over two hundred years, during which period it has succeeded in capturing hundreds of thousands of Jewish souls. Over a hundred years ago the historian Heinrich Graetz, incorrigibly biased against Hasidism and, for that matter, against any expression of kabbalistic fervour, viewed the rapid growth of the movement in his day with the kind of alarm of which only a thoroughgoing, German, Jewish, nineteenth-century rationalist was capable. Graetz concludes his chapter on Hasidism with these words:

> All efforts made to suppress the Chassidim were in vain, because in a measure they represented a just principle, that of opposing the excesses of Talmudism. Before the end of the eighteenth century they had increased to 100,000 souls. At the present day they rule in congregations where they were formerly persecuted, and they are spreading on all sides.[1]

Hasidism has, indeed, 'spread on all sides'. In the present century, despite the inevitable decline which attends every mass movement of rebellion once it has emerged victorious, and despite the appalling loss of the great centres of Hasidic life through the Holocaust, there has been a revival both of Hasidism itself and of keen interest on the part of sympathetic onlookers and fellow travellers. In New York and other cities in the United States, in the Stamford Hill district of London, and above all in the state of Israel, the old ideas, even the old interdynastic feuds, flourish with renewed vigour. The fires of Hasidic *hitlahavut* ('burning enthusiasm'), fanned by a curious mixture of winds, blithe disregard for worldly opinion, and recourse to high-powered Western business techniques and advertising, still provide warmth and illumination.

The mystic joy of Hasidism is infectious. An American father, whose son asked to be taken to see the Sotmarer Hasidim dancing in the streets on Simhat Torah, is said to have replied: 'OK. But don't forget, you are only going along to watch!' The writings of Heschel and Buber – whether or not the latter's interpretation of Hasidism is valid is another matter – have made Hasidism palatable and attractive for sophisticated Jews and non-Jews alike. The researches of Dubnow and the Scholem school have made the study of Hasidism scholarly respectable.

All of this presents a challenge to the contemporary Jew who is neither Hasid nor Mitnagged, neither friend nor foe of the movement, or, better, who is both friend and foe, reluctant to let his admiration still the questionings of his mind and equally reluctant to allow his intellectual misgivings to dampen the ardour of his heart. The question such a Jew asks himself is, How much of Hasidism can he swallow without suffering mental and spiritual indigestion? He cannot bring himself to pronounce either an unqualified yes or an unqualified no. At the most he finds himself able to give only 'a definite maybe'. I am thinking of a Jew loyal to his Judaism who at the same time feels bound to accept the admittedly somewhat nebulous yet very real categories of modern thought; in short, to get down to the personal, a Jew like you and me. Which aspects of Hasidic thought can we accept without being intellectually dishonest? How much of Hasidic life can we adopt as our own without our Jewish existence becoming disjointed and without an unending battle in the recesses of our psyche? And which criteria are to be utilized in our quest? It is to these questions that this lecture addresses itself.

First, let us examine those norms of Hasidic life which most of us find extremely difficult to accept and which, consequently, we reject totally as having no relevance for us. Prominent among these is the doctrine of the zaddik, the holy man who is not so much a teacher of the Torah, like the traditional rabbi, but more of a guru-type spiritual guide and mentor. Well known is the saying of a disciple of the Meseritcher Maggid, that he did not journey to the Maggid to learn Torah from him but in order to see how the master tied his shoelaces. It would be rash, let it be said at once, to reject the doctrine solely on the ground that it is un-Jewish, having come into Hasidism under the influence of other faiths (for which view, incidentally, a very good case can be made out). The idea of a 'normative Judaism', a pure essence of the religion from which later accretions can easily be removed once they have been detected, is a very dubious one. Even if, as seems likely, the doctrine of zaddikism did come into Hasidism from without, that would not in itself be sufficient reason for its rejection. If otherwise acceptable, it could be said, like many other Jewish institutions, to have become Jewish by adoption and assimilation.

The doctrine is, however, unacceptable because, for many of us, it is based on beliefs that we do not hold to be true. The occult nature of the doctrine is frequently overlooked, but it can readily be discerned if one takes the trouble to scrutinize any standard account of the institution, say, R. Elimelech of Lizensk's great paean to the zaddik, the *Noam Elimelekh*. The zaddik is said to have powers over life and death.[2] Even when God has decreed that a certain person should die, the zaddik's prayer can succeed in setting aside the evil decree.[3] It is extremely rare, though not impossible, for a man to become a zaddik through his own efforts in subduing his instincts and rising to God.[4] Normally there are only three ways in which a man becomes a zaddik: his ancestors may have been zaddikim, and he inherits his charismatic gifts from them; he may have been named after a famous zaddik, and this naming has a magical effect on his character; or he may have been a zaddik in a previous existence, so that he simply takes up in this life where he left off in the other.[5] Furthermore, the ability of the zaddik to give adequate spiritual advice depends on his knowledge of the previous existences enjoyed by his followers. He alone, because the mysteries of the universe have been revealed to him, knows for which purposes his followers have been sent down once again into this lowly world. Only he is aware of which matters they are called upon to rectify because of their failures in their previous lives.[6] The zaddik is not only called God's 'brother' but also God's "redeemer'.[7] To insult the zaddik or speak ill of him is equivalent to speaking evil of God Himself.[8]

The true Hasid believes his rebbe to be a spiritual superman endowed from birth with superhuman qualities. Having this belief, the Hasid is duty bound to accept all the rebbe's edicts as those of an infallible oracle. In a popular Hasidic saying, the word *mahatzit* is noted as having five Hebrew letters, the letter *tzaddi*, representing the zaddik, being in the middle. The two letters on either side of the *tzaddi–het* and *yod*–form the word *hai* ('life'), while the letters at either extreme of the word–*mem* and *tav*–form the word *met* ('dead'). Only those in close proximity to the zaddik are spiritually alive. Those remote from the zaddik suffer spiritual death. They are lifeless corpses lacking all true vitality. In the name of Judaism itself, those who cannot accept this whole theological doctrine must not surrender individual searching for truth and authenticity. Masters and guides we all need, but these are harder to find than Hasidism will admit, and even when found they can fail us and let us down, so that there is no ultimate substitute for personal evaluation and decision. R. Israel Salanter put it neatly when he said that both the Hasidim and the Mitnaggedim were in error. The Mitnaggedim were mistaken in thinking that they did not need a rebbe. The Hasidim were mistaken in thinking that they had a rebbe.

It is not only the doctrine of zaddikism that is off-putting. The whole kabbalistic scheme upon which Hasidism is founded must be accepted in its totality if one aspires to be a Hasid. No Hasid can remain such if he denies any of the following propositions: that the Zohar is a holy book composed under divine inspiration by the second-century teacher R. Simeon b. Yohai; that the Lurianic Kabbalah was imparted to the Ari by the prophet Elijah; that the Sefirotic tree is an accurate picture of how the hidden God becomes manifest in His creation and that there really is a female aspect of the Deity personalized as the Shekhinah or the Matrona; that the letters of the Hebrew alphabet are not mere symbols but are the representation on earth of those spiritual forces on high by means of which God brought the world into being and through which He now sustains it; and that reflection on these letters sends the most powerful impulses heavenwards and thus promotes harmony in the Sefirotic realm so that the divine grace may flow unimpeded throughout all creation. The Hasid must believe in metempsychosis (gilgul); in the power of Samael and Lilith and their demonic hosts to do harm to humans; in dybbukim and mazikim; in amulets and sacred relics and other superstitions, not, of course, considered as such by the Hasid himself. This is to say nothing of the obscurantism displayed by many of the Hasidic masters in their hostility to secular learning, so that 'enlightenment' is seen as a tool of the devil and anyone who dares to question the Kabbalah is seen as an *epikoros*.

There is no doubt at all that the kabbalistic system in all its complexity is a work of extraordinary genius, but those of us who are students of the subject without being confirmed adepts see it as a mighty product of the human mind, a series of powerful meditations and bold speculations, with many profound insights, to be sure, and yet hardly as a corpus of divinely revealed truth regarding the Deity in His relation to the world. Modern biblical and rabbinic scholarship, showing as it does the developing nature of even these classical sources of Judaism, has made it impossible to view revelation itself in any simple terms of a divine communicator and passive recipients; *a fortiori* we cannot in honesty accept the Kabbalah and the Hasidism based upon it as God's direct communication to His privileged saints.

Beside these weighty objections to the total acceptance of Hasidic doctrine, questions regarding the external forms of Hasidic life and their adoption pale into insignificance. Yet these, too, form a barrier which moderns cannot cross. How many of us can follow the regimen of Hasidic life–the special Hasidic garb, the kapote, streimel, gartle, and peot; the prayers with violent gestures; the frequent ablutions in the mikvah; the qvittel and pidyon;[9] the singing and dancing and partaking of alcohol and tobacco, all as techniques for the attainment of *devekut*? Yet all of these are essentials if Hasidism is to be followed in earnest rather than admired from afar because of its 'relevance'.

For all that, Hasidism is far more than a pleasant anachronism, and its masters are more than cosmic talkers spouting holy nonsense. When the selective process is allowed to operate, the relevance of Hasidism to contemporary religious life does become apparent. Allowing for the exceptions, the Hasidim were, and still are, highly gifted practitioners of the art of religion, pursuing, with the exercise of the full creative imagination and with a heart-warming naïveté masking a mature sophistication, their aim of bringing God down to man and encouraging man to rise on the rungs of the ancient ladder linking heaven and earth. Hasidic panentheism,[10] with its stress that all is in God, that He is 'closer than breathing and nearer than hands and feet', is a powerful antidote to reductionism in religion. Hasidism speaks clearly to affirm that for religion to be relevant it must be seen as *sui generis,* an ultimate end, not a means to another end, be that end family harmony, the avoidance of juvenile delinquency, the promotion of ethical conduct, the furtherance of world peace, or the survival of the Jewish people–all of them supremely worthy ends, but for the truly religious, by-products of the ultimate end, part of that totality we haltingly call the worship of God. Dean Inge has remarked with justice that the breakdown of authoritarian religion frequently results among people deeply committed to a religious outlook in an approach that stresses religious experience, which goes a long way towards explaining the lure of mysticism – religion in its most intense form, as this has been defined– for a generation bored with religious formalism and disillusioned with behavioristic patterns and passive obedience as substitutes for spontaneity and a fresh response to the call of the divine.

Here is the place to take issue with Buber's neo-Hasidism. As Gershom Scholem[11] and Rivkah Schatz-Uffenheimer[12] have noted, Buber's reinterpretation of Hasidism in terms of his *I and Thou* may be a valid philosophy in its own right, but it is emphatically not Hasidism. The marvellous Hasidic tales are related in their Buberist version so as to teach that man meets God in his use of God's world; in his appreciation of beauty, his love of truth, his meeting in dialogue with his fellows; at his table, in his work, even in his bedroom, man, according to Buber's understanding of Hasidism, meets his God. In fact, every version of Hasidism teaches the exact opposite. It is true that on the whole Hasidism is opposed to asceticism. The 'holy sparks' in the material universe can only be reclaimed through the Hasid's use of the world in a spirit of consecration. But for the Hasid the ultimate aim is 'self-annihilation' (*bittul ha-yesh*), a mystic state in which the physical universe dissolves and only the divine vitality is seen as pervading all. Contra Buber and Israel Zangwill,[13] the Baal Shem Tov, the founder of Hasidism, did not gaze with fond appreciation at pretty girls. If the legends are to be believed, when he was inadvertently confronted with a beautiful woman, he turned his gaze away from her and concluded that God had sent him this sight so that he would reflect on the source of the woman's beauty on high. As a result of this reflection he would be led on to forget all about the woman and the world she inhabited, all about his own ego and its concentration on the particular things in creation, to lose himself in his apprehension of the divine unity which alone enjoys ultimate existence and which constitutes the only true reality.

Buber's discovery of the I–Thou relationship as a basic feature of human existence is one of the most important contributions made to human thought in the twentieth century. Yet it has tended to eclipse that other aspect of the human situation, at least as important if not more important, in which the 'I' is abandoned in wondrous contemplation of the 'Thou'. The great artists of mankind – the painters, sculptors, and poets; the scientists and philosophers; the musicians and statesmen – have tended to speak less in terms of meeting their subject than of losing themselves in their subject. The artists of the religious life have similarly seen in their highest flights – the more powerful in that they are so rare – the total surrender of the 'I' to the 'Thou' in whom all things move and have their being. Unless we are prepared to adopt the pedestrian view that Judaism is intrinsically hostile to mysticism, Hasidism can act as a useful corrective to an earthly, entirely this-worldly religion with no sense of a beyond and no apprehension of the infinite.

In his delightful autobiography, Jacob Mazeh (1859–1924), Chief Rabbi of Moscow, tells of his boyhood days in Russia. Mazeh came from a non-Hasidic family, but his grandfather hired a Hasidic teacher to instruct him in Hebrew. When the time came for Mazeh to deliver his bar mitzvah *derashah* in the synagogue, he was afflicted with such a bad attack of nerves as to render him speechless. His Hasidic teacher rebuked him: 'Oy, you Mitnaggedim! You are so scared of people that you suffer agonies of fright when called upon to speak in public. But we Hasidim, who hold fast to the idea of *bittul ha-yesh,* know that there is really no public of whom to be frightened.' The rebuke enabled the boy to conquer his shyness, and he eventually became an outstanding orator. This brave defiance of the world, this total indifference to both praise and blame (an idea which the Baal Shem Tov is said to have derived from Bahya ibn Pakuda, who, in turn, had it from the Sufis), can result in escapism and in lack of concern for the well-being of others. Dubnow[14] argues in fact that because of this doctrine Hasidism is a religious outlook that is bound to turn away from the ethical, bound to result, if Kierkegaardian terms are used, in a conflict between 'ethical man' and the 'knight of faith' – overlooking the obvious that few religious movements have emphasized as much as Hasidism that God is to be found in a caring attitude for others. Among its best exponents, the doctrine of *bittul ha-yesh* may have resulted at times in a wild attitude of self-abandonment, but it never encouraged an irresponsible approach to the needs of the community and of other individuals.

So far as Jewish studies are concerned, the study of Hasidism is as relevant as the study of any other manifestation of the Jewish spirit. Scholem, Tishby, B. Dinur, J. G. Weiss, Schatz-Uffenheimer, and others have shown how objective methods of scholarly investigation can be effectively applied to the study of Hasidism so that a new field of inquiry has been added to the curriculum of Jewish studies. Even for the non professional reader there is a vast amount of fascinating material, some of it now available in English, in which the enormous variety of Hasidic thought provides ample opportunities for intellectual and emotional response. There are the profound probings of Habad into what can and what cannot be said of God. There is the challenge of Kotzk, recently described by Heschel, very harsh and uncompromising in its critique of human vanity, but counterbalancing by its very extremism any notion of religion as a palliative. There is the infuriating anti-Zionism and narrowness of the Sotmarer Rebbe,[15] but expressed in a magnificent, easy-flowing rabbinic Hebrew style that is a pleasure to read. There is the attempt of R. Arele Roth[16] to storm the heavens, and there is the 'existentialist' thought of R. Nahman of Bratzlav, considered by the late J. G. Weiss to be the most original Jewish thinker of the past few centuries.[17] Few religious thinkers of any period have been as daring in their religious determinism as R. Mordecai Joseph of Izbica.[18] There are the deep speculations in a proper philosophical spirit of the Zanzer, the Koznitzer Maggid, R. Solomon of Radomsk, and R. Zadok of Lublin.[19] Nowhere is the spiritual meaning of the Kabbalah expressed with such precision and admirable clarity as in the writings of R. Baruch of Kossov.[20]

Even the Hasidic tales, some of them complete rubbish and some offensive,[21] have a charm unequalled in Jewish literature, especially when told by consummate masters of the art[22] and retold in the spirit of the original by Buber,[23] Louis I. Newman,[24] Elie Wiesel,[25] and, best of all, Jiri Langer.[26] The majority of these tales are not simply exercises in hagiography, nor are they solely the stuff out of which Jewish folklorists can construct the material for their researches. The tales are shot through with a sense of religious wonder tied to a strong ethical and pyschological motivation in which the good are rewarded, the swindlers meet their downfall, the unbelievers are discomfited, the simplehearted triumph over the casuists, the wicked are seen to have their good points, and the verse vindicated which says that there is none righteous upon the earth who doeth only good and sinneth not.

To sum up. There is a darker side to Hasidism, notwithstanding the panegyrics of some uncritical modern writers who know Hasidism only from without and see it through rose-coloured spectacles. I like the story of the Catholic archbishop who preached an eloquent sermon on the joys of marriage. Two poor charladies were discussing the sermon. 'What a lovely sermon,' said one. 'Yes,' said the other, 'but I wish I knew as little about it as he does.' If we are aware of Hasidic life as it is actually lived we cannot fail to come to the conclusion that a good deal of it is irrelevant to the religious outlook of the modern Jew. A good deal of it, but certainly not all of it. Enough remains, as we have tried to suggest, to make its study and even, though to a lesser extent, its practice entirely relevant. Where does one draw the line? To this I have no answer, and even if I had, what is an answer for me would not necessarily be the answer for you. We can and should observe, however, that the problem of relevance and discrimination applies, for the critical mind, to the whole range of Jewish belief and observance. It is the old dilemma which the talmudic rabbis[27] speak of as breaking the jar while retaining the wine. Many would declare such a task to be impossible. Others, among whom I include myself, would note instead that the precious wine of Judaism has not lost any of its fragrance through being poured from one container into another. As many of us see it, the jar containing the wine of Hasidism is severely cracked, so much so that the wine is in real danger of seeping away. Even if some of the precious liquid is lost in the process, much of it can still be saved if newer and stronger containers are made ready to receive it.

NOTES

1. *History of the Jews* (Philadelphia, 1946), vol. 5, p. 394.
2. *Noam Elimelekh* (various editions) *va-erah*, to Exodus 6:13, states that when the zaddik promises his followers that a government official will do as they wish him to do, that official has no option but to do so.
3. Ibid., *Likkutey Shoshanim* to Song of Songs 1:9.
4. Ibid., *emor* to Leviticus 21:1.
5. Ibid., *be-midbar* to Numbers 1:2.
6. Ibid., *naso* to Numbers 4:22.
7. Ibid., *be-har* to Leviticus 25:25.
8. Ibid., *shelah* to Numbers 15:31.
9. The only systematic study of Hasidic practices is A. Wertheim, *Halakho ve-Halikhot ba-Hasidut* (Jerusalem, 1960).
10. *Panentheism* (all is *in* God) is a far more suitable term for the Hasidic doctrine than *pantheism* (all is God). See my study of R. Aaron of Starosselje: *Seeker of Unity*(New York, 1966), index, *s.v.* panentheism.
11. 'Martin Buber's Interpretation of Hasidism', in *The Messianic Idea in Judaism* (New York, 1971), pp. 227–50.
12. 'Man's Relation to God and World in Buber's Rendering of the Hasidic Teaching', in *The Philosophy of Martin Buber*, ed. Paul A. Schilpp and Maurice Friedman (La Salle, Ill., 1967), pp. 403–34.
13. 'The Master of the Name', in *Dreamers of the Ghetto* (Philadelphia, 1943), pp. 221–88.
14. *Toledot ha-Hasidut* (Tel-Aviv, 1967), pp. 349–54.
15. E.g., his *Va-Yoel Mosheh* (New York, n.d.).

16. E.g., his *Shomner Emunim* (Jerusalem, 1964).
17. *Mehkarim he-Hasidut Bratzlav* (Jerusalem, 1974) is a fine collection of J. G. Weiss's Hebrew essays on R. Nahman.
18. See J. G. Weiss, 'The Religious Determinism of Joseph Mordecai of Izbica' (Hebrew), in the Yitzhak F. Baer jubilee volume (Jerusalem, 1960), pp. 447–53.
19. The Zanzer: *Divrey Hayyim* (New York, 1962); the Koznitzer: *Avodat Yisrael* (Lemberg, 1858); the Radomsker: *Tiferet Shelomo* (Jerusalem, 1966); R. Zadok of Lublin: *Divrey Soferim* (Benai Berak, 1967), *Peri Tzaddik* (Lublin, 1901), *Yisrael Kedoshim* (New York, 1951), and other works.
20. Especially in his *Amud ha-Avodah* (Tchernowitz, 1863).
21. These have been the target of the anti-Hasidic Haskalah, e.g., in Joseph Perl's *Megalleh Temirin* (Lemberg, 1864).
22. E.g., by Berger, *Zekhut Yisrael* (Jerusalem, 1973); Kamelhaar, *Dor Deah* (Jerusalem, 1960); Ehrmann, *Devarim Arevim* (Jerusalem, 1973).
23. *Tales of the Hasidim* (New York, 1948) and his novel *For the Sake of Heaven* (New York, 1953).
24. *The Hasidic Anthology* (New York, 1944).
25. *Souls on Fire* (London, 1972).
26. *Nine Gates* (London, 1961).
27. Babylonian Talmud, *Bava Batra* 16a.

—12—

Praying for the Downfall of the Wicked

Religious individuals who believe in the efficacy of petitionary prayer and in blessings and curses, whatever their theological understanding of the phenomena, are faced with a severe ethical problem. If it is believed that prayers and curses directed against the wicked can actually bring about their downfall, is it ethically correct to employ methods through which God is invoked to do harm to His creatures? On the one hand, the existence of the wicked is contrary to God's ultimate plan so that such prayers and curses may be seen as acts of piety in that they express a desire for His will to be done. But, on the other hand, God is said to wait patiently, as it were, for the wicked to turn from evil. Does this not suggest that the more correct form of prayer is for the wicked to abandon their evil ways and live? Moreover, for good men to pray to God to harm the wicked appears to be an exercise in self-righteousness. The very prayer or curse bears the unworthy implication that the one who utters it is confident that he is on God's side and belongs in the ranks of the virtuous. Arrogance is highly objectionable, from the religious as well as from the ethical point of view, and what is more arrogant than an implied protestation to God Himself of the worshipper's moral superiority? The sources considered in this essay discuss this question.

The *locus classicus* for the discussion is the well-known Talmudic story of Beruriah, wife of R. Meir.[1] There were certain *baryone*[2] in R. Meir's vicinity who used to vex him and in response he prayed that they should die.[3] On hearing this prayer Beruriah pointed out to her husband that, undoubtedly, his action was justified by him on the basis of the verse: 'Let *hattaim* cease' (Psalm 104:35). But, Beruriah argued, the verse does not say: 'Let sinners (*hoteim*) cease' but: 'Let *hataim* ('sins', reading the word without a *dagesh* in the *tet*) cease'. Furthermore, she argued, the verse goes on to say: 'and let the wicked be no more', meaning that when sins have ceased there will no longer be any wicked men. As a consequence, Beruriah suggested to her husband that he should pray that the sinners repent and then they will no longer be wicked. The story concludes that R. Meir acted on Beruriah's advice and the *baryone* did repent.[4]

In the Talmudic passage[5] immediately preceding the story of Beruriah and the *baryone,* the verse 'Let the *hattaim* cease' is quoted by R. Judah son of R. Simeon ben Pazzi. This teacher notes that the verse ends with "Hallelujah", the first reference in the book of Psalms to that expression, from which it is concluded that while David composed many Psalms without exclaiming 'Hallelujah' he felt obliged to exclaim it once he had sung of the downfall of the wicked. This appears to be in direct contradiction to the Beruriah story and yet the editors of the Talmud have placed the two passages in juxtaposition. It might be replied that the editors were not bothered by contradictions and that their arrangement of the material depends solely on association of theme. However, such an explanation was not acceptable to the traditional commentators who suggested that the editors may have intended to teach that even if it is wrong to pray for the downfall of the wicked it is still right to praise God when their downfall is witnessed. Perhaps, too, the editors wished to make a distinction between those wicked men who are beyond repentance and those, like the *baryone,* who are not thoroughly bad and who can be saved from death by their repentance. It is also plausible to conjecture that the editors, by supplying the Beruriah story *after* the comment of R. Judah, intend to demonstrate that the subject is a complicated one, with arguments on both sides, but that the preferred attitude is that adopted by Beruriah.

Another Talmudic passage[6] is relevant to the discussion. Here it is first stated that an indication is available of the moment of God's wrath, when it is propitious to utter a curse. This moment can be determined by observing the changes in the comb of a cox. A certain *Min* (heretic) who lived in the neighbourhood of R. Joshua ben Levi used to vex this teacher with arguments from Scriptural verses.[7] One day R. Joshua ben Levi took a cock, placed it between the legs of his bed and watched it carefully in order to witness the change that indicated the moment of God's anger so that he could curse effectively the presumptuous heretic. When the moment came, R. Joshua ben Levi had fallen asleep. On awakening, he concluded that it is not right to curse heretics since it is written: 'His tender mercies are over all His works' (Psalms 145:9) and it is also written: 'To punish is also not good for the righteous' (Proverbs 17:26). It is, however, possible that all that is meant to be implied by this story is the inadvisability of attempting to coerce God by the magical means R. Joshua ben Levi had intended to employ. It is the attempted coercion to which there is objection; it is wrong to try to compel God to harm any of His creatures. To pray for the downfall of the wicked or to curse them is still to leave it to God. Whether or not this, too, is wrong is a different topic and it is this that is discussed in the Beruriah story.

From the above it would appear that if one can speak of a dominant trend in Talmudic thought, it is that the punishment of the wicked by supernatural means should be left to God and that it is ethically wrong for the righteous to entreat God to punish the wicked or for the righteous to attempt to use the power of the curse. It hardly needs saying that this whole discussion has nothing to do with punishments meted out by an earthly court in its administration of justice. We do, in fact, find the curse as a penal method.[8] The court imposes the curse as a punishment for wrongdoers by the dictate of the Torah. Here man obeys God, whereas the problem we are examining concerns the attempt by man to ask God to do his bidding in bringing harm to the wicked. Nor is the *Birkat ha-Minim* (the 'benediction in which the heretics are cursed'), in which God is entreated to cut off and destroy the heretics, which was added to the *Amidah* (The Eighteen Benedictions) relevant to our problem. In the Talmudic sources[9] this was introduced as a measure by which the *minim* would be compelled to separate themselves from the rest of the community; a crypto-*Min* would be exposed when he refused to recite the *Birkat ha-Minim*. God is, indeed, entreated to bring about the downfall of the *Minim*. But since this prayer has as its aim the separation of the *Minim* from the community, this justifies what otherwise would be wrong. It can be seen as a wrong done consciously in the service of a greater right, the principle of separation. Thus the *Birkat ha-Minim* is a special ordinance and, if anything, suggests that the norm is not to curse the wicked. Nor is the Mar Ukba incident[10] relevant to our theme. Mar Ukba, the Babylonian Exilarch, being troubled by certain men, inquired of R. Eleazar whether he was justified in handing the men over to the governmental authorities for execution. R. Eleazar advised Mar

Ukba to frequent the *Bet ha-Midrash* (House of Study) and then his enemies would perish of their own accord i.e. he should not have them executed but should leave it to God who would destroy them. The narrative concludes that no sooner had R. Eleazar uttered these words than Geniva, one of Mar Ukba's enemies, was put in chains. However, despite this result it is by no means certain that R. Eleazar advised Mar Ukba to pray for the downfall of his enemies. The meaning of frequenting the *Bet ha-Midrash* morning and evening might be, as the *Tosafists* to the passage suggest, for the purpose of study, the merit of which would stand Mar Ukba in good stead in his struggle with his enemies. Again, there appears to be some kind of political motivation here. It is possible that the challenge to Mar Ukba's authority as the Exilarch might result in danger to the whole Babylonian Jewish community. But apart from all this, the *Tosafists* to the passage rightly compare the episode to the statement[11] that if a man delivers his judgment to Heaven, i.e., if he prays to God to take his side in his dispute with his neighbour, he will be punished by God unless he can obtain no redress in the human courts. This is the real distinction between the two sets of narratives. In the matter of the *Min* and R. Joshua ben Levi there was no personal attack on R. Joshua. The *Min* vexed him by quoting Scriptural verses. We are not told how the *baryone* vexed R. Meir but, from the reference to them living in his vicinity, it appears that there was no personal attack on R. Meir. It was just that he was annoyed by their proximity. In the Mar Ukba episode, on the other hand, Mar Ukba's enemies evidently had designs on him personally. The narrative, then, is not about cursing the wicked *per se* but is rather about the extent to which one may go in self-defence against personal attack. Here, therefore, as the other Talmudic passage quoted by the *Tosafists* suggests, the ruling is that where no redress is obtainable in the human courts an appeal may be made for God to intervene. This is obviously a quite different question from that of whether it is permitted to curse the wicked who have no intention of doing harm directly to the one who is invoking the curse.

There is surprisingly little discussion of our problem in mediaeval Jewish thought, though there are a few incidental references to it in the works of the Commentators to the relevant Talmudic passage quoted above. R. Eliezer b. Joel of Bonn, *Ravyah* (1140–1225), should be mentioned here. On the passage about R. Joshua ben Levi, *Ravyah*[12] comments:

At the moment when the Holy One, blessed be He, is angry, a man must not have the intention of punishing his neighbour, as it is said: 'To punish is also not good for the righteous.' This means, because it is then as if he actually kills him and then he will certainly be punished. But otherwise it is correct and proper, where he cannot obtain redress in the courts and in connection with the prayer for the downfall of the *meshummadim*[13] [apostates] and as is found in the Book of Psalms.

Ravyah evidently refuses to make any distinction between the various passages, treating them all together. His novel idea is that an appeal to God to punish the wicked is only improper at the moment of God's anger because to curse at such a time is so effective that it amounts to an act of murder! This is the exact opposite of the view of the *Tosafists* to the R. Joshua ben Levi passage, that even when it is permitted to kill an offender it is improper to pray for his destruction. Nor does *Ravyah* make any distinction between the *Birkat ha-Minim* and other petitions for God to punish the wicked. It is difficult to know how *Ravyah* understands the narrative of Beruriah and the *baryone*. To understand that, too, as referring to the moment of God's anger is highly problematic. Probably, *Ravyah* understands the Beruriah narrative as referring to those instances where prayers for the wicked to repent will be effective and then it is wrong to pray that the wicked should die. *Ravyah* refers in his comment to the many imprecations in Psalms. The Psalmist does pray to God for the destruction of the wicked[14] which shows that, otherwise than at the moment of God's anger, it is proper to curse the wicked. It is somewhat surprising that the other Commentators do not refer to the imprecatory Psalms. Possibly, they considered these to be irrelevant since they are either not actual curses at all but praise of God for destroying the wicked or are prayers by the Psalmist concerning those bent on destroying him and against whom, as above, he has no means of defending himself in the human courts.

On the whole question it is also surprising that none of the Commentators seems to have noted that the heroes of all the three stories recorded in the Talmud in connection with our theme (R. Joshua ben Levi,[15] R. Meir and Abba Hilkiah) are men renowned for their extraordinary piety. It is thus possible, even probable, that the narratives were never intended to imply that it is improper for everyone to pray for the downfall of the wicked, only that it is improper for saints to do so. This would account for the strange silence on the whole question by the Codes, noted by

Isaac Arieli.[16] This would explain, too, why the theme reappears in the sixteenth century not in a legal but in an ethical treatise, based on the Kabbalah, for those with saintly aspirations, Moses Cordovero's *Tomer Devorah*.[17] Cordovero writes that a man should love even the wicked as if they were his brothers and even more so. He should love even the wicked, saying to himself: 'Would that they were righteous, returning to repentance, so that they were all great men, acceptable to the Omnipresent.' Cordovero quotes in this connection Moses' exclamation: 'Would that all the people of the Lord were prophets' (Numbers 11:29). The whole passage in Cordovero contains advice on how a man might attain to the ideal of *Imitatio Dei* in its Kabbalistic sense and the work as a whole is hardly addressed to the average Jew.[18]

There are a number of prayers for the downfall of the wicked in the standard liturgy in addition to the *Birkat ha-Minim* which we have already discussed. These include: 'Pour out thy wrath' (*Shefokh hamatekha*) in the Passover Haggadah, and the prayer '*Av ha-Rahamim* in the Sabbath liturgy in which God is entreated to avenge the martyrs. The Scriptural verses of which *Shefokh* is composed as well as those quoted in the '*Av ha-Rahamim* prayer all have to do with the cry to God for vengeance for the atrocities committed against the Jewish people. In this they resemble the individual's plea to God to take the side of the victim where redress is not available on earth. These imprecations had their origin in the Middle Ages at a time of severe tragedy for the Jewish community. For this reason, in modern times, especially when the fortunes of the Jewish people took a turn for the better, voices have been raised to omit these prayers and even when they continue to be recited in the Orthodox liturgy they are now generally seen more as memorial prayers than prayers calling down God's vengeance. It is worth noting in this connection that in the Messianic hope expressed in the *Rosh ha-Shanah* (New Year) liturgy, the prayer is for all 'wickedness' to cease not for all the 'wicked' to cease – *kol ha-rish'ah* not *kol ha-resha'im*.[19] After the rise of the Reform movement in the early nineteenth century, a definite tendency can be observed, especially in Hungary where the battle was joined with great ferocity, in the more extreme Orthodox circles not only to identify the 'wicked' with the Reformers but also to justify cursing them and praying for God to humble them. In addition, some of the more fiery Hasidic masters, zealous for the honour of God, as they saw it, did not scruple to use the power of prayer in their struggle against both the Reform and the Haskalah movements and to conclude that it is right and proper to invoke God's anger not only against the movements themselves but also against their individual adherents. It is against this background that the writings of the Hungarian Hasidic master R. Hayyim Eleazar of Munkacs have to be appreciated (1872–1937). It is a notorious fact that his ire was directed not only against Jewish secularists of every kind, but also against the Zionists.

The Munkacer Rebbe has a lengthy discussion on the meaning and implications of the Beruriah story.[20] The Munkacer protests that everyone seems to have accepted far too readily the alleged implications of the story that it is not permitted to pray for the destruction of the wicked, only for the cessation of wickedness. Such an understanding, he objects, is contradicted by the rest of the Book of Psalms and by many other Scriptural verses. He refers to the statement in the same talmudic passage we noted earlier, that David himself did not say 'Hallelujah' until he witnessed the downfall of the wicked. In other words, we ought not to follow the opinion of Beruriah. According to the Munkacer, so little store did the Rabbis set on Beruriah's view that they did not even bother to record that her opinion is not to be followed. This is because, the Munkacer startingly continues, 'A woman's wisdom is confined to the distaff',[21] and it applies even to a saintly woman like Beruriah. Women are tender-hearted and for them it is indeed improper to pray for the destruction of the wicked, which is why, in the Abba Hilkiah story, the cloud first appeared in the corner of his wife. But, while not womanly it is a manly thing to curse the wicked refusing to allow tender feelings to soften the rigours demanded by righteous zeal. In this connection he refers to another Talmudic passage[22] about some *baryone* in the vicinity of R. Zera. R. Zera used to befriend them in order to encourage them to repent but the Rabbis were displeased with R. Zera's attitude. He quotes further a saying in the name of the sixteenth-century teacher R. Hershel of Cracow: since the Talmud states[23] that whenever a heretic repents he dies at once, Beruriah herself intended the *baryone* to repent and die. As for the statement that it is not good for the righteous to punish others, this means that it is not good for the righteous man himself to be the instrument of God's wrath but for the world it is a good and beneficial thing and there is joy when the wicked perish. A disciple of the Munkacer Rebbe, N. S. Schlisel, adds some notes to his master's observations.[24] He points out that, in fact, in

Midrash Psalms to the verse: 'Let sinners cease' there is a debate between R. Judah and R. Nehemiah as to whether 'sins' or 'sinners' should be read. A further note was added by R. Hayyim Eleazar himself. He refers to a Zoharic passage in which it is said that it is forbidden to pray for the downfall of the wicked but he adds that in the recently printed notes to the *Zohar* by his great-grandfather, R. Zevi Elimelech of Dinov, author of *Beney Yisakhar* and himself a powerful opponent of anything smacking of heresy, this Zoharic statement is qualified as follows: 'It seems to me that the *minim*, informers and *apikorsim* are not intended here since according to the law of the Torah these must be lowered into a pit (to die there). *A fortiori* is it permitted, then, to pray to God that He should remove the thorns from his vineyard.'

On the whole subject there are a number of interesting letters by the contemporary halakhist Rabbi Menashe Klein in his seven-volume collection of Responsa *Mishneh Halakhot*. A letter, dated 1957,[25] to a Rabbi whose name is not mentioned for obvious reasons, refers to a debate Klein had had with this Rabbi. Klein had stated that one must pray even for the repentence of a heretic (*mm*). When the Rabbi had ridiculed this statement of Klein, the latter had referred to a Responsum of R. Moses Sofer (1762–1839) in which this famous Rabbinic authority severely attacks the Reformist views of Aaron Chorin (1766–1844).[26] For all the vehemence with which Sofer castigates Chorin and the other Reformers, he none the less concludes with a prayer that they repent sincerely and return to the way of the Torah. Klein refers to the *Tosafists*, mentioned above, that even when the law demands that the heretics be killed, it is wrong to pray that they should die. As for the *Birkat ha-Minim*, Klein remarks that he has many replies but will only note that the Gaon of Vilna[27] argues that the benediction should read 'and let all wickedness (*kol ha-rish'ah*) perish' not 'all the wicked (*kol ha-reshaim*) perish', and the Gaon refers in support to the Beruriah narrative. After quoting a number of passages in which it is stated that God accepts the sincere repentance of even the worst of sinners, Klein concludes that it is right and proper to pray that heretics repent and that 'this is the true way of the Zaddikim and teachers of our generation', i.e., the Hasidic masters and Orthodox halakhic authorities.

In another letter, dated 1971, Klein[28] returns to this subject. A questioner who had read his earlier Responsum referred to the practice of the Hasidic Rebbe of Skvire. This master was noted for his habit of finding excuses for Jewish waywardness yet he used to conclude the *Birkat ha-Minim* with the words: 'Blessed art Thou, O Lord, who breakest the enemies and humblest the *minim*' (i.e., instead of the conventional 'the arrogant' – *zedim*). Klein retorts that the Skvirer Rebbe did not pray for the destruction of the *minim* but that they should be 'humbled', that is, they should repent.

In the course of this reply Klein now refers to two new sources on the question. The first of these is the *Maharal* of Prague, R. Judah Loewe (d. 1609), Klein's ancestor, who discussed this issue in his *Beer ha-Golah*.[29] *Maharal* understands the reference in the *Birkat ha-Minim* to 'let there be no hope' to the *minim*, to mean not that they should be destroyed but that their 'hope' for their heresies to spread should be frustrated. So, too, the reference to the *minim* being 'cut off' means that there should be no more heresy because all men will have acquired the true faith. In referring to this material, however, Klein does not sufficiently indicate the real tenor of *Maharal*'s views, i.e., that the *Beer ha-Golah* is a work of religious apologetics and thus in the chapter to which Klein refers the *Maharal* is concerned with defending the Rabbis who composed the *Birkat ha-Minim* against the charge of religious intolerance and of hatred for non-Jews. *Maharal*'s defence against this accusation is that this malediction is directed against those, Jews or non-Jews, who wish to destroy all religion and even then it is not directed against particular persons since 'nowadays' there are no such persons. Thus, for obvious apologetic reasons, *Maharal* softens considerably the full impact of the *Birkat ha-Minim*.

The second source quoted by Klein is the *'Ari*, the famous sixteenth-century mystic of Safed, R. Isaac Luria, who is reported to have composed a special intention (*kavvanah*), a special mystical prayer with kabbalistic meaning, for a man whose son had become an apostate that the son should revert to Judaism.[30] A further source quoted by Klein is the *Kav ha-Yashar* of R. Zevi Hirsch Kaidenover (d. 1712). Kaidenover writes[31] that a man should pray for 'the wicked of the age' that they should repent and he refers to the Beruriah narrative in support. Yet another source is the *Peri ha-'Aretz* of the eighteenth-century Hasidic master R. Menahem Mendel of Vitebsk[32] where it is said that a man should seek in his prayers to draw down the divine mercies to all creatures, even to the wicked, since we cannot enter the heart of another and it is possible for a great sinner to achieve in one moment of repentance that which the greatest of saints is incapable of achieving.

Moreover, the Torah itself states that the purpose of levirate marriage is that the dead brother's name should not be erased (Deuteronomy 25:6) and, according to the majority opinion among the halakhists, levirate marriage applies even if the dead man was an apostate, which shows that it is wrong to use the common expression *yemah shemo* ('may his name be erased') even of a great sinner. Later on[33] Klein quotes this latter observation in the name of R. Abraham Bornstein (1839–1910), Rabbi and Hasidic master of Sochachov. Again, the Talmud[34] praises Moses for petitioning God that the sinners in Israel should return to Him in repentance. Klein also quotes the Zoharic passage, referred to above, that it is wrong to curse even the wicked and that one should pray for them to repent.[35]

Klein clinches his argument by quoting the prayer referred to in the Talmud[36] to be recited when one observes a place from which idolatry has been rooted out. The prayer thanks God for destroying the idols and continues 'may the hearts of the idolaters be turned to serve Thee'. Klein concludes that he has felt obliged to write all this because he has seen in our times small-minded, immature disciples who follow the practice of certain Hasidic masters of a former generation, failing to realize that when these masters did curse sinners they 'cancelled it out in their minds', i.e., the curse was immediately nullified mentally. It is unfortunate, to say the least, that these masters are not followed in all their other good practices but on this matter the immature disciples suddenly claim this precedent and do not scruple to attack even 'great men in Israel', i.e., even Rabbis of renown are not immune from the vituperations of these extremists. It is fairly obvious by the 'Hasidic masters' Klein means, particularly, the Munkacer and, possibly, the Satmarer school.

Klein returns to the fray in yet another letter, also dated 1971, but from the *Sidra* (weekly Torah reading) given this letter was, in fact, written a month or two earlier.[37] This letter is addressed to Rabbi Wolf Glick of Brooklyn who had similarly taken Klein to task for his contention that the proper way is to pray that the wicked should repent. Klein here states that he is not in possession of the work by the Munkacer, quoted by Glick, but finds the opinion that Beruriah's opinion is rejected very odd. It is certainly not rejected as is clear from the sources, which Klein then repeats.

Glick had evidently found Klein's reply unconvincing. In a further letter[38] Klein, with a degree of reluctance, again defends his position. Glick had argued that there is no proof to be adduced from the fact that Moses prayed for the worshippers of the Golden Calf since these were not real sinners but had been led astray by the 'mixed multitude'. But, retorts Klein, are not the sinners of our day led astray by those only too ready to cause devout Jews to deviate from the true path? Glick had also questioned Klein's reference to the Sochachover Rebbe that 'may his name be erased' must not be used even of an apostate. But what of the expression 'may his name rot' which is used of the wicked? To this Klein replies that the meaning of 'let his name rot', according to the Talmud,[39] is that people should not give their children the name of a wicked man but the other expression: 'let his name be erased' is objectionable in that it is a direct curse. Glick had further protested that he prefers to follow his own Hasidic masters who did curse the wicked. Even if their practice can be challenged he prefers them to the Sochachover; they were, at least, as great as he. To be sure, Klein replies, it is good for a disciple to follow the ways and opinions of his own master but never in the manner of blind faith and certainly not when the way of the master can be shown to be contrary to the Torah. Klein tellingly quotes the Munkacer Rebbe himself as rejecting blind hero-worship. The views of a Hasidic master, states the Munkacer, must not be followed where they seem to be in conflict with the law.[40] It is, moreover, Klein suggests, a canard that the Munkacer ever cursed famous Rabbis and, in any event, it is quite wrong to follow blindly today actions carried out by a great master in a previous age, the full circumstances of which we are not fully aware. It is clear that in this whole discussion the question of whether it is ever permitted to curse the 'wicked' is now extended to whether it is ever permitted to curse famous Rabbis who are 'wicked' because they oppose the views of a renowned Hasidic master. It is now argued, since the views of these Rabbis are opposed to the Rebbe's teachings (it looks as if the context is the Satmar Rebbe's opposition to the 'Zionism' of the Agudat Israel)[41] and since this makes them 'heretics', it is permitted to curse them. Religious separatism can hardly go to any further extremes and Klein rightly takes issue with such extremism, though he is not above a touch of extremism himself, as is evident from his excellent Responsa collection as a whole.

Our topic provides as good an example as any of how precarious it is to speak of *the* Jewish attitude to complicated moral, ethical and religious problems, as if there were only one attitude, especially where powerful emotions are engaged and where both the cultural background and individual temperament have their influence on the opinions of even the most determinedly objective thinkers. With regard to the Talmudic material, the most convincing way of looking at this is to see it not as an attempt at drawing up hard and fast rules but rather as spontaneous reactions to particular circumstances. If, for example, we knew more than we do about the precise identification of the *baryone*, we would be better equipped to appreciate why these called forth the attitudes they did from those who told the Beruriah and Abba Hilkiah stories. With regard to the 'heretics' (*minim-meshummadim*) these were obviously not all of one type and the responses to them may have been different depending on who they were and the circumstances in which they were found. The resulting tensions no doubt explain the considerable ambiguity in the talmudic statements, many of these being the work of the final editors not those who actually fought against the *minim*. *Maharal* of Prague, in the later period, is compelled by the aim and thrust of his thought in sixteenth-century Christian Europe, when Judaism was on the defensive, to adopt an attitude which found Judaism to be the more tolerant faith. The *'Ari's* desire to pray for the repentance of the wicked is based on his kabbalistic views on the need for reclaiming every Jewish soul before the advent of the Messiah. Many of the Hasidic masters, stressing love and God's tender mercies, could not bring themselves to hate any of God's creatures. Others, in their battle for the truth they had apprehended, saw no reason why the only real weapon they had in the struggle, that of prayer, should not be used. Moreover, the whole question is befogged by the lack of clarity in defining terms like 'the wicked'. One man's *rasha'* (wicked) is another man's *tzaddik* (righteous man). Even if it be granted that it is permitted to curse the 'wicked' or 'heretics', which individuals qualify as such so that it is permitted to curse them?

The question, naturally, only arises for those who believe in the objective reality of petitionary prayer. If prayer is understood in purely subjective ways, as having strong psychological value and the like, it is hard to see what value there can be in cursing the wicked or in calling down God's wrath upon them unless it be argued that in some circumstances it is good to cultivate feelings of hate towards those who are hateful or who do hateful things. But the arguments against petitionary prayer are not new – namely, from scientific determinism on the one hand, and the concern as to how it is possible that God needs to be told what to do on the other – and both can be refuted. It can and has been argued, for example, that as part of man's autonomy he has the free choice of turning to God in prayer; God making His decision dependent, as it were, on man praying to Him. Yet even those of us who do believe in prayer and blessing still find it hard to believe in the efficacy of a curse, though why this is so probably depends on modern ideas about tolerance. We are reluctant to invoke the power of God against those who oppose His will. This is because we are less sure than our ancestors were, in many situations, what that will really is.

NOTES

1. *Berakhot* 10a.
2. The meaning of this word is uncertain nor are we told how the *baryone* vexed R. Meir. In any event it would appear from the story that they provoked R. Meir in some way causing him to retaliate. There is nothing in the story about R. Meir wishing to curse wicked men in general, although, the reference to them being in his vicinity seems to suggest that it was their proximity to R. Meir that vexed him. The Soncino English translation of the Talmud, following Levy and Jastrow, takes the word from *bar*, 'outside', i.e., 'outsiders' or 'rebels' and here render the word as 'highwaymen' (p. 51 *ad loc.*) but in note 6 there is an admission that the word is of doubtful meaning and is very imprecise. Why should R. Meir wish to curse these 'highwaymen' in particular and how did they vex him? Rashi here understands *baryone* as *peritzim*, 'loose-livers', perhaps to suggest that their way of life was a constant affront to R. Meir since they were his neighbours. But in *Ta'anit* 23b Rashi renders *baryone* as *burim*, 'ignorant men'.
3. The Munich ms. has: 'He placed them under the ban and wished to destroy them' (i.e., by praying that they should die), see *Dikdukey Soferim, ad loc.*
4. R. Akiba Eger (*Gilyon ha-Shas ad loc.*) calls attention to the parallel passage in *Ta'anit* 23b. Abba Hilkiah and his wife both prayed for rain. When the clouds gathered they first came to the corner in which the wife stood in prayer because there were *baryone* in their vicinity and while he prayed for them to die she prayed for them to repent. In both stories the *baryone* are in the saint's neighbourhood. In both it is the wife who prefers to pray for their repentance not their death. But in the *Ta'anit* passage there is no reference to the *baryone* vexing Abba Hilkiah. It looks as if the *Ta'anit* story is the later and has been influenced by the Beruriah story. R. Akiba Eger also refers to the Zoharic passage on Abraham's prayer for the wicked to be spared (Genesis 18:23–33). The *Midrash ha-Ne'elam* (*Zohar* 1, 105a) states in the name of Rabbi Judah the Prince that it is praiseworthy to entreat God that the wicked repent of their evil ways so that they do not go to Hell but that it is forbidden to pray that the wicked be destroyed since if God had taken Terah from the world when he was an idol-worshipper Abraham would not have come into the world and hence there would have been no tribes of Israel, no King David, no Messiah, no Torah and no righteous men, saints and prophets. On the difficulty of how prayers for the wicked to repent can be effective see the note of R. Samuel Edels, the *Maharsha*, to *Berakhot* 10a.
5. *Berakhot* 9b.
6. *Berakhot* 7a; *'Avodah Zarah* 4b.
7. Note the similarity between this and the stories of Beruriah and Abba Hilkiah above. The *Min*, like the *baryone*, lives in the neighbourhood of the saint and, again like them, he vexes the saint, except that here the nature of the vexation is stated: the *Min* quoted

Scripture in support of his heretical opinions, to which arguments, evidently, R. Joshua ben Levi was unable to find easy replies.
8. See e.g., *Mishnah, Baba Metzia'* 4:1 and the discussion on it in *Baba Metzia'* 48b. Cf. Tosafists to *Berakhot* 7a *s.v. ha-hu* and to *'Avodah Zarah* 4b where the distinction is made between judicial punishments by courts and an appeal to God to punish the wicked: even if it is permitted to kill the *Minim* by law it is forbidden to curse them. Cf. Meiri to *Berakhot* 10a, the Beruriah story. Meiri writes: 'If certain people are vexing a scholar, it is not right for him to curse them but he should pray for their repentance. Nevertheless, there are occasions when it is right for him to curse them, place them under the ban and excommunicate them as will be explained in the proper place.' The reference is to *Mo'ed Katan* 16a–17a, see Meiri *ad loc.* Meiri evidently makes a distinction between a private curse or petitionary prayer for the downfall of the wicked and the curse or ban used by a scholar as a disciplinary measure, and the same applies to a curse by the court or the community, which is less of a supernatural invocation than a judicial procedure.
9. See *Berakhot* 28b–29a. On the *Birkat ha-Minim* in its historical development see the Hebrew translation of I. Elbogen's *Der jüdische Gottesdienst*, edited J. Heinemann and others under the title *Ha-Tefillah be-Yisrael* (Tel-Aviv, 1972), pp. 27–32 and the bibliography cited in the notes on pp. 390–1. See now also R. Kimelman, 'Birkat Minim and the Lack of Evidence for an Anti-Jewish Prayer in Late Antiquity', in E. P. Sanders (ed.), *Jewish and Christian Self Definition*, II (Philadelphia, 1981), pp. 235–40; and S. Katz, "Issues in the Separation of Judaism and Christianity after 7', *Journal of Biblical Literature*, forthcoming; and *idem.*, 'Minim' and 'Birkat ha-Minim' in the *Cambridge History of Judaism* 4, 1984.
10. *Gittin* 7a.
11. *Baba Kama* 93a.
12. *SeferRavyah* (ed.) H. N. Dembitzer (Cracow, 1882), No. 17, p. 2b.
13. I.e. the *Birkat ha-Minim*. It is likely that the original reading was *birkat ha-meshummadim*, altered by the censor to *ha-minim*. See the note of Isaac S. Baer in his *Siddur, Avodat Yisroel* (Berlin, 1937), on this benediction, p. 93, that the original beginning was not *ve-la-malshinim* but *ve-la-meshummadim*.
14. E.g. *Psalms* 7, 10, 18, 137, 139:21; 145:20 and freq.
15. See Jerusalem Talmud *Terumot* 8:4 (46b) where R. Joshua ben Levi is expected by Elijah to obey the 'rule for saints' (*mishnat hasidim*) and not be content with the law quite proper for ordinary men.
16. Isaac Arieli: *Eynayim le-Mishpat, Berakhot* (Jerusalem, 1947), p. 22.
17. Chapter 2 end (ed.) Zeev Wolf Ashkenazi (Jerusalem, 1975), pp. 21–22; in my translation: *The Palm Tree of Deborah* (London, 1960), pp. 78–79.
18. Z. Ashkenazi, op. cit. p. 21 note 3 finds Cordovero's statement, that a man should love the wicked, puzzling in view of Psalm 139: 21 but, apart from the fact that Cordovero is addressing himself to the saintly few, Cordovero does not mean that in every instance it is forbidden to curse the wicked. It all depends on the occasion and the type of wickedness. Ashkenazi, in fact, says that the verse refers to those wicked men who are beyond repentance. Cf. the little Hasidic work by Jacob Klein, *Rahamey ha-'Av* (Jerusalem, 1979) *s.v.* 'ahavah, p. 6b, which argues that the verse in Psalm 139 refers only to hatred where the honour of God is at stake; otherwise only love should be shown to the wicked. But Ashkenazi remarks that he has been unable to discover anywhere in the classical sources of Judaism that a man should, as Cordovero suggests, bring the love of the wicked into his heart. He notes that in the *Shevet Musar* by Elijah ha-Kohen of Smyrna (d. 1729), Chapter 37, beg., (Jerusalem, 1978), p. 297, this passage occurs: 'This is the meaning of the Rabbinic saying: *'There is no peace for the wicked* (Isaiah 57:2). From here it is derived that God loves the wicked.' There is no such saying in the extant Rabbinic literature and the meaning is, in any event, obscure.
19. See I. S. Baer's note to his *Siddur*, p. 386, that the prayer here is based on Isaiah 29:19–20 which the author of the prayer has consciously altered. Baer refers to the Beruriah story in this connection. This is by no means conclusive. It is doubtful whether the author of the prayer made any distinction between 'wickedness' and 'the wicked'. He may well have intended that when the wicked perish there will no longer be any wickedness, see the discussion by M. Fogelman: *Bet Mordecai* (Jerusalem, 1970), No. 35, pp. 73–74. Fogelman also makes the interesting suggestion that Beruriah's interpretation does not

mean that the word *kattaim* be read as *hataim* to mean 'sin'. Both *hattaim* and *hoteim* mean 'sinners' but the latter denotes those who only sin occasionally. Consequently, one can pray that they repent.

20. *Divrey Torah*, II, 4b (Munkacs, 1929), pp. 19a–20a.
21. *Yoma* 66b.
22. *Sanhedrin* 37a.
23. *'Avodah Zarah* 18a.
24. *Hashmatot*, printed at end of Vol. 2.
25. Latest edition, with complete index, 3, 29 (New York, 1979), pp. 22a–b.
26. Responsa *Hatam Sofer* (Jerusalem, 1973), *Hoshen Mishpat, Hashmatot*, No. 191, end; *Likkutim*, No. 85.
27. *Bi'ur ha-Gra, 'Orah Hayyim* 241 end.
28. Vol. 6, 27, pp. 16a–17a.
29. *Be'er ha-Golah* (London, 1964), Chapter 7, pp. 141–51.
30. *Shulhan 'Arukh. ha-'Ari* (Munkacs, 1930), *Hilkhot Tefillah*, No. 18.
31. *Kav ha-Yashar* (Warsaw, 1879), Chapter 5, No. 11 (incorrectly given by Klein as 17).
32. *Pen ha-'Aretz* (Jerusalem, 1965), *va-ethanan* end, p. 62.
33. Vol. 6, 28. Klein states that it is found in the Sochachover's *'Avney Nezer* but while the saying is often quoted in the Sochachover's name it is not found in his Responsa collection, *'Avney Nezer*.
34. *Sotah* 14b.
35. Klein wrongly gives the passage as *Zohar, lekh lekha*; it should be, as above, *va-yerah*.
36. *Berakhot* 57b.
37. Vol. 6, 28.
38. Vol. 6, 30.
39. *Yoma* 38b.
40. The reference is to the Munkacer's *Nimmukey 'Orah Hayyim* (Jerusalem and Brooklyn, 1968), No. 68, pp. 38-42.
41. On the Satmar Rebbe's theological opposition to Zionism see Allan L. Nadler, 'Piety and Politics: The Case of the Satmar Rebbe,' *Judaism* 31, 2 (Spring, 1982), pp. 135–52.

—13—

Rabbi Aryeh Laib Heller's Theological Introduction to his *Shev Shemat'ata*

Aryeh Laib Heller (d. 1813)[1], a pupil of R. Meshullam Igra of Pressburg, was Rabbi of the Galician towns of Rozhnyatov and, from 1788 until his death, Stry. He acquired world renown among traditional students of the Talmud and Codes for his commentary to the *Hoshen Mishpat,* entitled *Ketzot ha-Hoshen,* a model of acute reasoning on Rabbinic legal principles. Although a fierce opponent of Hasidism, Heller was revered by some of the Hasidic masters as the supreme example of the classical *talmid haham.* Until he became Rabbi of the important centre of Stry Heller lived a life of great poverty. It is said that in winter he had no money to buy fuel to heat his home so that he spent most of the day in bed in order to keep warm, writing his great work under these adverse conditions; which perhaps explains some of his ideas on the need for students of the Torah to give up the world and his implicit critique of those who claim to be pious but fail to be patrons of learning. The famous pioneer of *Jüdische Wissenschaft,* Solomon Judah Rapoport (*Shir*), was Heller's son-in-law. Rapoport edited Heller's posthumously published work *'Avney Miluim,* to which he provided an Introduction and an Index. It is an intriguing question whether Heller approved of his son-in-law's new method of Jewish study in a more 'scientific' spirit and whether Rapoport was at all influenced by his father-in-law but on both these matters there is no information at all.

Heller's work on the treatment of doubt in Rabbinic law, *Shev Shema'tata* ('Seven Discourses') was compiled while the author was still a very young man but was evidently later revised.[2] To this work Heller added an Aggadic Introduction, printed in all editions of the work, in which he considers a number of theological topics.

Each paragraph of this Introduction begins with a letter of the Hebrew alphabet, in order from *'alef* to *tav,* followed by paragraphs each of which begins with a letter of his name, *'Aryeh Laib ha-Kohen.* Though in parts very pilpulistic, this Introduction is of historical importance in so far as it reflects the theological views of an anti-Hasidic Rabbinic scholar who drew his inspiration from the classical sources of Judaism. Heller, in this Introduction, is an eclectic, quoting from the Talmudic and Midrashic sources, of course, as well as from the mediaeval Jewish philosophers, from the Zohar and Lurianic Kabbalah and, especially, from the writings of Judah Loew ben Bezalel, the *Maharal,* of Prague (d. 1609), whose works seem to have helped mould Heller's thoughts on Judaism. The remainder of this essay will attempt to provide a systematic analysis of Heller's thought as presented in this Introduction.

In his brief opening paragraph (which opens with words the initial letters of which form the Tetragrammaton, a practice far from unusual in Rabbinic works and which has the support, among many others, of Maimonides' opening words to his great Code) he quotes Maimonides[3] in support of the view that the whole cosmos is a single individual, united in all its parts, because the One created one, not many. It is therefore essential, Heller continues, to have the intention when carrying out a good deed that it is performed 'for the sake of the unification etc.'. Heller does not complete the quotation, relying on his 'etc.', but he is obviously referring to the Kabbalistic formula: 'For the sake of the unification of the Holy One, blessed be He, and His *Shekhinah,* in the name of all Israel'. These latter words 'in the name of all Israel' are quoted in full by Heller in support of his unitary theme and he adds that one should also have in mind when carrying out a good deed that one takes upon oneself the duty of loving one's neighbour as oneself. The Kabbalistic formula was well-known long before Heller but the Hasidic adoption of it had been severely attacked by the Rabbi of Prague, Ezekiel Landau (1713–93).[4] Landau urges the total abandonment of this formula as dangerous to faith. It is, therefore, curious that an anti-Hasidic Rabbi like Heller should have attached such significance to the formula, in view of Landau's opposition.[5] No doubt Heller only refers to the formula because of the support it gives his theme and, in fact, he does not quote the purely Kabbalistic part regarding the Holy One, blessed be He, and His *Shekhinah.* Moreover, it should also be noted that he does not advocate the actual recitation of the formula but states only that it should be kept in mind. Heller will return again and again to this idea of unification.

In the opening four paragraphs, alef to daled, Heller begins his discussion with a consideration of the purpose of man's creation. According to the Midrash[6] when God was about to create Adam the angels objected. But why should the angels have been so concerned whether or not man was created? To appreciate the reason it is necessary to examine why God created man. The purpose of man's creation was for the soul to inhabit for a time the earthly body so as to be tried and tested in carrying out God's laws in a world remote from God which provides serious obstacles to the pursuit of the good. If the soul emerges victorious from the struggle she can return to her Source on high with her glory enhanced, more resplendent than could ever have been possible without the probationary period on earth. In short, the soul has to inhabit the body so that, as a result of the struggle against temptation, the good she acquires is her own, earned by her own efforts, not given to her as a divine gift. God wishes man to maintain the sturdy independence with which he has been endowed from birth so that he finds true happiness only in a good that he has made his own through his own free choice.

Scripture says: 'Drink waters out of thine own cistern, and running waters out of thine own well' (Proverbs 5:15). The Zohar[7] explains the difference between a cistern (*bor*), which has no water of its own, and the well (*be'er*) with its own running and living waters. The *bor* has to be filled from without, the *be'er* replenishes itself. While on high, the soul enjoys the good but only in the category of the *bor*. But once the soul has descended to earth and has made the good her own by engaging in the struggle provided by bodily life in the material universe, the good she has acquired makes her category that of the well of living waters, the *be'er* that requires no other for its existence and refreshing powers. God's greatest gift to man is thus the opportunity to be no passive recipient of any gift, not even the divine gifts of grace; or rather to have these but as of right because they have been earned. For the soul to have enjoyed eternal bliss without any prior effort would be for it to enjoy 'bread of shame' (*nahama di-kesufa*), a Kabbalistic term for this very idea that God does not want to give away His goodness but wishes man to share in that goodness in its highest form by working to attain it. The poor man who eats the finest delicacies at another's table eats the 'bread of shame'. True life, real spiritual vitality, depends precisely on man being a giver and not merely a passive recipient of divine favour. That is why one who has nothing of his own is said to be as one who is dead, why the poor man is so referred to.[8] This thought of the distinction between the *bor* and the *be'er* was advanced by the *Maharal* of Prague, who remarks that this is why the waters of the well are referred to as 'living waters' (Genesis 26:19) and why 'he that hateth gifts shall live' (Proverbs 15:27). Thus the soul while on high is empty of all good except that which is given to her as a free gift, but when she has earned the good during her pilgrimage on earth she can then be said to be truly alive. That is why Scripture, speaking of man's creation, says: 'And He blew into his nostrils a *living* soul' (Genesis 2:7), i.e. through coming down to earth the previously 'dead' soul has the opportunity of acquiring life for herself. And this, too, is why Scripture speaks of man 'living' by carrying out God's laws (Leviticus 18:5).

We are now able to grasp the deeper meaning of the verses: 'Take to heart all the words with which I have warned you this day … observing faithfully all the words of this Torah. For this is no empty thing but your very life' (Deuteronomy 32:45–46). Moses is here refuting the view that man's acts are predetermined. If that were the case all the good that man does, since he is obliged to do it because it has been so determined, would leave him 'empty'. Moses therefore declares that it is not so but that the Torah is 'your very own life', providing you with the freedom of choice that will make the good your own. The Torah allows one to create the good and not merely to be the passive recipient of it. The whole purpose of creation is for 'all of you to be *alive*' (Deuteronomy 4:4). The Rabbis in 'Ethics of the Father' ('*Avot* 2:5) tell us: 'A sin-fearing man is not a *bur.*' This word should be read as *bor*, the cistern with no water of its own. All other talents a man has are given to him as a free gift. But his ability to be sin-fearing, to choose the good and reject evil, is his own. This is why we refer in our prayers to the Torah and the precepts as 'our life.' They are, indeed, *our* life, the means we have of acquiring eternal life by our own efforts. And this is why the wicked are said[9] to be dead even while alive. For the purpose of creation is for the single good man, out of a thousand, to acquire life for himself by his own efforts. He is the spiritual aristocrat who knows the true secret of human existence. All others enjoy their existence solely for his sake, risking their lives, as Maimonides remarks,[10] by a kind of folly God has put into their hearts, in order to make the world habitable for the spiritually elite who alone are truly sane. The wicked are as the dead because their existence is not for their own sake but for the sake of the righteous.

Moreover, man's conduct has cosmic significance. As the last created being all creatures have contributed to his nature, he is the apex of creation. Moreover, all have been made dependent on him. If he is virtuous all share in his perfection while his degradation is theirs. At the time of the Deluge, for instance, man's corruption brought about the corruption of all species, and this included the angels; the 'fall' of the angels dates from that period, being the direct result of human sinfulness. We can now see why the angels should have objected to man's creation. God had informed them that He intended to create man and give him this cosmic role as a consequence of which they perceived how their fate would depend on him. Furthermore God had informed the angels that He intended to give man a portion of his very Self,[11] as the Rabbis comment on the verse 'and blew into his nostrils' (Genesis 2:7), 'one who blows it is from his very self that he blows'.[12] Lurianic Kabbalah teaches that when man sins this divine portion of the soul returns to its Source and man is left in isolation from the divine, an isolation that is his fate because of his free choice of evil. True, the angels declared, we may rise to even greater heights through man but we do not wish to take the risk of suffering degradation if he fails in his lofty task. But God has greater confidence in man. He made all creatures, including the angels, dependent on him and as sharing in the good he attains. The virtuous man thus raises the whole of creation which, through his free choice of the good, becomes as a living well. This is the whole purpose of creation.

In the light of the above a further difficulty is removed. Why did God refuse to accept Adam's sincere repentance and thus avert the death decreed upon him? We can begin to understand this difficulty when we consider the view stated in the Lurianic Kabbalah that when man sins the divine portion of his soul departs from him. When man repents of his sin that divine portion returns to him and then he is as one reborn. Here the Kabbalists follow the lead of the Rabbis[13] who had interpreted the verse: 'And a people which shall be created shall praise the Lord' (Psalm 112:19) as referring to the repentant sinner who is like a new-born infant. It thus follows that before Adam sinned he was entirely the work of God's hands, the divine portion of his soul being a gift from God. Now the work of God endures for ever so that if Adam had not sinned he would have been immortal. Once he had sinned, however, even though he repented it was he himself, by that very act of repentance, who brought back the portion of the divine. Thus, in a sense, through his act of *teshuvah* he re-created himself and hence came into the category of the 'people which shall be created'. This new life that was now his was no longer a divine gift but something he had earned for himself. As such it was human and perishable. Man as a species could still be immortal but death had to follow inevitably for the individual. This is the meaning of the Midrashic comment[14] on the verse: 'Turn Thou us unto Thee, O Lord, and we shall be turned; renew our days as of old' (Lamentations 5:21). The Midrash understands 'as of old' as referring to the days of Adam. We pray that our return to God should be the result of an 'awakening from above', of God taking the initiative in causing us to return to Him. Then we shall be, as was Adam before he sinned, the work of God's hands and we will be immortal. Like Adam we shall then make the good our own by keeping God's laws and so preserve the divine soul within us, making it as the well whose waters never cease. This is the meaning of: 'The righteous shall live by his faith' (Habakkuk 2:4).[15] Through his faith and trust in God the good man realizes that his wealth is a gift from God and not his own. With his heart firm in trust in God the good man, by acknowledging that his wealth and talents are divine gifts to him, paradoxically makes them his own by virtue of that very trust, which is his own, and he therefore 'lives' by his faith. He is freed from dependence on his external wealth and enjoys a self-authenticating existence.

In paragraph *hey* Heller leads from the anthropological question into the two themes of trust in God and the methods of Torah study. Some men are naturally obliged to engage in business but it is necessary for them to be scrupulously honest in their business dealings. We are told in the Talmud[16] that the first question put to man on Judgment Day is: 'Did you conduct your business affairs with integrity?' The term used in Hebrew is *'emunah:* 'Did you conduct your business affairs with *'emunah?'* This is the word employed for 'faith' in the Habakkuk verse cited above and is, moreover, applied in the same Talmudic passage to the order of the Mishnah known as *Zera'im*, 'Seeds', dealing with agricultural pursuits. The *Tosafists* commented on this passage, in the name of the Jerusalem Talmud, that the connection between 'seeds' and the business conducted with 'faith' is this: '"because He has faith in the Life of all worlds and sows the seed'. Sowing the seed is, indeed, an apt metaphor for man's business activity. The sower casts his seed to the ground, abandoning it there but confident that by giving it away to God, as it were, by relinquishing his hold on it, the seed will be fed by the rains and the dew to grow and yield a rich harvest. This is precisely the attitude the man of faith should have in financial matters. He should never delude himself into believing that it is his own power or skill that will enable him to succeed. His own efforts should be seen as no more than the sowing of the seed, the rest being left to God.

In the same Talmudic passage it is reported that a second question is put to man on Judgment Day: 'Did you engage in the dialectics of wisdom?' (*pilpalta be+okhmah*). In explicating this notion, Bahya Ibn Pakudah in his *Duties of the Heart*[17] gives the following illustration: a missive is sent by the king to one of his loyal subjects. Loving the king, the letter's recipient will make every effort to understand the message and the instructions it contains. Likewise, the will of God is contained in the Torah. It is God's missive to mankind. The individual who loves his God will spare no effort in order to understand fully the divine communication. We can thus see why dialectics (*pilpul*) is referred to in the question put to man on Judgment Day. A simple, superficial perusal of the divine text will never succeed in unravelling its message; only the art of *pilpul* will enable man to grasp the Torah's deeper meanings. It is true that earlier generations did not require elaborate *pilpul* in order to arrive at the truth but that was because their intellect was of the highest calibre, enabling them to penetrate immediately to the very heart of whatever subject they studied. Yet even in the days of the Amoraim these great teachers decried their own intellectual ability to grasp the subtleties of the Torah in comparison with earlier sages.[18] If that was so with regard to such giants what shall we orphans of orphans say! How much time and effort, how much dedicated application, do we require if we are to grasp thoroughly even a single theory advanced by the ancients! And for this only a vast amount of *pilpul* will suffice.

Developing the theme of the importance of *pilpul* Heller, in paragraph *vav*, quotes the comment of Moses Almosnino (c. 1515–c. 80) of Salonika on the verse: 'Dead flies make the ointment of the perfumer fetid and putrid; so doth a little folly outweigh wisdom and honour' (Ecclesiastes 10:1). For Almosnino a 'little folly' outweighs wisdom and honour in the sense that it contributes to an even better understanding of the truth. That is to say, as Almosnino remarks, those with perfectly straight, uncomplicated minds are not generally very keen. Sharpness of intellect is due to the need to overcome errors and confusions which set up obstructions for the questing mind. It is *pilpul*, keen dialectics (*harifut*), that alone can overcome these obstacles to truth. Just as fire spurts and gains in power when a little water is poured on to it, so the mind that is obliged to grapple with problems becomes even more alert. This is the 'little folly' that acts as a spur to the scholar. We can now understand the otherwise strange saying of the Rabbis[19] on the verse: 'and behold it was very good' (Genesis 1:31). Had the verse simply said: 'and it was good' it would have referred to the 'good inclination'. Now that it says 'and behold it was very good' it refers to the evil inclination. How can the 'evil inclination' be referred to as 'very good'? Note that the evil inclination is called a 'fool', the good inclination a 'sage'.[20] Without the obstacles placed in the way of the pursuit of wisdom by the folly of the evil inclination the 'good' would still have been possible. But the 'very good' is only possible through the struggle with the folly that is the evil inclination. This, too, is the meaning of the Rabbinic comment[21] on the verse: 'Happy is the man that feareth the Lord, that delighteth greatly in His commandments' (Psalm 112:1). The comment is: Happy the *man* and not the *woman*? Rather the verse means, happy is he who repents while he is still a man, i.e. in the full strength of his passions. If he can overcome these in his pursuit of God's laws the very struggle will have the result that, he delighteth *greatly* in His commandments'. An old man whose desires and appetites have waned can also delight in God's precepts but for him there can be no *great* delight since this can only emerge from the tension between good and evil.

Heller, in paragraph *zayin*, continues to develop this theme by adding that it is essential for the study of the Torah to be undertaken with a deep and abiding love. He quotes the *Midrash Tanhuma* (section Noah) which elaborates on the need for God to have suspended the mountain over Israel in order to compel them to accept the Torah as follows. This cannot refer to the Written Torah which Israel accepted willingly without any need for coercion, saying: 'we will do and obey' (Exodus 24:7). The reference is to the Oral Torah, to the complicated dialectics found in the Talmud, demanding such intense application that it is only possible for the man who loves God with all his might, caring nothing for the lures of the world. There are promises of worldly success and happiness in the Torah but these are in the Written Torah and are for those inferior souls who follow only the Written Torah. No such rewards can be promised for those who study the Oral Torah since these cannot even begin their studies unless worldly successes have no appeal for them. The reward promised to these scholars cannot be of this world at all but is rather that unfathomable spiritual bliss which comes in the Hereafter.

Another Midrashic comment is quoted on the same theme. God compelled our ancestors to accept the Torah because the woman who is raped, who is forced to engage in the act of love, is bound to her lover, if she so wishes, for ever, 'he may not put her away all his days' (Deuteronomy 22:29). This was the purpose, for example, of God giving them the manna. As the mystical diary kept by R. Joseph Karo, the *Maggid Mesharim*, informs us, the manna the Israelites ate had the effect of compelling them to keep the Torah. And the *Yalkut Reuveni* (section *Beshallah*) similarly observes that it was the Prince of the Torah, the guardian angel of learning, who was responsible for causing the manna to rain down from Heaven. The Israelites had no free choice in the matter. The manna, from the Prince of the Torah, killed all earthly desires and automatically set their hearts on fire with the love of the Torah. This love of the Torah and the precepts became their inheritance to their chosen sons who came after them, to the 'enlightened ones' *(maskilim)* of whom it is said: 'This is the Torah: when a man dieth in a tent' (Numbers 19:14).[22]

Heller, paragraphs *het* and *tet*, now embarks on an exceedingly casuistic treatment – appropriate enough in view of his insistence on the need for *pilpul* – of the theme of the manna compelling the Israelites to keep the Torah. He begins by commenting on the biblical dictum that Aaron and Miriam criticized Moses (Numbers 12) 'because of the Cushite woman whom he had married'. The Rabbis interpreted this as meaning that they complained about Moses separating himself from his 'Cushite' wife, Zipporah, because God had spoken to him. This account is prefaced with: 'From Kibrot-hattaavah the people journeyed unto Hazeroth; and they abode at Hazeroth' (Numbers 11:35). Now the *Tosafists*[23] ask why Miriam and Aaron waited so long after the giving of the Torah, the time when God spoke to Moses, before they made their complaint. Their reply is predicated on the basis of the Rabbinic comment that it was at Kibrot-hattaavah that the seventy elders were chosen. Miriam said to Zipporah: 'Happy are the wives of these' but Zipporah replied: 'Unfortunate are the wives of these for from the day God spoke to him my husband has separated himself from me.' Thus it was at that time that Miriam became aware that Moses had separated himself from his wife.

If we read the verses which tell of the people's complaint against the manna (Numbers 11) we find that the mixed multitude fell lusting and they said: 'Would that we were given flesh to eat. We remember the fish, which we were wont to eat in Egypt for nought ... but now our soul is dried away; there is nothing at all; we have nought save this manna to look to. Now the manna was like coriander seed, and the appearance thereof as the appearance of bedellium' (verses 4–7). This last verse, in praise of the manna, contradicts their previous complaint so that Rashi comments that these final words were not spoken by those who complained. There follows the verse (10): 'And Moses heard the people weeping for their families, every man at the door of his tent.' Again Rashi comments that the reference to the 'families' means that they were weeping over family matters, distressed, in fact, because incest had been forbidden to them. It is hard to see what connection there is between the complaints about the manna and that of forbidden incest.

On the verse: 'And they stood beneath the mountain' (Exodus 19:17) the Rabbis comment[24] that, as above, God held the mountain suspended over their heads, threatening them with total destruction unless they agreed to accept the Torah. The difficulty, considered above, is that there should have been no need for divine coercion since they said: 'we will do and obey' (Exodus 24:7). The *Maharal* of Prague suggests that God did not want them to imagine that acceptance of the Torah was simply a matter of their own free choice. He wished to demonstrate that they had to accept the Torah whether they wanted to or not. Something forced on another is irrevocable; as already noted, the man who forces his love on a woman may never send her away (Deuteronomy 22:29). When Scripture says that they fell a lusting (verse 4) it is explained by Moses Alshekh (d.c.1595) that it means, they lusted to have lusts. Because of the manna all their natural desires had been stilled and they were compelled by their new spiritual nature to long only for spiritual things. As above, this was due to the Prince of the Torah from whom the manna came. They wanted to regain their natural desires for earthly things so that when they kept the Torah it would be of their own free will, as it was when they voluntarily declared 'we will do and obey'. No man wishes love to be thrust upon him.

We can now turn to a consideration of the relevant texts. They said: 'We remember the fish, which we were wont to eat in Egypt for nought' (*hinnom*). As Kimhi tells us the word *hinnom* means 'with grace' (from *ken*) that is, without any compulsion. 'But now our soul is dried away; there is nothing at all; we have nought save this manna to look to' i.e. we are now compelled to love the Torah whereas we wish to love it by the exercise of our own free choice. Verily, they said, even if we were free to choose we would still choose the manna since 'the manna is like coriander seed, and the appearance thereof as the appearance of bedellium'. There is thus no need to follow Rashi in stating that this verse was not recited by those who complained. Our love for the Torah, they intended to say, would then be free and not the consequence of any coercion caused by the manna.

'No sooner had they said this than their shame was revealed.' They began to weep for their 'families', over the incestuous relationships now forbidden to them. The *Maharal* of Prague in his book *Gur 'Aryeh* (section *Va-Yiggash*) raises the following difficulty. According to the Talmud[25] the Israelites who went out of Egypt required 'conversions in accordance with the *halachah*. The law is:[26] a convert to Judaism is as a new-born infant. Strictly speaking, then, such a convert has no blood ties any longer and he can marry his sister. Why, then, was incest forbidden to that generation? *Maharal* replies that the law only applies to one converted of his own free will while the Israelites were 'converted' by God holding the mountain above their heads. We can now see the connection between the manna and their weeping over the incestuous relationships forbidden to them. Were it not for the manna their choice of the Torah would have been free and then the law would have applied that they were as new-born infants and incest would have been permitted to them.

Now there is a debate in the Talmud[27] between R. Johanan and Resh Lakish regarding a Gentile who has children and then becomes converted to Judaism. According to R. Johanan he has fulfilled the duty of procreation since, after all, he has had children. But according to Resh Lakish the children he had when he was a

Gentile are not counted as his and he has not fulfilled the duty of procreation. This is because from the moment of his conversion he is like a new-born infant. The rival Schools of Hillel and Shammai debate how many children a man must have in order to fulfil the duty of procreation. According to the School of Shammai he must have two boys but according to the School of Hillel a boy and a girl. The reasoning of the two Schools is given in the Talmud.[28] The School of Shammai derive their opinion from Moses who separated himself from his wife once he had had two sons. The School of Hillel, on the other hand, derive their opinion from the creation narrative, Adam and Eve, one male and one female, being created. It is then asked why the School of Hillel does not derive its position from Moses and the reply is given that there is no proof to be deduced from Moses' action because Moses acted of his own accord, although later on God granted approval of his action. The School of Shammai, however, do derive it from Moses. But at that time the Israelites, including Moses, were converts to the Torah and hence as new-born infants. According to Resh Lakish this means that they had not fulfilled the duty to procreate with the children they had had beforehand. But if we accept the *Maharal*'s reasoning the difficulty is removed since the Israelites were compelled to accept the Torah and the law that they were as newborn infants was not applicable.

All this helps us to cope with the difficulty raised at the beginning of this discussion, the question raised by the *Tosafists*, why Miriam and Aaron waited until that occasion to complain. The answer is that until then they had imagined that the principle that a convert is like a new-born infant applied. Consequently, Moses' two sons, born before his 'conversion', did not count. Moses would not have disobeyed of his own accord the law of procreation so if he did separate himself from his wife it must have been, so they argued, at God's direct command. But from the incident at Kibrothattaavah, when it became clear that incest was forbidden to the people, it also became clear that the principle that a convert is like a new-born infant did not apply, since, as *Maharal* says, their 'conversion' was not of their own free choice. It follows, then, that Moses had fulfilled his duty to procreate with the two sons he had had beforehand (even according to the School of Hillel who only add that a son and daughter suffices).[29] In that case there was sound reason to suspect that Moses separated himself from his wife of his own accord, not because God had so commanded him to do, which is why Miriam and Aaron began to complain. But God said to them: 'With him do I speak mouth to mouth' (Numbers 12:8), meaning that God had communicated to Moses His approval of the separation.

Far-fetched though this involved *pilpul* is, it is impossible not to admire the brilliance of Heller's series of associations in building up his argument. Granted the completely homogeneous nature of all the sources from different periods that Heller quotes, it is not entirely unreasonable to suppose that in uncovering these associations one is simply revealing the true meaning of the Biblical episode. After all this notion that there is in all the Torah literature a single indivisible truth was held by all the traditional scholars of Heller's day. It was precisely this unhistorical view of the sources that began to be assailed by the new movement, energing soon after Heller and of which his son-in-law Rapoport was a foremost representative. The adherents of the new historical approach began to study Jewish sources in a more 'scientific' manner in order to show that ideas develop in response to social and religious conditions so that one cannot quote R. Johanan and Resh Lakish, the Schools of Hillel and Shammai, Moses Alshekh and the *Maharal* of Prague, in order to describe what actually happened in the days of Moses. It is worth noting that Rapoport himself, on the whole, limited his historical researches to mediaeval Jewish literature, a fairly safe subject even in the first half of the nineteenth century; however, his contemporary Nahman Krochmal, the outstanding Galician sage, would show that the Halakhah itself could be investigated more adequately by the application of the historical method. These new winds were soon to blow away the brilliant artificialities of Heller and his famous contemporaries. Yet the price that had to be paid was a virtual abandonment of theological concern. It was not until comparatively recent times that it has come to be appreciated that though, as a system, Heller's views and their like are untenable because unhistorical, this in no way ought to detract from the profundities of the ideas themselves. There is still considerable theological significance in the idea that man, in order to be true to his nature, desires to be free of coercion, even from God Himself, and that this is precisely the situation in which God has placed him for the greater fulfilment of His purposes. At the heart of theism is the idea that man has been given autonomy by God and yet without God and His law man is as nothing. Some degree of demythologizing is certainly called for but ideas such as these are what thinkers like Heller were trying to convey even if the only way they could convey them was within the framework of an extremely ingenious scheme that history has rendered obsolete.

Heller, in paragraphs *yod* and *kaf*, proceeds to develop the theme of complete devotion to Torah study. Isaac Arama (d.c. 1495), author of the work *'Akedat Yitzhak,* is quoted as commenting on the verse: 'And the dust returneth to the earth as it was but the spirit returneth unto God who gave it' (Ecclesiastes 12:7) as follows. The ideal state for man at his death is for body and soul to become completely separated from one another; the soul, severed now from all bodily associations, ascends to God on high. But if during his life on earth a man allows his soul to become subordinate to earthly desires, his soul cannot escape entirely from bodily desires even when it leaves the body at death. Such a soul suffers torments in that the earthly desires it still has can no longer be satisfied. The *Maggid Mesharim* of R. Joseph Karo is here quoted to the effect that this is the meaning of the punishment after death known as 'the hollow of the sling' (I Samuel 25:29). The soul is hurled in the sling of earthly desires which it longs to satisfy but no longer has the means to do. This is why it is said that the people who lusted after the meat in the wilderness continued to lust after it even when they had perished in the body.

The Midrash tells us further that these people lusted after the meat even though they knew full well that it would kill them if they ate it. Their offence, as above, was that they wished to be free from the compulsion to love the Torah brought about by eating the manna. Their punishment was in the nature of measure for measure. Theirs was now a terrible compulsion to eat the meat they had chosen to eat even though they knew of its death-dealing properties. Heller concludes: 'From this the enlightened ones will derive a lesson. If a strange lust such as this had the power to cause men to die for it, how much more should man's heart be on fire with love for the Torah and the precepts even in the midst of a strange, terrifying darkness. He should fulfil in his own person the precept "when a man dieth in the tent", having no thought for his sustenance and being cruel to his own self, meditating day and night in the Torah. Then will it be well with him in both this world and the next. Nothing of that which is banned will cleave to him at the time when his soul leaves the body and, as we have written, he will not have to suffer, God forbid, the fate of being hurled in the sling.' It is to this that R. Hisda refers in the Talmud[30] when he speaks of the scholar's death as 'the parting of the ways'. For the scholar's study of the Torah frees him from subservience to the body and his death is truly a 'parting of the ways', the body decaying in the earth and the soul free to soar unimpeded to her Source.

Heller, paragraph *lamed*, remarks that at first glance it is hard to understand how this complete separation of soul and body is possible since in this life the two are so inseparable. When Moses saw the vision of the burning bush (Exodus 3:2–5) he was instructed to remove his shoes. Maimonides in his *Guide for the Perplexed* understands this as a symbol of God's warning to Moses to strip off from himself all bodily powers at that holy moment. In the writings of the Lurianic Kabbalah it is stated that the reason why physical fire consumed whereas spiritual fire does not consume is because spiritual fire, even when manifested in material things, has no real association with the material. Physical fire, on the other hand, does consume because it has such an intimate association with the object it takes hold of, entering into its every particle. This is the symbol of the burning bush seen by Moses, of the fire that did not consume because it was spiritual fire. When Moses was shown this manifestation, that spiritual fire does not consume because it has no real association with the material, the lesson he had to learn was to 'take off his shoes', i.e. to be capable of keeping soul and body in only a loose association. By the same token all persons must strive to detach their souls from too intimate an association with their bodies. Understanding this notion helps us to grasp the idea of the separation of the soul and body at death.

Developing this theme still further, Heller, in paragraph *mem*, remarks that when Adam was first created his soul was in no way identified with his body but was the governor of his bodily faculties, standing aloof from these and in full control of them. The association that did exist between soul and body was purely relational not organic. When Adam sinned and thereby refused to allow his soul to govern his body, the result of his evil deed was a strange admixture of soul and body. A new and inferior type of man emerged. The scientists inform us that a mixture of two different substances has the form of neither but is a new hybrid with properties of its own. The sinner is not half human and half material but a different creature in whom the human and the material are combined. The good man, on the other hand, by virtue of the good he does and the Torah he studies, has his soul freed from the fetters of the body. He has a purely relational association between body and soul, one that is comparable, for instance, to the relationship between the different parts of the body. The hand, the eye and the foot, for instance, each has its own function and identity, the eye separate from the hand, the hand separate from the foot.

In this connection Rabbi Simeon ben Zemah Duran (1361–1444) reminds us[31] that there is a sound reason for a specific distinction of interest made in Rabbinic law. A man, half slave and half freeman, may not marry a woman half slave and half free since it is held that the half that is slave would be cohabiting with the half that is free. Yet two mules can be mated and we do not say that the half horse is mating with the half that is ass. The distinction between the two cases, however, is clear. The mule is not a creature that is half horse and half ass but an entirely different creature, a hybrid with an identity of its own. The purpose of the separation of soul and body at death is, as we have said, so that the soul can soar unfettered to God. The Rabbis assert[32] that when Scripture speaks of man and beast being saved by God (Psalm 36:7) it refers to a special type of man, to the spiritual superman. In his being man and beast are separate even though yoked together during his lifetime. Man's true humanity, however, resides in his soul and it remains distinct and apart from the beast in his nature. The whole purpose of creation is to allow for the emergence of such supermen of the spirit.

Pursuing the theme of man's animal nature still further, Heller, in paragraph *nun*, seeks to illumine it through an analogy to almsgiving. First he quotes the following Talmudic passage:[33] 'We have a tradition that a lion does not attack two persons. But we see that it does? That is only when they resemble animals, as it is said: "He is like the beasts that perish" (Psalm 49:13).' The plain meaning of the passage is, of course, that when a lion does attack two men it is because the lion imagines that they are not men but animals. Heller gives his own interpretation based on a Zoharic passage[34] as follows. The Zohar comments on: 'Let us make man in our image (*be-tzalmenu*), after our likeness (*kidemutenu*) ...' (Genesis 1:26). These two terms are said to refer to the male principle (*tzelem*) and the female principle (*demut*). Now the rich man represents the active male principle, the poor man, who is a recipient, the female principle. When a man gives generously to the poor and thus becomes associated with them he becomes both a giver and a receiver, realizing in himself both the male and female principles. He then resembles both the *tzelem* and the *demut* on high and is no longer merely half human but fully human. The beasts fear a man who is truly human, as it is said: 'And the fear of you and the dread of you shall be upon every beast of the earth' (Genesis 8:9). This is what the Talmud means when it says that a lion does not attack two persons i.e. the man who is two persons, who realizes in himself both the male and female elements in his personality, who is both giver and receiver. The Talmud, however, at first misunderstood it to mean that a lion does not attack two men and to this it objects that we see it does. The reply is then given that the text means a person resembling a beast i.e. one who is not truly human because he does not resemble Adam's original form created in God's image. This, concludes Heller, is the meaning of the verse: 'Surely man walketh as a semblance (*tzelem*) surely for vanity they are in turmoil; he heaps up riches and knoweth not who shall gather them' (Psalm 39:7). The uncharitable, hard-hearted individual who keeps his riches to himself has lost the full human image and is left only with the *tzelem*, the male element in his personality.

Developing the theme of almsgiving further Heller, in paragraph *samekh*, quotes another passage from the Zohar.[35] Here it is said that God hates the rejoicing on the festivals unless a portion is given to the poor. Alternatively, God does not 'hate' it if, on the Sabbath, man fails to give the poor their portion, though such an attitude is hardly meritorious. This is why Scripture says: '*Your* new moons and *your* appointed seasons My soul hateth' (Isaiah 1:14) i.e. when it is 'yours' alone with nothing for the poor. Since the verse makes no reference to 'your Sabbaths' it is implied that even a selfish enjoyment of the Sabbath is acceptable, though not ideal. That is why, the Zohar concludes, Scripture says of the Sabbath: 'It is a sign between Me and the children of Israel for ever' (Exodus 31:17).

At the same time, Heller finds a number of difficulties in this Zoharic passage. First no reason is given why rejoicing on the festivals is culpable unless the poor are given their portion. Secondly, why does the verse quoted refer to the 'new moon' since the Zohar speaks only of the festivals and makes no mention of the new moon. Thirdly, it is hard to see why the Zohar quotes the verse: 'It is a sign between Me and the children of Israel'. What is this supposed to prove? Heller replies to these questions as follows: the festivals are Heavenly guests and it is the duty of a good host to make his guests happy, which is here achieved by giving the poor their portion. In addition, Heller provides the following illustration in order to explain the distinction between the Sabbath and the festivals. A great king invited himself to the home of a peasant and became angry when the peasant failed to give him the honour that was his due. At that time a messenger came from another peasant inviting the king to sup with him. To the king's consternation this peasant, too, failed to pay him honour. Naturally the king was even more incensed at the conduct of the second peasant who had, after all, invited him to be his guest. Now according to the Talmud[36] the Sabbath is fixed from the beginning of creation whereas the festivals depend on the calendar fixed by the Sanhedrin. Thus, the Sabbath is the uninvited guest whereas the festivals are the invited guests and the new moon, on the fixing of which the dates of the festivals depend, is the messenger. That is why the Zohar quotes the verse: 'It is a sign between Me and the children of Israel' i.e. on the Sabbath it is God who takes the initiative whereas the festivals are 'between the children of Israel and Me' i.e. they take the initiative in fixing the new month. Furthermore, the festivals are pilgrim festivals when every male appears before the Lord (Deuteronomy 16:16). It is only fitting that man's appearance before the Lord should be as a complete human being, in line with what has already been discussed above, and not as a partial human being who fails to appreciate the needs of the poor.

Having demonstrated the great virtue of charity, Heller, in paragraph *'ayin*, now remarks that it applies especially to the support of poor scholars so as to enable them to study God's Torah undisturbed. In praise of the Torah-scholar Heller first points to an apparent contradiction between two Talmudic passages. In the first of these[37] it is said: 'How foolish are ordinary folk who rise when a Scroll of the Torah is carried before them but do not rise when a great man passes by! For the Torah writes: "Forty stripes" (Deuteronomy 24:3) and yet the Rabbis deducted one' (i.e. reducing the number of stripes to thirty-nine). While in a second passage[38] it is asked: how do we know that one has to rise when a Scroll of the Torah passes by and the reply is given, because Scripture says: 'Thou shalt honour the face of the old man' (Leviticus 19:32). 'Old man' (*zaken*) means an 'elder', a scholar.

Thus if one has to rise before a student of the Torah how much more so has one to rise before the Torah itself! From this latter passage it would seem that the Torah is greater than those who study it whereas from the initial passage it would seem, strange though this is, that those who study the Torah are greater than the Torah.

For his solution to this apparent contradiction Heller relies on the remarks of *Maharal* of Prague as given in his *Tiferet Yisrael*.[39] *Maharal* notes that, as the Midrash states,[40] all things were created unfinished, man having to bring them to perfection, by grinding the wheat and so forth. Thus man's intellect improves on the natural shape of things. This capacity, given by God to man, applies even to prophecy. God reveals His will to the prophet but only in its natural state, as it were, and it is the task of the sage to bring it to perfection by exercising his mind in uncovering all the meanings of the original prophetic message, which is why the Rabbis say:[41] 'a sage is greater than a prophet'. Thus the sages 'perfect' the Torah and are able to interpret the verse regarding forty stripes so that it is said to mean only thirty-nine. Like all other created things the Torah has been given in an unfinished state and requires the human intellect to bring it to completion. The Midrash[42] tells us that the Roman Turnus Rufus asked Rabbi Akiba which is better, the work of God or of man, to which Rabbi Akiba replied, the work of man! Do not be astonished at this, continues *Maharal*, for the human intellect is also from God. God created the world and gave man the skills to improve it. God created prophecy and gave man the mind to make it intelligible.

We are now able to understand the passage regarding the folly of ordinary folk who rise before the Torah but fail to rise before a sage. The Torah is the Lord's vineyard. Without the scholars who toil in the vineyard no grapes would be produced. There is not a single precept in the Torah which is fully intelligible in itself and which does not require the fuller elaboration and exposition the Rabbis provide. Consequently, it is truly a matter of folly to rise before the Torah without respecting the scholars who make the Torah what it is. For all that, and here the second passage is relevant, the workman is only worthy of his hire because he tends the vineyard. Thus it also follows that if one is obliged to rise before students of the Torah then *a fortiori* one is obliged to rise before the Torah itself.

Heller now proceeds to quote, in paragraph *peh*, another Talmudic passage[43] in praise of supporting students of the Torah. Rabbi Eleazar is quoted as saying that those ignorant of Torah learning will not rise up again at the resurrection of the dead. Rabbi Johanan was distressed to hear this but Rabbi Eleazar quoted the verse: 'For Thy dew is as the dew of light, and the earth shall bring to life the dead' (Isaiah 26:19). The light of the Torah revives those who make use of it in this life but does not revive those who do not make use of it. Yet, at the same time, Rabbi Eleazar declares that he has found a revivifying remedy even for those who are incapable of studying the Torah. They, too, can have a share of the life-giving power of Torah by supporting Torah scholars. The verse is quoted: 'But ye that cleave to the Lord your God are alive every one of you this day' (Deuteronomy 4:4). By 'cleaving' here is meant being attached to the Torah by virtue of supporting those who study it. We see accordingly that the resurrection depends on the dew of the Torah. Only scholars and those who support scholars have this dew and they alone will be raised from the dead. That is why the Talmud[44] states that only one who believes that the resurrection of the dead is 'from the Torah', i.e. a biblical precept, will be revived. In the context the phrase 'from the Torah' means those who believe that the doctrine of the resurrection is biblical, but Heller understands the phrase 'from the Torah' to mean that it is essential to believe that resurrection is only possible, as above, *from* i.e. as a result of, the Torah.

Elaborating still further on this theme, in paragraph *tzaddi*, Heller refers to the vivid Talmudic description of the dire state of affairs before the advent of the Messiah[45] when 'the sages are like school-teachers and the ignorant become more and more detached (from learning) and upon whom can we (then) rely except our Father in Heaven'. Heller understands this in accordance with the idea he has examined that the whole purpose of creation is ultimately for the sake of the Torah. The whole community of Israel is like a single individual, the scholars representing the heart, the ordinary folk the limbs. This is the meaning of 'detached' in our passage. When the ignorant fail to support the scholars (who, then, have only their Father in Heaven on Whom to rely) they are like detached limbs in the body, hanging only loosely by the skin without any vitality because the heart-blood cannot reach them.

As a corollary of this inter-connectedness it is essential for each Jew to love all the other members of the community, the pain of any single organ of the body being sensed by the other organs. Our Sages say:[46] 'Let the wealth of thy neighbour be as dear to thee as thine own.' *A fortiori* it follows that no man should rob another of his goods. This consideration now leads Heller, in paragraph *kof*, to turn to the offence of theft and robbery.

R. Levi in the Talmud[47] contrasts two verses. In the verse dealing with robbery from another human being it is said: 'If any man sin, and commit a trespass' (Leviticus 5:21), 'sin' thus being recorded before 'trespass'. But in connection with robbery of holy things the verse says: 'If any man commit a trespass and sin' (Leviticus 5: 15), thus recording 'trespass' before 'sin'. R. Levi concludes that this is to teach us that it is a worse sin to rob another human being than to rob from the Temple. Now at first glance it is hard to see what difference there can be whether 'sin' or 'trespass' is recorded first since in both instances there is both 'sin' and 'trespass'. The answer is to be found in the observation of Isaac Arama in his *'Akedat Yitzhak*.[48] Arama remarks that since man is by his very nature prone to sin he cannot really be blamed for any light sins he commits -provided he sincerely repents of them. The punishment for sin is not so much for the initial impulse to sin, which is largely beyond man's control, but rather for man's persistance in sinning. Scripture says: 'For this commandment, which I command thee this day, it is not too hard for thee, neither is it far off' (Deuteronomy 30:11). The Rabbis say[49] that the 'commandment' referred to here is that of repentance. The meaning is that although the sin itself may be too hard for man to avoid because of his essentially sinful nature, it is not 'too hard' for him to give up the sin and sincerely repent of it. This is what R. Levi means. With regard to robbery from the Temple the 'sin' only comes after the 'trespass' i.e. when the robber fails to repent. But with regard to robbery from another human being there is 'sin' right from the beginning. Here no superhuman powers are required to resist the initial impulse to sin. This is certainly not part of human nature, to rob from others, and here the 'sin' itself is culpable, the very intention to sin, even before the 'trespass' has actually been committed. Every decent person knows that it is wrong to steal from another whom he should love as himself and such a thing is easily avoidable.

From the theme of robbery Heller turns, in paragraph *resh*, to that of the similar offence of usury. Commenting on the verse: 'He that putteth not out his money to usury, nor taketh reward against the innocent, he that doeth these things shall never be moved' (Psalm 15: 5), the Talmud[50] quotes R. Simeon b. Eleazar as saying that this shows that whoever lends his money on interest his wealth is 'moved' i.e. it disappears, eventually he loses his money. To this the Talmud objects that we see from experience that even people who do not lend on interest sometimes lose their wealth. To this the reply is given that when usurers lose their wealth it is never again restored whereas when people who are not guilty of usury lose their wealth it is eventually restored. The obvious objection to this is that experience also shows that innocent people sometimes lose their wealth and yet never have it restored to them. But the Talmud does not say that the wealth of such people is restored *to them* but only that is is *restored*, the meaning being that the wealth does not vanish completely but is given to someone else, so that they can have the satisfaction of knowing that their efforts have not been entirely in vain. The userer's wealth, on the other hand, vanishes completely, no one ever benefiting from his ill-gotten gains. Heller finds this idea in the Midrash[51] that God takes wealth from one man and gives it to another. But money gained from usury is called by the Midrash[52] 'loathsome'. It is so tainted that it can only be utterly destroyed and is not worthy of ever being transmitted to another.

Heller, paragraph *shin*, now reverts to the theme with which he began his essay. That the universe is a single individual whole can be proved from the Talmud[53] which states that the world is judged according to the majority of its inhabitants. If the majority is virtuous the whole is treated as virtuous, if the majority is wicked the totality is so treated. This demonstrates that the collectivity of mankind is treated as if it were a single individual, otherwise how can the conduct of the majority for good or ill have any effect on the minority.

Heller then quotes a Midrashic comment[54] on the verse: 'He hath filled me with bitterness, he hath sated me with wormwood' (Lamentations 3:15). The Midrash comments: 'From the bitter herbs with which He fed me on Passover, as it is written: "they shall eat it with unleavened bread and bitter herbs" (Numbers 9:11), He sated me with wormwood on the Ninth of Av when the Temple was destroyed.' Heller quotes another Midrash[55] which tells of the Patriarch Abraham conversing with God on the night of the Ninth of Av. Abraham asks God why He has exiled Israel among the nations, were there no righteous among them? God replies: 'She hath wrought lewdness with many' (Jeremiah 11:15). But Abraham protests that God should have considered the righteous among them. To which God replies that there were many categories of sinners among them. This dialogue between God and Abraham is difficult to understand. Once God had informed Abraham that the majority of the people had sinned what does Abraham mean when he still protests that God should have regarded the righteous among them and what, in fact, is God's reply to this?

The solution to the difficulty can be found in an idea put forward by the sixteenth-century preacher Judah Moscato. This is how Moscato understands the teaching that the world is judged according to the majority. Even if all men commit sins, each particular sin is committed by only a minority of men. Thus a majority is always innocent of every particular sin and this majority cancels out the sins of the guilty. Just as we find in the Talmud[56] that if a man ate together a number of types of forbidden food he is not culpable since each of these is a 'minority' and is neutralized by the 'majority'. This is known as: 'forbidden things cancel one another out'. We can now understand the dialogue between God and Abraham. Abraham protests that even though the people have all sinned, each particular sin has been committed by only a minority and should, therefore, be cancelled out. To this God replies that 'forbidden things do not cancel one another out'. Now the Talmud[57] observes that Hillel, who used to eat the Paschal lamb, the unleavened bread and the bitter herbs together, taking literally the verse: 'they shall eat it with unleavened bread and bitter herbs', must hold that 'forbidden things do not cancel one another out', just as, according to Hillel, the precepts, of the Paschal lamb, the unleavened bread and the bitter herbs, do not cancel one another out. Hence the Midrashic association of the bitter herbs of Passover with the wormwood of the Ninth of Av. From the practice of Hillel with regard to the eating of the bitter herbs on Passover it can be seen that the precepts do not cancel one another out. From this it follows, as the Talmud states, that 'forbidden things do not cancel one another out' and hence Abraham's protest is stilled and the destruction of the Temple on the Ninth of Av justified. Here again Heller indulges in very ingenious but extremely far-fetched pilpul though in the process he touches upon acute problems regarding divine Providence and the doctrine of sin and punishment.

Heller now turns, in paragraph *tav*, to another aspect of social life, the appointment of judges. The Midrash[58] remarks that the appointment of judges is worthy enough to ensure the survival of Israel on its land. Why this strange expression 'worthy enough'? The Midrash,[59] in fact, waxes eloquent on the tremendous significance of justice in the state. Surely then it is not simply a question of the appointment of judges being 'worthy enough'. It is far more than that. Again Heller quotes Arama's *'Akedat Yitzhak*.[60] Arama faces the old problem of why the men of Sodom were condemned whereas the men of Gibeah (Judges 19), who appear to have been guilty of the same offences, were spared. Surely there is no divine favouritism. Arama replies that the basic difference between the two cities was that in Gibeah the laws were disregarded but at least they were not abolished. In theory, at least, they were still in force, whereas in Sodom it was not only a question of disobeying the laws. The laws themselves were perverse, justice being punished and injustice rewarded. There is still hope for men, even if the laws are widely disobeyed, if the laws, in theory at least, are on the statute books. The laws can acquire a new authority. But a state that has no laws at all or, still worse, perverse laws is doomed to extinction. We can now see what the Midrash means. The mere 'appointment' of judges, even if the laws they lay down are disregarded for a time, is sufficient to ensure Israel's survival. A state based on just laws will survive. This is the reward promised for the mere appointment of judges. For those who actually keep the laws their reward is incomparable bliss beyond all human understanding.

On the general theme of ethical conduct Heller, in paragraph *'alef* 2, quotes the Psalmist: 'When thou sawest a thief thou hadst company with him, and with adulterers was thy portion ... thou sittest and speakest against thy brother; thou slanderest thine own mother's son' (Psalm 50:18–20). Heller first refer's to the *Maharal's Netzah Yisrael*.[61] *Maharal* writes that Gentile friends asked him how he could possibly uphold the doctrine of Israel's chosenness in view of the fact that there is no more cantankerous people than the Jews. *Maharal* replies that the Jewish trait of lording it over their fellow-Jews is a fault to be sure but one which stems from the aristocratic nature of the Jewish soul. An aristocrat of the spirit finds it hard to give way to the opinion of another, his sense of pride refuses to allow him to yield. For all that it can be seen that no sooner is a Jew attacked than all the others spring to his defence. The attitude of the man who holds fast stubbornly to his own opinions is quite different from the lowly traits of lewdness and lust. Thus, says Heller, the Psalmist decries the man who is both an adulterer and one who speaks evil of his neighbour. Such a person is guilty of an inner contradiction since the adulterer is generally soft and easy-going and has too little self-regard and too little dignity to attack his neighbour who happens to disagree with his opinions. And on the basis of this thought it is possible to obtain a deeper understanding of the verse: 'Because they forsook the covenant of the Lord, the God of their fathers ... and went and served other gods, and worshipped them, gods that they knew not...' (Deuteronomy 29:23–24). Rashi explains 'that they knew not' to mean these gods brought them no benefits and the *Targum* gives a similar explanation. But this presents difficulties for surely it would still have been a great evil for them to have worshipped other gods even if these gods had been of benefit to them. In order to explain away this difficulty Heller makes recourse to the idea that at the time of the Deluge, the Rabbis say,[62] part of the earth itself, some of the actual soil, was destroyed. This was a punishment for the 'sin' of the earth which failed to follow God's instructions.[63] The meaning of this statement is that the earth itself was coarse and unrefined and this had an influence on men's deeds. At the same time, Maimonides[64] observes that terms like 'fierce anger' used of God are only used in connection with idolatry. But idolatry is a spiritual sin, not one caused by the grossness of matter. Thus in Deuteronomy, where the earth itself is said to have been consumed (verse 22), it must have been because of the gross, material sins the people had committed. However this raises a question regarding the wording of Scripture: 'Wherefore hath the Lord done thus unto this *land*, what meaneth the heat of this *great anger*?' (Deuteronomy 29: 25) i.e. if the sin was a grossly material one to warrant the destruction of the very soil, why this 'great anger', which, as Maimonides has said, is only appropriate to idolatry which is a terrible sin but not a 'coarse' one. We can now understand the reply Scripture gives. It was because they worshipped gods who brought them no benefits and this was no 'spiritual' sin but due to their depraved nature. Heller piously concludes that the opposite is true. If men conduct themselves virtuously the very soil is blessed and becomes fertile.

Heller, paragraph *resh* 2, now takes up the theme of purity of speech. The Jerusalem Talmud[65] quotes Rabbi Simeon ben Yohai as saying that if he had been at Sinai he would have requested to have been given two mouths, one for worldly matters and one for the study of the Torah. On the face of it this is a curious saying for what harm is there if the mouth is used for worldly matters as well as for study of the Torah? But *Maharal* writes[66] that the Written Torah, the Bible, is not peculiar to Israel and has now become the property of other peoples as well. The Oral Torah, on the other hand, represents God's special covenant with Israel which is why it was originally forbidden to record the Oral Torah in writing.[67] Thus the mouth is, as *Maharal* remarks in that passage, the 'parchment' on which the Oral Torah is recorded. Just as the parchment upon which the Written Torah is recorded has to be made from the skin of a kosher animal, ideally the 'parchment' of the Oral Torah, man's mouth, has to be sacred and pure, and dedicated solely to study. The scholar must guard his lips not only from evil but from all lengthy conversation on worldly matters.

The Psalmist (Psalm 17:1) declares: 'Give ear unto my prayer from lips without deceit.' The Midrash to this verse understands it as referring to the Oral Torah and the *Musaf* prayer. This can be understood on the basis of a comment by R. Menahem Azariah of Fano (1548–1620) that the *Musaf* prayer corresponds to the Oral Torah. When Miriam and Aaron spoke against Moses, Aaron said to Moses: 'Oh, my lord, lay not, I pray thee, sin upon us, for that we have done foolishly and for that we have sinned' (Numbers 12:11). The *Yalkut*[68] explains Aaron's plea as: if we have sinned unwittingly forgive us as if we had sinned intentionally, a very strange comment on the face of it. But on the verse: 'wherefore then were ye not afraid to speak against My servant, against Moses' (Numbers 12:8) Rashi comments: 'Against My servant, even if he were not Moses, and against Moses, even if he were not My servant. You should have realised that it is not for nothing that the King loves him. And if you will say, we did not appreciate his greatness, that is the worst offence of all.' Now a man may speak ill of his neighbour because he imagines the man against whom he speaks to be truly evil or he may recognise the man's worth but speaks evil of him, none the less, out of sheer malice. Thus if Aaron and Miram really thought little of Moses their offence against him would not have been so serious but their sin against God would have been of a considerable magnitude since how could they think little of Moses if God had spoken to him. On the other hand if they appreciated Moses' worth because, after all, God had spoken to him, their offence against God would not have been so serious but then their sin against Moses would have been more severe. That is why Aaron appealed to Moses to treat them as intentional sinners so far as he was concerned. True this would have made their offence against him the more serious but it would have had the effect of lessening their offence against God.

Heller continues, in paragraph *yod* 2, by quoting the Talmudic saying:[69] A man should always engage in the study of the Torah and the practice of the precepts even if his motives are impure for out of study and worship with impure motives (*shelo lishmah*) he will eventually come to study and worship with pure motives (*lishmah*). On the verse: 'Speak unto the children of Israel, that they take for Me an offering' (Exodus 25:2), Rashi comments '"for Me", that is "for My sake"'. Since the Talmud permits worship with an ulterior motive why was it essential for the offering to have been made for God's sake? There is, however, a debate between Rav and Levi[70] regarding the token delivery of an object (*kinyan sudar*) so as to effect a transfer of property. If A sells his field to B, even though the purchase price has not yet been given, the transfer is effected as soon as the token object has been delivered. Levi holds that it has to be given by A, the vendor, to B, the vendee, but Rav holds that it must be given by the vendee to the vendor. The law follows Rav's opinion. R. Nissim Gerondi (d.c.1375), the *Ran*, raises the following objection. The Talmud[71] rules that although normally for a valid betrothal to be effected the man has to give an object of value to the woman, not the woman to the man, yet if the man is an important person it is valid even if the woman gives the betrothal money. The reasoning here is that for such a man to be willing to accept a present from a woman is itself an act of 'giving' by the man wherewith the betrothal is effected. In that case, asks the *Ran*, if the vendee is an important person the transfer ought to be effected even if the token object is given by the vendor since the vendee's acceptance of the gift is itself a 'giving'. The *Ran's* solution is that in the case of betrothal the gift to the important man is permanent whereas the token object is generally returned. On the basis of the *Ran's* distinction, R. Josel Sirkes (1561–1640)[72] states that if a woman gives a gift to the important man with the condition that it be later returned, although such a conditional gift is treated, in law, as a gift, it cannot effect the betrothal. Thus we must conclude that even though for an important person to accept a gift is really for him to 'give', this only applies where the gift is not returnable.

Now both R. Moses Alshekh and R. Isaac Karo, author of the work *Toledot Yitzhak*, point out that the verse speaks of the children of Israel 'taking' an offering whereas we might have expected the verse to speak of them 'giving' an offering. Their answer is that just as a gift to an important person is considered to be 'taking' from him, not 'giving' to him, so *a fortiori* a gift to God really means that He is 'giving' by accepting the gift. Now with regard to all the precepts, alms-giving for instance, if it is done with the thought of reward it is still considered to be a valid act. If, for example, a man gave alms on the condition that God will give him a share in Paradise or that God will let his sons live, it is a valid good deed.[73] Thus if the children of Israel had given their offering with thoughts of being rewarded for it, their offering would still have been perfectly valid. But then the verse could not have said *'take for Me'* since, as we have noted, the gift to an important person is only said to be 'taking', not 'giving', when the gift is given outright, not when it is anticipated that the important person will later return the gift. For the children of Israel to have given their offering with the thought of reward would have made the gift conditional on its return, as it were, and it would not then have been a 'taking', hence Rashi's comment that the offering had to be for God's sake with no ulterior motive. Heller concludes that this is always the ideal, for the good to be pursued for its own sake.

Heller, paragraphs *hey* and *lamed* 2, now turns to discuss the high quality of the Jewish soul. The Talmud[74] states that before the soul is sent down to earth it is besworn to be righteous and not wicked but is told: 'And even if the whole world declares that thou art righteous be as wicked in thine own eyes.' This appears to be in flat contradiction to the saying in 'Ethics of the Fathers':[75] 'Be not wicked in thine own esteem' (*b:fney 'atzmekha*). The Psalmist declares: 'The sons of man are vanity, a lie are the sons of man; if they be laid in the balances, they are together lighter than vanity' (Psalm 62: 10). The *Yalkut*[76] explains this to mean that since the Israelites are the sons of Abraham, who is called a 'man', when their lies and vanities are weighed in the balance on the great judgment day at the beginning of each year, the scales are tipped in their favour. Why, of all sins, are those of lies and vanity mentioned? In order to answer this question Heller first introduces another Midrash[77] which states that as a reward for Abraham having said 'Let now a little water be fetched, and wash your feet' (Genesis 18:4) God, in the future, will wash away the sins of Abraham's children. But Heller realizes this does not suffice as an answer and thus another Midrash[78] must be quoted, this being one on the verse: 'Look not upon me, that I am swarthy, for the sun hath tanned me' (Canticles 1:6). The illustration given in the Midrash which elaborates on this verse is of an Ethiopian slave-girl who declared to her friend that her master will divorce his wife, whose hands are swarthy, in order to marry her. Her companion retorted that her claim is absurd. If the master is displeased with his wife because only her hands are swarthy is it likely that he will marry a girl whose whole body is swarthy. The black hands of the wife are, only temporary and they will soon become white again. Israel has no taint of 'original sin' and the blackness of her sins can easily be washed away. This, then, is the meaning of the earlier Midrash cited. Abraham's merit is sufficient to endow his descendants with 'original virtue'. This, too, is the meaning of the verse: 'Her princes were purer than snow, they were whiter than milk, they were more ruddy in body than rubies, their polishing was of sapphire' (Lamentations 4: 7). Heller takes the word *'etzem* ('body') in the mediaeval sense of 'essence'. In essence Israel is pure and its sins are only a temporary stain on the soul that can easily be washed away.

It is, in fact, this same word *'etzem* that occurs in the passage from 'Ethics of the Fathers', which can be translated: 'Be not wicked in thine own essence' i.e. while humility demands that the Jew sees himself as wicked, as a sinner, he must never imagine that he is tainted in his essence. Heller also uses the term *'etzem* in its mediaeval sense of 'essence' in contradistinction to *mikreh,* 'accident' (in the philosophical sense if non-essential). Sin is not of Israel's essence but is an 'accident' and as such can never be permanent. Now we can see why the Midrash speaks of Israel's sins as 'lies' and 'vanity'. The meaning is that the sins are not truly part of Israel's being. They are unreal and deserve to be ignored on judgment day. That is why the Talmud[79] informs us that God conducts Himself with respect to Israel in 'truth' and that He is also 'abundant in goodness'. This is because, in essence, in *truth,* Israel is not tainted. Just as a little of the light pushes aside a good deal of the darkness so a little of the truth pushes away a good deal of error.

The discussion now shifts to the theme of the fear of God. Heller, paragraph *yod* 3, quotes the verse: 'and the fear of the Lord is His treasure' (Isaiah 33:6). Bahya Ibn Pakudah in his *Duties of the Heart*[80] tells of a saint who was thoroughly ashamed to be afraid of bandits and wild beasts so great was his fear of God which cast out all other fears. It is this fear that preserves man's Torah and the precepts he carries out. In the Zoharic scheme the Torah is called *ben*, 'son', and the fear of the Lord *bat*, 'daughter'. There is perhaps a hint of this in the Talmudic saying[81] that if a daughter is born first it is a good sign for the sons who come after her since she will help to bring them up. The hint here is to the saying in 'Ethics of the Fathers'[82] that the fear of God should precede man's knowledge of the Torah. Thus if the 'daughter', the fear of God, comes first, it is a good sign for the 'sons', the Torah and the precepts man performs. The 'daughter', that is the fear of God, will help to rear the 'sons' and the Torah and precepts will endure. We can now understand the meaning of: 'And the Lord saw, and spurned, because of the provoking of His sons and daughters' (Deuteronomy 32:19) i.e. God was angry because they put their wisdom before their fear of Him – 'sons' and then 'daughters'. That is why the verse continues: And He said: "I will hide My face from them, I will see what their end shall be; for they are a perverse generation, children on whom there is no reliance"' (verse 20). This is to say, since they are perverse, in reversing the order of 'daughter' and then 'sons', there is no relying on them since the Torah does not endure unless there is the prior fear of God.

In further explication of the notion of the fear of God and its connection with the love of God, Heller, in paragraph *bet* 2, quotes the fifteenth century philosopher Joseph Albo[83] who observes that no one can love two things or two persons -with a perfect love, since, if he loves them both, neither love is perfect, divided as it is between them. That is why Scripture (Deuteronomy 6:4) first states that the Lord is One and then follows it with the command to love God. Heller notes that when Abraham was ordered to offer up his son Isaac as a sacrifice, Isaac is referred to as 'thine only son, whom thou lovest' (Genesis 22:2) but after Abraham had demonstrated his willingness to offer up Isaac it is said: 'and hast not withheld thy son, thine only son' (Genesis 22:15), with no reference to Abraham's love for Isaac. For once Abraham had shown his readiness to offer up Isaac as a sacrifice there was only one love left in his heart, the love of God. Heller concludes that the love of God and the fear of Him are complementary, one requiring the other.

Furthermore on the verse: 'And the fear of the Lord is His treasure' (Isaiah 33:6) Heller introduces two Rabbinic illustrations. In the Talmud[84] the illustration given is of the man who instructs his agent to take a measure of wheat into a loft, telling him that it will be of no use unless he mixes the wheat with a measure of *humton*, a preservative. The wheat of the Torah can only be preserved by the fear of God. But in the Midrash[85] the illustration given is of the man who instructs his agent to place the wheat in an adequate storehouse. In his work *Tur Barekhet*, Hayyim ha-Kohen of Aleppo (d. 1665) explains that the Talmud is thinking of the inner fear of God while the Midrash is thinking of the external fear of God. It follows that the more learning a man possesses the greater his need to have the preservative of the fear of God. And the way to attain it is by association with God-fearing men, just as the farmers arrange to preserve their wheat jointly in a common storehouse. Thus the Psalmist declares: 'I am a companion of all them that fear Thee, and of them that keep thy precepts' (Psalm 119:63) i.e. through man's association with the God-fearing his precepts are *kept*, that is, preserved.

Heller, paragraph *hey* 3, continues to discuss the demand that the scholar's life be one of the greatest purity. He cites the verse: 'How long, ye fools, will ye love folly? And how long will scorners delight in scorning?' (Proverbs 1:22). At first glance this verse presents difficulties in this context. Who but the foolish delight in folly and who but the scorners in scorning? The matter can best be understood if we note a passage in the early Kabbalistic work *Ma'arekhet ha-'Elohut* and the commentary thereon.[86] This work refers to a Rabbinic observation that the greater a man the greater is his evil inclination.[87] This cannot refer to the perfectly righteous man who is like an angel and is not afflicted by the evil inclination. Nor can it refer to the thoroughly wicked man whose evil inclination has gained complete control over him. It can only refer to the average man. The greater such a man is in his knowledge of the Torah the more intense are all his emotions since the north wind blows at all times and together with all other winds,[88] i.e. the 'north wind', representing the evil inclination, is strong because it is involved in the whole of man's psychic life and in the man of learning this is especially strong. The passage concludes by referring to the Talmudic saying that there were booths filled with food and drink all along the way for the benefit of the man who led the scapegoat into the wilderness on the Day of Atonement. This was because the man was fasting and unless food were available to him he might become faint and be unable to carry out his task. It never happened that the man actually ate any of the food since the very fact that he knew that he could eat if he wanted to was sufficient to remove the temptation. 'One who has bread in his basket cannot be compared to one who has no bread in his basket.'[89] The commentator is puzzled by this last remark but Heller explains it as follows. The lesser man knows that he can disobey God's law whenever he wishes. Consequently he has 'bread in his basket' and is rarely tempted, in fact, to disobey. The greater man finds it psychologically impossible to disobey God and for that very reason 'he has no bread in his basket' and thus the temptation to disobey is all the more severe. Now we can see why the author of Proverbs is astonished that the foolish love folly and the scorners scorning. The greater man cannot imagine himself behaving foolishly or scorning others and for that very reason the temptation to do so is greater. The foolish on the other hand, who can so easily yield to folly, should find it easy not to do so in practice. Since the student of the Torah has these great temptations it behoves him always to keep watch over his tongue, which, as above, is the 'parchment' upon which the Oral Torah is recorded.

Heller, paragraph *kaf* 2, now turns to the theme of prayer, which, the Rabbis say,[90] stands high in the world and yet people treat it lightly. The Prophet teaches: 'Forasmuch as this people draw near, and with their mouth and their lips do honour Me. but have removed their heart from Me ... Therefore, behold ... and the wisdom of their wise men shall perish' (Isaiah 29:13–14). The Psalmist declares: 'But they beguiled Him with their mouth, and lied unto Him with their tongue. For their heart was not steadfast with Him, neither were they faithful in His covenant' (Psalm 78: 36–37). At first glance it is hard to see why the Psalmist says that they lied with their tongue since the lie is really in the heart. In order to explain this Heller begins by citing the Talmudic[91] material which tells of the prayer leader who exhausted the praises of God and was rebuked for it. To understand the reason for this rebuke the illustration is given there of a king who had millions of gold pieces and was praised for having millions of silver pieces. Commenting on this Maimonides[92] notes that the distinction is made between gold and silver pieces. The very coin of praise is totally inadequate to describe the Reality. Nothing can really be said of God but man's imagination is given free rein in order for him to be able to recite the words of the prayers, always with the proviso that nothing is really being said to convey the Reality. It follows that there must always be a mental reservation that what is said with the mouth is not the truth and it is in this mental reservation that the true praise of God is to be found. Thus true praise is in the heart which negates, as it were, that which the tongue is compelled to utter if God is to be worshipped at all. Bahya Ibn Pakudah in his *Duties of the Heart*[93] gives the following illustration. The master of a slave paid a visit to his slave's house but the slave went off to amuse himself leaving his wife and children to entertain the master. Naturally the master will be wroth at the slave's disregard for his honour. We can add to the parable that the wife and children do not know the identity of their visitor and are entirely blameless in failing to pay him the respect that is his due. The slave alone is blameworthy since he knows the high rank of his lord. By the same token the mouth and tongue cannot be blamed for the poor words they utter in praise of God since words are essential if God is to be worshipped and words about God are all lies. It is when the heart is absent, when the reservation is not made inwardly that all that is said expresses nothing of the true Reality, that there is blame. That is why the Psalmist speaks of 'lying' with the tongue. It is only because the heart is absent, because the mental reservations are not made, that the tongue speaks lies. And that is why the prophet says that the people are far from God in their hearts but near to Him in their lips. They are, in fact, too near, too familiar in their approach to God, their heart failing to make the reservations that alone can rescue the words from becoming lies. That is also why the prophet goes on to say that the wisdom of their wise men shall perish. There is a verse in the book of Job (Job 28:12) which can be rendered: 'And wisdom is found in nought' i.e. true wisdom consists in negating all attributes so far as our praise of God is concerned whereas when the heart is absent it can only be because wisdom has perished. The faithful, concludes Heller, will always make this reservation in their heart that whatever they are permitted to say of God does not express any of the Reality but is, by God's grace, the only way we have in our human situation of offering praise to him.

Heller sums up his complex understanding in his final paragraph. Through the Torah and the precepts all Israel become as one. As the Zohar[94] has it, the One can only rest upon a united, not a divided, people. The *Shekhinah* rests upon an Israel united in carrying out God's laws, through the 22 letters of the Torah, comprising the 613 precepts, 365 negative precepts and 248 positive precepts, the latter corresponding to the limbs of the body.[95] It is then that the whole community of Israel becomes like a single individual. When the prophet speaks of the sins of the people separating them from God (Isaiah 59:2) he also means that their sins cause them to be separated from one another. This is why Hillel said to the would-be proselyte:[96] 'That which is hateful unto thee do not do unto thy neighbour. This is the whole of the Torah. The rest is commentary, go and learn.' By 'the rest' he meant the other precepts. They are all a profound commentary on the basic theme of unity. And this is the meaning of the Midrashic passage[97] that the precepts were given *le-tzaref* ('to refine') Israel. This word is from *tziruf* 'combination'. The purpose of the precepts is to weld Israel into one, undivided people. The Midrash says that Jacob was afraid that there would be no unity among his sons because they came from four different mothers but they reassured him that they were all united because they had only one father. Rashi explains the verse regarding man and wife become 'one flesh' (Genesis 2: 24) to mean that they are united in the child to which they give birth. The famous fifteenth century commentator Don Isaac Abravanel elaborates on this theme as follows. Through the child, formed from both of them, husband and wife become more closely attached to one another and love one another all the more. The branches produce love in the roots. In the same way Israel's unity has a cosmic effect, serving to unite the powers on high. This is the meaning of the Rabbinic comment[98] on the verse: 'And thou shalt love the Lord thy God' (Deuteronomy 6:5), interpreted as: 'Let the name of Heaven become loved through thee.'

Heller concludes as he began. Before carrying out the precepts it is necessary to have in mind the mystical formula of unification in the name of all Israel. When all Israel is as a single individual there is unity on high. This is why we are told at the end of tractate *'Eduyot* that Elijah, the herald of the Messiah, will come to make peace in Israel and then the world will be redeemed.

The essay concludes with Heller's personal prayer: 'As for me, I pray: Let Him hasten to redeem us. Let Him not chastise us further, though we know that all He has done is in His mercy like a father chastising his son. As the Psalmist, on whom be peace declares: "Hath God forgotten to be gracious? Hath He in His anger shut up His compassion?" (Psalm 77:10), meaning, that He hath forgotten His revealed compassion and has hidden that compassion in His anger, for it is out of His love for us that He chastises us. Yet we have taken the lesson to heart. We have been doubly smitten. Let Him now accept us. Let Him bring our scattered ones near and gather our exiles in. Let Him lead us in the paths of righteousness and tranquillity. Let our Beloved lead us and bring us to His holy mount. Let Zion rejoice and Jerusalem be glad, speedily and in our days. Amen. Selah.'

NOTES

1. On Heller see C. Tchernowitz, *Toledot ha-Posekim*, Vol. III. (New York, 1947), pp. 246–58; M. Waxman, *A History of Jewish Literature*, second ed. (New York, 1960), Vol. III, pp. 713–15; *Encyclopedia Judaica*, Vol. 8, pp. 306–7 and the bibliography cited there. Heller's works are: 1) *Ketzot ha-Hoshen* (Lemberg 1788–96), and printed subsequently in editions of the *Hoshen Mishpat*; *Shev Shema'tata* (Lemberg, 1804), printed in many later editions; 3) *'Avney Miluim* to *Even ha-'Ezer*, published posthumously (Lemberg, 1816), with the Index compiled by Rapoport, Heller's son-in-law, by Rapoport's second marriage. For more details see R. Margaliout in *Sinai*; Vol. 15, 7–8 (April–May, 1952), p. 94. Cf. Gerson D. Cohen's remarks on the affinity of Rapoport's style and methods with 'the later rabbinic literature in which Rapoport had been schooled'. Cohen's comments are found in the Introduction to the Ktav ed. of Jacob Mann's *Texts and Studies* (New York, 1972), p. xv. Heller's great-great-grandmother was a daughter of Yom Tov Lippmann Heller, hence his family name. The earlier Heller was a disciple of the *Maharal* of Prague, which may account for our author's fondness for this teacher's ideas.
2. Author's Preface. The Introduction was added by Heller after he had published his *Ketzot ha-Hoshen* and from quotations from the *Ketzot* in the body of the *Shev Shema'tata* it is clear that he revised his youthful effort for publication. The text of the Introduction is in a deplorable state in all the printed editions. It abounds in obvious misprints and there are hardly any references to Heller's sources. Cf. Rapoport's observation in his Preface to the *'Avney Miluim* (photocopy, New York, 1948, p. 180) that Heller's speed in writing caused him, at times, to supply incorrect references. All this involved a good deal of extremely laborious deciphering for the purpose of this study.
3. *Guide*, I, 72. Cf. Philo, who was, of course, unknown both to Maimonides and to Heller, *De Opificio Mundi*, trans. F. H. Colson and G. M. Whitaker (Cambridge, 1949). Chapter LXI, pp. 135–7. Philo holds the doctrine that the One created one to be a cardinal principle of the faith.
4. Responsa *Noda' Biyudah*, *Yoreh De'ah*, No. 93. Cf. Jair Hayyim Bacharach (1630–1702), Responsa *Havvot Yair*, No. 210, where Bacharach, himself a Kabbalist, states, when discussing this formula, that he does not know what it means and doubts whether anyone else in his generation understands it. For Landau's Polemic see the Chapter dealing with this issue in my *Hasidic Prayer* (London, 1972), Chapter XII, pp. 140–53.
5. Heller refers to the *Noda' Biyudah* a number of times in the *Shev Shema'tata*: IV, 17, 20; V, 14; VII, 1, 5, 6, 17. 21, and can hardly have been unaware of Landau's stance in this matter. The formula is referred to again at the end of the Introduction.
6. Gen. R., 8:5.
7. I, 60a.
8. Zohar II, 119a; Nedarim, 64b.
9. Berakhot, 18b.
10. Introduction to *Commentary to the Mishnah*, ed. M. D. Rabinovitz (jerusalem, 1961). p. 80. Maimonides' theory of a natural instinct by means of which man exercises his skills and even risks his life in order to make the world habitable is developed by the Maggid of Dubno, Jacob Krantz, *Sefer ha-Middot* (Vilna, 1870), pp. 163f. Cf. Rj. Zwi Werblowsky: 'Faith, Hope and Trust: A Study in the Concept of Bittahon' in *Papers of the Institute of Jewish Studies*, ed. J. G. Weiss (Jerusalem, 1964). pp. 128–30.
11. On this see my article: 'The Doctrine of the "Divine Spark" in Man in Jewish Sources' in *Studies in Rationalism, Judaism and Universalism in Memory of Leon Roth*, ed. Raphael Loewe (London, 1966), pp. 87–114. This doctrine, that there is a 'portion' of God Himself deep in the recesses of the human psyche, is especially prominent in the Habad school of Hasidism.
12. Heller quotes this in Hebrew as a saying of the Rabbis. In Habad writings it is frequently

quoted in Aramaic as if it were a Zoharic saying. In reality the saying is found in Nahmanides' comment to the verse in Genesis, *Commentary to the Pentateuch*, [in Hebrew] ed. C. B. Chavel (Jerusalem, 1959), pp. 33–4. Chavel refers to the *Sefer ha-Kanah* as Nahmanides' source but fails to give the reference. For Christian thought on this theme that man's freedom of choice is for the perfection of the cosmos and that the world is an arena against which the moral character of man can develop, see John Hick, *Evil and the God of Love* (London, 1966).
13. *Yalkut*, par. 855 to Psalm 102:19.
14. *Lam. R.*, 5:21.
15. Heller quotes this as a saying of the Rabbis, no doubt referring to the Rabbinic saying that 'faith' refers to trust in God with special reference to man's earning his living, as quoted by Heller in the next paragraph, *hey*.
16. *Shabbat*, 31a.
17. *Sha'ar* 8, Chapter 3.
18. *'Eruvin*, 53a.
19. *Gen. R.*, 9:7.
20. *EcclR.*, 4:13.
21. *'Avodah Zarah*, 19a.
22. Referring to the Rabbinic comment: 'The Torah only finds its fulfilment in the one who kills himself (in the 193 "tent" of learning) for its sake' (*Berakhot*, (63b).
23. *Yevamot*, 62a.
24. *Shabbat*, 88a and Tosafists *ad loc.*
25. *Yevamot*, 46a.
26. *Yevamot*, 93b.
27. *Yevamot*, 62b.
28. *Yevamot*, 61b–62a.
29. Heller quotes the Jerusalem Talmud *Yevamot*, 6:6 (7c).
30. *Sotah*, 23a.
31. Responsa, *Tashbetz*, II. 4.
32. *Hullin*, 5b.
33. *Shabbat*, 151b.
34. I, 13b.
35. II, 88b.
36. *Rosh Ha-Shanah*, 25a; *Berakhot*, 49a; *Betzah*, 17a.
37. *Makkot*, 25b, see *Maharsha ad loc.*; and Isaac Arama, *'Akedat Yitzhak* (Pressburg, 1849), *hukkat*, pp. 69a–b.
38. *Kiddushin*, 33b.
39. (London, 1955), Chapter 89, p. 216.
40. *Gen. R.*, 11:6.
41. *Bava Batra*, 12a.
42. *Tanhuma, Tazri'a.*
43. *Ketubot*, 111b.
44. *Sanhedrin*, 90a.
45. *Sotah*, 49a–b.
46. *Avot*, 2:12.
47. *Bava Batra*, 88b.
48. *Hukkat*, 87b
49. Actually this is not a Rabbinic comment but is found in Nahmanides' *Commentary* to the verse.
50. *Bava Metzi'a*, 71a.
51. *Num. R.*, 22: 8.
52. *Ex. R.*, 31:4.
53. *Kiddushin*, 40b.
54. *Lam. R.* 3: 5.
55. *Lam. R.*, 1:0.
56. *Zevahim*, 78a.
57. *Zevahim*, 79a.
58. *Sifre*, Deuteronomy, 144.
59. *Ex. R.*, 31:1.

60. *Va-yerah*, p. 144.
61. London, 1964, Chapter 25, pp. 126–7.
62. Gen. R., 31:7.
63. Gen. R., 5:9.
64. *Guide* I, 36. On the difficulty here that there are numerous passages containing expressions like 'fierce anger with no reference to idolatry, see K. Kahana': *'Lashon Haron 'Af be-A 'Avodah Zarah'* in *ha-Mayyon (Nisan,* 1974), pp. 37–40.
65. *Berakhot*, 1: (3b).
66. *Tiferet Yisrael*, Chapter 68, p. 213.
67. *Gittin*, 60b.
68. Par., 741.
69. *Pesahim*, 50b.
70. *Bava Metzia*, 47a.
71. *Kiddushin*, 7a.
72. To *Tur Hoshen Mishpat*, 30.
73. *Pesahim*, 8a–b.
74. *Niddah*, 30b.
75. *'Avot*, 2:13.
76. Par., 645.
77. Gen. R., 48:10.
78. Cant. R. 1:1,3.
79. *Rosh Ha-Shanah*, 17b.
80. *Sha'ar*, 10:3.
81. *Bava Batra*, 141a.
82. *'Avot*, 3:9.
83. *'Ikkarim* III, 35.
84. *Shabbat*, 31a.
85. Ex. R., 30:14.
86. *M'aarekhet ha- Elohut*, Chapter 6. On this work and its anonymous commentator, see *EJ*, Vol. XI, pp. (537–639).
87. *Sukkah*, 52a.
88. *Gittin*, 31b.
89. *Yoma*, 67a.
90. *Berakhot*, 6b.
91. *Berakhot*, 33b.
92. *Guide* I, 59.
93. *Sha'ar*, 10 (Chapter 3.
94. III, 176a–h.
95. *Makkot*, 23b.
96. *Shabbat*, 3 la.
97. Lev. R., 13:3.
98. *Yoma*, 86a.

—14—

Rabbi Meir Simhah of Dvinsk

Rabbi Meir Simhah of Dvinsk,[1] whose religious thought I want to discuss this evening, resembled in many ways Rabbi Dr Salzberger in whose memory the lecture is given. Both were active in the practical Rabbinate during the major part of a long and fruitful life; both were religious thinkers who refused to live in an ivory tower but were at home with people and deeply concerned with the real problems of men and women of flesh and blood; both were held in high esteem not only in their own communities but in world Jewry; and both belonged to the great Jewries of the continent that are alas no more. There, of course, the resemblance between the two Rabbis ends. Rabbi Salzberger had a doctorate in philosophy, was a Reform Rabbi, albeit one of a very traditional hue; his thinking dominated by Judische Wissenschaft and the problems and challenges Judaism had to face in the Western world. Rabbi Meir Simhah, on the other hand, was a Rabbi of the old school, albeit a somewhat unconventional one, and drew his inspiration from the classical sources of Judaism alone and who by no stretch of the imagination can be considered a modernist. It can be argued that Jewry today needs desperately for its continued vigour an outlook derived from the massive command of the old typical of a R. Meir Simhah with the openness to the new of a Salzberger. In any event I try to offer here, as a small tribute to Rabbi Salzberger, some of the ideas of Judaism found especially in R. Meir Simhah's *Meshekh Hokhmah*,[2] his commentary to the Pentateuch, but also in his Halakhic work, *Or Sameah*,[3] on Maimonides' Code the Mishneh Torah.

The facts of R. Meir Simhah's life can be stated briefly. He was born in the year 1843 in the townlet of Baltermantz near Vilna where his father was a leading member of the Jewish community.

It is said that at the age of thirteen he wrote his own learned notes on a Rabbinic manuscript a distinguished visitor to his home had left on the table. The guest, when he studied the notes, not only forgave the young genius for his presumption but forecast a brilliant future for him as an outstanding Talmudist. We find him studying in the Lithuanian town of Eishishok, renowned for its piety and learning, at the age of seventeen, his teacher being Rabbi Moses Danishevsky. He married Hayyah, the daughter of Zevi Paltiel of Bialystok, a wealthy merchant of that town. Here the young scholar for many years was able to devote himself to his Torah studies while, after the fashion of the time, his wife conducted a successful business. R. Meir Simhah was fond of punning on the Rabbinic saying: 'He who gives life (a pun on Hayyah) gives a livelihood'. They had no sons. Their only daughter married Rabbi Abraham Luftavir, author of the work *Zera Avraham*. In the year 1888 R. Meir Simhah was appointed the town Rabbi of Dvinsk, in which capacity he served until his death in 1926. In 1906 he refused to accept the position of Rabbi of Jerusalem that was offered to him, in his loyalty to Dvinsk. Of his two works he used to say that while he could have compiled the *Or Sameah* in his youth he could not have compiled the *Meshekh Hokhmah* until he was advanced in years. The *Meshekh Hokhmah* does, indeed, exhibit all the signs of mature reflection on life's meaning as well as displaying an astonishing familiarity with the whole range of classical Jewish learning, Bible, Talmud, Midrash, the writings of the mediaeval Jewish philosophers, the Zohar and the Kabbalah in general. The work is in the form of a running commentary to the verses of the Torah in which ideas are thrown out, as it were, in the course of the exposition of a particular verse, the main aim being to illumine the meaning of that verse. It is not possible, therefore, to construct a religious system out of his thinking and to attempt to do such would undoubtedly result in distortion. What I propose to do is rather to examine some of his central themes as they appear in his admittedly unsystematic treatment. The question of relevance to contemporary Jewish religious needs and modes of thought is complicated and very tricky in considering a work of this nature but I have tried to single out particularly those ideas which 'ring a bell' even today.

R. Meir Simhah is adept at interpreting the symbols of the Jewish faith. Take his understanding[4] of the law of tzitzit, the fringes to be worn on the corners of the garment. The whole universe is the garment of God. As a garment both conceals and reveals its wearer, covering his body so that it cannot be seen and yet, at the same time, matching the form of its wearer so that others know that he is present, so, too, the physical universe acts as a screen before the divine and, at the same time, reveals the glory of God as manifested in this marvellous universe. Marvellous this garment is but it is also unfinished and incomplete. The task of completion God has given to man who can freely choose the good and reject evil and by so doing elevate the universe to its Source. This is the deeper meaning of circumcision. When, in the Midrash,[5] Turnus Rufus, the Roman Governor of Palestine, asks Rabbi Akiba why God did not create man without a foreskin, if that is His will, Akiba replies that God wishes man to be responsible for his own perfection, sharing with God the task of removing that which is inessential and acting as a co-partner with God in raising the whole creation to ever greater heights. Thus the tzitzit represent the part of the garment still to be woven. When we gaze at the tzitzit we are reminded of the tremendous responsibility that is ours of doing God's work for Him and with His help. R. Meir Simhah had certainly never heard of George Eliot and would not have quoted her even if he had but what he says here is not too remote from her famous saying that God could not make a Stradivarius violin without Stradivari. But R. Meir Simhah goes a little further and deeper into the matter. The blue thread, the tekhelet, used, in ancient times, for weaving round the other threads of the tzitzit, represents, in the vision of Ezekiel, the glory of God (the reference is to the vision of the rainbow in Ezekiel chapter 1). Although it is given to man to complete the weaving of the garment that is the universe, he must realize that his free choice is in itself a gift from his Creator. Man is given control of the universe but he must exercise his control in accord with God's will and in the realization that without the God-given capacity he would be powerless to achieve anything at all.

In this and in other passages in his work there is to be observed a strong humanistic tendency, leading him, on occasion, to soften the apparent heinousness of some of the Biblical villains. Genesis chapter 19, for instance, seems to present both the inhabitants of Sodom and Lot in the worst possible light. The two angels, disguised as men, arrive at Sodom where they are offered hospitality by Lot. The men of Sodom, both young and old, encompass Lot's house and demand that his guests be delivered to them for, so it is generally understood, the purpose of 'sodomy', whereupon Lot offers them his two daughters. According to R. Meir Simhah,[6] however, the meaning of the passage is quite different. The men of Sodom use the expression 'bring them out unto us, that we may know them'. The meaning is not that they wished to have carnal relations with the men but rather 'to know' is to be understood literally, that is to say, they wished to get to know more about them, to conduct an investigation to see if the mysterious visitors were really spies. To this Lot retorted that he will bring out his two daughters and they will be witnesses to the truth, namely, that the visitors were no spies but had simply come to betroth Lot's single daughters.

The universalistic note is sounded by R. Meir Simhah in his comment to Exodus 4:22:[7] 'Thus saith the Lord: Israel is My son, My first-born.' A firstborn is special not because he is necessarily loved by his parents more than the children who come after him but because it is he who gives his father and mother their title. Through his first-born it is that a father becomes a father. By the same token the uniqueness of Israel consists in the fact that it was through this people that God became known as the Father of all men. It was this people which first called God 'Father'.

With a fine appreciation that no man is an island and that each person is influenced by his surroundings, is the interpretation[8] of the verse in Jeremiah 32:9: 'Great in counsel, and mighty in deeds; whose eyes are open upon all the ways of the sons of men, to give unto every one according to his ways, and according to the fruit of his doings'. God does not judge each individual on his own but against the background of the time and environment in which he lives. A scoundrel, brought up among thieves and murderers and in an age in which moral and ethical standards are low, cannot be as blameworthy as one whom life has provided with a more fortunate lot, nor can a good man, in an age and climate where goodness is admired and encouraged, be worthy of as much praise as the good man who has had to struggle against the pull of his environment. Before, in the language of the verse, God gives 'every one' – each individual – 'according to his ways, and according to the fruit of his doings,' God's eyes are 'open upon all the ways of the sons of men', that is, upon the age and period as a whole. This idea of relative goodness is also read into Abraham's plea for Sodom: 'What if there should be fifty righteous men within the city; wilt Thou indeed sweep away and not forgive for the fifty righteous men that are therein?' (Genesis 18:24). The words to be emphasized here are 'within' the city and 'therein'. Fifty men who are righteous in any absolute sense will not be found, says Abraham, but in comparison to the wicked men 'in the city' there will surely be found fifty who are at least 'righteous' in this relative sense.[9]

Very interesting is R. Meir Simhah's analysis[10] of the problem of authority in Judaism. Maimonides[11] understands the verse: 'thou shalt not turn aside from the sentence which they shall declare unto thee' (Deuteronomy 17:11) to be Scriptural warrant for Rabbinic authority. Thus, according to Maimonides, the obligation to obey Rabbinic law is Biblical. Nahmanides[12] takes issue with Maimonides. If Maimonides is correct why do the Rabbis themselves treat Rabbinic law in a more lenient fashion than Biblical so that, for example, a doubt in matters of Biblical law is decided according to the stricter view but a doubt in matters of Rabbinic law is decided leniently. After paying due homage to Nahmanides' great learning, R. Meir Simhah sides with Maimonides and offers this explanation. Laws stated explicitly in Scripture are the direct will of God. 'Thou shalt not bear false witness against thy neighbour' is a direct divine command regarding this particular offence so that one who does bear false witness against his neighbour contradicts the will of God. When Maimonides states that to obey the Rabbis is a Biblical injunction what he means is that there is an overall Biblical rule that the recognized authorities be heeded but it does not mean their particular enactments are directly the will of God. For instance it is a Rabbinic injunction to kindle the Hanukkah lights but this should not be understood to mean that it is the direct will of God that Jews should kindle the Hanukkah lights, only that since the Rabbis have ruled thus it is an obligation to follow their rulings. In order to have a legal system at all it is necessary for there to be legal authorities but it is this alone that is the direct will of God not that there is a kind of automatic assent by God to Rabbinic rules so that these, too, become Biblical commands. This enables us to understand why where there is doubt in Rabbinic law the lenient view is taken. A doubt of this nature is not a doubt whether there is present the will of God since that will is dependent on the ruling of the Rabbis and in matters of doubt there is no ruling to the contrary. It is for this reason that Rabbinic rules, unlike Biblical rules, can sometimes be repealed or can be shown to have been in error. It is, indeed, the will of God for these rules to be followed until they are repealed but that does not mean that there is a divine edict guaranteeing the rules against error. The rule may actually be opposed to the will of God but until this is shown to be the case it is the will of God that it be followed because it is the divine will that there be a system with authority in Judaism. For this reason it is impossible to offend unwittingly against Rabbinic law, as it is against Biblical law. Since the offence in matters of Rabbinic law is that of disobedience, not of doing a thing wrong in itself, there is no offence at all where the act is done unwittingly and is hence no act of disobedience at all. R. Meir Simhah does not explore the matter much further but there is much here for the reworking of a dynamic approach to the Jewish tradition.

Commenting on the verse:[13] 'If thou shalt hearken to the voice of the Lord thy God, to keep His commandments and His statutes which are written in this book of the Torah; if thou turn unto the Lord thy God with all thy heart, and with all thy soul' (Deuteronomy 30:10), R. Meir Simhah understands 'if thou turn' as a necessary condition for the correct reading of 'this book of the Torah' mentioned earlier in the verse. Only the pure-hearted will be able to read the Torah correctly. Those in thrall to their passions and ambitions will distort the meaning of Scripture by interpreting it in such a manner as not to conflict with their present conduct. That is why the following verse continues: 'For this commandment, which I command thee this day, it is not too hard for thee, neither is it far off.' The demands of the Torah for holiness, justice, righteousness and compassion are natural to man, his soul giving total assent to their worth unless he allows his judgement to be clouded by his base desires or by perverse ideas. Belief in God and in the way the Torah advocates is perfectly natural to man. It only seems hard and remote if man allows himself to be dragged down either by physical lust or by false notions.

The truth is patently obvious to every human being honest with himself. It is only the coarse materialist or the pseudo-sophisticate who strays from the path of the truth. This is why a man feels sorry for the wrong he has done. Once the heat of his desire to do wrong has evaporated he no longer has any incentive to distort the truth and acknowledges it as perfectly clear and obvious.

Man is prone to error in matters of religious belief because he is unaware of his human limitations. Torn as he is in this life between the material and the spiritual, his knowledge of God is bound to be obscure so that there is an element of the mysterious even in that which is otherwise perfectly clear and obvious and the result is that man frequently hankers after the unknown and unknowable. The new type of man that will emerge, according to Maimonides' statement at the end of his Mishneh Torah, in the Messianic Age, will be one who will comprehend the knowledge of God according to man's capacity, as it is said: 'The earth will be filled with the knowledge of the Lord as the waters cover the sea' (Isaiah 11:9). Why does Maimonides stress here 'according to man's capacity' and what is the significance of the prophet's comparison to waters covering the sea? R. Meir Simhah replies[14] that in that age man's heart and mind will be free of the distortions caused by man's physical nature. He will come to know that which finite humans can know about God and the result will be that he will be freed from the lure of the unknowable. Like the waters of the sea which keep to the limits imposed on them by their very nature, never encroaching on a domain that is not theirs, mankind will be content with that knowledge of God possible for humans. Truth will no longer be clouded by error so that none will be guilty of the error that a truth utterly beyond man can be his for the asking.

R. Meir Simhah,[15] on the impossibility of comprehending as opposed to apprehending, God, observes that God is beyond any comprehension, conception or grasp. Even when we say, as we must, that God is self-aware or that He knows Himself, we must say this without having any inner cognition of what this really means. For this reason the philosphers of old denied that man can have any intuitive awareness of revelation. But here they were in gross error since in their very attempt at removing from His nature all limits they place limits on His ability to reveal Himself to His creatures. It is this revelation of God to others of which the Kabbalists speak when they use terms like the Shekhinah and the Sefirot and its true meaning is known to the mystics who have had an experience of God. In any event, the fact that God can so reveal Himself to His creatures that they become directly aware of Him is a miracle far greater and more wonderful than any other miracle. This, according to R. Meir Simhah, is the meaning of the verse: 'Who is like unto Thee, O Lord, among the mighty? Who is like unto Thee, glorious in holiness, fearful in praises, doing wonders?' (Exodus 15:11). The 'wonders' referred to in the verse are those by which He who is 'giorious in holiness' and 'fearful in praises', Who can only be thought of, as Maimonides remarks, by means of negative attributes, yet communicates with finite human beings so that they can have an awareness of His presence.

Although, as we have noted, R. Meir Simhah's thought is not generally presented in a systematic fashion but in the nature of comparatively brief observations and homilies, he does have a systematic investigation of the age-old and most stubborn problem in mediaeval religious philosophy: how God's foreknowledge can be compatible with human free will. The essay[16] opens with a detailed critique of religious determinism and a defence of free will. The following arguments are presented against the views of religious determinists i.e. those who argue that since God does know beforehand how men will conduct themselves they are not really free to choose the good and reject evil. First, these determinists also admit to the existence of good and evil. But if all is determined this can only mean that God, by His foreknowledge, has determined the existence of evil. This is impossible since God is all good. R. Meir Simhah here no doubt means that the conventional defence of the problem of evil, since God is good, is on the basis of the free-will argument, that God must provide an arena in which men freely choose the good. That solution is ruled out if good and evil doing are themselves determined. Secondly, if religious determinism is true it is very hard to see why God should have made some men good, others wicked. It will not do to reply that this is a meaningless question, like the question why did God create some creatures as flies and others as animals, because there the simple reply is that God knows the kind of world in which freedom can be exercised. In other words it is, indeed, meaningless to ask why God has created a great variety of creatures since all these are presumably necessary to serve the good. But if the doing of good and of evil are themselves determined the problem is then acute: where is the justice in God making some men good and others evil? Thirdly, how, if all is determined, is God's glory increased by the good man since he is compelled to do good and is a mere machine. As for the objection that if this is the case the angels are like machines, the answer is that the angels are compelled to do only good because of a divine decree that they should so do but rather, because of their very nature; as purely spiritual beings, trembling in awe before the Throne of God, they are compelled to choose the good. God does create beings with so pure a nature that they can only do good but it is hard to see how He can have created beings like man who can do evil but who are compelled to do good for then they would be mere instruments in His hand. God's glory is enhanced by this creature man, able to do evil, but choosing, instead, to do good. Fourthly, there is the old question of why the righteous suffer and the wicked prosper, not too difficult to grasp if there is free will since then it can be said both that men bring evil upon themselves and that the difficulties in the path of the righteous make goodness even more admirable. But if all is determined why should men be made to suffer?

On the basic question of how human free will can be reconciled with divine foreknowledge R. Meir Simhah, after examining and rejecting as unsatisfactory the various solutions that have been attempted, remarks that we are obliged to fall back on Maimonides' statement that we cannot know the answer because God's knowledge is really God Himself and of God's nature we can have no comprehension whatsoever. To ask the question is akin to asking what is the true nature of God. This does not mean, as Maimonides' great critic, R. Abraham Ibn David suggests, that Maimonides has been unwise in stating a problem and then replying that there is no solution. Maimonides is not, in fact, saying that there is no solution. He is rather saying that the solution, having to do with God's essence, is bound to be, by its very nature, utterly beyond the scope of the human mind. R. Meir Simhah points to certain mathematical problems, that, even in this world, are insoluble. Again he returns to what seems to be a favourite theme of his, the limitations of the human mind which, paradoxically, can only be appreciated by those whose intellect is sound and deep.

When the third-century Palestinian teacher, R. Johanan, teaches that God, seeing that the righteous are few, planted them in every generation, this must not be understood literally in a deterministic fashion. The meaning is that God has decreed that every generation must have its good men, otherwise that generation would be hopelessly corrupt, but it is not determined who is to belong in that select company. Every man in every generation can, by the exercise of his free will, be of the company of the righteous. Here R. Meir Simhah adds an interesting note. According to the Kabbalists the meaning of R. Johanan's saying is that God 'plants' the souls of the righteous who have died into each generation i.e. their souls are reincarnated to assist the men of later generations. R. Meir Simhah approves of this doctrine and declares it to be a true Jewish belief, but aware as he is that thinkers like Maimonides do not refer to it and Saadya Gaon rejects it explicitly he prefers to give an explanation in accord with what he calls the plain meaning.

Finally, he quotes a comment of his grandfather Rabbi Hananiah Ha-Kohen. Scripture says: 'Now the man Moses was very meek, above all the men that were upon the face of the earth' (Numbers 12:3). The philosophers have raised the general difficulty about humility. How can a man with high worth and many talents and achievements imagine himself to be inferior to those lacking in these qualities? If we recognize the worth of others is it not merely a lack in perception to fail to recognize our own worth? R. Meir Simhah observes that much can be and has been written on this question but his grandfather's comment on Moses has a point to it. Moses did know himself. He was certainly not guilty of self-delusion. How could he not have been aware that he alone has ascended to Heaven to receive the Torah. But by virtue of that very fact Moses, in his humility, imagined that he was no longer a freely choosing human being. Having seen God 'face to face' all doubt had become impossible for him. Having seen the value and significance of the mitzvot how could he possibly choose not to obey them. Thus Moses was humble in the sense that he believed he could no longer claim any credit or merit in being a good man. His experiences had made him into an automaton, virtually obliged to do good. This is perhaps the meaning of the words 'all the men that were upon the face of the earth'. Moses felt himself to be inferior to men on earth who had not ascended to Heaven as he had and who were still capable of pursuing the good by their own free choice. Faith had become impossible for Moses since faith involves acceptance on trust of that which one cannot actually comprehend. Moses had actually 'seen' God and for him there was never again any need to invoke faith. This is reminiscent of the Hasidic master who once remarked that, while there are stories of Elijah appearing to the saints, if he were offered a vision of Elijah he would refuse it, because such a confirmation of the truths he had hitherto held by faith would serve to deprive him of man's most precious gift, his freedom of choice and his moral autonomy.

A thinker such as R. Meir Simhah would hardly have failed to comment on the Shema. The following are some of his comments[17] on the verse: 'And thou shalt love the Lord thy God with all thy heart, and with all thy soul, and with all thy might' (Deuteronomy 6:5). It is psychologically true, R. Meir Simhah notes, that religious warmth and enthusiasm are awakened when there is strong opposition to them. For instance, when in times of martyrdom attempts are made to force Jews to embrace a rival faith, there bestirs itself a holy resolve to be true and loyal, so that even a lukewarm adherent of Judaism will be ready to lay down his life for his faith. The difficulty is to have this enthusiasm amid life's daily routine. We are creatures of habit so that we do carry out the rules of our religion but in a cold and unfeeling way. That is why the Rabbis tell us[18] that the righteous love every penny of their wealth. The meaning is that they cultivate a love of wealth not for its own sake but in order that feelings of restraint might be brought into play when they are called to give away some of their wealth for charitable purposes and other good causes. In this way the struggle with self is always present for them and through the struggle itself the resolve to give is with the powerful desire that can only follow on the attempt to stifle it, just as a fire will burst into spurts of flame when attempts are made to extinguish it. This is why the verse states both 'with all thy soul', that is when martyrdom is demanded, and also 'with all thy might', this latter meaning that even in the day-to-day routine one should try to overcome the lifelessness that is the result of habit and so not only live Jewishly but with the joy and enthusiasm of worship.

In another comment on this verse R. Meir Simhah sees in the verse a reference to man's threefold duties: to God, to himself and to his neighbour. 'With all thy heart' refers to his obligation to recognize that all is from God who watches over him continually. 'With all thy soul' refers to his need to improve his own character and to strive for perfection. 'With all thy might' refers to his relations with his fellow-men, doing nothing that will cause them harm or injury and having a sense of belonging to the human race, a trait that distinguishes man from the animal creation.

The Sifre to 'with all thy might' observes: 'With every quality by which He deals with thee, whether good or bad'. According to R. Meir Simhah the meaning is that the word *meodekha* can mean 'with all thy excellence' (from *meod* in the sense of 'very', 'superiority'). We are commanded to love God with that by means of which we are superior to animals. Animals have instinctive reactions to pain and pleasure. Incapable of thinking of their future and concerned only with the immediate satisfaction of their needs they can never appreciate why they should suffer. Not so human beings who, by nature, have a profound sense of destiny. The noble human being is capable of loving his God even when he meets with suffering, in his belief that in any ultimate sense this is not evil but good, either because it wins him pardon for his sins or because it helps to refine his character or for the purpose of some future good or for some other reason that belongs to God's providential purposes. Furthermore, as Maimonides holds,[19] humans are superior to animals in that God's providence over animals is only for the species not for the individual. God does not determine that this spider shall catch this fly, for example, but He does bring this particular form of suffering on this particular human being as part of his cosmic scheme. When man comes to recognize this aspect of divine providence he will accept even his sufferings in love, he will love God in his thanks for his superiority over the brute creation.

Occasionally, R. Meir Simhah allows himself to refer to contemporary events. An amusing example is when he comments on Maimonides' ruling that one should not build palatial halls, like the heathen do, for the purpose of public assembly, that the reference is to what we call a 'club'.[20] In singing the praises of Israel's loyalty to its faith he refers to the emigration of vast numbers of Russian Jews to America where, despite the strangeness of their surroundings and the lure of a new civilization they retain their Jewish identity by creating the institutions of Jewish communal life.[21] Obviously with the conditions of his own country in mind, he refers to the fact that every social philosophy finds its precedence in the Torah.[22] Thus at the time of the Deluge when the earth was filled with violence there is an anticipation of a tyranny (without actually saying so R. Meir Simhah is obviously thinking of Tzarist Russia which he calls *'shittat ha-egrof'*, 'the theory of the fist' i.e. that might is right). The story of the Tower of Babel anticipates the theory of *'kis ehad le-khulanu'*, 'a common purse for all' i.e. Communism. The purpose of the Torah hinting at all this is to point the way to the kind of life represented by the Patriarchs, of striving for perfection, and which is the heritage of their descendants the Jewish people.

It is over fifty years since R. Meir Simhah departed this life. He lived through the First World War, the Communist Revolution and amid the upheavals of his time. He could not have envisaged the destruction of a third of the Jewish people in the Holocaust and he can have had no idea of the emergence of a Jewish State. Living for forty years in Latvia where the Jewish community was not uninfluenced by the new winds of change that had begun to blow in

Germany at the end of the eighteenth century, he, too, this old-time Rabbi, seems to have tried to face the new challenges to Jewish life with an astonishing breadth of mind, the most thorough acquaintance with the classical Jewish sources and with complete sincerity and intellectual honesty but without the tools forged in the German Jewish community that enabled Rabbi Salzberger to achieve all that he did. Both men have now gone to their eternal rest but both live on here on earth in Jewish lives made better for having known them personally or through their works.

NOTES

1. On R. Meir Simhah see the article in *Encyclopedia Judaica*, Vol. 11, pp. 1260 –61; S. J. Sevin: *Ishim ve-Shittot*, Tel-Aviv, 1952, pp. 137–65; H. R. Rabbinovitz in *Shanah be-Shanah*, Jer., 5739, pp. 457– 466; *The Jews in Latvin*, Tel-Aviv, 1971. Index: Cohen, Mrir Simcha (Rabbi). Z. A. Rabiner: *Maran Rabbenu Meir Simhal ha-Kolen*. New ed. Jer., 1972.
2. Z. A. Rabiner: *Maran Rabbenu Meir Simhal ha-Kolen*. New ed. Jer., 1972 ed. Riga. 1927. Abbreviated MH.
3. ed. Friedmann, New York, n.d.
4. MH, shelah, end, pp. 360–1.
5. *Tanhuma*, ed. Buber, tazria 7.
6. MH, va-yera, p. 23.
7. MH, shemot end, p. 68.
8. MH, va-yelekh, end, p. 540.
9. MH, va-yera, p. 21.
10. MH, shofetim, pp. 463–465.
11. *Sefer ha-Mitzvot*, shoresh rishon, ed. Warsaw, 1883, pp. 1–26.
12. Nahmanides to Sefer ha-Mitzvot *ad loc.*
13. MH, nitzavim, p. 529.
14. OS to Melakhim 12:5.
15. MH, be-shallah, p. 98.
16. OS to Teshuvah 4:4; R. Meir Simhah states here that he composed this essay in his youth.
17. MH, va-ethanan, pp. 430–1.
18. Hullin 91a.
19. Guide, III, 17.
20. OS to akum 11:1.
21. MH, kedoshim, p. 264.
22. MH, kedoshim, p. 265.

Zionism after 100 Years

Rabbi Spectre, our Chairman, has told you that a book of mine is about to appear on *teiku*, the unsolved problem in talmudic literature. This is a suitable introduction to the topic we are to discuss this morning. If I may digress, just for a moment, my thesis in the book is that *teiku* is not the response to an unsolved problem but to an insoluble one, the two halves of which are so equally balanced that it is quite impossible to come to any conclusion. There are problems to which no solution will ever be found.

The problem we are discussing this morning is not that kind of problem. Many would say, in fact, that the problem has already been solved, that it is now pointless to talk about the future or the challenge of Zionism or what meaning there is now to Zionism. The emergence of the State of Israel and its many achievements have made it all obsolete. It is rather like the building committee of a synagogue. This committee discusses ways and means of raising funds. It engages the architect and considers his plans. There is great excitement until eventually the synagogue is built. It would then be the height of stupidity for the committee to continue to function as a building committee. No doubt its members will wish to participate in the work of the synagogue, but hardly as a building committee, and if they persisted in so doing all that would be required would be to point to the synagogue and say, there it is.

Many would argue, this is precisely the situation of Jews today now that the State of Israel is a reality. How conscious we are of it as we have the privilege of meeting together in Jerusalem. It is here. The dream has been realized. What point is there in continuing to speak of Zionism? You are aware, no doubt, that in some circles in Israel, *tzionut* is a synonym for nonsense.

Others are aware that a problem does exist. They do want to know what Zionism can mean now that there is a State of Israel.

Now the only competence I have to speak on the subject, and I am far from sure that I have any competence even here, is that I have dabbled a little in theology. The Chairman referred to Schechter on Zionism. The passage in question is typical of Schechter's excellent English prose; after all he did spend some time in Cambridge before he went to the United States! The passage is also typical of Schechter's well-known view that the best theology is not consistent. One can see what he means. To speak consistently of God is ridiculous. But when we discuss Zionism, theologically we are talking about the human situation. The question to which my remarks are addressed is, what can be a theological approach, in the sense of a Conservative Judaism coming to grips with the problem, now that the State of Israel is flourishing?

Some years after the Balfour Declaration, many years before the Holocaust and the establishment of the State of Israel, Rabbi Meir Shapiro of Lublin examined the prayer in the *maariv* service: 'Let our eyes see it, let our heart rejoice, and let our soul be glad' when it is said unto Zion, thy God reigneth. Three things are spoken of here – our eyes seeing, our heart rejoicing and our soul being glad. Rabbi Shapiro commented that priority had to be given to the first of these. It had become absolutely essential for the Jewish people to regain its independence for it not to be ordered around, for it to have a homeland and bring an end to Jewish homelessness. Let our eyes but see it. Let us be free from subservience to the whims of every petty tyrant and Jew-hater. For this, any country would do. As you know, there were schemes advanced by serious people for Jews to found a State in places like British Gehinna, as it has been called, or anywhere else remotely hospitable to the idea. This did not satisfy the Jewish heart. And so the prayer continues: 'Let our heart rejoice.' The only place where the Jewish heart could be contented was here in the Holy Land. Rabbi Shapiro went on to say that following the Balfour Declaration these two aims, of eye and of heart, were coming closer to being fulfilled.

But what of: 'Let our soul be glad'? He saw this as the ultimate aim of religious Zionism, though, as an Agudist, he would not at that time have expressed it quite in this way. We can admit that the political and emotional aims of Zionism have been realized. We cannot say the same for the spiritual aim. *Vehanefesh lo timmalei*, which, with preacher's licence, we can render: 'There is no limit to spiritual striving and so there will always be a task for spiritual Zionism to perform.'

Rabbi Shapiro was speaking as an Agudist. He believed that this soul fulfilment had to wait in large measure for the coming of the Messiah, which is why the Agudah was then anti-Zionist, though no longer so. Nowadays, things have changed. With very few exceptions, the State of Israel is seen as fulfilling, in part at least, the third of these aims as well, the growth of the Jewish soul, or, if you wish to put it that way, the re-emergence of the Jewish soul.

So far this would presumably be accepted by all religious Zionists – that Zionism is not only a political movement, not simply an attempt at solving the problem of Jewish homelessness. It is a movement to restore Judaism, and where can this be done except in Eretz Yisrael? What ought to be the specific Conservative approach? Wherein do we differ from the Agudah, the Mizrachi and from other religious Zionists? There are, I submit, three areas of difference.

The first of these is in our understanding of the concept of Torah. We are just as much committed to the Torah as other religious Zionists. We have heard during these few days the stirring achievements of the Mesorati movement in Israel. We differ from the majority of religious Zionists in adopting a non-fundamentalist approach to Torah. We cannot, as these others frequently do, conceive of the Torah as a body of static and sacred texts to be quoted as direct and infallible guidance on the problems facing Jews everywhere, and especially Jews in the State of Israel.

We find it hard to accept the view that Eretz Yisrael is a divinely promised land in a direct sense, because we have become accustomed to the dynamic view of Jewish history, including sacred history. I once had occasion to remark that it is all very well speaking of *Torah mim Hashamayim* but it all depends on what you mean by Torah, what you mean by *shamayim* and, above all, what you mean by *min*! Those of us who have been influenced by thinkers like Zachariah Frankel and Solomon Schechter and by the historical school generally have been taught to see it rather differently. I did not have the privilege of studying at the Jewish Theological Seminary but I am told by colleagues who did that Professor H. L. Ginsberg used to tell his students that the figure of Abraham is best seen as akin to that of Uncle Sam in the United States or John Bull in my country, though, I am sure, Ginsberg would not have denied the historicity of the Patriarchs. Abraham is a symbol of the Jewish spirit. On Abraham there have been fathered, quite literally, all the ideas and ideals Jews found of value. On this view it is obviously an over-simplification to speak of Eretz Yisrael as the land 'promised' to Abraham. On the other hand, we need be no less devoted to the land of Israel as the Holy Land or, indeed, as the Promised Land, provided we understand the holiness and the promise as conveyed through the historical experiences of our people. We would tend to see it as holiness and promise through association rather than by divine fiat; through the fact that in this land and in no other did God reveal Himself to the prophets; that here and nowhere else did Isaiah see God on His Throne with the seraphim singing "Holy, holy, holy'; that here Amos taught us justice and Hosea love and compassion; that here Rabban Johanan ben Zakkai and Hillel and Akiba made the mighty attempt at translating prophetism into a wondrous way of life whose power has not abated.

Just as we have accepted for a long time now that our observance of shall we say *kashrut* or Shabbat need not depend on a fundamentalist view of revelation, so should it be with regard to our attitude towards the Holy Land. The other Professor Ginzberg, Louis, often spoke of the genetic fallacy, that origins do not matter. Shabbat may have had its origin in some kind of Babylonian fear of certain days. The dietary laws may have originated in primitive taboos. Yet, the Jewish people, under God's guidance, have made something altogether sublime of Shabbat and a means of promoting holiness in daily living of the dietary laws. By the same token this land and no other has become sacred to Jews and a central feature of the Jewish religion because of the tremendous associations between land and people through a history of three thousand years.

Arising out of this we would no doubt be less ready than the fundamentalists to see *kedushah* as residing in a quasi-physical way in the soil. We would be more inclined to follow the lead of the Rabbis when they commented on the verse: 'Seek ye the Lord while He may be found.' 'When is He to be found?' ask the Rabbis. They have two replies. One reply is, during the ten days between Rosh Hashanah and Yom Kippur; the other is, in the synagogue. Here the Rabbis surely were grappling with the problem of transcendence. Professor Heschel speaks of Shabbat as a Temple in Time. The land of Israel, theologically speaking, is the location of God in space. But how can the Infinite be confined to particular times or particular places? Thus the Rabbis imply that

God indeed is beyond space and time, but He can be *found* in these since the humans who are finding Him are space- and time-bound, and for them associations matter. You recall the rabbinic passage in which the angels ask God, 'When is it Rosh Hashanah?' God replies, 'Let us go down to see when the people Israel celebrate Rosh Hashanah, for that day *is* Rosh Hashanah.' The same applies to the location of God in space. He is everywhere and beyond all places, but by historical association Jews can find Him here more than anywhere else. This is the first area where a non-fundamentalist view of Judaism differs, and it frees Jews from a static picture in which all the problems of land and statehood can find their direct solution in the pages of the Bible.

The second area where a non-fundamentalist approach to religious Zionism can be helpful is that of universalism. The early Zionists so far as I know – Professor Avineri is the expert – wished to create a new kind of nationalism, one that would not be chauvinistic or narrow but which would make a contribution to all mankind and would look outwards towards the wider world as well as within the Jewish camp. They were great dreamers thinking of a new society based on social justice and the other ideals of Judaism. Ahad Ha-Am is somewhat outdated today but let us not forget that he and the other Zionist thinkers were men of strong moral principles. Their ethical stance, which they rightly believed is that of Judaism, was sufficiently broad to go beyond the confines of the particular. I am far from suggesting that this vision has departed, but it does seem to be the case that religious Zionism – for very natural reasons – has tended increasingly to prefer the particularistic biblical texts to the more universalistic, those which refer to God's special concern for His people.

'How odd of God to choose the Jews.' Wherein lies the oddness? Not in the choice of the Jews – after all if He had to choose, what better choice could He have made? No, the oddness lies in the choice itself, and it is odd unless the choice is interpreted as taking place through the Jewish historical experience and implying that the choosing God is interested, as it were, in all men. With the greatest respect to the distinguished thinker whose hundredth birthday we are celebrating at this Convention, we can still say: *asher bahar banu*, provided that we understand this in a way that is not an affront to the very concept of Deity. Maybe, though such a thought is heresy to many present-day Zionists, the *Golah* has a contribution to make not only by helping Israel, supreme though this duty is, but also by widening the scope of Zionism. Jews in other lands, each with its own specific outlook, can further the universalistic aspects of Zionism. There need not be any contradiction between the Zionist vision and the universalistic since the Torah does, after all, *go out* of Zion to be a blessing for all men.

The rabbi of the *Toledot Aharon* synagogue in Meah Shearim, notorious for his fierce anti-Zionism, writes in one of his letters to some followers in Brazil that Jews have to live in such distant lands in order to reclaim the 'holy sparks' scattered there, according to the Lurianic Kabbalah, whereas in France and Germany this need is far less, the task having been undertaken in the Middle Ages by Rashi and the Tosafists. Quaint though this is, may there not be some truth in the idea that there is a specific American approach to Judaism which can enrich the idea of Jewish peoplehood as a whole? I must be frank with you. I am not totally enamoured of the American approach any more than you might be of the English approach. Yet there are Jews in England – only a few and not terribly significant on the world scene – and there are Jews in other parts of the world, each with a philosophy of life based on Judaism as mediated in a particular environment. When these Jews, dedicated and committed to eternal Judaism, pool their spiritual resources, the result is an enriched universalism.

The third area where a non-fundamentalist understanding has something to say is that of individual needs, especially of individual spiritual needs. Inevitably in the struggle for the survival of the State of Israel the individual tends to be overlooked. A theological approach to Zionism can never be content with the total subordination of the individual to the group, which has not, of course, happened but which *can* happen if no voices are ever raised to redress the balance. It is an impertinence to say it, and one who does not reside in Israel dares say it only because Israelis are saying it: the individual exists for and in himself. He is not a cog in the machine of state. The group is essential. Brave men and women have been prepared to lay down their lives that the State of Israel may endure, but the theological basis for their sacrifice is that their courage and martyrdom was that of freely choosing individuals on behalf of other individuals. To sacrifice one's life for a state, no matter how nobly conceived, is idolatry. Indeed, the nobler the conception the greater the danger of idolatry.

There was a man who lived in the State of Israel, who rejoiced in it and wrote about it, Rabbi Abraham Chen. This man's writings have been overlooked. I came across them by accident. Chen's book, *Bemalkhut Hayahadut*, tries to analyse the relationship which ideally ought to obtain between the individual and the state. In his Preface to the book, Rabbi S. J. Sevin recounts a story told to him by the author about which he, Sevin, has reservations; ones that perhaps you will share when I repeat the story.

Rabbi Levi Yitzhak of Berditchev, mighty pleader for his people, was once leading his congregation in prayer at the *neilah* service on Yom Kippur. Everyone present could see that the moment was fraught with spiritual power, the saint prolonging his prayers with excessive concentration, pouring all his being into them. It was clear that something of tremendous significance was about to take place. Suddenly, Rabbi Levi Yitzhak called a halt to his devotions, rushing through the prayers at great speed and sending the congregation home. Later his disciples asked him to tell them what it was all about. 'You are right,' he replied, 'I was engaged in an activity of the utmost, wondrous significance. I was assured that if I persisted I could bring the Messiah to our oppressed people. But then I noticed in a corner of the synagogue a frail old man who would not dream of leaving the synagogue before the service was over in order to break his fast, and I knew that he might die. That was my dilemma. Was I to ignore the old man and let his life be endangered, or was I to bring the service to a speedy end that he might be spared? I came to the conclusion that my immediate and present duty was to the old man. The Messiah would have to wait.'

Sevin is right to express his reservations. After all, the Messiah is sorely needed and why should the life of a single old man stand in the way? But the point of the story is that the individual matters. He is an end in himself, not a means to an end, no matter how elevated that end may be. 'Therefore was a single man created to teach you that he who saves a single human life is considered as if he had saved a whole world, and he who destroys a single human life is considered as if he had destroyed a whole world.'

Please allow me a little further homiletical licence. The *Yalkut* at the beginning of Psalms has the theme of each great figure from Abraham onwards taking up the challenge recorded in the words of a leader who preceded him. King David, says the *Yalkut*, took it up from Moses. Moses said: 'Happy art thou, O Israel' and David began the book of Psalms with: 'Happy is the man.' Can we apply this to our situation? We have all responded to the call of Israel. We have answered a fervent Amen to Israel's blessing. We have said and will continue to say: 'Happy art thou, O Israel.' But a religious Jew is obliged at the same time to say: 'Happy is the man,' the individual, and not only the individual Jew but the individual *man* since every human being is created in God's image. The early Zionists were certainly no theologians, but did they not see it in terms not too dissimilar from these?

There is one further idea I would like to put forward for your consideration. One can hardly discuss religious Zionism without referring to the Messianic hope. Conservative Jews may have differing ideas on how the doctrine of the Messiah is to be understood, but they all consider the doctrine basic to Judaism. Traditionally the Messiah comes at the culmination of human history. Partly in response to the challenge of secular Zionism, many religious Zionists now speak of the emergence of the State of Israel as: *athalta de-geulah*, 'the beginning of the Redemption', thus wishing to introduce Messianism into the realities of present-day political life. This is a very dangerous thing to do, since realized, or even partly realized, eschatology tends to justify actions and thoughts that otherwise would be unjustifiable. If the Messianic age has already dawned, if God has already intervened in a direct way, then we can leave many of our responsibilities to Him instead of facing our problems honestly with dignity and with *sekhel*. The expression *athalta de-geulah*, used in such a context, is misleading. The only passage in which this expression occurs is in tractate *Megillah*, and there the reference is to events which take place during the seventh year of the son-of-David's coming; that is, the expression belongs to eschatology, not to the pre-Messianic age in which we are now living. There is no such concept in traditional Judaism as a partial *Geulah*. Either we are redeemed or we are still unredeemed. This is not simply a question of semantics. Yes, we have to dream of a Zionism for the future; dreams are very important. But they ought not to be feverish dreams.

Hayinu ke-holemim. This is generally translated as 'we were as they who dream'. The New English Bible, however, following the *Targum*, renders *ke-holemim* as 'healthy', We acquired a new lease on life. How true. With the establishment of the State of Israel, Jews have become a healthier people, more complete and integrated, less fearful and more outward-looking. And yet is it healthy for the Jewish people to be content simply to be cured of its sicknesses? With all due respect to the *Targum* we must continue to render *ke-holemim* as 'they who dream'. We refuse to give up the dream of Zionism. Now that, thank God, the State of Israel is a reality, that dream should now embrace the wider, universalistic vision as well as the spiritual needs of the individual Jew, and all this dreaming occurs in the pre-Messianic age in which eschatology is invoked neither as an excuse for inactivity nor as a spur to actions we ought not to undertake. Maybe our dream of the Zionist future is a poor dream. Maybe we would prefer to see a profounder vision, but for that, our tradition teaches, we have to wait for the Messiah. Nevertheless, the lesser dream is still powerful and still has much to give to us and to the whole world. Religious Zionists can still say:

> Had I the heavens' embroidered cloths,
> Enwrought with golden and silver light,
> The blue and the dim and the dark cloths
> Of night and light and the half-light,
> I would spread the cloths under your feet.
> But I, being poor, have only my dreams;
> I have spread my dreams under your feet;
> Tread softly, because you tread on my dreams.

—16—

Sanctity and Meaning of Human Life in Relation to the Present Situation of Violence

If I understand my brief correctly it is to suggest some guidelines for the future, as these emerge from the Jewish teachings of the past, on the sanctity and meaning of human life with special reference to the present situation of violence in human affairs. The task is a daunting one. How do we begin to grapple with terrible problems with which decent human beings of every religion, and of none, are faced today? Who can dare to come up with new ideas when these have not been forthcoming in the ranks of the most distinguished theologians and ethical philosophers, when, indeed, many contemporary philosophers limit their activity to analysis of concepts and refuse even to consider, as beyond the scope of this activity, the question of what ought to be done? All one can offer for discussion are very tentative guidelines. To claim any authority in laying down such guidelines is in itself to be guilty of a form of violence, in that it seeks to brush aside legitimate doubts and anxieties and pretends to certainties where no certainty is to be had.

A number of propositions should first be stated regarding the sanctity of life according to Jewish teaching. These would be accepted as true by the majority of professing Jews. (I am fairly sure that they would be acceptable to the majority of professing Christians as well but I can only try to speak on behalf of Judaism.)

MAN IS CREATED IN GOD'S IMAGE

However this concept is understood – it has, of course, received many different interpretations – it implies that there is something God-like in man and that in this man differs from all members of the animal kingdom. The difference between man and animal is qualitative. It is a difference not of degree but of kind. Animals, too, are God's creatures but they have nothing of the God-like quality man has.

THE IMAGE OF GOD IS IN ALL MEN

However the concept of the Chosen People is understood (and this, too, has received many different interpretations), the image of God is found in all human beings not only in members of the Chosen People. In *Ethics of the Fathers* (3:14) this saying is attributed to Rabbi Akiba: 'Beloved is man, for he was created in the image of God; but it was by a special love that it was made known to him that he was created in the image of God; as it is said: *For in the image of God made He man* (Gn 9:6). Beloved are Israel, for they are called children of the All-present; but it was by a special love that it was made known to them that they are called children of the All-present; as it is said: *Ye are children unto the Lord your God* (Dt 14:1).' The particularism of the second part of Rabbi Akiba's statement is explicitly made not to refer to God's image in man. It is *man*, not only Israel, who is beloved of God and created in His image. There is a story regarding some Nazi storm-troopers who forced their way into a synagogue, holding the congregants at gunpoint and compelling the aged rabbi to deliver a sermon at which they intended to mock. The rabbi took as his text the verse about the image of God in man and, turning to his persecutors, declared that this, with all the responsibilities and privileges it entails, applies to them as well. The Nazis retreated in confusion. True or not, the story expresses the authentic Jewish attitude.

COMPASSION IS A HIGH VIRTUE

Implied in the image of God concept is the Rabbinic version of *Imitatio Dei* expressed by the Rabbis as: 'Just as He is merciful be thou merciful. Just as He is compassionate be thou compassionate.' Cruelty to animals is sinful in the Jewish tradition, *a fortiori* cruelty to human beings. To be cruel to human beings offends doubly against the image of God concept. The perpetrator of cruelty to humans is false to the concept both in the act he performs and in carrying out the act on one to whom the concept applies.

VIOLENCE IS EVIL

It follows from the first three positions that it is exceedingly sinful to behave aggressively to any human being, whether the aggression is physical or even only verbal. Aggressive acts deny the dignity of the human person.

MURDER IS THE GREATEST EVIL

If it is wrong to harm a person, to take away his life is to commit the greatest of all sins. According to Jewish teaching, it is forbidden for one man to kill another even if it is in order to save his own life, where, for instance, he is ordered by a tyrant to kill an innocent man and if he refuses his own life will be forfeit. In the words of the Talmud: 'How do you know that your blood is redder? Perhaps the blood of your intended victim is redder.' That is to say, it is not given to humans to play God by making judgements on the relative value of one human life against another. In the eyes of God, for all we know to the contrary, the life of a notorious sinner may be of greater 'value' than the life of the greatest saint. Some commentators argue that it is forbidden for even a large number of persons to save their own lives by taking life. Murder must be categorically forbidden since no human being dare assume God's mantle by assessing the value of a single human life against the lives of others who are bent on destroying that life, even when their motive is to save their own lives. The Sabbath, for example, may be profaned in order to save the life of a person dangerously ill and that person may eat on Yom Kippur if to fast may result in danger to his life. Murder must be an exception to the rule that a sin or a crime may be committed in order to save life since the crime of murder, unlike all the others, involves the taking of life.

Are there any circumstances in which recourse to violence is legitimate? Two such circumstances, according to the Classical Jewish sources, are:

        judicial punishments;
        self-defence.

Judicial punishments

The Bible appears to sanction both capital and corporal punishment. The very same verse in which murder is condemned enjoins the taking of the murderer's life: 'Whoever sheds the blood of man, by man shall his blood be shed; for in His image did God make man' (Gn 9:6). It can, of course, be said that there is no contradiction. Judicial punishments have as their aim the protection of society against aggressors and, if the most effective way of achieving this aim is for violence to be done to the violent, it must be done. A thing may be evil and yet a necessary evil. For all that, there is a marked tendency in post-Biblical Jewish thought to limit severely the legitimacy of pursuing violent means even if the aim is that of compassion and the eradication of violence in society. One must not make too much of the saying of Rabbi Akiba and Rabbi Tarfon in the Mishnah (*Makkot* 1:10) that if they had been members of the Sanhedrin no one would ever have been executed, or the saying in the same section of the Mishnah that a Sanhedrin which was responsible for one execution in seven years was a bloodthirsty court, and some say once in seventy years. When these things were recorded there was, after all, no Sanhedrin so that it was all theoretical and theory can afford to be idealistic. Yet in theory, at least, the tendency is present and was, in fact, given practical expression in the State of Israel when the Knesset decided, *on the basis of Jewish tradition,* to abolish capital (and corporal) punishment. (The death penalty for Eichmann was the sole exception.)

In the same manner as the Jewish tradition could see nothing strange in departing from the surface meaning of the Biblical passages enjoining capital and corporal punishments, it relegated other extremely violent injunctions – the command to exterminate the Canaanites and to blot out the memory of Amalek, for example – to ancient history never to be emulated by Jews. The Rabbinic doctrine of the 'Oral Torah' includes the idea that the authority for Jews is not the bare Biblical texts but the manner in which these have been interpreted and applied through the historical experiences of the Jewish people. To give another example, the Deuteronomic law regarding the stoning to death of the stubborn and rebellions son (Dt 21:18–21) is treated in the tradition as no more than a stern warning against the evils of juvenile delinquency. It was held to be quite inconceivable that the Torah would ever tolerate parents having their child executed or that parents would ever wish to have this done to their child. So far as judicial punishments are concerned it was further stated that once the Sanhedrin had ceased to function it was illegal for a Jewish court to impose corporal or capital punishment. It would be less than honest if we were to leave it at that. In the Middle Ages harsh punishments were meted out by the Jewish courts, the mutilation of certain classes of offenders and, in Spain, even the death penalty on occasion. This was in obedience to the Talmudic principle that for the protection of society 'illegal' methods of control could be exercised by the courts, the law giving back with one hand what it had taken away with the other. That this right was at times abused is undeniable. Jews, like others, have been guilty of religious intolerance, especially against their own. Yet an outstanding Orthodox Rabbi, Isaiah Karelitz, could say, and his opinion is quoted with full approval in the standard work of Jewish law, the *Encyclopedia Talmudit*, that in our age of little faith heretics cannot be blamed for their unbelief and that the persecution of heretics, tolerated and even advised in the earlier sources, cannot be allowed nowadays; the only way to win back unbelievers is the way of love. Cruel punishments have gone the way of other out-moded traditions in the name of the tradition itself. There is room for progress in Judaism and in this area, at least, progress has been hailed enthusiastically.

Self-defence
Violence is also held to be legitimate in self-defence. In the old Rabbinic formulation: 'If someone intends to kill you get in first and kill him.' The difference between killing in self-defence and killing an innocent man in order to save one's own life is obvious. Where the aggressor takes the initiative he is not innocent and it is intolerable that defence against his aggression should be disallowed. Unless there is resistance to aggression the world will be delivered into the bloody hands of the violent and the takers of life. Indeed, for the intended victim to allow himself to be killed rather than kill his attacker is for him to be guilty of suicide. By the same reasoning it is forbidden to stand by and witness a murder rather than protect the intended victim, by slaying the would-be murderer if that is the only way. If that is the only way – for the Rabbinic teaching urges that if the would-be victim can be saved by other means than by taking the attacker's life, by maiming him, for instance, it is an act of murder to slay him.

Thus, while there is no fully developed doctrine of the 'just war' among the ancient and mediaeval Jewish thinkers (how could there be when there was no Jewish state in which the question was otherwise than theoretical?), the principles out of which such doctrine can be developed are clearly stated in the Jewish sources: warfare is an abomination, resort to violence of any kind is evil and must be avoided utterly unless it be for the purpose of self-defence. War and aggression in self-defence are still evil but necessary evil in that the killing of the victims of the aggressor who takes the initiative or of the violent who attacks the innocent prevents the perpetration of an even greater evil.

Having come so far, the agonizing problem now confronts us: how is self-defence to be defined? There is a tale about a man who went to a psychiatrist for help. He was bothered, he said, by a cat scratching away inside him. The psychiatrist put the man under hypnosis, produced a black cat, woke the man up from his hypnotic sleep and declared: 'Your troubles are over . Here is the cat that was bothering you. I have taken it out of you.' 'No, doctor,' said the man, 'You see the cat that is bothering me is grey and that cat is black.' The trouble with any attempt to deal with contemporary issues of violence on the basis of our religious sources is that these state the principles in stark terms of black and white whereas we are bothered by the many questions which arise in the grey areas of life. Granted that self-defence is permitted, what of those circumstances where it is none too clear who is the aggressor and who the intended victim? In a war against an aggressor is the killing of civilians also allowed if that is the only way the aggressor can be vanquished and, if it is, are there any limits to the extent of the carnage permitted? Where does one draw the line between simple defence and a pre-emptive strike against a would-be aggressor? How do we guard against miscalculating the intentions of an enemy and against our own miscalculations that he intends us harm? The Rabbis, anachronistically but significantly, say that before king David would go out to battle he would consult the Sanhedrin to discover if the war he intended to engage in was legitimate. But even a Sanhedrin (or its modern equivalent in teachers of religion whose duty it is to bring to bear the principles of their faith on human relationships) will be impotent where it is not the principles themselves that are in doubt but their detailed application in very complex situations.

Does this mean that religion has nothing to say to a world torn apart by violence and conflict? By no means. The principles, at least, require to be stated by religious leaders loud and clear.

Human life, it is essential for religion to affirm and reaffirm, is sacred and violence evil. The leaders of society – the statesmen, the politicians, government and civic bodies and all who are responsible for initiating plans for human betterment – must be constantly reminded that violent means are not to be resorted to in the achievement of their laudable aims except in those very few circumstances (far fewer than most seem to imagine) where the alternative is far greater outbreaks of violence. This implies surely that the spokesmen of religion should not themselves engage in war-mongering or rabble-rousing, not even on such high-sounding but very dubious grounds of national honour and religious triumphalism, to say nothing of class-warfare or revenge. Surely we have all, at last, learned the lesson that God must not be invoked to destroy or cripple human life, that holy wars are the worst kind of wars, that a too-ready acceptance of the notion that God is on our side is to take the name of God in vain. Religion, and I include my own religion, has too often been the cause of violence. The lesson requires constant reiteration: God did not create in order for His creation to be destroyed by men. All men are created in His image. The real enemies of the human race are those bent on destruction, not least, when the praises of God are on their lips and a two-edged sword is in their hands. This is implied in the great dream of the Hebrew Prophets, Messianic to be sure but summoning mankind in the here and now, that nation will not lift up sword against nation, the wolf will lie down with the lamb, there shall be no hurting and no harming but the earth filled with the knowledge of the Lord as the waters cover the sea.

The Concept of Power in Jewish Tradition

An examination of the concept of power in the Jewish tradition must draw on the classical sources of Judaism, particularly the Bible and the talmudic literature, but the task is rendered especially difficult because of the diverse nature of these sources. The Hebrew Bible is not a single, homogeneous work but is rather a collection of books produced by different authors over a long period of time with, except for fundamentalists, a variety of responses influenced by the social, political and economic conditions which obtained at the time the books were compiled, to say nothing of the composite nature of most of the books themselves as uncovered by the massive researches of modern biblical scholarship. There is much agreement among the biblical authors but there is also disagreement. There is consent but there are also many contradictions. The same applies to the Rabbinic literature, produced in the rival schools of Palestine under Roman rule and Babylon under Persian, in which individual temperament and disposition have their part to play, so that, strictly speaking, it is almost as absurd to declare that the Talmud says as to declare that English literature says this or that. It is for this reason that it is extremely precarious, when discussing a complex moral issue, to speak of *the* biblical or Rabbinic or traditional Jewish point of view. It is tempting here to emulate the apocryphal leader-writer of *The Times* who settled down to his task with a long, blank sheet of paper on which he had written in the middle the single word: however. Yet on some questions, such as the one we are considering, it is still possible to detect a general thrust sufficient for certain conclusions to be drawn as to broad principles, always provided that confident assertion is tempered with a healthy degree of scepticism.

The concept of power implies a capacity to achieve ends by exerting control over something or someone. The man of power is able to manipulate things or persons so as to make them serve his interests or those of the causes in which he believes or for the sheer joy the heady experience of dominion gives him. Since power is self-serving, many moralists have tended to see it as intrinsically evil, liable, as in Lord Acton's famous dictim, to corrupt and in its absolute form to corrupt absolutely. It should be said right away that this is not the Jewish attitude to power, in so far as we can speak of a Jewish attitude, having in mind our previous reservations. A perusal of the Jewish sources seems to demonstrate that they see power either as morally neutral or, occasionally, even as a good, certainly not as an evil, provided that power is exercised to control nature, not to coerce other human beings, and provided that no attempt is made by man to imagine that he can achieve without divine aid the power to which he is entitled.

LIMITATIONS OF POWER

In the creation narrative at the beginning of the book of Genesis man is described as coming on to the scene after all other creatures had been brought into being:

> *And God said: 'Let us make man in our image, after our likeness; and let them have dominion over the fish of the sea, and over the fowl of the air, and over the cattle, and over all the earth, and over every creeping thing that creepeth upon the earth.' And God created man in His own image, in the image of God created He him; male and female created He them. And God blessed them; and God said unto them: 'Be fruitful and multiply, and replenish the earth and subdue it; and have dominion over the fish of the sea, and over the fowl of the air, and over every living thing that creepeth upon the earth.' (Genesis 1:26–28)*

Yet this 'dominion' or 'power' is not given to man unconditionally. He is obliged to acknowledge his indebtedness to God for the capacity with which he has been endowed of exercising control over God's world. His position in life is that of steward, not of owner. In later Judaism, the Sabbath, on which 'work' is forbidden, was interpreted as a weekly reminder to man that God alone has absolute control of His universe, man enjoying his privileges as a permission, not as a right. We read in the Babylonian Talmud (*Shabbat* 119b): 'Rabbi Hamnuna said: "He who prays on the eve of the Sabbath and recites *and the heaven and the earth were finished* (Genesis 2:1) Scripture treats of him as though he had become a partner with the Holy One, blessed be He, in the work of creation."' In another passage (*Sanhedrin* 10a) it is said that when a judge gives a true and fair decision Scripture treats it as if he had become a partner with the Holy One, blessed be He, in the work of creation. This idea of man's co-partnership with God was extended by the Kabbalists so as to make the flow of divine grace through all creation dependent on the prior efforts of man. Every deed of man has cosmic significance. 'The impulse from below awakens the impulse from above.' God has given man the power to empower God Himself as it were.

Yet, according to the classical sources of Judaism, for all the power man has, he is obliged to acknowledge that without God he is nothing. As the Deuteronomist puts it:

> *And thou shalt keep the commandments of the Lord thy God, to walk in His ways, and to fear Him. For the Lord thy God bringeth thee into a good land, a land of brooks of water, of fountains and depths, springing forth in valleys and hills; a land of wheat and barley, and vines and fig-trees and pomegranates; a land of olive-trees and honey; a land wherein thou shalt eat bread without scarceness, thou shalt not lack any thing in it; a land whose stones are iron, and out of whose hills thou mayest dig brass. And thou shalt eat and be satisfied, and bless the Lord thy God for the good land which He hath given thee. Beware lest thou forget the Lord thy God, in not keeping His commandments, and His ordinances, and His statutes, which I command thee this day; lest when thou hast eaten and art satisfied, and hast built goodly houses, and dwelt therein; and when thy herds and thy flocks multiply, and thy silver and thy gold be multiplied, and all that thou hast is multiplied; then thy heart be lifted up, and thou forget the Lord thy God, who brought thee out of the land of Egypt, out of the house of bondage; who led thee through the great and dreadful wilderness, wherein were serpents, fiery serpents, and scorpions, and thirsty ground where there was no water; who brought thee forth water out of the rock of flint; who fed thee in the wilderness with manna, which thy fathers knew not; that He might afflict thee, and that He might prove thee, to do thee good at thy latter end; and thou say in thy heart: 'My power and the might of my hand hath gotten me this wealth.' But thou shalt remember the Lord thy God, for it is He that giveth thee power to get wealth; that He may establish His covenant which He swore unto they fathers, as it is this day.* (Deuteronomy 8:6–18)

In the same vein a talmudic passage (*Hullin* 89a) observes:

> *It is written:* It was not because you were greater than any people that the Lord set His love upon you and chose you for you are smallest of all peoples *(Deuteronomy 7:7). The Holy One, blessed be He, said to Israel: I*

> love you because even though I bestow greatness upon you, you humble yourselves before Me. I bestowed greatness upon Abraham, yet he said to Me, *I am dust and ashes (Genesis 18:27); upon Moses and Aaron, yet they said,* And we are nothing *(Exodus 16:8); upon David, yet he said,* But I am a worm and no man *(Psalms 22:7). But with the heathen it is not so. I bestowed greatness upon Nimrod, and he said,* Come let us build a city *(Genesis 11:4); upon Pharaoh, and he said,* Who is the Lord? *(Exodus 5:2); upon Sennacherib, and he said,* Who are they among all the gods of the countries? *(2 Kings 18:35); upon Nebuchadnezzar, and he said,* I will ascend above the heights of the clouds *(Isaiah 14:14); upon Hiram, king of Tyre, and he said,* I sit in the seat of God, in the heart of the seas. (Ezekiel 28:2)

And, of course, there is the great verse that became in later Jewish literature and thought the supreme text for this idea of human insufficiency: 'This is the word of the Lord unto Zerubabel, saying: Not by might, nor by power, but by My spirit, saith the Lord of hosts' (Zechariah 4:6). A dominant theme in the Hebrew Bible is the power of God working through men so that while human achievement is recognized as a good, the constant implication is that human beings are the instruments and God the true Author of all. As Chesterton has said: 'God is not the chief character of the Bible. He is the only character.'

The use of power to manipulate nature so as to serve human needs is, then, perfectly legitimate and is seen as one of God's gifts to man. If such is needed, this is the biblical warrant, the religious justification, for the advancement of science and technology and the development of human culture. 'The heavens are the heavens of the Lord; but the earth hath He given to the children of men' (Psalms 115:16). On the other hand, the use of power by humans to bend other humans to their will is the oppression that is so ruthlessly condemned in all the classical sources of Judaism. The problem is posed in its most extreme form when a man can only preserve his own life by using his power to deprive another man of his life. This question is discussed in the Talmud and the conclusions codified as authoritative in the standard Codes of Jewish law. Here the principle of self-defence is accepted. 'If someone comes to kill thee get in first and kill him' is the rule as stated in the Talmud (*Sanhedrin* 72a). The victim of a potential murderer is not obliged to remain passive and allow himself to be killed. He must take up arms in his own defence to slay the aggressor (if there is no other way of escape) who, as the initiator, forfeits his claim to life. But otherwise than in self-defence a man is not allowed to purchase his life by depriving another man of his.

The example given in the Talmud *(Pesahim* 25b) is of a local tyrant who ordered a man to kill someone, telling him that if he failed to carry out the terrible order he himself would be killed. The case came before the fourth-century Babylonian teacher, Raba. Raba ruled: 'Let him kill you but do not kill that man. How do you know that your blood is redder; perhaps the blood of that man is redder?' As the great French mediaeval commentator, Rashi, explains it, a sin or a crime can be committed in order to save life but this cannot apply to the crime of murder, since a life is lost in any event in the very commission of the crime. The only justification for a murder to be committed in order to save life would be that the life of the murderer is more valuable than the life of his victim. Since no human being can possibly assess the value of one life over another, it follows that murder is never justified, not even where the motive is the saving of life. The commentators agree that the rule would apply even if the potential murderer were a great saint and the victim a profligate and even if a number of men were ordered to murder a single individual. The rule would still apply: 'How do you know that your blood is redder; perhaps the blood of that man is redder?'

EVIL POTENTIAL OF POWER

That the use of power by an individual or group to exploit other individuals or groups is an intolerable evil is implied throughout the Hebrew Bible. The biblical villains such as Pharaoh, Nebuchadnezzar and Haman are chiefly condemned because of their tyrannical abuse of power to enslave and destroy. It is true that in these instances the victims of agression are Israelites, yet it would be a complete distortion of the biblical record to read the biblical authors as disapproving of aggression only when it was directed against their own people by its enemies. The prophets condemn with equal vehemence the powerful among their own folk who take advantage of the weak, the poor and the stranger and they are sufficiently interested in the moral quality of the life of the other nations around them to castigate these nations for the crimes and atrocities they perpetuate against one another. Such is the constant burden of the prophet and is referred to repeatedly by the law-giver. A few illustrations among many will suffice for our purpose.

And a stranger shalt thou not wrong, neither shalt thou oppress him; for ye were strangers in the land of Egypt. Ye shall not afflict any widow, or fatherless child. If thou afflict them in any wise – for if they cry out at all unto Me, I will surely hear their cry – My wrath shall wax hot, and I will kill you with the sword; and your wives shall be widows, and your children fatherless. (Exodus 22:20–23)

And if a stranger sojourn with thee in your land, ye shall not do him wrong. The stranger that sojourneth with you shall be unto you as the home-born among you, and thou shalt love him as thyself for ye were strangers in the land of Egypt; I am the Lord your God. Leviticus 19:33–34)

Nowhere is the ideal more emphatically set forth than in the famous prophetic visions. It is true that these are messianic and so of little help amid the realities of power politics in an unredeemed world, and it is also true that some modern scholars are inclined to interpret some of these passages in a less than purely universalistic sense, e.g., let the nations stop fighting among themselves and then we will not become involved in conflict. For all that, these passages have been understood by generations of Jews in their universalistic sense and, at the very least, have established the principles by which Jews are expected to conduct their affairs in the here and now.

And it shall come to pass in the end of days,
That the mountain of the Lord's house shall be established as the top of the mountains,
And shall be exalted above the hills;
And all nations shall flow into it.
And many peoples shall go up and say:
'Come ye, and let us go up to the mountain of the Lord,
To the house of the God of Jacob;
And He will teach to us His ways,
And we will walk in His paths.'
For out of Zion shall go forth the law,
And the word of the Lord from Jerusalem.
And He shall judge between the nations,
And shall decide for many peoples;
And they shall beat their swords into ploughshares,
And their spears into pruning-hooks;
Nation shall not lift up sword against nation,
Neither shall they learn war any more. (Isaiah 2:2–4)

The same vision in almost identical words occurs in the book of the prophet Micah where the verses are added:

But they shall sit every man under his vine and under his fig-tree;
And none shall make them afraid;
For the mouth of the Lord of hosts hath spoken.
For let all the peoples walk each one in the name of its god,
But we will walk in the name of the Lord our God for ever and ever.
(Micah 4:4–5)

It is no departure from the plain sense of passages such as this to interpret it as a prophetic statement of the right of every people to self-determination and to be free from those who would enslave it by force. Again in the book of Isaiah there occurs the marvellous vision:

And there shall come forth a shoot out of the stock of Jesse,
And a twig shall grow forth out of his roots.
And the spirit of the Lord shall rest upon him,
The spirit of wisdom and understanding,
The spirit of counsel and might,
The spirit of knowledge and of the fear of the Lord.
And his delight shall be in the fear of the Lord.
And he shall not judge after the sight of his eyes,
Neither decide after the hearing of his ears;
But with righteousness shall he judge the poor,
And decide with equity for the meek of the land;
And he shall smite the land with the rod of his mouth.
And with the breath of his lips shall he slay the wicked.
And righteousness shall be the girdle of his loins,
And faithfulness the girdle of his reins.
And the wolf shall dwell with the lamb,
And the leopard shall lie down with the kid;
And the calf and the young lion and the fatling together;
And a little child shall lead them.
And the cow and the bear shall feed;
Their young ones shall lie down together;
And the lion shall eat straw like the ox.
And the sucking child shall play on the hole of the asp,
And the weaned child shall put his hand on the basilisk's den.
They shall not hurt nor destroy
In all My holy mountain;
For the earth shall be full of the knowledge of the Lord,
As the waters cover the sea.   *(Isaiah 11:1–9)*

In the admittedly late passage, considered by many scholars to be an interpolation, there is stated as clearly as possible that every nation, including the traditional foes of the Israelites, Egypt and Assyria, has its right to existence and its special role to play in God's world:

In that day shall there be a highway out of Egypt and Assyria, and the Assyrian shall come into Egypt, and the Egyptian into Assyria; and the Egyptians shall worship with the Assyrians. In that day shall Israel be the third with Egypt and with Assyria, a blessing in the midst of the earth; for that the Lord of hosts hath blessed him, saying: 'Blessed be Egypt My people and Assyria the work of My hands, and Israel Mine inheritance.'

(Isaiah 19:23–24)

ABUSE OF POWER

Most remarkable of all in this connection is the teaching of the prophet Amos that God's anger is kindled against the abuse of power even when both perpetrator and victim have no connection with the prophet's own people. Far from adopting towards his people's enemies an attitude of, 'Let them do what they like to one another and if they destroy themselves in the process so much the better,' the prophet seems to be saying that justice is indivisible and injustice and aggression are to be condemned wherever they occur and condemned in the name of God who created all men:

> *Thus saith the Lord:*
> *For three transgressions of Moab*
> *Yea, for four, I will not reverse it:*
> *Because he burned the bones of the king of Edom into lime.* (Amos 2:1)

The same prophet is as severe on the oppressors among his own people:

> *Thus saith the Lord:*
> *For three transgressions of Israel,*
> *Yea, for four, I will not reverse it:*
> *Because they sell the righteous for silver,*
> *And the needy for a pair of shoes;*
> *That pant after the dust of the earth on the head of the poor,*
> *And turn aside the way of the humble;*
> *And a man and his father go unto the same maid,*
> *To profane My holy name;*
> *And they lay themselves down beside every altar*
> *Upon clothes taken in pledge,*
> *And in the house of their God they drink*
> *The wine of them that have been fined.* (Amos 2:6–8)

Very revealing on this question of the abuse of power are the biblical attitudes towards the monarchy, the institution in which power was chiefly vested. When Samuel, at the command of God, finally yields to the request of the people to have a king appointed over them, he is ordered at the same time to warn them of the despotism inseparable from the royal rule:

> This is the manner of the king that shall reign over you: he will take your sons, and appoint them unto him, for his chariots and to be his horsemen; and they shall run before his chariots. And he will appoint them unto him for captains of thousands, and captains of fifties; and to plough his ground, and to reap his harvest, and to make his instruments of war, and the instruments of his chariots. And he will take your daughters to be perfumers, and to be cooks, and to be bakers. And he will take your fields, and your vineyards, and your olive-yards, even the best of them, and give them to his servants. And he will take the tenth of your seed, and of your vineyards, and give to his officers, and to his servants. And he will take your men-servants, and your maid-servants, and your goodliest young men, and your asses, and put them to his work. He will take the tenth of your flocks; and ye shall be his servants. And ye shall cry out in that day because of your king whom ye shall have chosen you; and the Lord will not answer you in that day. (I Samuel 8:11–18)

This devastating critique of the power of the monarchy is paralleled by the fearlessness of the prophets in admonishing kings for their tyranny; Nathan rebuking David in the affair of Uriab (II Samuel 12:1–15); Elijah foretelling Ahab's doom because the king had listened to his pagan queen to have Naboth executed so that he could take the vineyard he coveted (I Kings 21:1–26); Amos prophesying King Jeroboam's downfall despite the threats of the 'establishment' figure, Amaziah the priest of Beth-el (Amos 7:10–17). The Deuteronomist is less uncompromising but none the less lays down strict rules to restrict the king's powers. The king was not to be a foreigner who would have no brotherly feelings towards his subjects. He was not to multiply to himself horses, wives, silver and gold. He was to write for himself a copy of the law to be with him always 'that he may learn to fear the Lord his God, to keep all the words of this law and these statutes, to do them; that his heart be not lifted up above his brethren, and that he turn not aside from the commandment, to the right hand, or to the left' (Deuteronomy 17:14-19). King and subject were both members of the covenant people. Their relationship to one another was not to be that of Lord and master to his subordinates but that of brother to brother.

A typical statement in the Rabbinic literature occurs in the Mishnah (*Sanhedrin* 4:5) which discusses the procedure to be adopted in the ancient law courts when a man was on trial for his life. The witnesses to the charge, says the Mishnah, had to appreciate the heinousness of taking the man's life if he were innocent. They were to be warned of the enormity of destroying life by being referred to the Genesis narrative of Adam and Eve, in which all mankind is descended from a single pair. The Mishnah continues:

> *Therefore but a single man was created in the world, to teach that if any man has caused a single soul to perish Scripture imputes it to him as though he had caused a whole world to perish; and if any man saves alive a single soul Scripture imputes it to him as though he had saved alive a whole world. Again (but a single man was created) for the sake of peace among mankind, that none should say to his fellow: 'My father was greater than thy father'; also that the heretics should not say: 'There are many ruling powers in heaven.' Again (but a single man was created) to proclaim the greatness of the Holy One, blessed be He; for man stamps many coins with the same seal and they are all alike; but the Holy One, blessed be He, has stamped every man with the seal of the first man, yet not one of them is like his fellow. Therefore everyone must say: 'For my sake was the world created.'*

In this passage all the theological principles on the question of power are adumbrated. Every individual man is unique. He is a special divine coinage and is irreplaceable. Moreover, to destroy him is to destroy his whole potential, in fact, to destroy a whole world, while to assist his growth is to assist in the emergence of a whole world. And all men are brothers, the descendants of a common ancestor and the children of the One God. The gods of polytheism have their human favourites. The God of all the earth has infinite concern for every human being. It follows that no person is allowed to treat other persons as things to be used for his own advantage. It would be less than honest not to admit that in some texts the words 'of Israel' ave been added after 'saves alive a single soul' but this narrow interpretation is in none of the authentic texts. As the proof-text and the whole tenor of the discussion clearly demonstrate, the reference is to every human being, Jew or Gentile.

No discussion of the classical Jewish attitudes towards power can afford to ignore one of the worst examples of its abuse, the institution of slavery, which is tolerated in biblical law and which seems to be in flat contradiction to all we have said regarding the enormity of using human beings as tools. It must be realized, however, that slavery like polygamy is never enjoined but is tolerated. Social historians have been able to advance cogent reasons why, in ancient societies, it was not possible to outlaw slavery entirely. Yet the law severely curtailed the power of the master over his slaves. The Deuteronomist declares:

> *Thou shalt not deliver unto his master a bondman that is escaped from his master unto thee; he shall dwell with thee, in the midst of thee, in the place which he shall choose in one of thy gates, where it liketh him best; thou shalt not wrong him.* (Deuteronomy 23:16)

The slave was to be allowed to rest on the Sabbath

> *that thy man-servant and thy maid-servant may rest as well as thou. And thou shalt remember that thou wast a servant in the land of Egypt, and the Lord thy God brought thee out thence by a mighty hand and by an outstretched arm; therefore the Lord thy God commanded thee to keep the Sabbath day.* (Deuteronomy 5:14–15)

Most significant of all, the institution of the jubilee year, when slaves were set free, theoretical though it may well have been, is the form in which the ancient Hebraic protest against slavery expressed itself.

> *And ye shall hallow the fiftieth year, and proclaim liberty throughout the land unto all the inhabitants thereof it shall be a jubilee unto you; and ye shall return every man unto his possession, and ye shall return every man unto his family.* (Leviticus 25:10)

A fine comment by Rabbi Joshua Falk (1680–1756) notes that the verse does not speak of proclaiming liberty to all the slaves but to all the inhabitants. For, he said, a society in which there are slaves is a society which affronts every one of its inhabitants. Masters as well as slaves are the beneficiaries when the slaves are set free.

LEGITIMACY OF POWER

One of the conclusions which seems inescapable is that, according to the Jewish sources, power exercised for the realization of legitimate ends, one of which is the enrichment of human life, is a God-given right. There is nowhere any suggestion that power is evil in itself. It is not unknown in the history of religion for power to be relegated to the sphere of the demonic. The danger of such an approach is that it leads men to argue; since power is in any event evil but requires to be embraced for the sake of survival, logic dictates that it be given its head come what may. It is hard to appeal to ethical standards in an area acknowledged to be intrinsically unethical. Once, however, the legitimacy of power is acknowledged, ethics can step in to make the distinction between its lawful and unlawful exercise. It can then be declared that power is unlawful when it is exercised at the expense of the rights and ambitions, the property and life, of others. On the practical level, it hardly needs saying. The real problem is to define when power is being used to frustrate aggression and when it is being used as a means to aggression. So far as individuals are concerned, the man of integrity can generally recognize whether or not he is the initiator of the aggression and so whether the use of power against it is justified, and even when he is in doubt he may prefer to err in favour of others. In relations between groups or nations or federations the problem becomes far more complicated, both because the demarcation line between illegal aggression and legitimate self-defence is far more finely drawn and because in relations between groups excessive altruism is at the expense of the individual members of the group. A saintly individual can well be praised for a voluntary surrender of his power, for enriching another at the expense of himself. In the language of the Rabbinic book *Ethics of the Fathers* (5:10), the man who says, 'What is mine is thine and what is thine is thine,' is a saint. For the leaders of a group to say to the leaders of another group, 'What is ours is yours and what is yours is yours,' is far more questionable since those leaders would then be engaged in the extremely dubious activity of being saintly at the expense of those to whom their greatest loyalty is due. It is perhaps unlikely but not entirely impossible that this is the meaning of the much discussed verse 34 of the fourteenth chapter of the book of Proverbs, the Hebrew of which can be rendered: "Righteousness exalteth a nation; But the practice of *hesed* (i.e., excessive generosity) by a people is sinful."

A final word requires to be said on the wider question, with which we began our investigation, of the use of the classical sources for guidance with regard to a moral question such as this. In addition to the factors to which we have already called attention, the compositeness and lack of systematic thought in the sources and the difficulty of distinguishing between aggression and self-defence, one of which is condemned in the sources, the other advocated, new conditions not envisaged in the classical literature render some of the problems more acute. The problem of the emergent nations and their use of power in order to achieve self-determination, for instance, is one that could only have arisen in a world made much more sophisticated by the advance of technology, more divided by a variety of social and political theories, and made much smaller by the increase of communications. To be sure the principles are there in the sources. How they are to be applied is another matter.

Our investigation has, consequently, remained within the realm of pure theory. But in a religion like Judaism, which, for all its stress on activism, knows of the idea of midrash, of searching the Torah in order to discover the truth, theory is far from unimportant. The practical Jew is less than practical unless he has a sound Jewish philosophy to guide and inspire him. In *Ethics of the Fathers* (1:17) Rabban Simeon ben Gamaliel sounds a cautionary note: 'All my days I have grown up among the wise and yet I have found nothing of better service than silence. Not midrash in itself but doing is the main thing. And whoever is profuse of words causes sin.' Yes, midrash may not be in itself 'the main thing' yet it is through midrash that the eyes of the blind are opened. In the area we are considering, especially, theory counts. It is the theoreticians, for good or ill, who have moved men to action.

> We are the music makers,
>   We are the dreamers of dreams,
> Wandering by lone sea-breakers,
>   And sitting by desolate streams; –
> World-losers and world-forsakers,
>   On whom the pale moon gleams:
> Yet we are the movers and shakers
>   Of the world for ever, **it** seems.

Contemporary Judaism

The traditional view of Judaism as a revealed religion governing every aspect of life had to face severe challenges from the end of the eighteenth century when the Jews began to participate in the life of Western society and share in its values, often in contradiction to traditional Jewish life and values. This period saw the rise of the *Haskalah* (Enlightenment) movement lead by Moses Mendelssohn, a child of the ghetto who became renowned as a foremost German philosopher to become the inspiration for the Maskilim, as Mendelssohn's followers were called, who sought to influence Jewish intellectuals towards a greater appreciation of the need to adapt to the new order. The Maskilim saw themselves, not as rejectionists of the tradition, but rather as the promoters of a new approach in which the tradition could live side by side with the new learning and social forms. The *Haskalah* was, in a sense, a Jewish Renaissance in which, as the historian Zunz said, the Jewish Middle Ages came to an end. The *Haskalah* spread to Eastern Europe where it met with considerable hostility on the part of the traditionalist rabbis but its impact was such that no Jew could be impervious to its claims.

Even more severe challenges to the whole tradition were presented in the twentieth century by the Holocaust, in which 6,000,000 Jews, a third of the world population of Jewry, perished, and by the establishment of the State of Israel. These two events, the one catastrophic beyond belief, the other providing a new measure of hope for Jewish survival, both demanded a complete rethinking of the whole philosophy of Judaism. Questions have been raised for contemporary Jews hitherto unparalleled in the long history of Judaism. Are the Jews an ethnic group or are they the adherents of a religion? Is the main thrust of Judaism universalistic or particularistic? Can the doctrine of God's providential care of His people still be maintained in the light of modern historical investigation into the origins of Judaism and after the Holocaust? Is it still intellectually respectable to continue to affirm the doctrine that the Torah (the Jewish religion) is 'from heaven' or does this doctrine now require drastic revision? These kinds of questions have haunted contemporary Judaism, every version of which has now to be seen as a re-interpretation so that even Jews who opt unreservedly for the tradition do so, unlike their mediaeval counterparts, by a conscious act of the will. This article surveys the various responses, their reasoning and their practical implications, as well as the new institutions to which these have given rise.

The divide between Orthodox Judaism and Reform Judaism is ostensibly on the question of whether the tradition can be changed in the face of new situations, that is, whether the Torah is totally immutable in theory. Yet, since the emphasis in Judaism has been on practice rather than theory, the term Orthodoxy, denoting correct opinions, is somewhat misleading. The differences between Orthodoxy and Reform are especially marked with regard to the rules and regulations of Judaism, Sabbath observance and the dietary laws, for example. The Orthodox, in theory at least and with differing degrees in practice, are committed to keeping all the observances, this being for them the direct will of God. The Reformers, on the other hand, see many of the traditional observances as time-conditioned and not necessarily binding in all their details on contemporary Jews; the degree of observance being decided by individual choice. As the famous nineteenth-century Reform leader, Samuel Holdheim, put it, 'The *Talmud* (the source of the detailed rules) was right in its day and I am right in mine.' The vast majority of Reform Jews still observe male circumcision, 'the covenant of Abraham'; many Reform Jews do not eat pork and some observe the other dietary laws and keep the Sabbath in its strict, traditional form, refraining, for example, from writing or riding on the day, but all as a matter of free personal choice. Yet the reformers tend to see Judaism best expressed in the call of the Hebrew prophets for the pursuit of justice and the life of compassion and holiness rather than its strict observance of the ritual side of Judaism. The Orthodox view such attitudes as heretical. For the Orthodox the ritual observances are of the same order as the ethical, both commanded by God in the Torah, so that there can be as little picking or choosing in the one as in the other. For the Orthodox, the *Halakhah* (the legal side of Judaism), as the very word of God, has never suffered and can never suffer change. Conservative Judaism adopts a middle way, in which the *Halakhah* is seen as binding but in dynamic terms, in which the *Halakhah* has been and can be developed in the future in response to changing conditions. To give only one example, Reform Jews would argue that the Pentateuchal prohibition of kindling fire on the Sabbath (Exodus 35:3) is the product of the particular age in which it was first promulgated and has no eternal binding force. The Orthodox see the prohibition as eternally binding and extend it to the switching on of electric lights and the use of electrical appliances. Conservative Jews, while agreeing with the Orthodox that the prohibition is still binding, tend to interpret the *Halakhah* in such a way that a simple operation as switching on an electric light, one which adds to the enjoyment of the Sabbath, is not covered by the prohibition but they would not cook food or bake bread on the Sabbath.

On the doctrinal level, Orthodoxy understands the belief that the Torah is from heaven to preclude all biblical criticism with regard to the Pentateuch and is uneasy with the application of the new discipline to the rest of the Hebrew Bible and even with historical investigation into the other classical source of Judaism, the *Talmud*. Reform accepts modern historical, critical methodology as applied to all the Jewish sources and tends to see the sacred texts as the product of a purely human response to God rather than as divine revelation. Conservative Judaism, like Reform, accepts the findings of modern historical, critical investigation, but, unlike Reform, sees the process itself as a form of divine revelation, God giving the Torah not only *to* the people of Israel but *through* the people in its quest for the divine will.

Both Reform and Conservative Judaism is particularly strong in the USA, where Reform synagogues, or temples, as these are usually called, are organized under the Union of American Hebrew Congregations and Conservative synagogues under the United Synagogue of America. The major institution for the training of Reform Rabbis is the Hebrew Union College–Jewish Institute of Religion (in Cincinnati, Los Angeles and Jerusalem) and for Conservative Rabbis the Jewish Theological Seminary in New York and Los Angeles. In England there is a movement known as Liberal Judaism, very close in attitude to American Reform, and a Reform movement, closer to, though not identical with,

Conservative Judaism in the USA. The institution for the training of English progressive (that is, both Liberal and Reform) rabbis is the Leo Baeck College in London. In England there is also a comparatively small Masorti ('traditional') movement, very close in attitude to the version of Conservative Judaism in Israel with the same name. In recent years there has emerged in the USA a more right-wing version of Conservative Judaism known as Traditional Conservative Judaism in reaction to the decision by the Jewish Theological Seminary to ordain women as rabbis and other moves to the left in American Conservative Judaism.

Formerly it was unheard of for a rabbi to officiate at the marriage of a Jew to a Gentile but a fairly large minority of Reform rabbis, nowadays, do officiate at such marriage ceremonies in the belief that it is better in this way to retain the loyalty of the Jewish partner than to reject him or her completely. A furore has erupted over the decision by American Reform rabbis to accept as Jewish the child born to a Jewish father and non-Jewish mother, a decision running counter to the traditional rule that the Jewish status of a child is determined by matrilineal descent. Reform Judaism generally does not require the traditional *get* (bill of divorce) for the dissolution of a marriage, relying solely on the civil divorce. While all three groups accept proselytes, the Orthodox procedures are stricter and far more demanding of the prospective convert to Judaism than the other two groups.

With regard to eschatological beliefs, Orthodoxy holds fast to the traditional scheme according to which the soul, after the death of the body, awaits the time when it will be reunited with the body at the resurrection. Preceding the resurrection, the *Messiah* will come to redeem the Jewish people from its exile among the nations and, through Israel, usher in for all mankind a state of peace, justice and the establishment of God's kingdom on earth. The Messiah will cause the Temple to be rebuilt in Jerusalem and the ancient sacrificial system restored. This state will endure until the resurrection of the dead when a completely new state of existence will be brought about for all the righteous, Gentiles as well as Jews. Reform Judaism has abandoned belief in a bodily resurrection, substituting for it the belief in the immortality of the soul. And instead of the belief in the coming of a personal Messiah, Reform stresses the advent of the Messianic age in which the ancient hope of redemption will be realized. There is no official Conservative view on these topics but the majority of Conservative Jews no longer pray for the restoration of sacrifices. Naturally, there is considerable vagueness in all three camps about these tremendous mysteries and it might be said that generally the stress is on Judaism as a this-worldly religion in which the will of God is to be realized in the here-and-now with the eschatological scheme left in the hands of the Almighty. Even among the Orthodox, while belief in *Gehenna* (the place of afterlife punishment) is still maintained, there is very little hell-fire preaching and few attempts at exploring the geography of heaven and hell.

All contemporary versions of Judaism reject totally, of course, the Christian dogma but there has emerged in modern times a belief in the value of a dialogue with Christianity (and, to a lesser extent, with Islam), though many of the Orthodox grant this low priority.

The comparison in the last century of the division between Orthodoxy and Reform to that between Roman Catholicism and Protestantism, implying the strongest element of schism, is no longer in vogue. Nowadays, all three groups co-operate willingly in welfare work, in supporting the State of Israel and in other spheres of activity. Bodies such as the New York Board of Rabbis have as members rabbis from all three groups, although the more right-wing Orthodox have expressed strong disapproval of this kind of fraternization as weakening Orthodoxy by blurring the distinction between what it considers to be authentic Judaism and spurious substitutes. It is still rare, however, for Orthodox and Reform rabbis to exchange pulpits or to participate together in religious services. Some of the Orthodox deny the right of Reform and Conservative Rabbis to assume the title.

On the contemporary scene, there are few differences among the various groupings with regard to the State of Israel and its centrality in Jewish life. Zionism was at first opposed by the Reformers on the grounds that it tended to favour Jewish particularism against universalism; many of the Reform rabbis viewing the *Diaspora* not as exile but as the fulfilment of the prophetic ideal of the people of Israel as a 'light to the nations'. The Orthodox rabbis opposed Zionism on the different grounds that it tended to replace the Messianic hope of direct divine intervention with, to them, an impious anticipation of the redemption through human, political activity. But some of the Orthodox founded in the Mizrahi (in the State of Israel this is now the Mafdal, the National Religious Party) a movement of religious Zionism in which human efforts to secure a home for Jews in the land of their fathers are praiseworthy as 'the beginning of the redemption', that is, as human preparation for the ultimate realization of Messianism. After the Holocaust and the establishment of the State of Israel, most Jews, whether Orthodox or Reform, gave up the old opposition, which seemed now to be anachronistic granted the fulfilment of the Zionist promise and the burning need to repair the devastation caused by the Holocaust. The Agudat Israel party, formerly among the fiercest religious opponents of political Zionism, have now accepted, more out of necessity than conviction, the State of Israel and there are members of this party in the Israeli government. The older attitude of opposition only persists among the Hasidim of Satmar and the Neturei Karta. Sephardi and Oriental Jews were originally largely unaffected by the European movement of Zionism but are now fully active in Israeli political life with their own party of Shas.

With a brave insistence that Hitler should not have the last word, there has been an astonishing revival of Orthodoxy in the post-Holocaust world, including an extreme right-wing trend towards the preservation intact of the life of traditional Judaism as it was lived in the great centres of Orthodoxy in Eastern Europe. This trend is often described as that of Ultra Orthodox Judaism and its followers as the haredim (God-fearing), embracing many Ashkenazi Jews and a lesser number of Sephardi and Oriental Jews who seek to perpetuate, so far as possible, the way of life adopted by their ancestors, different in many respects from that of Eastern European Jewry. The Ashkenazi *haredim* are followers of Hasidism or the heirs to the tradition of Lithuanian Jewish piety and learning, hence known as the Litvaks. There are also *haredim* who follow the uncompromising way of Hungarian Orthodoxy, that of Rabbi Moses Sofer in the early nineteenth century whose slogan was, 'anything new is forbidden by the Torah'. The main Hasidic groups on the contemporary scene are: Belz Satmar, Lubavitch, Bratslav, Bobova, Gur, Klausenberg-Zanz, Vizhnitz and Karlin-Stolin. Each of these has its own *rebbe* (the name given to the Hasidic master, to distinguish him from the traditional rabbi) and its own rules and regulations. The Hasidim favour enthusiastic prayer in which the soul soars to its source in the divine. The ultimate aim of the Hasid is to attain to the state of *devekut* (attachment, of the mind to God), a mystical state in which the limitations of the material universe are transcended. This state is only held to be fully possible for the *rebbe* himself, his followers approximating to it through their to him. The *rebbe*'s word is law for his followers, who turn to him for guidance not only in the spiritual path but are advised by him on how to conduct themselves in every aspect of life.

The central institution for the Litvaks is the *Yeshivah*, the college of higher learning, based on the pattern of the great Lithuanian Yeshivot in the pre-Holocaust period. Today many thousands of young men spend years in a Yeshivah, where the main subject studied is the *Talmud*. The major 'Lithuanian' Yeshivot today are those of Lakewood in New Jersey; Telz in Cleveland, Ohio, and in Telstone near Jerusalem; Mir, Hevron and Kamenitz in Jerusalem; and, the largest of all, Ponievezh in Bene Berak. The Yeshivah caters to young men, from the age of eighteen, already fairly advanced in their studies. The main pattern in the Yeshivot is for the students to study by themselves in groups of two; reading through the particular Talmudic tractate designated for the term, and there are twice-weekly lectures by the Rosh Yeshivah, the principal or his assistants. In the majority of the Yeshivot, the language of instruction is Yiddish, as in Eastern Europe of former times, though in some modern Hebrew and English are also used. The usual method adopted is that of keen logical analysis of the difficult legal concepts, with the emphasis on in-depth learning. In these Yeshivot, too, a period is set aside each day for a period of reflection in which the classical works of Musar are rehearsed in a melancholy tune, with the aim of perfecting the moral and religious character. In the older Yeshivot of Lithuania there was, at first, strong opposition to the Musar movement, in the belief that the Torah (that is, the study of the Talmud) is sufficient for the improvement of the character. But, eventually, the opposition was silenced and, nowadays, Musar sessions are the norm, with a special moral tutor, known as the Mashgiah, to supervise this aspect of Yeshivah life. In addition to the large Lithuanian-type Yeshivot, there are a number of 'Hungarian' Yeshivot in which greater emphasis is placed on the practical rules of Judaism and there are some few Sephardi Yeshivot with their own traditions. In the Hasidic Yeshivot, the study of Hasidic texts is substituted for Musar. Many of the Yeshivot have attached to them a Kolel, in which married students are supported financially so that they can continue their studies without financial care. The aim of the Yeshivot is not to produce rabbis but to encourage the study of the Torah for its own sake (*Torah lishmah*), though, naturally, some students do eventually become practising rabbis. There has emerged as a result a Yeshivah 'world' of elitist scholars with a language and vocabulary of its own.

The Yeshivah world is not only opposed to secular studies, unless these are pursued for the furtherance of a career, never for their own sake, but has little use for the modern historical, critical approach to the sacred texts of Judaism. The whole notion of historical development is viewed with strong suspicion as introducing a human element into the revelatory scheme.

Reference should here be made to the recent Baal Teshuvah (penitent) movement. Many hitherto estranged young people have become attracted to the full Ultra-Orthodox life. Their progress towards this aim is assisted by special Yeshivot catering for their special needs, the heads of which are conversant with the inevitable traumas associated with the transition and favour a gradual approach foreign to the either/or of the general Yeshivah world.

The majority of the Orthodox, however, follow, in various degrees, the trend known as Neo-Orthodoxy, in which modernity and secular studies are embraced not only as means to an end but as good and valuable in themselves. As one of the leading figures in the Neo-Orthodox camp put it, 'You can have Shakespeare and the Talmud'. The two main colleges for the training of modern Orthodox rabbis are Yeshivah University in New York and Jews' College in London. The main organizations of modern Orthodox synagogues are: the Union of Orthodox Hebrew Congregations in the USA and the United Synagogue in Greater London. A phenomenon not to be overlooked or underestimated is the powerful swing to the right on the part of modern or centrist Orthodoxy in which the attitudes of the Ultra-Orthodox are becoming increasingly popular.

Judaism has not been unaffected by the tendency towards greater equality between the sexes and there are a number of Jewish Feminist Groups. In Orthodox synagogues women and men sit separately, women do not officiate in the services and are not called to the Reading of the Torah. The view of Maimonides is generally followed among the Orthodox that women may not occupy any communal office and they cannot serve as rabbis or cantors. But the ongoing debate about rabbinic ordination is concerned more with traditional norms rather than, as in the Church debate, with questions of dogma or doctrine. In Reform synagogues and in a majority of Conservative synagogues men and women sit together and women are ordained as rabbis and as cantors. The older view which excluded women from participation in the study of the Torah is no longer held even by the Orthodox, with few exceptions, though women are not admitted as students in the Ultra-Orthodox Yeshivot. In the circle of these Yeshivot, the graduates, whether in the Kolel or studying independently, are not the breadwinners, their wives earning the family living outside the home, usually by teaching children or by secretarial work.

Among all the various groups there has emerged a renewed interest in the Jewish theosophical, mystical system known as the Kabbalah, once attacked by the rationalists as sheer superstition but now popular not only in the circle of Jewish New Agers but for many other Jews seeking the mystical dimension to the religious life. Hasidism is in any event based on the Kabbalah but, under the influence of Martin Buber and others, Neo-Hasidism has emerged in which an attempt is made to translate Hasidic and Kabbalistic ideas and values into the language of the modern world. Followers of this trend will admire the Hasidic masters but, unlike in Hasidism proper, will not owe allegiance to any one particular master. The study of the Kabbalah is also engaged in by Sephardi Jews and there are even one or two Kabbalistic Yeshivot in which this science is an important part of the curriculum together with the *Talmud* and the *Codes*. Some few Jews adhere to what may be termed 'pop-Kabbalah' bordering on the occult, far removed from the study of the Kabbalah as a scholarly discipline introduced by Gershom Scholem and his school. But the Scholem approach is purely objective and scientific without any necessary attachment to the Kabbalah as relevant to contemporary religious life. Not all religious Jews see value in the contemporary interest in Kabbalah. Professor Saul Lieberman once introduced Scholem by declaring, 'The Kabbalah is nonsense but the scientific study of Jewish nonsense constitutes Jewish scholarship.'

Reconstructionist Judaism, founded by Mordecai Kaplan, was originally not a separate movement but had as a general aim one that cut across the different groups: the reinterpretation of Judaism in naturalistic terms; God as the power that makes for righteousness, not the personal, transcendent God of Jewish tradition. This philosophy of Judaism was popular among scientifically influenced religious Jews who found difficulties with the idea of a God who sets aside the laws of nature to perform miracles and can be dissuaded from His decrees by the act of petitionary prayer. These Jews found attractive Kaplan's description of Judaism as a 'religious civilization', embracing art, music and literature, rather than a pure but limited religion. Judaism was seen more as 'a way of life', the means of best realizing the Jewish potential and individual Jewish self-expression than as the fulfilment of the commands of a divine being outside the universe. But the renewed interest in the mystical dimension of Judaism and the stark reality of the human situation after the Holocaust seemed to demand, for many Jews, a belief in the God of tradition with whom human beings co-operate in overcoming evil. Consequently, Reconstructionism in the contemporary Jewish world is a philosophy of Judaism adopted by only a comparatively small group as a separate Jewish religious movement, with its own college for the training of Reconstructionist rabbis in Philadelphia.

External evidence of the particular group to which religious Jews belong is often provided by the mode of dress they adopt. Men belonging to the Ultra-Orthodox are usually bearded and dress in sombre garb, a long black coat or a shorter black jacket. Ultra-Orthodox women dress modestly in long dresses with sleeves reaching to the wrist and have their heads completely covered with a kerchief or, more usually, with a *sheitel*, a wig made of hair other than their own. The modern Orthodox usually adopt Western-style fashions and the men are clean-shaven but many of the modern Orthodox women still have their heads completely covered. Hasidic men usually wear on the Sabbath the sable hat known as the *streimel*, originally the type of head covering worn by the Polish nobility but into which various mystical ideas have been read. To the informed observer, subtle distinctions can be observed between the different Hasidic groups. The Lubavitchers, for instance, do not cultivate the curled side-locks (*peot*) worn by other Hasidim and they do not don the *streimel*. The Hasidim of Gur have larger fur hats than the others and the followers of some *rebbes* wear white socks on the Sabbath. All Hasidim attach great significance to regular immersion in the specially constructed ritual bath (*mikveh*) as an aid to purity. All the Orthodox observe the rules of 'family purity', according to which a married woman must immerse herself in the ritual bath after her periods before she can be reunited with her husband. The Ultra-Orthodox cover their heads with the prayer-shawl (*tallit*) during the morning prayers and the Hasidim don for all the prayers a girdle made of silk or other materials to divide the upper part of the body from the lower. A number of Hasidim do not wear ties since this belongs to a Gentile form of dress. Reform, Conservative and some of the modern Orthodox Jews adopt unreservedly Western forms of dress although some Conservative Jews and many of the modern Orthodox still observe the ancient law against wearing a garment made of both wool and flax (*shaatnez*).

As if to compensate for the destruction of millions of Jewish books in the Holocaust and as a powerful instrument for the renewal of Jewish life, there has taken place an astonishing amount of publications on every aspect of Judaism. The Yeshivot and other Ultra-Orthodox institutions publish journals of scholarship and monthlies such as The *Jewish Observer* in the USA. Modern Orthodoxy publishes the journal *Tradition* in the USA and *Le'Elah* in England, both of high standard. Among Reform publications are *Reform Judaism* in the USA and *European Judaism* in England. Conservative Judaism publishes in the USA a monthly with this name. It might be remarked that, while the non-Orthodox journals open their pages to all, hardly any of the Orthodox contribute to them and non-Orthodox writers are not normally welcome to contribute to the Orthodox journals. However, the journal *Judaism*, published in the USA by the World Jewish Congress, opens its pages to contributors from all the Jewish groups and has published important cross-group symposia; on the question of the role and importance of Jewish law for example. *Commentary*, a monthly published by the American Jewish Committee, is not, strictly speaking, a religious journal but often publishes articles of religious significance such as the symposium in the 1960s in which rabbis and scholars belonging to all the groups replied to a number of questions regarding their stance on Jewish theology, later published in book form. On the level of pure scholarship, the learned journals *Zion, Tarbitz,* and the excellent biographical journal *Kirvat Sefer* are published in Israel; the *Hebrew Union College Annual* and the *Jewish Quarterly Review* in the USA; and the *Journal of Jewish Studies* in Oxford. Most of the larger Jewish communities publish a newspaper though none remotely approaches the London *Jewish Chronicle*, a paper that has been in regular publication for 150 years and which, in addition to general Jewish themes, covers religious topics in articles, letters and editorial comment, succeeding on the whole in fairly representing all the different viewpoints.

Mossad Ha-Rav Kook in Jerusalem has published hundreds of critical editions of the ancient and mediaeval Jewish religious classics as well as the commentary *Daat Mikra* to the whole of the Bible, carrying through successfully its avowed aim of presenting the modern reader with a digest of the best scholarship, though it does tend to fight shy of biblical criticism, lower or high, in connection with the Pentateuch. The gigantic undertaking, *Enzyklopedia Talmudit* covers the whole range of Talmudic and post-Talmudic learning. The *Encyclopedia Judaica* gives a full account of every aspect of Jewish life with much information on the different religious groupings and their history. The Ultra-Orthodox, attractively produced, *ArtScroll* series, in English, covers large parts of the *Bible*, the *Mishnah*, the *Talmud* and other classics, and has produced prayer books for weekdays, the Sabbath and the Festivals; the attitude is that of fundamentalism throughout. The very capable Jewish scholar, Adin Steinsaltz, has produced singlehanded fine editions of many Talmudic tractates with his commentary in modern Hebrew. Some of these have also been translated into English, complementing but not supplanting the older translation of the complete *Talmud* into English published by the Soncino Press in London. Numerous works in Hebrew, English and other languages have streamed forth on Hasidism. The Musar movement, too, once somewhat shy of publishing its teachings in print, has now a large number of works to its credit. In the area of traditional Jewish law, hundreds of *Responsa* volumes have seen the light, either as original publications or as photocopies of works long out of print. The work *Otzar ha-Posekim* is a digest of all the *Responsa* on marriage law, now very widely used by Orthodox rabbis.

A particularly strong cult of personality has emerged among the Ultra-Orthodox, not only in Hasidism where it has always been prominent. Photographs of famous rabbinic personalities are on sale in bookshops, despite the earlier reluctance of rabbinic leaders to be photographed. A spate of rabbinic biographies describe the rabbinic and Hasidic heroes in hagiographical terms. Especially among Sephardi/Oriental Jews, the saints are depicted as miracle workers for whom healing the sick, levitation and the ability to turn water in wine are everyday occurrences. There are regular pilgrimages to the graves of the saints, though this stops short of actual intercession.

The departure from tradition is perhaps nowhere to be observed more strikingly than in the rabbinate. The main function of the traditional rabbi, still maintained among the Ultra-Orthodox and some of the modern Orthodox, is to render decisions in Jewish law in all its ramifications and, otherwise closeted in his study, to set the example of total dedication to the study of the Torah. Modern Orthodox, Conservative and Reform rabbis, on the other hand, model their role on that of the Christian clergyman in that they preach regularly, engage in pastoral work, officiate at marriages and funerals, and act as representatives to the non-Jewish world. When a spokesman for Ultra-Orthodoxy was asked what he thought about women rabbis, he replied that, in his book, men rabbis of the new type are also not acknowledged as true rabbis.

It must finally be noted that for all the views from extreme to extreme, Jewish religious life has not yielded to sectarianism and it is incorrect to speak of the various groupings as 'denominations'. With the exception of those who have embraced a different religion – the 'Jews for Jesus', for example – the members of the various groups may dub the others reactionaries or obscurantists or heretics or sinners or even as *goyim* (Gentiles), yet the others still remain in their eyes part of the Jewish community of faith; misguided Jews but Jews nevertheless.

Angels and Feminism

Jewish Feminism has challenged the use of exclusively male terminology for the Deity but, so far as I am aware, has found nothing objectionable in the use of the masculine form *malakhim* for angels; probably because belief in angels is peripheral in any event in contemporary religious thought, which, contrary to the conventional view, does know of women Rabbis[1] but seems to have little to say about angels in the guise of women. As a purely theoretical exercise, it is perhaps worth discussing whether traditional Jewish thought ever knows in fact of lady angels.

Years ago, I came across a Responsum of R. Hayyim Eleazar Spira (1872–1937)[2] in which he elaborates on the statement by R, Abraham Gumbiner (d. 1683)[3] to the effect that women need not wear white garments as men do on Yom Kippur since the reason for wearing white garments on the holy day is to resemble the angels and he quotes a Midrash[4]) to the effect that angels are male. The Midrash, on the verse: 'A wise man scaleth the city of the mighty' (Proverbs 21:22), interprets this to mean that Moses, the wise man, scaled the city of the angels when he went up to Heaven. The Hebrew word for mighty, *gibborim*, is read as *gevarim*, meaning men. Thus Heaven is the abode solely of male angels. As the Midrash puts it: 'The written form is *gevarim*, for all of them are males; there are no females among them.' Thus, apparently, Heaven is a celestial male club through whose august portals females are not allowed entrance; hardly a happy text for Jewish feminists.

This, however, is not the whole story. Surprisingly, neither Gumbiner nor Spira refers to another Midrash[5] in which it is stated explicitly that the angels do appear, occasionally at least, in the guise of women. The 'flaming sword which turns every way'

(Genesis 3:24) is interpreted as referring to the angels on the basis of 'His ministers are as flaming fire' (Psalms 104:4) and 'which turns every way' is taken to mean that the angels change their forms: 'sometimes they appear as men, sometimes as women, sometimes as spirits, sometimes as angels'. In yet another Midrash[6] it is said that God is called 'the Lord of hosts' (Hosea 12:6) because He does His will among the angels, i.e. He makes the angels assume various guises. 'Sometimes He makes them assume the guise of women, for it says: "And, behold, there came forth two women, and the wind was in their wings" [Zechariah 5:9], and at others, the form of men, for it says,"And, lo, three men" [Genesis 18:2].'

Maimonides (Guide, I, 49)[7] combines these last two Midrashim.[8] Maimonides was hardly a feminist yet he follows these Midrashim, albeit understanding them in the light of his own theological views. Maimonides writes (in the translation of Shlomo Pines): 'The angels are not endowed with bodies, but are intellects separate from matter. However, they are the objects of an act, and God has created them, as will be explained. The Sages say in *Bereshith Rabbah*: "The flaming sword which turns every way is called thus with reference to the verse: His ministers are as flaming fire. The expression 'which turns every way', alludes to the fact that sometimes they turn into men, sometimes into women, sometimes into spirits, and sometimes into angels." Through this dictum they have made it clear that the angels are not endowed with matter and that outside the mind they have no fixed corporeal shape, but that all such shapes are only to be perceived in the vision of prophecy in consequence of the action of the imaginative capacity, as will be mentioned in connection with the notion of the true reality of prophecy. As for their dictum, sometimes into women" – which implies that the prophets likewise "sometimes see the angels in the vision of prophecy in the form of women – it refers to the dictum of Zechariah, peace be on him: "And behold, there came forth two women, and the wind was in their wings."'

Maimonides here is, of course, true to his own view that an angel, as a disembodied spirit, cannot really appear on earth so that all such appearances in the Bible are in the mind of the prophet, that is, as Maimonides states here, in the prophetic vision. Thus, for Maimonides, there are no female angels but, for him, there are no male angels either. The various guises the angels adopt are solely in the psyche of the prophet. The Rabbis of the Midrash, on the other hand, do seem to take the appearance of the angels in their various guises quite literally. It is not clear how Maimonides would cope with the Midrashic statement that the angels are 'all male'. Maimonides makes no reference to this Midrash. As for the Rabbis, there is no real reason to postulate any difference on this matter between the Midrashic sources[9] since it can, without distortion, be suggested that in Heaven all the angels are male, whereas when they appear on earth they can, on occasion, assume the guise of women.

NOTES

1. See e.g. R. Hayyim Joseph Azulai, the *Hida*, in his *Shem Ha-Gedolim* under *rabbanit* where a list is given of learned women who functioned as Rabbis.
2. Responsa *Minhat Eleazar*, ed. Brooklyn, New York, 1974, II, No. 64.
3. *Magen Avraham* to *Shulkan Arukh, Orah Hayyim*, 610, note 5.
4. Gumbiner gives as his source the *Yalkut*, Proverbs 959 to Proverbs 21:22 but the parallel Midrash is in Leviticus Rabbah 31:5, ed. M. Margolis, Jerusalem, 1972, p. 723.
5. Genesis Rabbah 21:9, ed. Theodor-Albeck, p. 203.
6. Exodus Rabbah 25:2.
7. English translation by Shlomo Pines : *The Guide for the Perplexed*, Chicago University Press, 1963, pp. 108–9.
8. Actually, Maimonides gives the Genesis Rabbah version but in quoting the verse from Zechariah uses the Exodus Rabbah version as well since this quote is only found there.
9. As does Ginzberg: *Legends of the Jews*, Vol. V, note 63 on page 22.

Index

Aaron, 98, 167–8, 170, 171, 184
Abbaye, 29, 127
Abraham ben Isaac of Granada, 128, 131
Abraham (Hebrew Bible): *Akedah* (sacrifice of Isaac), 39–50, 188; Rabbi Aryeh Leib Heller, and *Shev Shemat'ata*, 180–1, 186; Rabbi Bana'ah, Talmudic tale by, 119; Sodom, plea for, 199–200; as symbol of Jewish spirit, 211–12
Abravanel, Don Isaac, 192
Adam and Eve, 58–9, 84, 92, 161, 170, 175, 234; sin of Adam, 163, 164, 173
'additional soul', notion of, 91
Aggadic statements, 106
Agudah, 211
Ahad Ha-Am, 213
Ahavat 'Olam, 122, 123
Akedah (sacrifice of Isaac), 39–50, 188; interpretations in Jewish tradition, 47, 48; place of sacrifice, 54, 58; as 'test', 40, 44, 47
Akedat Yitzhak (I. Arama), 60, 172, 179, 182
Akiba, Rabbi: on circumcision, 198; cosmology and, 27; on image of God, 219; Rabbi Aryeh Leib Heller, and *Shev Shemat'ata*, 177; on Torah, 76, 80–1; on violence, 221
Albo, Joseph, 188
Algazi, 123
Alkabetz, Solomon, 92
Almosnino, Joseph (Rabbi of Belgrade), 120–3
Almosnino, Moses (of Salonika), 165–6
Alshekh, Moses, 61, 168, 186
American Conservative Judaism, 240, 241
Amidah (Eighteen Benedictions), 146
Amoraic period, 31
amora'im, 127, 131
Amos, 232
Angel of Death, 96
angels, 161, 163, 213, 251–3
anthropomorphisms, 6, 11, 56, 60
apostasy, act of, 103, 104, 106
Aquinas, St Thomas, 11
Arama, Isaac, 62; *Akedat Yitzhak*, 60, 172, 179, 182
Arieli, Isaac, 149
Aristotelianism, 11
Ark, holy, 98
asceticism, 85–6
Asher, Jacob ben, 89

Ashkenazi Jews, 89, 243
athalta de-geulah (beginning of Redemption), 216
atheism, 6, 10, 67; Jewish people as 'atheists', 2
authoritarian religion, breakdown of, 138–9
averah lishmah (sin for the sake of God), 81
Av ha-Rahamim (Sabbath liturgy), 149
Avineri, Shlomo, 213
Avney Miluim (Rabbi Aryeh Leib Heller), 159
Avodah Zarah (idol worship), 102–3
Avot (Fathers), 66–7, *see also* Ethics of the Fathers
Ayin (Nothingness), 16
Azriel of Gerona, 16

Baal, 4, 41
Baal Shem Tov, Rabbi Yisrael, 126, 128, 139, 140
Baal Teshuvah movement, 245
Babylonians, 105
Balaam's ass, 30
Balfour Declaration (1917), 210
Bana'ah, Rabbi, 119
Baruch of Kossov, Rabbi, 141
baryone (ignorant men), 144, 145, 148, 150
Bedersi, Jedaiah, 119
Beer ha-Golah, 152
be'er (well), 161, 162
Belz (Hasidic group), 243
Bemalkhut Hayahadut (Rabbi Abraham Chen), 215
Beney Yisakhar, 151
ben Gamaliel, Rabban Simeon, 237, *see also* Ethics of the Fathers
ben Isaac, Abraham (of Granada), 128, 131
ben Levi, Rabbi Joshua, 145–6, 147, 148
ben Maimon, Moses (Rambam) *see* Maimonides, Moses
Ben Sira, 27
ben Yohai, Rabbi Simeon, 183–4
ben Zakkai, Rabban Johanan, 212
ben Zemah Duran, Rabbi Simeon, 174
Berachiah of Modena, Aaron, 96
Bereshith Rabbah, 252
Berger, Israel, 130–1
Berit menuhah, 128, 130
Bet ha-Midrash (House of Study), 147

Bet Knesset, 56
Bible: anthropomorphisms in, 6; creation myth, 4–5, 27–31; Criticism, Biblical, 71; Genesis, 17, 24, 26, 34, 84; God, descriptions in human terms, 2; goddess, lack of Hebrew word for, 4; Hebrew, 225, 240; linguistic problem, 66; mercy of God, 15; New English, 216; picture of world portrayed in, 23, 24, 25, 27; rending of garments, 97; on self-sacrifice, 39; villains, 229; Zohar and, 11
Binah Sefirah (Understanding), 16, 88
Birkat ha-Minim (benediction in which heretics are cursed), 146, 148, 149, 151, 152
bittul ha-yesh (self-annihilation), 139, 140, *see also Ayin* (nothingness)
Boaz, Joshua, 76
Bobova (Hasidic group), 243
Book of Psalms, 150
Bornstein, Rabbi Abraham, 153
Bratslav (Hasidic group), 243
'bread of shame' (*nahama di-kesufa*), 161
Buber, Martin, 135, 139, 141

Cain and Abel, 58
Canaanites, 62
Cassuto, Umberto, 56
Chardin, Teilhard de, 34
Chariot, Ezekiel's vision of, 20, 69
charity, virtue of, 175–6
Chassidim *see* Hasidism
Chen, Rabbi Abraham, 214–15
child sacrifice, 39
Chorin, Aaron, 151
Chosen People doctrine, 7, 182, 219
Christianity: contemporary Judaism and, 242; conversion of Jews to, 106, 110, 111; *Halakhah*, attitudes of towards, 102–16; idolatry, as form of, 105, 106, 107, 108, 109; Incarnation, 105, 107; Jesus, 13, 107, 111; as monotheism, 108; mysticism, 11, 13; Scholasticism in, 13; Trinity doctrine, 105, 107
Christmas, 112
circumcision, 198, 239
cistern (*bor*), 161, 162
Cloud of Unknowing, 11, 12, 13, 17, 18, 19, 20
Code of Jewish observances *see Shulhan Arukh* (Code of Jewish observances)
Commentaries to the Pentateuch, 71
Commentary (journal), 248
compassion, as high virtue, 219–20
Conservative Judaism, 72; eschatological beliefs, 241–2; publications, 248; in USA, 240, 241; women, position of, 246
Cordovero, Moses, 20, 149
corporal punishment, 221
corpse, preparations for burial, 95–7
cosmic cycles (*Shemmitot*), 33–4
cosmology, Jewish, 22–38; firmament (*rakia*), 24, 25, 26, 28; Heaven (*shamayim*), 23, 24, 25, 26; Mesopotamian cosmologies, 26; waters, 24–5

'cosmos', no word in Bible for, 24
Court of the Israelites, 55
Court of the Priests, 55
Court of the Women, 55
creatio ex nihilo doctrine, 26–7, 31
creation, purpose of, 161, 162
creation myths, 4–5, 27–31; world of Creation, 19
Criticism, Biblical, 71
Crusaders, 43
cycles, 128, 129

Daat Mikra, 249
Daniel, 30
Danishevsky, Rabbi Moses, 197
David, 150, 215, 223, 233
Day of Atonement *see* Yom Kippur (Day of Atonement)
Decalogue, 54, 58, 80
decline of generations dogma, and Hasidism, 126–33
de Leon, Moses, 14
Deluge, 24, 163, 183, 207
demonic powers, 94
demut (female principle), 174, 175
determinism, religious, 203
deus absconditus/deus revelatus, 15
Deuteronomy, 4, 118, 183, 221
devekut (attachment), 75, 76, 138, 243
dialectics (*pilpul*), 165, 166, 167, 171
Diaspora, 242
dietary laws, 212, 239
Dionysius, 12, 13
Divine Being *see* God
Divine Presence (*Shekhinah*) *see* Shekhinah (Divine Presence/female principle)
doubt, psychological phenomenon of, 6
dualism, 5, 16
Dubnow, Simon Markovich, 140; school, 135
duchaning (solemn rites performed in prayer before Ark), 97
dukhan (platform), 97
Duties of the Heart (Bahya Ibn Pakudah), 165, 187, 191
dybbukim, 137

Ecclesiastes, 24, 84
Ein Sof, and Kabbalah: body and soul, 87–8, 89; cosmology, 33; location of God, 52, 53; *Via Negativa* theology, 15, 16, 17, 18, 19, 20
Eishishok (Lithuanian town), 197
Eleazar, Rabbi, 85, 129, 146–7, 178
Eliezer ben Joel of Bonn, Rabbi, 147
Eliezer, Rabbi the Great, 68
Elijah, Prayer of, 18, 19
Elijah Gaon of Vilna, 16
Elijah (prophet), 80, 128, 137
elilim (non-entities), 4
Elimelech of Dinov, Rabbi Zevi, 151
elohim, 117, 118, 119, 121, 122
emanation theory, 28, 33, 88; world of Emanation, 19
emunah (faith), 67, 164, *see also* faith

Encyclopedia Judaica, 249
Encylopedia Talmudit, 222, 249
En Sof *see* Ein Sof, and Kabbalah
Enzyklopedia Talmudit, 222, 249
Ephraim, Rabbi Jacob ha-Kohen, 117–25
epikoros, 137
Eser orot, 130
et ha-elohim, 118
Ethics of the Fathers, 4, 66–7, 100, 219, 236, 237; Rabbi Aryeh Leib Heller, and *Shev Shemat'ata*, 162, 186, 187
etzem (body), 187
European Judaism, 248
evolutionary theory, 34
existentialist school of thought, 47–8
Exodus, the, 67, 80
Ezekiel, 56; Chariot, vision of, 20, 69, 198

faith: articles of, 8; direct experience, 80; *emunah*, 67, 164; God, Jewish concept of, 4, 5, 6–7, 8, 9; linguistic problem, 66, 67; tradition, and, 78, 79, 81
Falk, Rabbi Joshua, 235
fear of God, 77, 187, 188, 189
Feinstein, Rabbi Moses, 71
feminism, 251–3; Jewish Feminist Groups, 245; rabbis, women ordained as, 241
festivals, Sabbath distinguished, 176
firmament (*rakia*), 24, 25, 26, 28–9
forbidden food, 181
Formation, world of, 19
Franco, Joseph Rahamim (Rabbi of Jerusalem), 110–11
Frankel, Zachariah, 211
Free Will doctrine, 118–119,168, 203–4
Friedländer, M., 75

Gamaliel, Rabban, 27
Gaster, T. H., 23–4
Gehenna (afterlife punishment, place of), 242
Genesis, 17, 24, 26, 34, 84; Adam and Eve *see* Adam and Eve; Isaac, sacrifice of *see* Akedah (sacrifice of Isaac), problem of
Gentiles: business relationship with Jews, Talmud on, 106, 107; idols, worship of, 103, 106; Jews, married to, 241
Geonim, 103, 104, 128; Geonic principle, 105
Gerondi, Rabbi Nissim (*Ran*), 185
Gershom of Mainz, Rabbenu, 110, 111
Gersonides, 31, 32
get (Jewish divorce), 102, 110, 241
Gevurah (God's sternness and judgments), 88, 121
gezerah shavah (Talmudic method), 69
Gibeah, men of, 182
Ginsberg, Harold Louis., 211
Glick, Rabbi Wolf of Brooklyn, 153–4
God, 2, 3, 13, 15, 24, 28, 219; anger of, 121, 183, 232; attributes of, 14–15; faith in *see* faith; fear of, 77, 187, 188, 189; goodness of, 5, 15; in His essence/in manifestation, 1, 6, 15, 87, 204; image of, 218–19, 224;

Jewish conception of, 1–9; location of, 51–4, 212–13; man's knowledge of, 201–2, 204; nearness/remoteness, 2, 7; as 'One' *see* 'One'; sternness and judgments, 121; will of, 39–40, 165, 200–1, 239
goddess, lack of Hebrew word for, 4
Godhead, 88; female principle in *see* Shekhinah (Divine Presence/female principle); three equal Persons in, 108
Golden Calf, 117, 118, 119, 120, 154
Gombiner, Abraham, 89, 98
Graetz, Heinrich, 134
Gumbiner, Rabbi Abraham, 251
Gur 'Aryeh' (Judah Loew ben Bezalel, Maharal of Prague), 169
Gur (Hasidic group), 243, 247

Haggadah, Passover, 149
haggadot shel dofi, 70
Hagiographa, 16
Hakham Zevi, 123
Ha-Kohen, Rabbi Ephraim *see* Ephraim, Rabbi Jacob ha-Kohen
Ha-Kohen, Rabbi Hananiah, 205
Ha-Kohen, Rabbi Hayyim (of Aleppo), 189
Halakhah: Christianity, attitudes towards, 102–16; conversions and, 169; God's will, duty to obey, 45; Orthodox/Reform differences, 240; theological *motif* introduced into, 104
Halevi, Judah, 61, 62
halitzah ceremony, 104, 110
Ha-Makom (the Place), 60, *see also* God
ha-midrash (house of study), 57
Hanina b. Dosa, Rabbi, 127
Haredim (Strictly Orthodox Jews), 243
Hasidism: attire, 138, 247–8; body and soul, 89; cosmology, 33; decline of generations dogma, 126–33; groups, 243; growth of, 134; *lishmah* concept, 75; Mitnaggedim compared, 76; mystic joy, 135; of Neturei Karta, 243; relevance/irrelevance, 134–43; on Sabbath, 91; of Satmar, 243; Zaddik, doctrine of, 75, 91–2, 135, 136–7
Haskalah (Enlightenment) movement, 150, 238
hataim (sins), 144–5
havdalah (division) ceremony, 94
Hayyim Eleazar of Munkacs, Rabbi (Munkacer Rebbe), 150, 151, 153, 154
Heaven (*shamayim*): cosmology, 23, 24, 25, 26; Torah from, 69, 70, 71, 72, 211, 239, 240
Hebrew College Annual, 248
heemidan, 79
Heller, Rabbi Aryeh Leib, 159–95
heretics (*minim*), 102, 146, 151, 152, 155, 222
hermeneutical principle, 69
Hershel of Cracow, Rabbi, 150
Heschel, Abraham Joshua, 135, 141
Hesed Sefirah (Love), 88, 99
Hevra kaddisha (Holy Brotherhood), 96, 97
Hevron Yeshiva (Israel), 244
Hezekiah, 33

'Higher Garden of Eden', 96
High Priest, 54, 55
Hilkiah, Abba, 148, 150, 155
Hillel (sage), 88, 181, 192, 212
Hillel, School of, 27, 170, 171
hinnom (with grace), 169
Hisda, Rabbi, 173
hitlahavut (burning enthusiasm), 134
Hiyya bar Abba, Rabbi, 74
hiyyuvi (divine attribute), 11
Hod Sefirah (Splendour), 88
Hoffman, Rabbi David, 109
Hokhmah Sefirah (Wisdom), 16, 17, 20, 88
Holdheim, Samuel, 239
Holocaust, 134, 238, 243, 248
Holy of Holies, 26, 54, 55, 56, 58
holy places, 51–65; mediaeval philosophers, 57–63; sources, 54–7, 63
'holy sparks' doctrine, 89, 139, 214
Horowitz of Frankfurt, Rabbi Markus, 109
Horowitz, Shabbetai Sheftel, 98
Hoshen Mishpat, 159
human life, sanctity and meaning, 218–24; compassion as high virtue, 219–20; Man created in God's image, 218–19, 224; murder, as greatest evil, 220–4; violence as evil, 220
Hurwitz, Rabbi Phineas Elijah, 34

Ibn Adret, Solomon (Rabbi of Barcelona), 119
Ibn Asher, Bahya, 45
Ibn David, Rabbi Abraham, 118, 204
Ibn Ezra, Abraham, 26, 43, 71, 93, 129–30
Ibn Pakudah, Bahya, 14, 15, 79, 85, 140; *Duties of the Heart*, 165, 187, 191
idolatry: Christianity, and, 102–9; God, Jewish conception of, 2, 4; as spiritual sin, 183; tradition and, 77, *see also* paganism
Igra, Meshullam (Rabbi of Pressburg), 159
Imitatio Dei, 149, 219
Imrei kodesh, 130
Inge, Dean, 138–9
intermarriage, 103, 241
Isaac, binding of *see Akedah* (sacrifice of Isaac)
Isaiah, 212; book of, 231
Ishmael, Rabbi, 27
Islam, 103, 104, 111
Israel: children of, 62, 186; Conservative Judaism in, 241; establishment of State, 238, 243; Land of, 55, 212; Mesorti movement, 211; Promised Land, 54, 212; sins of, 187; unification of, 191, *see also* Zionism
Israelites, Court of, 55
Isserles of Cracow, Moses, 89, 94, 107, 108, 109, 110, 111, 112
I–Thou relationship, 139–40

Jacob, 192
Jacob of Izbica, Rabbi, 77
Jael, sinful act of, 81
Jeremiah, 41

Jeroboam, King, 233
Jesus Christ, 13, 107, 111
Jewish Chronicle, 248
Jewish cosmology *see* cosmology, Jewish
Jewish Feminist Groups, 245
Jewish Observer, 248
Jewish people: as adherents of religion, 238; as 'aetheists', 2; Ashkenazis, 243; business relationship with Gentiles, Talmud on, 106, 107; chosen doctrine, 7, 182; as chosen by God, 7; church, permission to enter, 108; conversion to other religions, 102, 104, 106, 110; as ethnic group, 238; Sephardim, 89, 243, 246, 249, *see also* Judaism
Jewish Theological Seminary (New York), 211, 240, 241
Jews' College (London), 245
Job, book of, 5
Johanan, Rabbi, 27–8, 169, 171, 178, 204
John of Salisbury, 127
Jonah, 30, 41
Joseph, Rabbi, 73, 74
Joseph, Rabbi Mordecai of Izbica, 141
Joshua, 33, 41
Joshua ben Levi, Rabbi, 145–6, 147, 148
Journal of Jewish Studies, 248
Judah, Rabbi, 127, 145, 151
Judaism, 248
Judaism: Aristotelianism in, 11; authority problem in, 200; Conservative *see* Conservative Judaism; contemporary, 238–50; conversion to, 169; dogmas, 68, 69; God, conception of, 1–9; Liberal *see* Liberal Judaism; mysticism, 11; 'normative', 135–6; Orthodox *see* Orthodox Judaism; publications on, 248; Reconstructionist, 246–7; Reform *see* Reform Judaism; symbols of faith, Rabbi Meir Simhah on, 197–198, *see also* Hasidism; Jewish people; Kabbalah
Judgment Day, 3, 164, 165
Judgment (*Sefirah*), 34
judicial punishments, murder, 221–2
Jüdische Wissenschaft, 159, 196
'Just War', notion of, 222–3

Kabbalah, 15, 23, 53, 137, 141, 160; body, and, 87, 88, 96; contemporary interest in, 246; cosmology, and, 33, 34; emanation theory, 28, 33; God, revelation of, 202; Lurianic *see* Lurianic Kabbalah; 'popKabbalah', 246; power of, 137–8; Sabbath, and sexual activity, 93–94; Sefirot *see* *Sefirot, Ten*; terminology, 66, 80; on 'upper worlds', 33, 94; Zohar *see* Zohar, *see also Ein Sof*, and Kabbalah; Hasidism; mysticism, Jewish
Kadushin, Max, 68, 99
Kaidenover, Rabbi Zevi Hirsch, 152
Kamenitz Yeshiva (Israel), 244
kanefot (corners or wings), 24
Kaplan, Mordecai, 246–7

Karelitz, Isaiah, 222
Karlin-Stolin (Hasidic group), 243
Karo, Rabbi Isaac, 186
Karo, Rabbi Joseph, 89, 94, 119; *Maggid Mesharim* (mystical diary) of, 167, 172
Kattina, Rabbi, 29
Kav ha-Yashar, 152
kavvanah, 86, 152
kedushah (sanctity), 73, 212
kelippot (shells), 89
Keri, 119
keriah (rending/tearing), 97
Keter Sefirah (divine will), 16, 17, 88
Ketiv, 119
Ketzot ha-Hoshen, 159
Khazar, King of, 61, 79–80
kiddush (sanctification), 92
Kierkegaard, Soren Aabye, 3, 40, 42, 43, 44, 45, 46, 48, 140
kinyan sudar (delivery of object), 185
Kirvat Sefer, 248
kis ehad le-khulanu (common purse for all), 207
Klausenberg-Zanz (Hasidic group), 243
Klein, Rabbi Menashe, 151–4
kohen: conversion to Christianity, 110–11; defined, 95
Kohen, Rabbi Hayyim, 95
Kolel, 244
kol ha-rish'ah (wickedness), 149, 151
Kook, Rabbi A. I., 34
Koran, 70
Korhah, Rabbi Joshua b., 78
Kotzk, Menahem Mendel of, 141
Koznitzer Maggid, 141
Krochmal, Nahman, 70, 171
Kuzari, 61, 79

Lakish, Resh, 169–70, 171
Lamm, Rabbi Norman, 35
Landau, Ezekiel (Rabbi of Prague), 107, 160
Lange, I. S., 71
Langer, Jiri, 141
Le'Elah, 248
Leo Baeck College (London), 241
Leviathan, 31
Levi, Rabbi, 179, 185
levirate marriage, 153
Levites, 98
Levitical laws, 54
Levi Yitzhak (Rabbi of Berditchev), 215
Liberal Judaism, 240
Lieberman, Saul, 246
Lilith, power of, 137
lishmah (for the sake of Torah), 74, 75, 185
Litvaks, 243, 244
Loew ben Bezalel, Judah (*Maharal* of Prague): *bor/be'er* distiguished, 162; *Gur 'Aryeh'*, 169; on Judaism as tolerant religion, 155; Klein's references to, 152; *Netzah Yisrael*, 182; Rabbi Aryeh Leib Heller, and *Shev Shemat'ata*, 160, 168, 170, 177, 182, 184

Loewe, Rabbi Judah, 152
Lot, inhabitants of, 198–9
Lubavitch (Hasidic group), 243, 247
Luftavir, Rabbi Abraham, 197
Luria, Isaac (*Ari*, mystic of Safed), 87, 122, 152, 155
Lurianic Kabbalah: on body, 87, 89; Hasidism and, 137; Rabbi Aryeh Leib Heller, and *Shev Shemat'ata*, 160, 163, 173; on Sabbath, 91; Zionism, and, 214

Ma'arekhet ha-'Elohut (Kabbalist work), 189
maariv service, prayer of, 210
Maavar Yabok (Ford of Yabok), 96
Maccabees, second book of, 27
Mafdal (National Religious Party), 242–3
Magen Avraham, 89
Maggid Mesharim see Karo, Rabbi Joseph
Maggid Mesharim (mystical diary), Karo, Rabbi Joseph, 167, 172
Maggid of Rovno, 129
Maharal of Prague *see* Loew ben Bezalel, Judah (*Maharal* of Prague)
Maharit, 119–20
Maimonides, Moses: on *Akedah* (sacrifice of Isaac), 44–5, 47; on angels, 252, 253; on body and soul, 85, 87, 89, 100; Code of Jewish law, 57, 160; cosmology of, 30, 31–2; on God, 1, 6, 8, 15, 202, 207; on Golden Calf, worship of, 118; on good and evil, choice of, 162–3; 'Guide for the Perplexed', 15, 58, 59, 173; on holy places, 58, 59, 62; on Islam, 104, 105; Jewish tradition, and, 68, 70, 71; Rabbi Aryeh Leib Heller, and *Shev Shemat'ata*, 190; on Rabbinic authority problem, 200; on Sabbath, 90; on Talmud, 128; on women, 245, *see also* Nahmanides
malakhim (angels), 161, 163, 213, 251–3
Malkhut Sefirah (Sovereignty), 88, 91, 92
man: animal nature of, 174; conduct of, 163; creation of, 161, 162; duties of, 206; God, image of, 218–19, 224
Manasseh (wicked king), 70, 71
manna, 167, 168, 169, 172
man's cosmic significance, doctrine of, 35
Marduk, 4
marital relations, 92–3
marriage, as religious duty, 3
martyrdom, 39, 104, 105
Mar Ukba incident, 146–7
Mashgiah (moral tutor), 244
Maskilim (followers of Moses Mendelssohn), 167, 238
masorah, 66
Masorti movement (England), 241
Matrona, 137
matzo (unleavened bread), 181
Mazeh, Jacob (Chief Rabbi of Moscow), 140
mazikim, 137
Meah Berakhot (One Hundred Blessings), 86, 93
Megillah, 216

Index

mehokek (copyist), 70
Meiri, Menahem (Rabbi of Perpignan), 105
Meir, Rabbi, 144, 145, 147, 148
Meir Simhah (Rabbi of Dvinsk), 196–208; appointment as Rabbi, 197; life of, 196–7, 207–8; *Meshekh Hokhmah*, 196, 197; *Or Sameah*, 196, 197
melekh ha-olam (King of the Universe), 24
Menahem Mendel of Vitebsk, Rabbi, 152
Mendelssohn, Moses, 68, 238
Meroz, 34
Meseritcher Maggid, 135
Meshekh Hokhmah (Rabbi Meir Simhah), 196, 197
meshummad, 102, 104
Mesopotamian cosmologies, 26; creation myths, 31
Mesorti movement (Israel), 211
Messiah, 155, 178, 211, 215; Messianic Age, 63, 130, 202, 241; Messianic hope, 216, 217; Orthodox/Reform position contrasted, 241
met (death), 136
metempsychosis (gilgul), 137
Middle Ages, 95, 102–3, 149
Midrash: Adam, creation of, 161; and *Akedah* (binding of Isaac), 45; on angels, 251–2; body and soul, 88; circumcision, 198; Golden Calf, worship of, 118; Jewish tradition, 74, 75, 79, 81; Rabbi Aryeh Leib Heller, and *Shev Shemat'ata*, 172, 177, 180, 182, 187, 189; Rabbis of, 252–3; Sabbath, 92
Midrash Tanhuma, 166
mikveh (ritual bath), 247
Min (heretic), 145, 147, 211
minim (heretics), 102, 146, 151, 152, 155, 222
miracles, 29, 32–3; miracle-working, 126–7; Talmud, tales in, 131
Miriam, 167–8, 170, 171, 184
Mir Yeshiva (Israel), 244
mishkan (Tabernacle), 56
Mishnah: *Akedah* (binding of Isaac), 40; body and soul, 84; compilation, 90; cosmology, 27; death and burial rites, 95, 96–7; Fathers of, 30; on holy places, 55; on murder, 233–4; on Sabbath, 90; *Shema*, 78; Torah, revelation of, 69
Mishneh Torah (Code), 89, 90
Mitnaggedim (opponents of Hasidism), 75, 76, 135, 137, 140
mitzvot (precepts): body and soul, 86, 87, 88, 89; Jewish tradition, 72, 74, 75, 78
Mizrachi movement, 211, 242–3
Moed Katan (Talmudic statement), 95
Moloch worship, 42
monotheism: Christianity, 108; cosmology, 26; holy places, and, 51; Muslims, 103, 104; *Shema*, as affirmation of, 4
Moriah, Mount, 40, 43, 54
Moscato, Judah, 181
Moses, 42, 69, 97, 149, 162, 205, 215; Aaron and Miriam, criticism by, 167, 171; belief in, 67–8; holy places, and, 60, 61; Jewish tradition, 67–8, 69, 70, 80; Rabbi Ephraim Ha-Kohen, and, 117, 118; Song of, 73
Mossad Ha-Rav Kook (Jerusalem), 249
motives, pure and impure, 185, 186
mourning, 111–12; rending of garments (*keriah*), 111
Munkacer Rebbe (Hayyim Eleazar of Munkacs, Rabbi), 150, 151, 153, 154
murder, as greatest evil, 220–224; judicial punishments, 221–2; Mishnah on, 233–234; self-defence, 222–4, 228–9
Musaf prayer, 184
Musar, 244, 249
Muslims, 103, 104, 111
mysticism: Christian, 11, 13; Jewish, 11; 'normal', 9, 99, see also Hasidism; Kabbalah
'myth and ritual' school, 26

nahama di-kesufa ('bread of shame'), 161
Nahman of Bratzlav, Rabbi, 141
Nahmanides, 62, 78, 100, 200, see also Maimonides, Moses
Nahum of Gimzo, 118
Nathanson, Joseph Saul (Rabbi of Lemberg), 109
National Religious Party (Mafdal), 242–3
Nazirite, the, 86
Nazis, 219
Nebuchadnezzar, 28, 105, 229
nefesh hayyah (living soul), 84
nefesh (lowest part of soul), 96
Nehemiah, Rabbi, 151
Neo-Hasidism, 139, 246
Neo-Orthodoxy, 245
Neo-Platonists, 1, 11, 15; Proclus, 12
neshamah (highest part of soul), 96
Netzah Sefirah (Victory), 88
Netzah Yisrael, 182
New Year festival, 26, 39, 149, 212, 213
New York Board of Rabbis, 242
Ninth of Av, 180, 181
Nittel (Christmas), 112
Noah, 103
Noahide laws, 103, 104, 106, 107, 108
No'am Elimelekh, 129, 136
'normal mysticism', 9, 99
Notzerim, 105
Numbers, book of, 97

oaths, taking, 106, 107
olam, meaning, 24
'One': meaning, 5; *Via Negativa* theology, 11, 12, 15
oneg shabbat (Sabbath delight), 90, 91, 94, 99–100
Orak Hayyim, 94
Oral Torah, 72, 166, 167, 184, 190, 221
Oriental Jews, 89, 243, 249
Or Sameah (Rabbi Meir Simhah), 196, 197
Orthodox Judaism, 72, 96, 100, 149; Neo-Orthodoxy, 245; Reform contrasted, 239–42; Strictly Orthodox Jews, 243, 249, 250; synagogues, 245

Orthopraxy, 72
Otzar ha-Posekim, 249

paganism, 4, 102–104; Christians, and, 105; see also idolatry
Paltiel, Zevi, 197
Papa, Rabbi, 127
Pappa, Rabbi, 118
particularism, 8, 61, 239, 242
Paschal lamb, 181
Passover, 149, 181
Pentateuch, 16, 69, 73, 240, 249; Commentaries to, 71
Pharaoh, 229
Pharisees, 95
Philo, 42, 84
philosophers, mediaeval, 57–63
Phinehas of Korets, Rabbi, 129, 130
pilpul (dialectics), 165, 166, 167, 171
Pines, Shlomo, 252
Pinhas b. Yair, Rabbi, 127
planets, 32, 34, 35
Plato, 31
Plaut, Rabbi W. Gunther, 35, 46–7
Plotinus, 11
pluralism, religious, 53
polytheism, 15; rejection of, 4, 5
Ponievezh Yeshivah (Bene Berak), 244
Porch, the, 55
power: abuse of, 232–235; evil potential of, 229–32; Jewish tradition, 225–37; legitimacy, 235–7; limitations of, 226–9
Prayer of Elijah, 18, 19
Prayer of St Denis, 18, 19
priestly blessing, 97–9, 111
priests, worship of idols, 110
Priests, Court of, 55
primordial light, 28
Prince of the Sea, rebellion of, 31
Proclus, 12
Prometheus legend, 7
Promised Land, 54, 212
prophecy, 177, 212, 230
Prophets, 16, 45, 224, 239, 252; Abraham as, 42–3; Amos as, 232
Proverbs, 92; author of, 190
Psalms, 22, 67, 79, 145; Book of, 150; *Yalkut* at beginning of, 215
Pseudo-Dionysius, 12

Rabban Gamaliel, 27
Rabbinic authority problem, 200–1
rakia (firmament), 24, 25, 26, 28–9
Rampart, 55
Ran (Gerondi, Rabbi Nissim), 185
Rapoport, Solomon Judah, 159, 171
Rashba, 119
Rashi (Solomon ben Isaac): on 'additional soul', 91; on Christianity, 106; on priestly blessing, 99; Rabbi Aryeh Leib Heller, and *Shev Shemat'ata*, 168, 183, 184, 185, 192; on self-defence, 229; tradition and, 73; Zionism, and, 214

rationalist school of thought, 47
Rava, 73–4
Rava bar Zamina, 127
Ravyah (Rabbi Eliezer b. Joel of Bonn), 147–8
Rav (third-century teacher), 74, 185
Rayya Mehemna, 14
rebbe (Hasidic master), 243–4, 247
Reconstructionism, 246–7
Reform Judaism, 72, 100, 149, 150
Reform Judaism, 248
Reform Judaism: Orthodox contrasted, 239–42; in USA, 240, 241; women, position of, 245–6
Regensburg, Saint of, 71
reincarnation of souls, 204
relativism, religious, 54
Responsa: Franco, Rabbi Joseph Rahamim, 110–11; Ha-Kohen, Rabbi Ephraim, 117–25; Klein, Rabbi Menashe, 151; publications, 249; Sofer, Rabbi Moses, 151
resurrection, doctrine of, 84, 178, 241
Righteous, as foundation of world, 28
robbery, 179
Rosenzweig, Franz, 46
Rosh ha-Shanah (Jewish New Year), 26, 39, 149, 212, 213
Rosh Yeshivah, 244
ruah (part of soul), 96
Rufus, Turnus, 177, 198

Saadiah, Gaon, 59, 205
Sabbath, 90–4; cooking on, 240; festivals distinguished, 176; fire, kindling of, 240; *havdalah* ceremony, 94; and man's power, limitations of, 226–7; marital relations, 92–3; meals, sacred, 91–2; *oneg shabbat* (Sabbath delight), 90, 91, 94, 99–100; Orthodox/Reform differences, 239, 240; saving of life, 220; Talmud on, 4, 90; as Temple in Time, 212
Sadducees, 95
Safed mystics, 92
sages, talmudic, 127
St Denis, 12; Prayer of, 18, 19
Salammbo (G. Flaubert), 48
Salanter, Rabbi Israel, 137
Samael, power of, 137
Samuel, 92
Sanctuary, the (Temple), 54, 55, 56, 59
Sanhedrin, 221, 222, 223
Sarah (Hebrew Bible), 40
Satan, 5, 45
Satmar (Hasidic group), 154, 243
Schatz-Uffenheimer, Rivkah, 139, 140
Schechter, Solomon, 210, 211
Schlisel, N. S., 150–1
Scholasticism, 11
Scholem, Gershom, 17, 139, 140; school, 135, 246
School of Hillel, 27, 170, 171
School of Shammai, 27, 170, 171
Sefer Ha-Berit (encyclopedia of human

knowledge), 34
Sefer Hasidim (Book of the Pious), 97
Sefirot, Ten: cosmology, 33; Jewish tradition, 77; priest, fingers of representing, 98; Sabbath, 91, 92; summary of, 88; tree, 137; *Via Negativa* theology, 15–16, 17, 18, 19, 20
self-defence, murder, 222–4, 228–9
Sephardim, 89, 243, 246, 249
Septuagint, 71
Sevin, Rabbi S. J., 215
sexual relations, 92–3
Sha'ar Efrayim (Responsa collection), 117–25
shaatnez (garment), 248
Shabbatai Zevi, 81
Shabbateanism, 120, 123
shamayim (heaven) *see* Heaven (*shamayim*)
Shammai, School of, 27, 170, 171
Shapira, Rabbi Zevi Hirsch, 108
Shapiro, Meir (Rabbi of Lublin), 210–11
Shefa Tal, 98
Shefokh hamatekha (Pour out thy wrath), 149
shehitah, act of, 102
sheitel (wig), 247
Shekhinah (Divine Presence/female principle): 'additional soul', 91; Hasidism, 137; holy places, and, 56, 58, 60; Israel, uniting of, 191; priestly blessing, 99, 100; Sabbath, 92
shelo lishmah (impure motives), 185
Shema, the, 4, 5, 78, 205–6
Shemmitot (cosmic cycles), 33–4
Sheol (abode of the dead), 24
Shev Shemat'ata (Seven Discourses), 159–95; Aggadic Introduction, 159–60; opening paragraphs, 161
shittat ha-egrof (theory of the fist), 207
shittuf (association), 106, 107, 108
Shiur Komah (Measurements of God's Stature), 87
Shulhan Arukh (Code of Jewish observances): on Christianity, 110, 112; Jewish tradition, 76; Karo, Rabbi Joseph, statement of, 119; rituals, Kabbalist meaning, 89; Sabbath, 94, *see also* Maimonides, Moses: Code of Jewish law
Sidra (weekly Torah reading), 153
Simeon ben Eleazar, Rabbi, 180
Simeon ben Pazzi, Rabbi, 145
Simeon ben Yohai, Rabbi, 128, 137
Simlai, Rabbi, 79
Simon, Ernst, 47, 48
Sinai, Mount, 54
Sirkes, Rabbi Josel, 185
Skvire, Hasidic Rebbe of, 151–2
Sochachover Rebbe, 154
Sodom, inhabitants of, 198–9
Sofer, Rabbi Moses, 112, 151, 243
Solomon of Radomsk, Rabbi, 141
Solomon's prayer, 55
Soloveitchick, J. B., 45, 46, 48
Soncino Press (London), 249
Sotmarer Hasidim, 135

soul: high quality of Jewish, 186; Jews and non-Jews, 8; parts of, 96; reincarnation of, 204, *see also* body and soul; death and burial rites
Spain, Zohar originating in, 11, 14, 87
Spectre, Rabbi, 209
Spiegel, Shalom, 43
Spira, Rabbi Hayyim Eleazar, 251
spiritual decline, doctrine of, 128
stars, 32
Steinberg, Milton, 42, 48
Steinsaltz, Adin, 249
streimel (fur hat), 247
sun-worship, 105
Supreme Being *see* God
synagogue: sale to Christians for use as church, 108; sanctity of, 56, 57, 61

Tabernacle, 56
taharah (purification rite), 96–7
tallit (prayer-shawl), 247
talmid haham, 159
Talmud, 3, 6, 11, 41, 103, 146, 220, 226–7; on *Akedah* (sacrifice of Isaac), 42, 43; ancient teachers of, 127–8; asceticism, 856; body, and, 84, 96, 99; dialectics in, 165, 166, 167, 171; Ephraim, Rabbi, sermon by, 117–18; Jewish tradition, and, 76, 77; Orthodox/Reform differences, 239; Sabbath, 4, 90, 91, 92, 100; self-defence, 228, 229; Yeshivah, 244
Tam, Rabbenu, 95
tanna'im, 129
Tannaitic period, 31, 102
Tarbitz, 248
Tarfon, Rabbi, 221
Targum, 216–17
Tehom (great deep), 24, 26
teiku, 209
Teilhard de Chardin, 34
Teitelbaum, Yekuthiel Judah (Rabbi of Sighet), 112
tekhelet (blue thread), 198
Telstone Yeshiva (Israel), 244
Telz Yeshiva (Ohio), 244
Temple Mount/Temple: blessing, priestly, 97; destruction (Ninth of Av), 180, 181; holy places, 54–5, 57, 58, 61; illuminations, 129–30; institutions of Judaism, and, 77; priests, garments worn in, 97; rebuilding of, Orthodox position on, 241; stealing from, 179
teshuvah, act of, 164
Tetragrammaton (Hebrew name for God), 98, 121, 122, 123, 160
Theism, 5, 10, 53
theophany, time of, 54
Tiferet Sefirah (Beauty), 88, 92, 121
Tiferet Yisrael (God of Israel), 123, 177
Tikkuney Zohar, 14, 18–19, 87
Tohu, 27
Toledot Aharon synagogue (Meah Shearim), 214

Toledot Yitzhak (Isaac Karo), 186
Torah: acceptance of, 166, 167, 168, 170; on *Akedah* (sacrifice of Isaac), 44–5; Christmas, and, 112; fear of, 77; as God's vineyard, 177; Heaven, from, 69, 70, 71, 72, 211, 239, 240; on holy places, 57, 58; on levirate marriage, 153; negative and positive precepts, 34; non-fundamentalist approach to, 211, 212, 214; Oral, 72, 166, 167, 184, 190, 221; parchment, 184; Prince of, 167, 168–9; reading of, 201; Scrolls of, 76, 95; Written, 166, 167, 184
torot, 126
Tosafists (mediaeval rabbis): on business activity, 164–5; on Christianity, 106, 107; on death/burial rites, 95; on giving of Torah, 167–8; on heresy, 151; on wickedness, 147, 148; Zionism, and, 214
Tradition, 248
Traditional Conservative Judaism, 241
tradition, Jewish, 66–82; animals, cruelty to, 219; capital/corporal punishment, abolition, 221; departure from, 249–50; faith, and, 78, 79, 81; Orthodox/Reform differences, 239, 240; power concept, 225–37
Trani, Rabbi Joseph of Constantinople, 119
Trinity doctrine, Christianity, 105, 107
Tur, 89, 98
Tur Barekhet (Hayyim ha-Kohen of Aleppo), 189
tzaddi/tzaddik (zaddick), 136, 155, *see also* Zaddik, doctrine of
tzelem (male principle), 174, 175
tzionut, 209
tzitzit, law of, 197–8

Ugaritic texts, 56
Ultra Orthodox, 243, 249, 250, *see also* Hasidism
Union of Orthodox Hebrew Congregations (USA), 245
United States: American Jewish Committee, 248; Conservative Judaism in, 240, 241; Jewish publications, 248; New York Board of Rabbis, 242; Reform movement in, 240; Union of Orthodox Hebrew Congregations, 245; United Synagogue of America, 240; Yeshivah University (New York), 245
United Synagogue of America, 240
United Synagogue (London), 245
universalism/universal law, 8, 29, 30, 214, 230, 239, 242
'universe', no word in Bible for, 24
'upper worlds', 33, 94
Uriab, affair of, 233
Uri of Strelisk (hasidic master), 130

Via Negativa (negation theology), 10–21; Cloud of *Unknowing*, 11, 12, 13, 17, 18, 19, 20; *En Sof*, 15, 16, 17, 18, 19, 20; Sefirot, 15–16, 18, 19; Zohar, 10–11, 14, 17, 18
Via Positiva, 11, 19

Vilna, Gaon of, 81, 151
violence: as evil, 220, 224; justification for, 220–4
Vizhnitz (Hasidic group), 243
von Holbach, Baron, 6

waters, 24–25
Weiss, J. G., 140, 141
well (*be'er*), 161, 162
wicked, praying for downfall of, 144–58
Wiesel, Elie, 141
wine, 103–4, 105
Wisdom of Solomon, 27
Wittgenstein, Ludwig, 1
Women, Court of, 55
Woolwich, Bishop of, 3–4
'Work of Chariot'/'Work of Creation', 68
World to Come, 100, 101
World Jewish Congress, 248
worship: *Avodah Zarah* (idol worship), 102–3; Golden Calf, 117, 118, 119, 120, 154; holy places, 56; of idols *see* idolatry; Moloch, 42; Torah, fear of, 77
Written Torah, 166, 167, 184

Yalkut Reuveni, 167
Yeshivah University (New York), 245
Yeshivot, 244–245, 246, 248
Yesod Sefirah (Foundation), 88
Yom Kippur (Day of Atonement), 54, 55, 189, 212; garments, wearing by women, 251; justification for eating, 220

Zaddik, doctrine of, 75, 91–2, 135, 136–7
Zadok of Lublin, Rabbi, 141
Zangwill, Rabbi Israel, 30, 66, 139
Zeitlin, S., 56
Zera Avraham (Rabbi Abraham Luftavir), 197
Zera'im (seeds), 164
Zera, Rabbi, 150
Zion, 248
Zionism, 209–217; aims of, 210–11; Reform movement, 242; religious, 210, 216, 242–3; secular, 216; spiritual, 211; universalistic aspects of, 214, *see also* Israel
Zipporah, 167, 168
Zodiac, signs of, 32
Zohar: 'additional soul', 91; Almosnino, quotation by, 121; cistern/well distinguished, 161; Genesis, 17; language of, 11; man's animal nature, 174; mystical contemplation, 18; priestly blessing, 98, 99; Rabbi Aryeh Leib Heller, and *Shev Shemat'ata*, 160, 175–6, 188, 191; Sefirot *see* Sefirot, Ten; Simeon b. Yohai, Rabbi, 128; Spain, originating in, 11, 14, 87; Tikkuney Zohar, 14, 18–19, 87; on Torah, 77; *Via Negativa*, 10–11, 14, 17, 18; Zoharic corpus, 14, *see also* Kabbalah
Zoroastrianism, 5
Zunz, Leopold, 23